P9-EMB-703

Managing Quality in America's Most Admired Companies

Managing Quality in America's Most Admired Companies

Jay W. Spechler, Ph.D., P.E.

Berrett-Koehler Publishers
San Francisco

Industrial Engineering and Management Press
Institute of Industrial Engineers
Norcross, Georgia

Library of Congress Cataloging-in-Publication Data

Spechler, Jay W., 1934-
    Managing quality in America's most admired companies / Jay W. Spechler.
        p.   cm.
    ISBN 0-89806-118-0
    1. Total quality management--United States--Case studies.
    2. Malcolm Baldrige National Quality Award--Case studies. I. Title.
    HD62.15.S646 1993
    658.5'62--dc20   92-44147

Additional copies may be obtained by contacting either of the following co-publishers. Quantity discounts are available.

Institute of Industrial Engineers
Customer Service
25 Technology Park/Atlanta
Norcross, Georgia 30092 USA
(404) 449-0460 phone
(404) 263-8532 fax

Berrett-Koehler Publishers, Inc.
155 Montgomery St.
San Francisco, CA 94104-4109
(415) 288-0260 phone
(415) 362-2512 fax

To Marilyn who always provides much guidance and inspiration for my work in quality management.

Contents

Part III. Appendices

Preface

While working as a senior examiner for the Malcolm Baldrige National Quality Award Committee, I noticed that many of the hundreds of thousands of companies that requested award applications expressed an interest in using the award criteria to implement a total quality management process, but were at a loss as to how to begin. How to begin to implement a total quality management process, how to build a solid foundation for continuous improvement and profitability became the genesis for this book.

Our first chapter provides a proven ten-step strategy designed to enable management to establish a results-oriented culture with supporting systems that will serve as a springboard for launching a total quality management initiative. Those wishing to enhance or fine tune their existing quality processes will also benefit from the strategy.

The ten strategies mentioned above are a combination of the successful approaches of companies that have won the Malcolm Baldrige Award, were finalists for the award, were identified by *Fortune* magazine as being outstanding quality providers, or singled out by the *Economist* magazine as companies providing the greatest added value for their customers. The latter sources also provided the principal criteria for selecting the companies whose case studies appear in this book.

The first chapter then serves as an overall implementation model for total quality management. Subsequent chapters provide greater depth of understanding of the most critical steps in the model; i.e., creating a corporate vision and set of values that galvanizes and hurtles an organization toward outstanding quality performance; developing significant improvements in quality and productivity through using business process analysis to identify performance gaps; understanding the internal customer concept; establishing quality performance measures that people believe in; and structuring customer satisfaction surveys to provide a sound basis for action planning.

My friend and professional associate, Curt Reimann, who serves as director of the Malcolm Baldrige Award Committee, has contributed a chapter that describes the origin, strategic mission, and the unique scoring model contained within the award design.

Another important element—the role of leadership in establishing a solid foundation for quality—is covered in a separate chapter. Many senior executives hesitate to involve themselves in implementing total quality processes. These executives have told me that they simply do not know how to get started, or they fear that they will not have enough time to devote to the effort. This chapter presents the results of research and personal investigation into the leadership practices of three-hundred successful quality companies. Sixty-one action steps taken by some of the most effective business leaders in America are presented. These action steps take very little time to accomplish, but they exert enormous leverage for enhancing organizational motivation and performance.

The case studies are models of quality excellence that span many industrial classifications. Large and small companies in both the manufacturing and service sectors and companies employing varying levels of technology are represented. Each case study demonstrates how the company has utilized the quality management principles and criteria embodied within the Malcolm Baldrige Award to enhance their competitiveness and the well-being of their people. A matrix is presented in the Appendix that shows the Malcolm Baldrige criteria referenced in each of the case studies.

It is worth noting that my co-authors, who devoted so much energy in developing their case studies, are individuals who have been personally responsible for making quality happen within their organizations. These people are the best in their fields because they have learned by doing, they lead by example, and their creativity knows no bounds.

Finally, while the genesis for the theme of this book stems from managements' need for a total quality implementation model, the author recognizes and is indebted to the founders and fellow trainers of Neuro Linguistic Programming (NLP). NLP knowledge elicitation and modeling skills have been used extensively in the development of this book.

Part I
Guidelines for Implementing Quality Management

The Malcolm Baldrige National Quality Award: Design, Criteria and Application Review

Curt W. Reimann
National Institute of Standards and Technology

In the 1980s, the United States experienced a decline in its balance of trade. Though many factors contributed to this trend, evidence is mounting that quality—real and perceived—of U.S. goods is one of the significant factors. Surveys show that buyers are becoming more quality conscious, and that in the minds of some, Made in America is no longer a symbol of quality.

The growing concern over quality, particularly as it related to U.S. competitiveness, led some members of Congress and the administration to consider options for raising corporate quality awareness. One mechanism considered was a national quality award for businesses, akin to Japan's Deming Prize, which is credited with having played a major role in reversing Japan's earlier reputation for poor quality.

In the mid 1980s, some members of Congress became interested in the quality issue, stimulated in part by John J. Hudiburg, Chairman of Florida Power and Light Company. In 1986, legislation was introduced to create a national award. In 1987, following the accidental death of Secretary of Commerce, Malcolm Baldrige, the national award legislation, then pending, was named for Mr. Baldrige, and the legislation quickly passed both Houses of Congress. President Reagan signed the Malcolm Baldrige National Quality Improvement Act of 1987 (P.L. 100-107) into law on August 20, 1987.

Responsibility for the Malcolm Baldrige Award was assigned to the Department of Commerce. The National Institute of Standards and Technology (NIST), an agency of the Department of Commerce, was given responsibility for the development and management of the award program.

KEY PROVISIONS OF THE ACT

The Malcolm Baldrige National Quality Award Improvement Act of 1987 sets specific requirements for the award and for the management of the award program. Requirements include:

- *Categories for award:* 1) manufacturing companies or subsidiaries; 2) service companies or subsidiaries; and 3) small business. (Up to two awards may be given each year in each category.)
- *Criteria for qualification:* Apply in writing to the Director of NIST, and permit rigorous evaluation.

- *Awards:* A medal bearing the inscription "Malcolm Baldrige National Quality Award" presented by the President or the Secretary of Commerce. Award recipients may publicize and advertise receipt of the award.
- *Award examination:* NIST shall rely on a Board of Examiners to conduct reviews and site visits.
- *Information transfer:* The NIST director shall ensure feedback to applicants and publicize successful quality improvement strategies.
- *Program oversight:* The Secretary of Commerce shall appoint a prestigious board of overseers to review award processes and suggest improvement.
- *Funding:* The Secretary of Commerce is authorized to seek and accept gifts and to impose fees upon applicants.

In summary, these requirements show that awards are to be made to companies for excellence of quality management and achievement as judged through detailed evaluations made by peers. Development and operating costs are to be borne by the private sector. The government's primary roles are creating, validating, and improving award processes and ensuring effective technology and information transfer.

DESIGN FEATURES
The law sets a number of key requirements for the U.S. national quality award, but nevertheless affords considerable latitude in award criteria and processes.

To ensure broad input to the design of the award, many quality leaders — manufacturing, service, academic, consultants, and retired —were contacted regarding characteristics that should be incorporated into the award. The requirements specified in the law and the advice of quality leaders were synthesized into a value system for the award. Key elements of the value system are as follows:

- *Total quality management:* The award should stress total quality control—all operations and functions. This should include integration of quality planning with business planning.
- *Human resource utilization:* The award should emphasize training and development of all personnel with particular stress on quality training.
- *Performance:* The award should give considerable weight to quality improvement results, in preference to specific techniques or processes for achieving results.
- *Measurables:* Award criteria and application evaluation should focus on quantitative results and positive trends, rather than on narrative descriptions of processes and anecdotal information. To be convincing, firms need a good quality measurement system, along with associated analytical capabilities.
- *Customer satisfaction:* The Award criteria should give major consideration to customers' views of products and services, and to the functioning of the entire customer interface in planning products and services.

- *World-class quality:* Award evaluation should, where appropriate, explore the degree to which firms recognize the quality requirements of international markets, their systems for assessing where they stand, and their plans for establishing a leadership position.
- *Quality early in the process:* Award criteria should reflect the need to address quality early in the design phase, both to reduce delays in bringing products to market and to enter markets with high-quality products.
- *Innovation:* Award application should permit firms to highlight and get credit for unique approaches to achieving high quality.
- *External leadership:* Award evaluations should give some weight to applicants' efforts to lead and support national and local activities in support of quality and its related infrastructure. This includes assisting suppliers, supporting quality standards, and creating community councils.

STRATEGIC DESIGN

The award program has been strategically designed to achieve all of the aims of the legislation as well as those of the quality community. It is also designed to minimize the problems inherent in setting up a program involving many people with different quality expertise, viewpoints, and organizational ties. Though the design strategy involves many facets, there are four key elements of the design.

CRITERIA

The award value system has been embodied in criteria organized into seven categories. This was done to convey the meaning of a total quality control system that would be useful for businesses whether or not they apply for an award. Each category probes areas of quality management that are most likely to reveal characteristics of excellent companies. The categories provide a balance between process and results, and adapt to differing definitions of quality. Criteria are written to minimize the distinctions between manufacturing and services so that one examination may be used for all businesses.

SCORING SYSTEM

The scoring system—created for the Award Program—is designed to provide high resolution at the upper end of the scale, suitable for distinguishing characteristics of the excellent companies expected to apply for awards. The system is three dimensional—based upon approach, extent of deployment, and results. The scoring system and the scoring method are integrated, and form the basis for evaluation and for providing feedback to applicants.

EVALUATION PROCESS

The evaluation is built around multiple, independent reviews, followed by a consensus process. High-scoring applicants are visited by examiners for further evaluation. Award recipients are recommended by a panel of judges who use scoring information and site visit reports to make their judgments.

The evaluation process is designed to minimize the effects of variability in scoring and potential conflicts of interest. This process also recognizes the need for a balance between scoring and judgment owing to many factors including the need to have award recipients serve as national models.

ORGANIZATIONAL STRUCTURE

The organizational structure is designed to ensure the integrity of award processes and to help promote information transfer. Since some organizations provide funding, and other groups evaluate and advise, the organization must ensure proper separation of functions. Since many U.S. organizations participate in or have a stake in quality improvement activities, the award organization needs to permit easy access to the award and to award results.

AWARD ORGANIZATION

The award organization was designed to carry out the specific responsibilities spelled out in the law as well as to facilitate the larger purposes—information transfer and quality awareness—that motivated the creation of the law. Through formal and informal linkages among new and existing organizations, the award organization serves as a vehicle for quality awareness and information transfer. The award organization is shown in Figure 1.

DEPARTMENT OF COMMERCE

The department of commerce is the federal department assigned responsibility for the basic directions of the award program. The Secretary of Commerce, together with the President, present the awards.

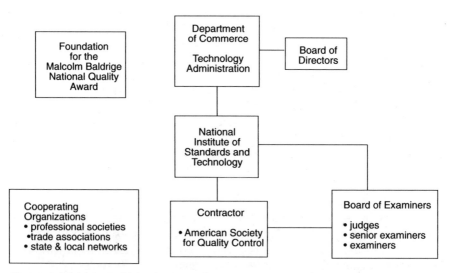

Figure 1. Malcolm Baldrige National Quality Award organization.

NATIONAL INSTITUTE OF STANDARDS AND TECHNOLOGY (NIST)

An agency of the Department of Commerce, NIST is assigned day-to-day program management of the award program. Responsibilities include creation of award criteria and processes, staffing of boards, contract monitoring, feedback to applicants, and information transfer.

CONTRACTOR

The contractor is the American Society for Quality Control. The contractor carries out a number operations such as management of the application review, preparation of promotional materials, and assistance with publicity.

BOARD OF OVERSEERS

The Board of Overseers, appointed by the Secretary of Commerce, advises the Secretary and the Director of NIST on broad directions of the award program. The recommendations of the board will guide the evolution of the award program so that it best serves the national interest.

BOARD OF EXAMINERS

The Board of Examiners, appointed by the Director of NIST, consists of quality experts selected on the basis of expertise, experience, and peer recognition. Beginning in September 1987, NIST began networking with a variety of organizations and individuals to identify leaders from around the country who could take part in the review process. Membership on the board of examiners is determined through an application process. Application materials include information on terms and conditions of involvement. Each September, applications are made available for those who wish to serve on the board of examiners during the following year.

EXAMINER PREPARATION

All examiners take part in a three-day preparation course. The course focuses on understanding of criteria, scoring system, evaluation process, and on developing consensus evaluations. Case studies developed for the preparation courses are used as the principal means to orient the examination team. The main emphasis throughout the course is reducing variability in scoring.

To maintain a team identity among examiners and to keep examiners informed of developments in the award program, *Update,* a newsletter, was created.

FOUNDATION

The law authorizes the secretary of commerce to seek and accept gifts to support the award program. Secretary of Commerce C. William Verify, invited Mr. John Hudiburg, CEO of the Florida Power and Light Company, and Mr. Sanford McDonnell, Chairman emeritus of the McDonnell Douglas Corporation, both strong supporters of the national quality award concept, to organize the

Foundation for the Malcolm Baldrige National Quality Award. The foundation is entirely independently of both the government and the organizations that conduct application review and program oversight.

COOPERATING ORGANIZATIONS

Many organizations in the U.S.—trade associations, professional societies, state organizations, etc.—have a stake in quality improvement in the United States. Most of these organizations have members who could participate in some way in the award program. All such organizations could play a major role in information transfer.

The principal purpose of working with cooperating organizations is to create a vehicle to make available the award findings for use in education and training programs throughout the United States. This approach is being taken because NIST does not wish to duplicate the many excellent programs now available. Rather, it seeks to strengthen these programs through encouraging greater emphasis on quality and the incorporation of the unique findings of the award program. Cooperative workshops, symposia, and publications are developed according to need and opportunity.

AWARD CRITERIA AND PROCESSES

The award is based on well-defined criteria as detailed in the application guidelines. The criteria are organized into seven categories as follows. The dynamic relationships among the award criteria categories are shown in Figure 2. (See Appendix for further details.)

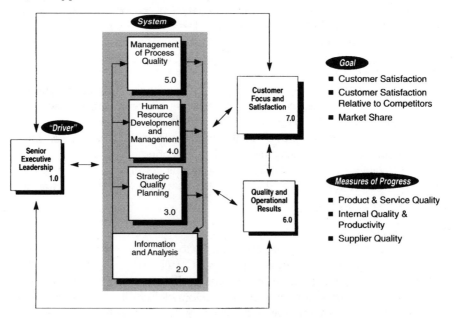

Figure 2. Dynamic relationships between Baldrige award criteria.

1.0 LEADERSHIP

This category examines senior executives' personal leadership and involvement in creating and sustaining a customer focus and clear and visible quality values. Also examined is how the quality values are integrated into the company's management system and reflected in the manner in which the company addresses its public responsibilities.

2.0 INFORMATION AND ANALYSIS

The information and analysis category examines the scope, validity, analysis, management, and use of data and information to drive quality excellence and improve competitive performance. Also examined is the adequacy of the company's data, information, and analysis system to support improvement of the company's customer focus, products, services, and internal operations.

3.0 STRATEGIC QUALITY PLANNING

The strategic quality planning category examines the company's planning process and how all key quality requirements are integrated into overall business planning. Also examined are the company's short- and long-term plans and how quality performance requirements are deployed to all work units.

4.0 HUMAN RESOURCE DEVELOPMENT AND MANAGEMENT

The human resource development and management category examines the key elements of how the company develops and realizes the full potential of the work force to pursue the company's quality and performance objectives. Also examined are the company's efforts to build and maintain an environment for quality excellence conducive to full participation and personal and organizational growth.

5.0 MANAGEMENT OF PROCESS QUALITY

The management of process quality category examines the systematic processes the company uses to pursue ever-higher quality and company performance. Examined are the key elements of process management, including design, management of process quality for all work units and suppliers, systematic quality improvement, and quality assessment.

6.0 QUALITY AND OPERATIONAL RESULTS

The quality and operational results category examines the company's quality levels and improvement trends in quality, company operational performance, and supplier quality. Also examined are current quality and performance levels relative to those of competitors.

7.0 CUSTOMER FOCUS AND SATISFACTION

The customer focus and satisfaction category examines the company's relationships with customers and its knowledge of customer requirements and of the key quality factors that determine marketplace competitiveness. Also examined are the company's methods to determine customer satisfaction, current trends and levels of satisfaction, and these results relative to competitors.

In the 1992 examination, applicants are required to address twenty-eight examination items. They are instructed to provide factual information, data, and trends to demonstrate both continued progress and high levels of success. While these criteria cover the process by which companies address quality, the emphasis of the award and the challenge to applicants is on the achievement and consequences of quality, as indicated by the high weight placed on results and customer satisfaction.

APPLICATION REVIEW

Award applications are reviewed by the Board of Examiners in a four-stage process:

1. FIRST-STAGE REVIEW

A review of the application report is conducted by at least four members of the board of examiners. At the conclusion of the first-stage review, the panel of judges determines which applications should be referred for consensus review.

2. CONSENSUS REVIEW

A review of the application report is conducted by at least four members of the board of examiners and led by a senior examiner. At the conclusion of the consensus review, the panel of judges determines which applicants should receive site visits.

3. SITE VISIT REVIEW

An on-site verification of the application report is conducted by at least five members of the board of examiners led by a senior examiner. The site visit review team prepares a report for the panel of judges.

4. JUDGES' FINAL REVIEW

A final review of all evaluation reports from site visits is conducted by the panel of judges to recommend award recipients. The panel of judges develops a set of recommendations made to the National Institute of Standards and Technology. The Institute presents the judges' recommendations to the secretary of commerce for award decisions.

FEEDBACK REPORTS

Feedback reports are sent to all applicants. The reports include general information on the evaluation process, scoring and overall results. Specific feedback to applicants is primarily in the form of comments on strengths and weaknesses in the seven categories that make up the examination. The reports also include statements of the scoring ranges reached by each of the applicants, along with the distribution of all scores.

INFORMATION TRANSFER

The information transfer strategy focuses upon promoting awareness among key organizations which have a stake in quality improvement and which must participate if the national quality effort is to succeed. Organizations contacted make up what might be called the quality system of the United States (Table 1).

Table 1. Quality System of the United States

- Professional and technical associations
- Trade associations
- Business groups
- Universities and schools
- State and local governments and organizations
- Federal government
- Accrediting bodies
- Health care organizations

AWARD CRITERIA AS INFORMATION TRANSFER DEVICE

A major element in the national quality awareness campaign is to promote the use of the award criteria in quality improvement. As of July 1992 several hundred thousand copies of the application guidelines have been disseminated. In addition, other groups have duplicated copies and made them available in their companies or among their member organizations. Through contacts with application requestors, examiners, and others, a number of use patterns have been revealed (Table 2).

Table 2. Use of Malcolm Baldrige National Quality Award Criteria

- preparation for awards
- self-assessment
- training and education in companies
- coordination among divisions in companies
- companies working with suppliers and customers
- trade associations promoting quality among members
- business school education
- basis for state, local, and company awards
- general training courses
- long-term goal setting

Organizations using the award criteria include many which are currently ineligible to apply for awards. Such organizations include business schools, community colleges, federal agencies, non-profit institutions, and others.

ACTIVITIES OF AWARD WINNING COMPANIES

A major element in the information transfer strategy underlying the Baldrige Award is built around the activities of the award winning companies. Beginning with the first award ceremony (November 14, 1988), the winning companies have conducted and participated in more than ten thousand information sharing activities. In addition, they have held numerous celebrations and advertised in major U. S. media The activities of the award winners have proven to be perhaps the most significant generators of awareness. More importantly, perhaps, the winners have reinforced the definition of world-class quality.

Ten Critical Success Factors for Implementing Quality Management

Astrophysicists at NASA recently presented their Big Bang Theory, which describes how outer space was formed. This theory holds that our entire known and unknown universe formed from a single particle of matter and gas smaller than a single dot on a TV screen. What I believe and have experienced in high quality performing companies is that residing within each person, within our inner space, is an energy source that when released through constructive leadership and direction, using appropriate quality models and principles, results in an extraordinary level of productivity and quality achievement.

This chapter describes a model for implementing a quality process in either manufacturing or service organizations that is based on in-depth research, personal application in client companies and discussions with management and employees in over three hundred companies. Applying this model will release the positive energy within peoples inner space. Further, this implementation model provides the foundation for a full adoption of the Malcolm Baldrige Award criteria and a continuous improvement process.

The following pages cover the full scope of ten critical success factors (see Figure 1) that form the implementation model. In applying this model, it is important to consider that total quality management is achieved within a well-balanced, three-part system (see Figure 2). The first part of this system is the *cultural system,* which is represented by the sum of beliefs and resulting behaviors that take place throughout the organization. If a company wishes to effect real change, its leadership must come to grips with its true beliefs and convey them convincingly to people at every level. Timing is an important element in addressing cultural factors. While desirable, a company may not be in a position to start its quality implementation efforts in the cultural area. Xerox, for example, made the decision in the early 1980s that its priorities lay in improving product and service quality. At that time Xerox was losing market share to Japanese competitors at an alarming rate. The company found itself in a survival state. Having regained market share and firmly established its position as a quality producer, it is now beginning to address cultural issues that it believes will result in an even more effective organization.

The second part of the total quality management system is the *technical system.* The technical system is composed of such factors as the technologies used and the physical infrastructure (including ergonomic considerations, com-

1. Create a vision and values statement.
2. Integrate strategic quality goals into the corporate strategic planning process.
3. Select a total quality management model.
4. Develop an organizational structure to implement quality improvement.
5. Establish a design team to tailor quality process implementation to the company's culture.
6. Design training for quality improvement team efforts.
7. Prepare a communications plan for quality.
8. Determine key business processes for cross-functional analysis and improvement.
9. Develop quality performance measures for all business processes.
10. Benchmark operations against world class quality companies.

Figure 1. Ten-step strategy for implementing quality management and continuous improvement for competitiveness.

Figure 2.

puter software and hardware configurations, and the capital investments needed to accomplish the company's mission).

Finally, the *management system* defines the effectiveness of those processes by which an organization manages its human and physical assets. The case studies in this book reflect the many ways in which management and employees are achieving greater operating effectiveness. If framing or defining effectiveness as an algorithm we would say that

$$\text{Effectiveness} = \frac{\text{Productivity} \times \text{Quality}}{\text{Investment}}$$

Increased effectiveness can be achieved by changing the value of a single factor in the above formula or by fine tuning the inter-relationship among all three. At the micro or operational level, there are many possible combinations.

Ritz Carlton Hotels has, for example, increased its effectiveness through developing an employee hiring and selection model that resulted in creating a work force that delivers quality performance to a demanding clientele. Through its emphasis on hiring quality people, the Ritz Carlton also achieved greater productivity without increased investment.

Cadillac made relatively minor capital investments that resulted in major increases in productivity and quality. Overall effectiveness increased. Knight-Ridder increased operating effectiveness through creating quality improvement teams that found ways to enhance productivity and quality without adding cost (investment).

The successful quality companies devote considerable energy and attention to the management system. They have created information systems that enable them to manage by fact. They use data to surface existing and potential problems, and they are driven to solving them. These companies are also focusing on their people. They are redefining manager-employee relationships toward the end of optimizing internal and external customer satisfaction.

THE TEN-STEP STRATEGY FOR IMPLEMENTING QUALITY MANAGEMENT AND CONTINUOUS IMPROVEMENT FOR COMPETITIVENESS

1. CREATE A VISION AND VALUES STATEMENT

My previous book on the subject of quality management, *When America Does It Right,* was published in 1988 following a three year research effort. At that time, half of the companies whose case studies were included in the book had created formal vision and values statements. Today, virtually every company that is considered world class or striving to achieve world class quality status has prepared a vision and values statement. Importantly, these statements contain the principle beliefs that the leadership and the people within these organizations wish to live by. The vision and values statements provide the spiritual and directional guidance that is a significant factor in motivating entire organizations toward excellent performance. Interestingly, no two values and visions statements are the same. Each one reflects individual needs, cultures, customers, and environmental factors.

In some cases, a top management team develops the vision and values statement, while other organizations involve all employees in the effort. In both situations considerable, ongoing effort is made to communicate the final product to all of the people. Further attention is given to determine if the company's values are truly being employed over time.

2. INTEGRATE STRATEGIC QUALITY GOALS INTO THE CORPORATE STRATEGIC BUSINESS PLANNING PROCESS

The development of strategic quality goals conveys the message to the entire organization that quality is an important element to success. Their development and subsequent implementation also provides a means for demonstrating how quality initiatives are being implemented.

Typical strategic quality goals include the following:
- 100 percent customer satisfaction.
- 100 percent employee satisfaction.
- 100 percent accuracy of products and service delivered to customers.
- The time to deliver products and services will at least meet customer expectations.
- New products and services will be added that exceed customer expectations.
- The measurement of total quality management is the Malcolm Baldrige criteria and each operating unit and the company will assess progress against the criteria.
- Appropriate, value added new techniques will be introduced to improve the productivity of our operations and the quality of our products and services.

Having developed quality goals, consideration should then be given to their deployment within the organization. The following approaches have been found to be successful in implementation efforts:
- Action plans will be developed by each department in support of the quality service objectives. Progress reports will be submitted to the Executive Quality Service Council at least quarterly.
- Internal and external assessments of customer and employee satisfaction levels will be performed regularly as a basis for continuous improvement and identification of new service opportunities.
- An annual assessment using the Malcolm Baldrige criteria will be performed to measure progress of the quality service approach and deployment.
- Improve knowledge and skills of employees, at all levels, regarding the quality service process and the tools and techniques to improve quality service. Involve employees and recognize desired behaviors.
- Key processes will be measured from the customer's point of view and an overall process measurement system will be established to share information with all employees and serve as a basis for improvement efforts and recognition.
- A formal communications plan will exist that conveys strategy, efforts, events, and results to the organization.

3. SELECT A TOTAL QUALITY MANAGEMENT MODEL

A piecemeal "quality flavor of the month" approach toward implementing a total quality management process is almost a certain guarantee of failure. Selecting a total quality management model is one of the key starting points in achieving world class quality performance. There are several models available including those developed by Deming, Juran, Crosby, and the European ISO 9000 series. Each organization needs to thoughtfully consider which model or combination of attributes from several models best suits their own needs. The most successful companies design their own pathways and time lines for implementing selected models. Further, their main thrust is to strive for continuous improvement—not to win a prize.

The Malcolm Baldrige Award criteria has emerged as the single, most comprehensive model for total quality management that is available. It has a unique and effective scoring component that enables a company or organization to measure its current level of quality achievement, and to then evaluate its progress over time. No other quality management model has this vital feature. While the Malcolm Baldrige Award criteria is administered by the Department of Commerce, it was designed by leading business experts, and has been enhanced since its introduction through annual, critical reviews conducted by leading business practitioners, academicians, and consultants. A study conducted by the United States General Accounting Office conclusively demonstrated that the application of the Malcolm Baldrige Award criteria has resulted in improved productivity, competitiveness, and profitability (U. S. General Accounting Office 1991).

Since the introduction of the Malcolm Baldrige Award in 1988, several other countries have introduced their own national quality awards utilizing the Malcolm Baldrige Award criteria. Numerous states, municipalities, government, and non-profit organizations in America have also adopted the criteria in whole or in part. For example, in 1992 the State of Florida created the Sterling Award for Quality and Productivity. The criteria for this award draws heavily on Malcolm Baldrige criteria.

4. DEVELOP AN ORGANIZATION STRUCTURE TO IMPLEMENT QUALITY IMPROVEMENT

Organizing for quality management implementation requires the establishment of five elements (shown in Figure 3).

The service quality or quality support department. A function within the company is needed to coordinate quality initiatives, assist in implementing corporate quality strategies, serve as the central reporting agency for quality performance reporting, design certain quality training and awareness programs, and conduct quality performance reviews.

The trend in establishing these functions or departments is to keep them small. Typically, they are staffed with five to eight persons in business units employing 3,000 to 8,000 employees. The purposes for keeping these departments small is to prevent the creation of bureaucratic practices that impede quick reaction to business issues, to push responsibility for quality into the operating departments, and to focus recognition for quality achievements most directly on the people who are accomplishing them.

The Quality Organization Structure

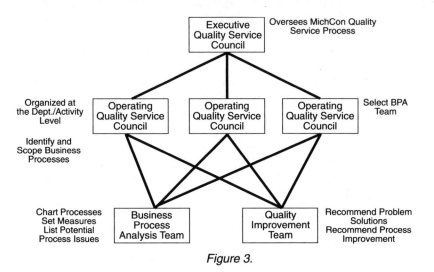

Figure 3.

The Executive Quality Council. The Executive Quality Council is a key organizational feature in initiating and sustaining a quality process over time. It serves to create quality strategies, objectives and initiatives, to lend encouragement to the entire organization as people strive to improve, to maintain a positive attitude as a model for the entire company in dealing with problems and striving for higher levels of achievement, to provide human and capital resources necessary to accomplish quality objectives, to apply forward thinking in adopting new technologies and methods, and to provide recognition for outstanding quality achievement by individuals, departments, and business units.

The Executive Quality Council is typically composed of the chief executive officer and/or the president, the president of the union where applicable, and direct reporting vice presidents.

The Operating Quality Council. The Operating Quality Council is composed of the respective department vice president or director, their direct reports, and union vice presidents where applicable. Its purpose is to ensure the implementation of quality policies, the achievement of quality goals, the evaluation and improvement of performance and the identification of business processes for cross-functional administration.

Typical action items or initiatives of Operating Quality Councils include the following:
• focus on safety issues
• celebrations for quality

- ensure vendor quality
- visit customers
- call recently visited customers
- benchmark local companies with reputations for quality

Business Process Analysis teams. Business Process Analysis (BPA) teams are formed to improve the operating effectiveness of both line and staff functions in manufacturing and service organizations. The formation of these teams gives recognition to the cross-functional nature of business processes rather than inter-departmental activities. For optimum results, BPA teams are structured to involve supervisors and non-management representatives from all departments and external customer groups involved in the respective processes. Further, the participants must be expert in their knowledge of operations.

Some typical business processes include:
- accounts payable/receivable
- billing
- purchasing
- public affairs/public issues management
- production control
- inventory management
- order entry
- complaint management
- closing the books
- new product or service design

Outcomes from BPA team efforts include:
- understanding of quality performance gaps
- identification and recommendation for improvement opportunities
- reduced operating cycle times
- creation of quality performance measures
- heightened awareness of intra-departmental communication needs
- activities to benchmark

Quality Improvement Teams. Quality Improvement Teams (QIT) are formed to address improvement opportunities identified by the BPA teams. Quality improvement teams are usually composed of volunteers within affected departments and stakeholder groups. The Operating Quality Council or any company manager may also invite or assign specific individuals with requisite skills to join a QIT.

To be most effective in their improvement efforts, trained facilitators should be assigned to work with the QITs. The facilitators need to have training skills in problem and decision analysis, basic statistics, presentation techniques, professional team building, and other quality management subjects.

5. ESTABLISH A DESIGN TEAM TO TAILOR QUALITY PROCESS IMPLEMENTATION TO THE COMPANY'S CULTURE

Whether a company is utilizing its own staff or retaining a consultant to implement a total quality management process, it is essential that a design team be established at the outset.

The design team is composed of members from all major departments. It has the functions of coordinating quality implementation efforts with other programs, assuring resource availability, and evaluating the effectiveness of all steps in the implementation process. Through the informal personal networks within the organization, the design team also serves to allay the fears that people have as new quality management initiatives such as creating performance measurement systems, are introduced.

6. DESIGN TRAINING FOR QUALITY IMPROVEMENT EFFORTS

The case studies in this book and those in *When America Does It Right*, indicate that the successful quality companies are investing considerable resources to providing quality training programs to their people. The Malcolm Baldrige Award winners and runner-ups typically devote forty to eighty hours per year, per person to training. Executives in these companies believe that employee knowledge is a critical element and differentiator in the ability of U.S. companies to compete.

The importance of training in quality tools and techniques may be seen in the case of Digital Equipment Corporation. Senior executives announced the implementation of their new quality process with a flourish and with a sincere voice of support in both moral and financial terms. A year after the initial start-up, an internal evaluation showed virtually no progress toward continuous improvement goals. Management then surveyed the employees to find out what was going wrong. The feedback from this survey was that the people felt that management wasn't serious in its intentions to strive for quality, and that the employees were doing the best they could under the circumstances. If there was training available that could help them to find the ways to improve, they said, give it to them and they would in turn do their best to improve further. Management took this feedback to heart, provided the necessary training and then saw the expected results in improved operating effectiveness.

Examples of specific quality training programs may be seen in several case studies in this book, and they fall into two general categories: general quality awareness training, and specific, results-oriented training.

General awareness training includes items such as: the available quality models and their applicability to the company's operations; team building; creating a customer focus; forming executive and operating quality councils; conducting business process analysis sessions; creating quality service measures; forming quality improvement teams, and conveying the company's overall plan to move forward in implementing a quality process.

Specific, results-oriented quality training programs include items such as: project planning and control techniques (i.e. PERT, CPM, and Gantt); decision making and analysis; statistical process control; value engineering; quality function deployment; benchmarking; Pareto analysis; process flow charting; cause and effect diagrams; customer perception survey design; designed experiments control charts, and scatter diagrams.

7. PREPARE A COMMUNICATION PLAN FOR QUALITY

A communications plan to support a quality process implementation effort has the following virtues:
- conveys the message to everyone in the organization that quality is a team effort
- includes recognition for quality achievements
- informs all employees of short- and long- term quality goals and initiatives
- creates a shared understanding and language for quality

Quality communication plans should initially span a period of at least two years and should be established as an ongoing effort. In implementing a new quality management process, the following elements need to be considered as they apply to the organization's culture, scope of operations, and organization structure:

- Create a vision and values statement with the participation of all employees. Display the final document prominently throughout the organization and provide the entire work force and new employees with a pocket and desk display piece.
- Establish an Executive Quality Council or Steering Committee. Provide company-wide understanding and awareness as to its mission, membership, and purpose. Convey this message through video tapes and internal news media.
- Create strategic quality goals and incorporate them into the general strategic business planning process. All business units should prepare action plans in support of the latter goals. These action plans should be documented in writing and presented personally by managers in quarterly updates to the Executive Quality Council.
- Establish Operating Quality Councils at the vice president or director level in all line and staff departments. Communicate to all employees the mission, membership and purpose of these councils through quarterly video updates, internal news media, and electronic notice boards.
- Organize BPA teams to enhance cross-functional communications. Develop BPA educational material and conduct real-time workshops where attendees work on actual processes of their choice. Show video tapes of actual BPA sessions to all managers and employees. Use internal news media to present interviews of BPA workshop attendees' perceptions of benefits of the workshop to themselves and to the organization.
- Educate the entire management group on the Malcolm Baldrige Award criteria (or other quality model) and how it applies to their operations. Conduct workshops, offer certification in the model to attendees, use video tapes of the sessions to all employees, and use executive interviews in internal news media to discuss the need and appropriateness of the model to all employees.

- Present quality motivational and awareness seminars on a quarterly basis to management groups. Utilize outside speakers for this purpose.
- Establish a quality information library and periodically distribute a list of available books, periodicals, news clippings, and videos.
- Publish opportunities to attend special quality conferences and seminars.
- Create numerous, non-financial quality recognition awards at all levels of the organization. Publish the winner's names and achievement in every issue of internal news media; develop video presentations showing recognition for both major and minor achievements.
- Publish noteworthy national and regional quality events and organizational achievements (i.e., state quality award recipients, national quality month, Malcolm Baldrige winners).
- Create annual quality day or quality month celebrations that involve all employees. Tie these celebrations into the results of quality performance measures.
- Offer QIT participation to all employees. Publish results and show videos of team presentations to management.
- Publish the results of all departmental quality performance measures, and provide to all employees. Utilize on-line systems with strategically located video displays, videos, and internal news media.
- Conduct daily or weekly, quality performance review sessions at the senior vice president or general manager level utilizing information from the quality performance measurement system. Invite all direct reports to attend, and rotate invitations to all other members of the organization.
- Establish recognition awards for suppliers, and invite suppliers to attend and participate in the organization's quality events.
- Conduct annual, Malcolm Baldrige Award assessments and publish the results to the entire organization. To achieve the maximum communication benefit from the assessment effort, the report that is produced for assessment (similar in scope to a Malcolm Baldrige application) should be prepared by internal managers. The assessment of results and scoring should be conducted by objective third parties.

8. DETERMINE KEY BUSINESS PROCESSES FOR CROSS-FUNCTIONAL ANALYSIS AND IMPROVEMENT

Business Process Analysis is proving to be one of the best analytical and action tools for achieving quality and productivity improvements. The employees who participate in BPA team efforts say that they gain a much better understanding of their own and other departments' operations, that they become aware of the concept of the internal customer, that they are able to convince team members from other departments of actions and changes needed to improve quality and productivity, and that they are given recognition and support for their ideas by management. Senior executives who have seen the results of BPA team efforts comment: "In all the years I have been President of this organization, I have never seen union members, other non-union employees and management work so well together." "The BPA teams develop tougher performance standards than we could have imposed on them"; and "The BPA teams' improvement ideas are being implemented by the people themselves. Productivity has improved beyond what we believed to be possible."

Business process analysis utilizes industrial engineering flow-charting tools to map business processes across departmental boundaries, and applies the concept of internal and external customer satisfaction as a principle vehicle for identifying improvement opportunities and establishing critical points of quality performance measurement.

The way in which BPA is applied is critical to achieving successful results. The strategies and tactics involved in achieving significant results from BPA efforts is presented in a later chapter.

9. DEVELOP QUALITY PERFORMANCE MEASURES FOR ALL BUSINESS PROCESSES

Any company wishing to achieve high levels of quality performance *must* develop a quality measurement system. Our extensive research into the state-of-the-art of quality management is conclusive on this point.

Quality performance measures cover three areas: accuracy, timeliness, and responsiveness. All three of these can be measured objectively and reliably and to statistically valid parameters. This is true in both manufacturing and in service environments.

Volumes have been written on the subject of product quality measurement and control. We have nothing new to offer as a contribution to the literature in this area. However, very little information is available on quality measurement in service companies or in service operations within manufacturing organizations. A chapter in this book is devoted to service quality measurement.

10. BENCHMARK OPERATIONS

Robert W. Galvin, former chief executive officer of Motorola, commented in one of his presentations that he considered benchmarking efforts in his company to be a key element in its outstanding success in the marketplace. In fact, he said that he personally went on twelve benchmarking visitations each year.

Benchmarking is a process that involves determining the key leverage points in a company's operations which, if improved, will have a significant impact on operating effectiveness and profitability; identifying the companies or organizations whose practices in the areas identified above are world class; and modeling the strategies, tactics and techniques used by the organizations identified in step two above.

For many individuals, step two, identifying the outstanding quality organizations is a difficult hurdle. Listed below are a number of sources for benchmarking:

Published data sources
- annual reports
- 10-K reports
- prospectuses
- trade journals
- general business periodicals
- company newsletters
- Wall Street analysts reports
- conference proceedings
- competitor sales literature
- local newspapers
- government and regulatory agency filings
- union agreements
- industry association publications

Unpublished data sources
- site visits
- direct competitor interviews (current and former)
- employees of companies being benchmarked
- supplier interviews
- distributors, agents and manufacturer's reps
- interviews with industry observers and experts for the following information:
  - corporate and division level strategies
  - operations technologies
  - product technology
  - products and processes under development
  - strategic alliances with other companies
  - proprietary practices in functional areas such as logistics, product development, distribution, and recruiting
  - product and service cost
  - internal synergy
  - organizational structure
  - areas of new breakthroughs

Customer interviews. For information on:
- purchase price of products and services
- purchase terms and conditions
- quality of customer service
- components of customer service
- product quality
- delivery practices
- sales approach/strategy
- strengths/weaknesses of your company's products and services

REFERENCES

U. S. General Accounting Office. 1991. *Report*. Doc. no. GAO/NSIAD-91-190. Washington, DC: USGAO.

Aligning Total Quality Management
and the Corporate Culture

Many of the leading quality companies have addressed the relationship between their cultures (defined as the sum of an organization's principle beliefs and behaviors) and the ability of their people to achieve high levels of performance. For these companies achieving an alignment between their strongly held beliefs regarding the need for extraordinary quality performance, motivating their people to achieve stretch goals, and maintaining a posture of continuous improvement over time, has been a vision realized. Once realized, they work hard at maintaining that vision.

The big question is, how does an organization achieve such a high degree of unity of purpose among all its people? The model presented in this chapter replicates the processes used by the successful companies in achieving this unity of purpose. The model was developed by Maxcomm Associates, a consulting firm located in Sandy, Utah. To this writer's knowledge, it is the only model that so effectively addresses the crucial issues described above, and has been successfully applied to developing a corporate culture that is receptive to the adoption of the Malcolm Baldrige criteria.

MAXCOMM's model has six major elements:
- anticipating four phases that the organization will experience as it modifies its culture, i.e. reactive, responsive, creative and productive
- implementing the change process through involving people
- undergoing a five-step transitional process from executive team development through creating a set of organizational vision and values coupled with a business focus
- challenging the new cultural direction to assure the right fit
- achieving a critical mass in attaining people's buy-in
- determining critical success factors

TQM—THE END OR A MEANS?

Theoretically, embracing total quality management (TQM) organization-wide produces many positive benefits; it eliminates non-value-added work from the system; it provides employees with a context to discuss and design how they work together in a results-oriented environment; it increases effectiveness while decreasing costs; and the quality of both products and services improves.

Yet, TQM has taken some heavy hits over the past few years. Current periodicals and business journals are full of stories on quality efforts that have fallen on hard times. In organizations with well-publicized quality efforts in place, people have been laid off, market share has dropped, and profits are flat.

Winners of the Malcolm Baldrige Award are under particular scrutiny. With several winners contributing to this book, what are we to think? One thing is clear, TQM is not a "quick fix." It will not solve all the problems an organization is facing and, in fact, may not necessarily be the best way to solve any of those problems.

To fully capitalize on an investment in TQM, it needs to be viewed as one of many tools to leverage a corporate culture change effort. TQM is not an end in and of itself; it is a means to bring about organizational transformation. Any other approach gambles a short-term focus on quality at the risk of ultimate regression to the way things were. Using TQM as a key element in a culture change effort is very different than viewing TQM as an event or program, as many organizations do.

Quality is just one of many possible strategies involved in shifting a culture, albeit a very significant one. As leverage for change, TQM may be the business focus of an organization for five-to-ten years before the basic quality tenets and behaviors are fully integrated into a new corporate culture. For a quality effort to produce the projected long-term results, it must be well-planned, well-capitalized, and well-executed. Most importantly, quality must become an integral part of an organization's culture.

If not, TQM can result in yet another short-lived "flavor-of-the-month" gimmick. If results do not come quickly enough, management may pull the plug on the effort because no one considered or prepared for the short-term downside risks of implementing a quality effort. Once the plug is pulled, it's a tough sell to "have at it" again with any subsequent efforts. This is why it is ironic that quality efforts are often deemed successes or failures after only a year or two.

The world today is very different from the world of just ten-to-fifteen years ago. We are in a fast-paced global marketplace. Technological change is rapidly accelerating. Geopolitical boundaries and cultures are shifting dramatically. The thinking and business practices we inherited from the industrial age are no longer formulas for success in the 1990s.

We don't have the luxury of time to guess at what we want to target. We must determine where we want to go and have a powerful reason why we want to go there. A shift in perspective looking at the organization as a living entity—is a necessity. Most importantly, we must be persistent and consistent in order to bring about lasting change. Setbacks are inevitable, and it is easy to get sidetracked; yet, people can more effectively overcome short-term obstacles if they believe that what they are trying to achieve truly represents something worthwhile.

What is missing for many companies at present is the capacity to continuously adapt and rethink strategies and tactics—to explore as they go. Organizations need to identify employee expectations; restructure roles and accountabilities quickly; and design appropriately to customer demands. Leaders who can recognize and tap into the enormous potential, creativity, and knowledge represented by their employees increase their ability to anticipate future opportunities and challenges while still facing day-to-day concerns.

Nowhere, then, is one of the basic principles of quality, "Doing right things right," more applicable than in capitalizing on the investment in quality. We can ill afford to waste our time, energy, or resources on something short-lived or mercurial in nature.

Consequently, when designing, implementing, and leading a cultural change effort with TQM as the business focus, emphases should be placed on:
• understanding the dynamics of change
• implementing the three "I's" of change
• designing a model organization
• employing the five-step transition process

UNDERSTANDING THE DYNAMICS OF CHANGE*

We simply cannot ignore the impact TQM can have on individuals, teams, and the organization. Regardless of how excited or resistant people are going into a quality effort or how positive the long-term outcomes promise to be, there is a drop-off in results and morale as everyone adjusts to different ways of thinking, behaving, accomplishing tasks, and conducting business.

Despite this natural reaction to change, expectations for immediate increases in productivity are usually very high (as seen in Figure l). Corporate executives and stockholders expect instantaneous results and ever-increasing returns on investment. Employees expect their long-standing frustrations with management, other departments, and even each other to be addressed and resolved. Suppliers expect exclusive contracts once they meet the quality standards. Customers expect flawless service levels and products that continually exceed expectations and still decrease in price.

Unfortunately, effectively leading and implementing a cultural change does not happen overnight. In fact, implementing any major change initially results in a downward slump in morale, effectiveness, and even quality. Each phase of the change cycle is characterized by issues that must be resolved before people can move to the next phase. Consequently, change evolves to form a dynamic, four-phased "U-shaped" profile for everyone and everything involved (see Figure 2).

Over time, the slope does level off and is followed by an upward trend in which effectiveness improves. However, successful passage through each phase of the change cycle depends on how well the prior one was negotiated. Each of the four phases of change presents distinct issues to be resolved before the next phase can begin.

---

* Much of the content of this section was developed in collaboration with The Leadership Edge, a consulting organization in Palo Alto, California. (Nelson and Black 1990)

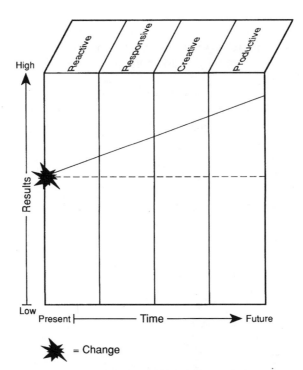

Figure 1. Expectations of implementing change.

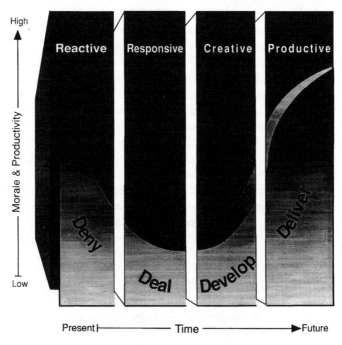

Figure 2. The four phases of change.

THE REACTIVE PHASE

During the reactive phase, people respond to the loss of the familiar and grapple with uncertainty about the way things will be in the future. The issue that must be resolved is denial. Many people react by feeling stunned, overwhelmed, or betrayed. They either avoid talking about the change or they drift off when the subject comes up. They often exhibit a variety of stress symptoms ranging from emotional outbursts and depression to withdrawal or even physical illness.

THE RESPONSIVE PHASE

The responsive phase begins as people start accepting the reality of the change and sort out how they fit in. When people stop dwelling on the way things were, let go of the past and respond to the present, they are ready to move into this phase. Although there is still no light at the end of the tunnel, the concern switches from, "Oh no, they can't do this!" to "How can I deal with this?"

THE CREATIVE PHASE

The sense of being without direction and struggling with the ambiguity of the responsive phase serve as needed catalysts to set off the third phase of change. The creative phase begins when people can entertain a notion that change is an opportunity to be explored—a new future to be developed. This period provides fertile ground for an emerging new vision to take shape as people, tired of looking backward, create forward momentum. When people are eager for a new direction, they are invigorated and a potent creative energy appears.

THE PRODUCTIVE PHASE

The productive phase occurs only if the other three stages have been successfully completed. If the organization has effectively moved through the initial resistance to change, dealt with uncertainty, and developed a new vision of the future, it is in a position to fully capitalize on the investment in quality. This phase supplies the final ingredient precipitating the successful completion of the change cycle— the emotional involvement of organizational members. A deep feeling of commitment to realize a new vision propels the organization toward achieving the desired productivity and profitability.

If the stage has been set for quality and the four phases of change are led and managed effectively, the organization can move quickly through the first two phases and on to the upward slope. If the stage has not been set, implementing a quality effort may trigger a chain reaction that drives the organization deep into a hole causing it to be reactive and rigid. In other words, the investment in change keeps escalating while the return on that investment is never realized. Despite a widely-held belief to the contrary, quality is not without a cost (see Figure 3). Poorly planned changes can drive the organization into financial and emotional ruin.

The objective in guiding the design, implementation, and leadership of a TQM effort is to apply the principles and dynamics of cultural change that not only provide a significant return on investment, but, over time, help develop a learning

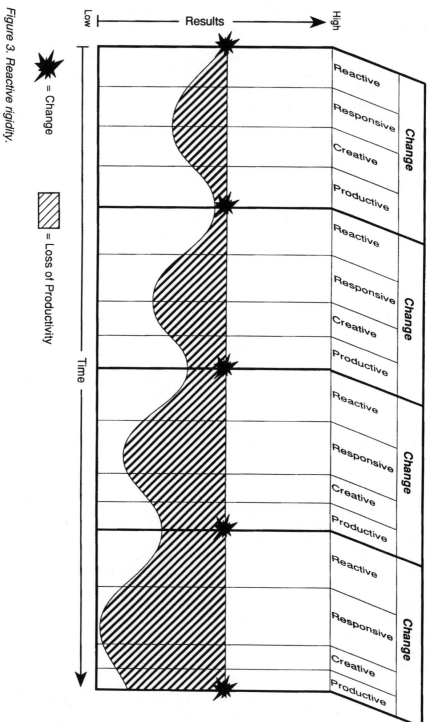

Figure 3. Reactive rigidity.

= Change

= Loss of Productivity

organization that responds with creative resiliency to change. Such an organization learns how to consistently take advantage of the opportunities inherent in change and makes continuous improvement a way of organizational life (see Figure 4).

In short, the quality effort does not become the end result. Rather, the, quality effort can become the catalyst for the overall cultural shift and prepare the organization for a future characterized by change, uncertainty, and unlimited opportunity.

IMPLEMENTING CHANGE: THE THREE I's OF CHANGE

Change can be implemented in any of three ways. It can be imposed, informed, or involved. The challenge is in selecting the best benefits that will justify the necessary expenditure of time, money, and resources (see Figure 5).

IMPOSED CHANGE

Imposed change is fairly straightforward and quick once a decision is made on the direction to go. The decision-makers often work hard over a long time period to devise a change strategy and think through the mechanics of implementing it with very little involvement from the rest of the organization.

When the plan is complete, it is simply dumped on the employees, and everyone is expected to comply. If leaders have sufficient power and influence, they can probably make the change viable. That's the easy part. Unfortunately, ownership and commitment rest entirely with those same decision-makers.

The result is often resistance and confusion from employees coupled with impatience and disappointment from senior management. The immediate tendency is to resist or reject the change; sabotage often follows. Consequently, management is forced to spend a significant amount of time and energy teaching employees how to implement the change and continually selling them on its value.

INFORMED CHANGE

When compared to imposed change, informed change demands more time and energy prior to implementation. This method does not involve employees when devising and planning the change. However, when the plan is complete, it is presented to the employees and their input is sought. Employees have an opportunity to consider the plan, understand it, and respond with any suggestions they have for improving it. To use this method successfully, decision makers must be willing to accept and act upon employee feedback.

In this case, people are not caught off guard; yet, wide-spread ownership and commitment are still lacking. At best, people tend to be reluctant and take a wait-and-see attitude until they determine what is in this change that will benefit them. Even though the result is implied acceptance—saluting—without any show of outright rejection or resistance, managers constantly have to nudge and encourage hesitant, cautious employees to persuade them to implement the change.

In this case, expanding ownership and commitment means going to those affected and saying, "From where we sit, here is our best take on what needs to

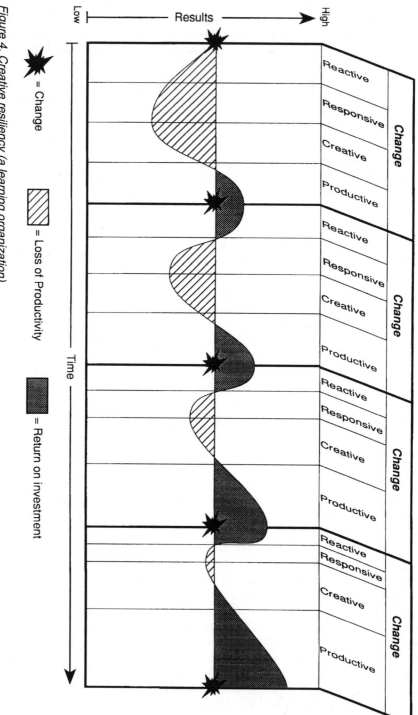

Figure 4. Creative resiliency (a learning organization).

	Imposed "Do It"	Informed "Here it is"	Involved "Let's plan together"
Change	resisted	considered understod	enhanced
Ownership Commitment Responsibility	at the top	wait and see	shared
Time Spent	crisis management	continually selling	up front

Figure 5. Dimensions of change.

be done. We want your feedback and input before we are comfortable with a final decision. Tell us what you think."

INVOLVED CHANGE

Both imposed and informed change can eventually lead to compliance. Involved change, on the other hand, leads to commitment and ownership. Involved change includes those who will be impacted by the change early in the decision making process. At the beginning of the process, leaders introduce their ideas about changes to employees and say, "Let's plan it together!" Considerable time and energy is spent going over strategies and creating implementation plans (see Figure 6). In essence, people determine their destination and contribute to the design of the vehicle that will transport them there.

As a result of this united effort, people come to understand and appreciate the change and develop personal ownership for and commitment to it. It is not something being "done" to them. Although the plan takes longer to create, the implementation is quicker and smoother because people are naturally receptive to the change and embrace it more willingly at all levels.

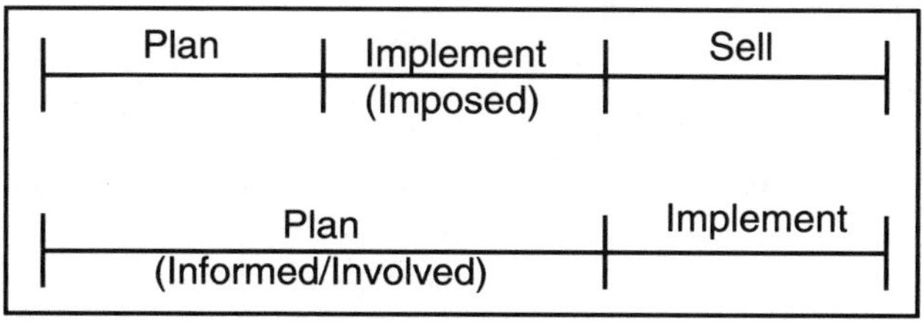

Figure 6. Change implementation timeline.

DESIGNING A MODEL ORGANIZATION

Over the years, organizations have become proficient at creating functional autonomy within their various departments and divisions. Organizational charts encourage this autonomy; reward systems reinforce it; and, in many instances, the walls built between functions are virtually impenetrable even if employees really did want to communicate or cooperate. This autonomy creates a smoke stack effect—each function stands alone, with no doors or windows, nor avenues for communication and interchange. Everyone does their own thing and blames poor results on others.

TRADITIONAL ROLES AND RESPONSIBILITIES

Our culture has defined roles for senior executives, managers, and supervisors that, in many instances, are very restrictive. For example, in many organizations, a supervisor's role is akin to that of a police officer. After all, someone needs to keep employees in line and headed in the right direction. The job of a supervisor, therefore, is to continually watch for mistakes, monitoring employees and prodding them back in line when they blunder. As everyone eventually stumbles, a shoving match results as supervisors apply pressure to employees, and employees naturally resist that pressure and push back.

Depending on the specific organization, shoving back can assume many forms. For example, some employees try to beat the system by abusing benefits such as sick days and health insurance. Others sabotage equipment and products. Mistreating the customer to get even with management is a particularly destructive example of shoving back. Whatever the method, everyone ultimately suffers, and a tremendous amount of energy is lost.

Add managers to the equation. They are traditionally in place to ensure that supervisors do their jobs. If supervisors fail to achieve results, then managers start pushing supervisors in line. In all likelihood, supervisors can take this strain for only so long before they, too, start resisting and push back. Consequently, the shoving expands to involve more combatants.

Then the senior executives, who are ultimately held accountable by the board and stockholders, see results slide or perceive things are not happening quickly enough and put the squeeze on their managers. If the situation is considered serious enough, they eventually position themselves behind the massive shoving match and endeavor to move everyone in the direction of achieving the organization's goals and objectives.

As senior executives apply more and more force, employees, supervisors, and managers dig in their heels and push back with all their strength. Now the shoving match has not only grown to gigantic proportions, it has the potential to turn ugly! It is easy, then, to understand how quickly an organization's energy can be directed inward. The competition is not another company; the competition is down the hall in the corner office or in the department next door. The customer is ignored, or worse yet, resented because they demand time and attention that is in short supply.

The organization tends to drift aimlessly because senior executives cannot provide necessary focus and direction when they are busy pushing. As they struggle from behind to move the gigantic mass of wasted energy, there is little hope they will have an unobstructed view of the future. Everyone is working hard, but no one is producing tangible results. No wonder people feel burned out. No wonder a company in this dilemma has trouble competing in a global economy.

We had just such an experience while working with an air line (no longer in business) whose senior management focused their attention internally on the unions, not externally on the competition or the rapidly changing marketplace. Most of their time and energy was devoted to eliminating the union control. Not surprisingly, the union was just as intent on bringing down management. Lost in this internal struggle was the customer and other stakeholders—namely employees. Needless to say, this air line was infamous for its poor financial performance and lack of quality service.

THE NEW VIEW

At the opposite end of the continuum, imagine an organization where everyone's energy is aligned to produce results, where employees take ownership for corporate performance, and everyone takes personal responsibility for pleasing the customer. There is cooperation and teamwork at every level. Unions and management partner to create the working relationships of the future, instead of dwelling on the past. Functionally autonomous units are virtually non-existent and in their place is an organizational structure that mirrors key business processes.

Managers and supervisors now serve as coaches and team leaders. Employees are self-managing. Senior executives are leading the organization—breaking down barriers, overcoming obstacles, and providing a clear focus and direction. Customers and suppliers are heard, and in many cases, have a voice in the decision-making process.

Non-value-added work is eliminated daily. Costs are down; quality is improving. Market share and profitability are both up. Employees feel good about coming to work each day and believe they are making a meaningful contribution to the organization's success. Customers are loyal, committed, and satisfied.

This may sound a little like "Pollyanna" yet it aptly describes the "new" organization that is vision-led, values-guided, and business-focused. Everything may not be as perfect as it sounds and many challenges lie ahead; however, this organization is capable of anticipating change and leading it, rather than just reacting to it.

The bottom line effectiveness of any organization is a function of how well it uses its energy, resources, and information. In system terms, the high-performing organization is one that is maximizing its full potential as a well-integrated, finely-tuned set of subsystems, strongly focused and aligned by a common purpose.

Sharing a strong sense of direction allows everyone in an organization to realize their contributions are relevant to the company's success. Applying a common set of values permits each individual to determine the effectiveness of their daily behaviors and encourages more self-management. Focusing on well-defined business objectives enables everyone to follow the game plan. We work to create this alignment—leveraging a strategic business focus such as TQM to effect this organizational shift.

TQM AS A BUSINESS FOCUS

It is possible, but highly improbable, to leave the old culture intact if TQM is not used as a means to leverage a cultural shift. Leaving the existing culture intact constantly risks that the old patterns will supersede what is being attempted through TQM. At best, the old way of doing things may simply not support the quality approach. At worst, the old ways of doing things may be in direct conflict with TQM principles.

Over and over again corporations have tried to reorganize by restructuring. In every case, the old structure supersedes the reorganized one. Problems that existed prior to the restructuring continue to exist after the restructuring. In the final analysis, the restructuring turns out to be an exercise in futility rather than a vehicle for improving organizational effectiveness.

For example, in one client organization (a resort property), the competition was really the other functional departments. Employees tended to view guests as an imposition and as trespassers into their private playground. In this organization, no amount of quality-based training could ever override the prevailing corporate culture. Only after completing extensive work on vision and values, building teams throughout the organization, restructuring reporting relationships, and concentrating on financial accountability was the organization finally able to shift its focus and attention to serving the customer with excellence.

Through our experience, we have identified components that ensure lasting change occurs. These include:

1. a committed, unwavering, and highly visible leader
2. a well-articulated vision, values, and business focus
3. a strategic emphasis on direction and education
4. personal responsibility and accountability
5. an accurate, reliable, and timely measurement system
6. effective means of communication—formal and informal
7. a systematic way of designing, implementing, and leading future changes
8. a commitment to be persistent and flexible based upon what the environment or situation dictates

Our systems approach to large-scale cultural change focuses on exchanging old habits and attitudes for purposeful actions aimed toward achieving the company's vision and desired state. This focus provides a foundation that translates TQM into individual and team commitment and a willingness to be accountable for results.

EMPLOYING THE FIVE-STEP TRANSITION PROCESS

The framework for our approach includes a high-involvement strategy and a model for learning that will bring about continuous, ongoing improvement. We have discovered from our experience that individuals, teams, and organizations produce outstanding results when they share a common sense of direction and are aligned with that direction.

Our model for learning is a proven five-step process that provides the canvas and pallet for initiating, leading, and capitalizing on change. Even though structural components of each effort share common traits, the actual design is, by necessity, customized to the unique needs of the client organization.

The model is comprised of the following five steps:

1. set the stage
2. diagnose the situation
3. design solutions
4. implement the plans
5. evaluate results

The process is designed in such a way that when the fifth step of evaluating results is achieved, the cycle begins anew. The process and its benefits are ongoing. Even though we present the steps in a linear form, they do not represent a linear process. At any given time, steps may be concurrent (see Figure 7).

Thoughtful action and results occur during all five steps of the process. Each step represents an interruption to and a reassessment of the traditional ways of doing things. Going through a culture shift does not denote a "time out" for the organization. Rather, it represents a seamless integration of daily activities and tasks with purposeful goals and objectives. The culture shift is set in motion as soon as we begin setting the stage. What happens in the stage setting step is of primary importance. Quite literally, it determines the success or failure of the

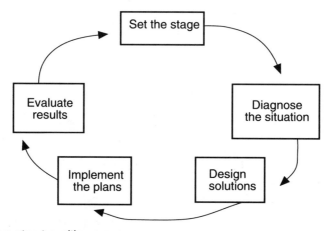

Figure 7. Five-step transition process.

remaining four steps. For this reason, we describe the first step in more detail than the others.

STEP 1: SET THE STAGE

This step is the first and most crucial of the change process. The introduction of any major change, such as quality, into an organization creates a ripple effect that can either propel the organization forward to a compelling future or thrust it back into resistance and confusion.

In setting the stage, our goal is to make the drop in the change curve less pronounced (see Figure 8) representing a decisive strategy for capitalizing on the investment in quality. Time and energy not invested up front will later become an added expense in reselling, restarting, and recovering from unexpected disasters.

Orienting the executive team. Our preliminary work with a president or CEO is referred to as reality testing. Before we embark on a major cultural change effort, we want to confirm that the client understands the effects the change will produce in them and the organization.

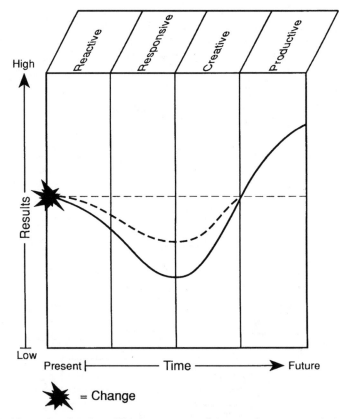

Figure 8. Managing the drop. The investment of time and resources during the stage setting step reduces the costs of change.

We explain the dynamics of change and explore what that means in terms of employee morale and bottom-line results. We challenge them to answer the following questions, "Can the organization afford the chaos that will be created at this time?" and "How will we minimize the negative impact the change may have on the organization and stakeholders?"

The concept of TQM is very seductive, so we take our time before deciding whether to embark on this journey that requires commitment to a long-term relationship. It cannot be interpreted as a one-night stand. Once senior executives have made the commitment, they travel a one way street. Turning back early in the journey threatens their credibility; turning back farther along the way can very well threaten the viability of the entire organization.

We also explore the critical role the leader plays in the change effort— fundamentally reshaping the organization. As the change unfolds, leaders become models for the organization. They must understand that they are constantly going to be under the magnifying glass. If they do not model what they espouse, their inconsistency will become a convenient excuse for everyone else to continue doing the same old things in the same old ways.

Leaders do not have to be perfect in order to ask people to stretch; however, they must challenge their own development if they wish others to view them as having integrity, authenticity, and credibility. In addition, they must be honest about their own struggle as leaders. In short, leadership in a cultural change effort is by example, not by delegation!

After we work with the president or CEO, we then guide the senior executive team through a similar process. Without understanding and support at this level, bringing about cultural change is virtually impossible. Again, we look for ownership and support. In many cases, extensive team building is necessary to prepare the executive group to lead the effort. In all cases, additional education is required. After all, true commitment is directly proportional to the level of comprehension. In other words, "How can I commit to something I don't understand?"

Creating the vision, values, and business focus. Much of the senior team development is centered around identifying, discussing, and articulating the corporate vision and values. Often, there is already "something" in place; however, typically there exists very little ownership for or commitment to its ultimate achievement. From the start, ownership for the change must reside with leadership, not with outside consultants. If ownership is vested externally, the results of the change leave the organization when the consultants do.

Without ownership for and commitment to the vision, values, and business focus at the senior executive level, there is little chance of stimulating ownership and commitment throughout the ranks of the organization. Eventually, if the objective is to have everyone in the organization share in the ownership of the effort, leadership must be committed to the long-term nature of the change process. Things can and will go wrong. Commitment must be there to support the effort through the bad times as well as the good. Without expressed ownership and commitment from the top, the process has the potential to collapse.

We work with the senior executives on envisioning a compelling future until they are ready to articulate that vision to the organization and open it up to challenge. Without an articulated vision, a statement of values, or an identified business focus, we have only random, unconnected bits and pieces of activity that contribute to confusion and increase the workload. Further, this fragmentation never produces lasting, positive change. By contrast, an effort that is vision-led, values-guided, and business-focused can produce significant and long-term change.

Vision-led. If people do not know where they are going, they are not likely to ever know when they have arrived. Articulating a clear vision—the first challenge in creating a model organization—creates passion in people. It defines a worthwhile, compelling future. The vision provides people with a meaningful purpose for where they are and what they are doing. However it is presented, the vision must evoke an emotional response to be effective.

Without a compelling future, there can be no long-term commitment to the organization. Without a vision, people have little to inspire them when things become difficult.

In our experience, a compelling vision:
- describes a preferred and meaningful state that evokes a powerful emotional image in people's minds
- helps give people a better understanding of how they can manifest their own purpose
- motivates people even during hard economic times, crisis, or conflict
- is perceived as achievable but still a stretch for individuals and the organization
- is genuine and comes from the heart
- is lofty and challenging
- is easy to understand
- is expressed in the present sense

Values-guided. Values—the second challenge in creating a model organization—are the nonnegotiable ethical code of conduct for the organization. They define how employees treat each other, customers, and suppliers. The values become the parameters within which people work. The values statement from Perot Systems is an example of a code an organization may agree to share (see Figure 9).

Eventually, all employees, hold each other accountable for living the values rather than this being the key responsibility of only supervisors and managers. Each employee assumes personal responsibility to be self-managing freeing up supervisors and managers to become coaches and team leaders as opposed to acting as police officers.

The process of defining values is straightforward; however, it is not necessarily easy. Asking people to establish an ethical standard of behavior they are willing to uphold requires them to examine their personal belief systems and core convictions. A major challenge is stating the values so they represent a desired state rather than reflecting the current status.

For example, in one organization, a heated debate occurred within the operating committee over whether the correct wording for one value statement should be "integrity" or "uncompromising integrity." Some felt that given the business they were in uncompromising integrity was an unrealistic standard for them to uphold.

Perot Systems

Vision

Perot Systems will become the premier computer services and communications firm in the world; it pledges that the company will belong to the people who build it; earn after-tax profits in excess of $100 million within 10 years; have the strongest balance sheet in the industry and no debt; maintain an atmosphere of mutual trust and respect; and listen to the people who do the work. Perot Systems will not be sold or merged.

Values

- We will have only one class of team member—each member will be a full partner.
- We will recognize and reward excellence while the individual is still sweating from his efforts.
- We will build and maintain a spirit of one for all and all for one.
- We will encourage every team member to take risks, make decisions, exercise initiative, and never be afraid to make mistakes.
- We will hold team members accountable for results, with great flexibility in deciding how to achieve results and the clear understanding that ethical standards must never be compromised.
- We will eliminate any opportunity for people to succeed by merely looking good.
- We will promote solely on merit.
- We will ensure that our ethical standards with our customers and suppliers are impeccable.

Perot Systems also has a code of conduct

- We will not tolerate anyone who
  - acts in a manner which will bring discredit to the company;
  - discriminates against another with regard to race, religion, sex or any other reason
  - looks down on others
  - becomes a corporate politician;
  - tries to move ahead at the expense of others;
  - uses illegal drugs

Figure 9. A sample values statement.

The conversation around this verbiage took months to resolve. The stalemate was finally broken when someone suggested the wording should be "convenient integrity." The point was made; everyone objected to the word "convenient" and agreed that the word "integrity" inherently means that it is not subject to compromise. In this case, the members of the operating committee learned about themselves, each other, and the business they were in while they were engaged in conversations about the appropriate wording of the values.

Wrestling with articulating an ethical code of conduct is an important exercise for all. It forces employees to think about their belief systems collectively and establishes their willingness to accept personal accountability for living to this standard. It also surfaces the gaps between where they are currently compared to where they say they desire to be. This can be a very painful, yet enlightening, experience.

Business-focused. The business focus begins to take shape in this step. However, it is not set in concrete until after the organizational assessment is conducted during Step two of the transition process. Derived from an analysis of internal and external forces that have an impact on the organization, business focus provides a yardstick to measure economic success. Over time, the business focus evolves to account for shifts in market conditions, the current state of the organization, and technological advances. It serves as the business directive on which to concentrate people's attention, time, and energy.

It also supplies a framework for organizing daily tasks. By constantly returning to the business focus, every employee can effectively prioritize their work. Everything in the organization must be centered on accomplishing the business focus. In other words, "if what I am doing is not moving the organization toward achievement of its business goals and objectives and is not aligned with long-term strategies, I should not be doing it."

To assist senior executives in better defining their business and creating well conceived strategies, we lead them through an assessment related to marketplace demands, competition, customers, and product/service differentiation strategies. Completing the assessment is key in nurturing an environment where people will address issues honestly and then challenge each other's thinking in constructive ways.

Once the business focus is defined, the dialogue about it is never finished. This dialogue must continue as the marketplace is constantly in flux. Successful companies not only anticipate customer needs, they create them. In other words, the business focus has to evolve and change over time to ensure the long-term viability of the organization.

CHALLENGING AND VALIDATING THE DIRECTION
Initially, the work on the vision, values, and business focus is the responsibility of the senior leadership the organization. However, if the ownership and commitment begins and ends with them, little has been achieved.

The purpose behind the vision, values, and business focus is to clearly lay out what the organization stands for, where it is headed, and how it plans to meet its goals ethically and strategically. It is not about changing anyone; rather, it is a call for membership, commitment, personal responsibility, and accountability. Unless everyone has an opportunity to provide feedback and input, ownership and commitment will be lacking. The direction will be nothing more than a framed piece of paper hanging on the wall collecting dust.

For this reason, we recommend organizations go through an extensive challenge process for validating the vision, values, and business focus. The process begins with the senior executive team. Over the course of several structured sessions, the senior executive team has an opportunity to articulate their vision, values, and business focus. Once they are comfortable with conveying their ideas out to the organization for feedback and input, the challenge process begins.

There is no magic formula for a challenge process design. We create each design in partnership with the client, taking into account the existing culture and desired outcomes of the process. We have found the process works best when senior executives and staff are trained to facilitate it. This allows senior executives to gather unfiltered feedback and input while addressing the issues face-to-face with those most affected. Trained facilitators are present to ensure an open and honest exchange takes place.

The challenge process is a lengthy and time-consuming undertaking, but in the end, people who have been through the process see the business in a way they have never seen the business before. Energy and enthusiasm are unleashed when all employees participate in the process

One of our client organizations is entering the second year of their challenge process. Eventually, almost ten thousand employees in over fifty countries worldwide will participate in sessions conducted in their native language. During these sessions, each employee explores how they fit individually and collectively into a worldwide vision, challenges the area mission statement, and rates current behavior against the stated values. In addition, barriers and obstacles to living the values are identified and captured for future reference. This information is compiled and serves as a basis for action planning at the appropriate levels.

So far, two vision statements have been discarded because feedback indicated these statements did not create a compelling future for everyone in the organization. In this particular company, employees clearly have a strong voice in creating and shaping their future. There can be little doubt about where the ownership and commitment to vision and values resides.

In another client organization, the finalized vision and values document was the result of 262 challenge sessions. Of the 3,500 employees in the organization, 75 percent took part in these sessions. The process extended over a period of more than a year from initial work. Even after a significant investment in time and energy, the challenge process is not complete. Every new employee goes through a modified challenge process as part of their orientation. Most importantly, the vision and values direct every aspect of the business internally and externally.

Members of the organization are working to integrate the vision and values into the way they operate on a daily basis.

For both organizations, the vision and values have provided, and continue to provide, the foundation on which to launch quality efforts. Because the concepts of quality have already been articulated in these statements, it is only natural for TQM to be the vehicle that will carry the vision and values from the conceptual to the practical. The vision and values process can establish the base and prepare people to appreciate the thinking and strategy represented by quality thus allowing the organization to capitalize on future opportunities.

The precise words on a printed page do not tip the scales regarding how people view their future with the organization. Any outside advertising agency could probably be more articulate and considerably more poetic. Rather, it is the challenge process the organization goes through to arrive at those exact words. Contemplating a compelling future, discussing business strategies with senior executives, and responding in an open, honest, and direct way regarding current behavior creates a sense of membership that company parties, picnics, and company-wide meetings never achieve. It begins a dynamic process that grows and develops over time and sets the stage for lasting cultural change.

When people leave these challenge sessions, they have a sense of feeling connected to each other and to the organization vision emotionally and intellectually. They begin to understand the significance of their contribution to the overall business strategy and the value of that contribution to the organization. Taking an entire company through the vision and values process unleashes tremendous amounts of energy and creativity. This challenge process is a must if the goal is total employee commitment and involvement.

On completion of the challenge process, the message is clear and unambiguous, "You now know where we are headed and why we are going there. The choice is yours and yours alone. Either come aboard now or deplane. We will depart momentarily!"

ANTICIPATING AND PLANNING FOR THE FUTURE

In conjunction with articulating clear vision and values, we also draft preliminary plans during stage setting. Here we try to anticipate what will be needed downstream of the change effort. Instead of kicking off the effort and then chasing along behind the organization reacting to every immediate crisis, we get out in front of the effort and have supplies waiting for us when we arrive.

For example, long before any business process analysis teams are ever formed, we address the hardware and software that will be needed to track results. Long before business process improvement teams begin eliminating non-value-added work from the system potentially undermining the unions, union leadership is involved in the decisions about the design, implementation, and management of the effort. Covering all the bases up front clearly takes time, but the benefits downstream are more than worth the effort.

Failure to anticipate future needs can lead to missed opportunities. For example, we put approximately 300 supervisors through a two-day team building session over a one-month period. Now if we had followed our own advice, we would have foreseen that a significant number of those supervisors would want their people to participate in a similar experience. This would have meant having twenty to thirty staff facilitators trained and ready to go as soon as we received the requests.

In reality, however, we were caught off-guard in a reactive mode and did not initiate the wide-spread training of facilitators soon enough to capture the momentum. By the time the facilitators were ready to present the sessions, many of the supervisors had lost interest or taken action on their own. Eventually, we conducted additional team building but not with the impact we could have achieved if we had anticipated the needs earlier in the process.

In fact, this is a common occurrence when supply depots are not in place. Those organization members who embrace the change early are the natural catalysts for cultural change. When you don't anticipate their needs, you miss the window of opportunity. It is critical to anticipate future needs and stock the supply depots as early as is feasible. Otherwise, you soon find yourself chasing after change and leaving the early adopters unsupplied, unsupported and, in some cases, unprotected.

ACHIEVING CRITICAL MASS

In our planning sessions, we also identify those areas of the organization that may initially be so averse to the change that confronting them head on at this time is not worth the time, energy, or effort. To do so requires more resources than the return on the investment justifies. In other words, we might eventually win them over, but we sacrifice the momentum in the rest of the organization to garner their support.

In this situation, a better strategy is to concentrate resources on the early adopters and use them to form the core of the critical mass necessary to create momentum for lasting change. By using this strategy, the change-resisters are isolated and their negativity rendered harmless. Later in the process, after their resistance has been worn down and their negative energy dissipates, we can go back and more effectively work with them.

This means designing the change effort around the highest common denominator, rather than the lowest. If we wait for everyone to come aboard, very little is likely to change. Our objective is to engage, support, and protect the five-to-ten percent who are willing to take a risk and make the difference early in the process. This focus promises a high return on investment.

Once another twenty-to-thirty percent of the organizational members see how the change benefits them, they, too, come aboard and constitute the critical mass that propels another twenty-to-forty percent of the organization along with them. It becomes evident to the remaining ten percent they no longer fit into the new culture. Eventually, they self-select out of the organization or are asked to leave.

After developing these initial plans, we are careful not to get locked into viewing them as the only viable alternatives. When implementation begins and more information is gathered, we continually review and revise the plans in light of new understandings. This contingency planning is supported by General Colin Powell's observation on the eve of the land invasion of Iraq, "Our plans are only good until the moment of execution. Then we have to change them."

Our working model for this is "double loop learning" (Figure 10). Rather than always measuring our actions only against the original plan—"single-loop learning"—we constantly ask the question, "Should we be doing what we set out to do given additional information?" Double-loop learning forces us to continually monitor the situation and make necessary adjustments (Argyris 1977).

Approaching the change effort from a systems perspective. Our approach to planning stems from a systems perspective which constantly reminds us that any intervention will eventually impact the entire organization, each supplier, every customer, and all other stakeholders in one way or another.

In other words, we cannot work with just one part of the organization, with just the senior team or with just one business process. Each and every action will cause at least a ripple effect throughout the organization and beyond. And the potential exists for each and every action to evolve into a devastating tidal wave.

In designing, implementing, and leading the change effort, we continually anticipate the consequences of our intervention beyond the immediate circumstances. Clearly, we can never anticipate or prepare for the myriad of possibilities that may occur. However, embarking on a TQM effort with the understanding that it is not just about quality is significant. Our experience with TQM

Single-loop Learning

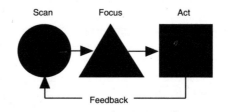

Double-loop Learning

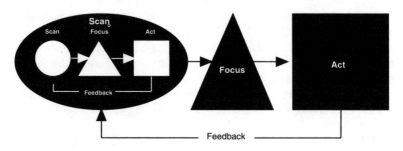

Figure 10. Single-loop and double-loop learning.

demonstrates repeatedly that such an effort can surface everything that is functional as well as dysfunctional in the organization.

Because the stage setting step can last anywhere from one to two years, we must carefully time any general announcement of the impending change effort with our readiness to begin the process publicly. We want to be as prepared as possible from the beginning so we can set and manage realistic expectations within the organization. It is often difficult to keep from prematurely sharing the excitement and energy that results from early discussions. However, the more planning that occurs during this step, before the general announcement, the easier the process becomes downstream.

Designing the communication plan. In the stage setting step, we also develop a comprehensive communication plan. We have found that timely, accurate, and reliable communication is the glue that holds a change effort together. The communication plan covers not only mass communication, publications, videos, and other formal channels, it also includes the informal, interpersonal ones.

For example, every time the Executive Quality Council meets, a communication specialist needs to be present. At the conclusion of each meeting, council members then discuss the key message points they will verbally pass on to their direct reports and how they desire their reports to move the information on through the organization.

On the formal side of the plan, in-house publications carry stories to support and report on all activities associated with the change effort. The importance of a well thought out communication plan cannot be over-emphasized. It prepares and informs the organization and provides an excellent feedback mechanism to verify the effectiveness of the communication process.

In reality, setting the stage never ends. We are always preparing the organization for something new. Time spent in this step is well-invested.

STEP 2: DIAGNOSE THE SITUATION

People are motivated to change either because they want to or because they have to. The vision and values process establishes a compelling future that can inspire people to want to change. Our experience indicates that until people understand how a compelling future involves them, they are not interested in the future. Step two allows us to determine the current state of the organization and determine where employees are, individually and collectively.

Conducting an organizational assessment. During this step, we capture a picture in time of the organization through traditional avenues such as employee opinion surveys, one-on-one interviews, focus group sessions, customer surveys, and a review of in-house documents. This research gives us a well-grounded understanding of the key issues for the organization and all employees. In other words, we assemble concrete data to support the perceptions of what is working, what isn't working, what's missing, and what needs to change. This awareness helps identify the opportunities that may provide the greatest leverage for positive change and thus justify the expenditure of time, energy, and resources.

It is also during this step that we determine if TQM is the appropriate business focus to bring about cultural change in the organization given what is occurring internally in the organization and externally in the marketplace. In some organizations, generating cash flow needs to be the business focus. In others, the most pressing need might be working with the senior team and the president. The important point is to determine the business imperative only after a thorough analysis of both the internal and external forces influencing the organization.

Diagnosing the situation also helps generate energy in the organization necessary to direct the culture change. When we compare the current reality of the organization with the desired state—the vision—a clear gap typically emerges. This gap creates frustration and dissatisfaction—energy we channel for positive change and toward realizing the vision and values.

In fact, in organizations not outwardly manifesting motivation to change, we actually stimulate motivation by graphically illustrating the size of the gap between where they are and where they say they want to be. When they get a glimpse of what can be rather than what is, they can't help but feel impatient to get there.

At this point, we also evaluate the corporate measurement system. If one exists, we make sure it will meet the long-term needs for ongoing organizational assessment. In addition, we use all the data gathered to create base line indicators that can be used to gauge organizational progress.

STEP 3: DESIGN SOLUTIONS

In this step, we design with the client the means for individuals and the organization to increase their effectiveness and move toward the vision. With one of our clients, key issues centered around poor service to the customer and little cross-functional teamwork or cooperation.

With this focus in mind, we began designing a quality effort that addressed the lack of cross-functional teamwork and cooperation to move them toward their vision of providing outstanding customer service. The key issue that supplied the impetus for the quality effort came from inside the organization. It was not imposed or implemented because all the president's associates were into TQM.

As previously mentioned, when designing solutions from a systems perspective, we take into account the ripple effects that any and every action will have beyond the immediate situation and time. For instance, if we are encouraging a team environment, we also look at the potential need to redesign reward and recognition systems. These systems reinforce desired behaviors and indicate the hiring process that can surface candidates who will thrive in a team environment. We endeavor to establish as many resource depots as possible ahead of time so we don't find ourselves in a reactive mode downstream.

As soon as the plans are actually implemented, the culture, people, and systems naturally begin to change. It is not long before our target shifts enough that our initial thinking is off the mark. General Dwight D. Eisenhower once said,

"Plans are nothing. Planning is everything." For us, this translates into continual redesign in one form or another.

STEP 4: IMPLEMENT THE PLANS

Although we are constantly anticipating and planning, it does not mean we wait to take action. As stated earlier, action and results occur in all five steps. In Step four of the process, however, we implement the long-term plans.

During this step, we bring on-line those specific activities that will keep people moving toward the vision. Extensive team building may be needed to develop cross-functional cooperation. At the same time, business process analysis teams may be working to identify existing bottlenecks that functionally obstruct cooperation.

Having all the activity coordinated and focused quickly results in noticeable changes in the organization while producing bottom-line results. Both are needed to give people a sense of accomplishment and the incentive to keep doing things differently.

STEP 5: EVALUATE RESULTS

Even though Step five is listed as "evaluate results," in reality, evaluation is ongoing during every step of the process. This perpetual monitoring provides the feedback and input necessary for continuous improvement. It also allows us to track progress and measure against established milestones. It is important to build yardsticks into the system so worthwhile results are tracked on a regular basis. We firmly believe in the adages: "you get what you inspect, not what you expect" and "you can't manage what you don't measure."

Anything measured in an organization serves very much like a reward in communicating to people what is valued by the organization. The key question then becomes, "Given where we are trying to take the organization, does what we measure lead us there?" If the answer is no, then we are sending mixed messages, and people are no doubt confused as to what is expected of them.

We believe an essential step in any TQM effort is determining the critical success factors for the organization and how to measure those factors (Figure 11). Critical success factors in the organization need to be aligned to a common vision, guided by shared values, and focused on collective objectives and goals with people at the core. This is crucial for aligning energy and behavior toward the vision, values, and business focus. In other words, the measures help direct the overall performance of the organization.

The five steps give us a structured way of thinking about and categorizing our work. In practice, however, the steps are never linear. In one organization, we may begin by implementing a communication plan because accurate information and formal channels are nonexistent, and we cannot proceed without some structure in place. As a rule, we follow the sequence, even though parts of the steps may be concurrent, because it continually forces us and the client to look at the change effort in a systematic and logical way.

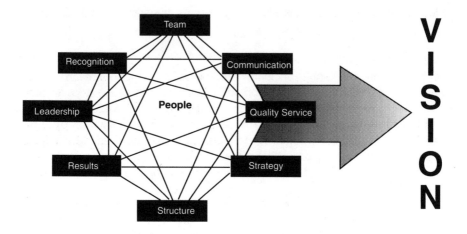

Figure 11. Eight element model

TQM—THE MEANS TO AN END!

Substantively changing the culture of an organization requires short- and long-term thinking combined with appropriate strategies. The long-term approach is what we call the "occupation" strategy. In other words, how do we occupy the organization with vision, values, and the business-focus of quality long enough to achieve the critical mass necessary to shift the culture.

Achieving this critical mass requires extensive education, development, and training at all levels. Massive resources are needed to execute this approach. In the process, early adopters must be protected from the organization until that critical mass is achieved. This protection is best provided by the senior executives. Finally, a formal structure is required to support the cultural change effort.

Clearly, there is much more to a quality effort than business process analysis, quality improvement teams, and basic statistical training. Implementing a quality effort alters the culture of the organization in profound ways. Such dramatic change always has emotional and financial costs associated with it.

By seeing the quality effort as one element to systematically shift the culture, we can capitalize significantly on the investment in TQM. More importantly, if a cultural change is well-designed, strategically implemented, and carefully managed, the organization can achieve a level of unequaled employee commitment, performance, and results. It is this organization that truly deserves the recognition of its peers and competitors, for the successful implementation of TQM enables a company to literally become a world-class organization.

The greatest leverage to be gained from implementing a TQM effort comes in employing it as the means rather than using it as an end—a process that never ceases but takes on a life of its own, continuing to blossom as employees at all levels nourish its growth.

REFERENCES

Chris Argyris, "Double Loop Learning in Organizations," Harvard Business Review, Sept./Oct. 1977.

Nelson, L. Tyler, Ph.D. and Joe D. Black. 1990. "The Leadership of Change." Seminar presented by the University of Utah DCE Business Institute, Salt Lake City.

Leadership for Quality: Best Practices of Top Quality Companies

Having studied the quality initiatives implemented by corporate leaders of several hundred successful organizations, it is absolutely clear that their actions and commitment to quality are the most important elements in achieving high levels of quality and productivity performance. This is true in starting a quality process and maintaining a momentum for continuous improvement over time.

Many executives who have been making the effort to familiarize themselves with quality management concepts have asked me to describe what is involved— what would be required of them in providing their organizations with leadership in the quality area. A number of these executives express the concern that their having to lead the way would occupy more of their time than they could afford to give. Interestingly, a number of executives who have lived through implementing a quality process in their organizations say that they now have more time to devote to planning and thinking about strategic issues than they had before they implemented a quality process. They explain this by pointing out that their business processes work more smoothly; that *potential* problems are dealt with at lower levels of the organization; that employee teams rather than management are setting tough performance standards and solving customer satisfaction issues; and that better and more effective planning techniques have reduced production and service delivery cycle times which has enabled their companies to be more profitable and competitive.

Research into the best practices of successful quality companies reveals the following series of actions by their leadership.

SENIOR LEADERSHIP

Senior executives lead by personal involvement and visibility in developing and maintaining a customer focus and an environment for quality excellence. For example, Motorola's CEO formally stated that the company's central theme is quality. Total customer satisfaction was presented as the company's fundamental objective. Key quality goals for Motorola are:

- to be the best in class in terms of people, technology, marketing product, manufacturing, and service
- focus on very specific numerical goals; i.e. 10X (10 times improvement), 100X, and Six Sigma product reliability
- a thrust towards cycle time reduction

- provide recognition through a CEO quality award bestowed on a deserving individual, team, operation, or higher level by the CEO
- the senior management team takes the lead in benchmarking world class companies.

Xerox embarked on its development of a formal quality strategy in the early 1980s. The following are highlights of their leadership approach to quality:
- senior executive team conducted extensive benchmarking of world-class companies
- quality effort was driven from the top, with customer satisfaction as the top priority
- utilized an Employee Satisfaction Measurement System to receive employee input about quality and instituted actions to effect improvements
- senior managers participate on quality teams and act as quality role models
- objectives based on quality priorities and on Xerox quality policies are developed at the corporate level and cascaded down throughout the company, becoming more specific at each succeeding level
- worked closely with the Amalgamated Clothing and Textile Workers' Union to develop a contract that includes clauses supporting joint quality efforts
- places emphasis on recognition for efforts of cross-functional teams

At IBM, the senior management
- places emphasis on continuous improvement through recognition and reward systems
- can receive up to forty percent annual performance bonus for meeting quality goals.

Leadership highlights from a variety of other high quality companies are summarized as follows:
- Provide training to all employees in various aspects of quality management and analysis.
- Re-organize to maximize customer satisfaction.
- President conducts a daily meeting of officers, directors, and department managers in reviewing prior day's performance against customer value factors.
- The president and members of the senior management team lead an Annual Quality Improvement Conference for all employees.
- The CEO and the president lead and participate in monthly quality review meetings. The focus is on progress toward achieving quality plan goals. All officers must attend these meetings.
- Senior executives originated and contributed quality articles to a monthly publication issued to employees and customers.
- The president delivers a video quality message each month to all employees.
- All senior managers routinely sponsor and participate in celebrations to reinforce quality improvement teams that evidence measured and docu-

mented progress toward quality plan goals. These are company paid and take place during the normal work day.

- Senior executives use personal, handwritten notes to their employees.
- Significant efforts are made to remove distinctions or symbols between levels in the organization. For example, the offices of all senior managers resemble those of service center managers—very spartan in nature. Additionally, former executive parking spaces are offered in a lottery for associates who have documented quality improvements in the current month.
- The CEO, president, and other senior executives personally teach courses on the vision, mission, core values, beliefs, and customer satisfaction.
- Senior executives and officers give numerous presentations on quality leadership and employee empowerment throughout the nation to business and government groups.
- The chief operating officer (COO) champions the cause of the customer in the organization. He is the voice of the customer in formal and informal planning sessions. The COO meets regularly with customers and key supplier partners.
- Created a Quality College to meet the needs of customers. Uses this also as a forum to answer questions on the company's quality performance, internal quality processes, ideas for improvement, and implementation. Information shared includes how the company developed its quality processes and how these processes contribute to their commitment to excellence efforts. The company's senior managers and hourly paid employees serve as teachers.
- Produce a quarterly in-house video magazine on quality. This consistently showcases service centers to reinforce those that have engaged in behavior-specific actions in quality improvement.
- All senior executives conduct informal, monthly meetings with a diverse group of employees.
- To emphasize the importance that senior management places on quality training, the president attends the graduation ceremonies for each of the three-day quality of customer service training classes to offer his congratulations to participants and to share the company's quality vision.
- New employees are introduced to the company's quality culture through a variety of activities:
  - The CEO meets for lunch with all new managers in small groups.
  - The CEO meets with all new employees for breakfast as part of the company's orientation program.
  - The president hosts small-group lunches with exempt employees of the assistant vice-president.
  - The president has breakfast meetings with groups of non-exempt employees by department.

- The CEO, president, and senior staff regularly call on corporate customers to determine if their needs are being met.
- The CEO created a program titled, Special Assistant to the Chairman. Area managers are encouraged to nominate talented junior officers for a five month

appointment to the chairman's office, where they observe and participate in corporate operations at the highest levels.

- Employees are encouraged to recognize outstanding service by a fellow colleague by nominating them for a Star Award. Star employees receive a certificate and are automatically entered into the pool of nominees for the quarterly Chairman's Awards. These honorees receive a pay bonus and meet with the chairman. Their various perspectives on what constitutes quality service are publicized within the company.

MANAGEMENT FOR QUALITY

Managing for quality includes how the company's customer focus and quality values are integrated into day-to-day leadership, management, and supervision of all company units. Listed below are actions taken by a variety of manufacturing and service organizations.

- Initiated the maintenance of a complete spectrum of quality measures in a corporate office chart room.
- Implemented a suggestion system which received special recognition from the U.S. Department of Labor's Bureau of Labor Management Relations and Cooperative Programs.
- Established facility housekeeping as a leading quality indicator, utilizing a Quality Workplace Critique (checklist) to arrive at a White Glove award.
- Fully integrated business and quality plans. Specific quality and growth items are integrated in the same planning document.
- Bi-monthly staff meetings focusing on quality issues are extended to the department level. Minutes are published and sent to regional managers who in turn send them to all operations center managers in order to document progress, confirm plans, and provide feedback.
- Any employee at any location can use a toll-free number to reach any senior executive. Senior executives frequently call employees directly to maintain personal contact and survey status of operations at the grass-roots level.
- Initiated cross-functional quality improvement teams involving all different levels of people.
- Established a policy whereby any level employee may communicate with anyone in the company or with suppliers to solve problems.
- Located key positions such as manager of field systems, director of business development, director of industrial relations, etc., in field locations to facilitate interaction with the people doing the work.
- Customer value factors (measures) and critical support areas are reviewed daily by the officer group.
- Each operating center holds a monthly planning meeting with all personnel where performance standards and business goals are discussed.
- Developed an upward appraisal system where each manager's subordinates prepare evaluations on their direct superiors and which are confidential to that manager.

- Utilize internal employee satisfaction surveys.
- Created a program for rotation of managers to provide individuals with broader business perspectives.
- Provide daily, weekly, and monthly quality performance tracking.
- Have a management reporting system on results achieved against strategic quality objectives.
- Exercise a high level of senior management involvement in quality awareness and improvement processes.
- The executive quality council meets monthly to review progress against quality plans, the status of quality improvement teams, quality measurement activity, and other quality issues such as problems that require interdepartmental attention. The CEO and chief quality officer meet weekly to share ideas and discuss issues involving the quality process.
- During the annual planning process, senior management members are responsible for developing the quality and business plans for their reporting units, which then become the foundation for performance assessments and rewards in the following year.
- Internal, Malcolm Baldrige assessments are conducted annually.
- Departmental quality councils provide input to the senior management quality council in the development of the annual quality plan.
- A Quality Improvement Team tracking report is produced each month by department, giving each project's purpose, status, and team make-up. This report is reviewed by the executive quality council.
- The key strategy used to promote cooperation among managers is through cross-functional quality improvement teams.
- Each manager and supervisor is required to have an annual quality plan as a prerequisite to salary increases.
- The company has four key strategies for encouraging quality leadership in all levels of management: TQM education; the quality steering team network; annual quality plans, and the employee improvement support system.
- Heavy emphasis is given to promoting internal customer-supplier relationships through education and through annual plans designed to satisfy internal customer expectations.

The leadership of each organization needs to determine what actions they can implement to motivate their people to improve customer satisfaction and operating results. There is no simple prescription for this. The appropriate approaches and implementation priorities will be determined by such factors as: the corporate culture and management's perception of any need for change; market structure; size of the company; competitive forces; and the type of business—manufacturing or service. Importantly, the quality leaders in America are very visible, creative, and energetic in promoting their personal commitment and focus on quality throughout all levels of the organization.

Business Process Analysis for Cross-Functional Improvement

Business Process Analysis (BPA) is a tool used to understand and improve work activities cross-functionally. Too often, efforts to improve business operations are isolated or focused within single business functions. While it is necessary to continually improve individual operations, it is also critically important to consider the impact of improvements on other related functions within and outside the company. American automotive companies have, in their quest for quality, adopted the concept of BPA in the design of new automobiles. In this case, examination of the existing automobile design process led to the awareness that individual, departmental efforts often negatively impacted other functions and resulted in sub-optimization of production efficiency, cost effectiveness, product quality, and customer satisfaction. The latter approach was replaced with a cross-functional team methodology that involved product design, production, market-ing, customers, dealers, suppliers, and others at the beginning of new automotive design programs.

Motorola's management maintains that cross-functional process analysis has played a key role in the company's achieving outstanding improvement in product quality. American Express applied business process analysis to its credit card emergency replacement activity and reduced the time to replace a lost or stolen card from twenty-eight days to one day. The company also applied process analysis to the introduction of its Platinum Card product. The total introduction time for this product including marketing development, computer and manage-ment systems design, employee hiring and training, equipment purchase, installation, testing and, space preparation was accomplished in three and one-half months. The chairman of American Express said at the conclusion of this effort, "At any other time in the history of this company, it would have taken two years to introduce the Platinum Card."

Business process analysis has its roots in industrial engineering systems design techniques. For example, the project management tool, Program Evalu-ation and Review Technique (PERT), significantly enhances the capability of BPA. Originally developed by Admiral Hyman Rickover's management team in the construction of the first nuclear powered submarine, it was reported that this cross-functional approach to project management led to the nuclear submarine's being the first occasion where a new capital ship design had been introduced on schedule and within cost estimates. Florida Power and Light Company applied a computerized version of PERT in improving its process of replacing spent nuclear fuel rods. Process time to bring its nuclear power plants back on line was reduced several days (with savings to its customers of $1 million per day in offsetting fossil fuel charges) and safety to its employees was enhanced.

Business process analysis is effective in improving quality and reducing costs in both line and staff activities within manufacturing and service organizations. Business process analysis is a significant aid to those companies whose businesses are changing rapidly as a result of accelerated new product design, competitive forces, organizational restructuring, advances in technology, and reduced operating cycle times.

As the above changes take place, many companies find that BPA enables them to implement new programs more effectively. Since BPA cross-functionally examines the impact of changes, all affected departments are brought into a cooperative, team structure that dramatically increases the opportunity to implement change successfully.

The purpose of this chapter is to present a proven and successful model for using the business process analysis system effectively. How BPA is implemented is as important to a successful outcome (i.e. improved quality, reduced costs, employee involvement, commitment, and enhanced self-worth) as the system itself.

Strategic factors discussed include organizational issues, selecting the best processes to improve, the roles of the participants, and the structure to use in introducing and conducting BPA workshops. Specific tactical considerations presented include team development, program facilitation, preparation of business process scope and mission statements, process mapping, understanding the importance of internal and external customers, establishing quality performance measures, developing recommendations for quality and productivity improvement, and final presentations to management.

BPA IMPLEMENTATION STRATEGY

OPERATING QUALITY COUNCILS
As described in the chapter "Ten Step Strategy For Implementing Quality Management and Continuous Improvement For Competitiveness", operating quality councils have the responsibility of identifying the key business processes in each operating area for analysis and improvement. See Figure 1 for a flow chart showing the relationship between executive and operating quality councils, the BPA system, and continuous improvement efforts.

The following criteria are used by the operating councils in determining their key business processes:
• Is the process related to key business issues?
• Does the process have a direct impact on the external customer?
• Is the process visible in the company?
• Would the executive council agree it's important to analyze?

The Quality Organization Structure

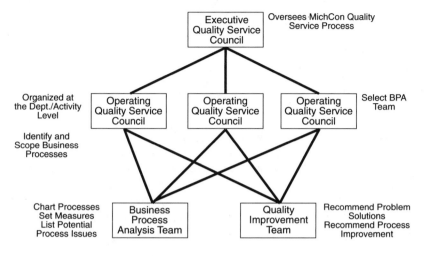

Figure 1.

- Does the process cut across functional boundaries?
- Is the process currently being studied by any other group?
- What is the monetary and resource impact?
- What are the areas of current significant customer satisfaction?
- Does the process have clearly defined start and finish points?
- Does the process recycle quickly?
- Does the process affect many employees?

The operating quality council has the additional task of assigning a sponsor to each BPA team. The sponsor is usually a member of the council.

THE ROLE OF THE BPA SPONSOR

1. Administrative actions—the BPA sponsor
- considers teaming up with a co-sponsor who learns the role and takes the lead on the next BPA;
- contacts the appropriate corporate department (i.e., usually quality assurance or human resources) for the assignment of a BPA workshop leader, a facilitator, and materials for the team members;
- arranges for an off-site location with enough tables and flip charts for every two people, and plenty of wall space to hang flow charts;
- distribute materials for homework assignments to all team members at least two weeks in advance of the BPA workshop;

- follow-up as necessary to ensure that arrangements have been made for travel; and
- as a final step in the BPA workshop, work with the team to arrange for a presentation of their results to the operating council and all stakeholders. In addition to selecting a date and location for the presentation, this may involve preparing a presentation agenda and conducting rehearsals.

2. Initial meeting with stakeholders—the BPA sponsor

- arranges meetings with stakeholders individually or in one group, as appropriate;
- discusses the emphasis on quality;
- explains that the objective of BPA is to identify the current process as it exists today, to develop critical measure points and future areas for improvement;
- describes the visual representation that will result—a map of the existing process;
- explains the selection criteria that identified this process as key;
- discusses the benefits of a cross-functional approach versus a functional approach;
- describe how the process selected drove the functional departments involved—not the other way around;
- discusses the review process that will take place with all stakeholders after the team has documented the flow and recommended critical measures;
- summarizes the time commitments necessary by the participants as best as can be predicted (the initial workshop to map the flow, additional days if necessary to complete the map, subsequent meetings to prepare for reporting to the stakeholders and operating council, and the actual meeting to make the presentation);
- invite stakeholders to drop in to observe the process and review the team's work;
- discusses the need for employees and their direct supervisors to be responsible for making travel arrangements; and
- describes the type of people who should be involved—experts in their part of the process who are available for the entire workshop. If some cannot attend the entire session, their participation should be postponed to a later team.

3. Initial BPA team mapping

To begin the meeting, the BPA sponsor

- greets team members the first morning;
- describes the sponsor's role as facilitative when necessary, not as team member or leader;
- summarizes the time commitments necessary by the participants as best as can be predicted;
- briefly reviews the agenda;
- provides a summary of the BPA process and describes how it fits in with the company's overall quality process;

- explains the selection criteria that identified this process as key;
- explains how the team and team members were selected (cross-functional, knowledge of operations, credibility within their organizations, etc.)
- discusses the review process that will take place with all stakeholders after the team has documented the flow and recommended critical measures;
- discusses the opportunity to identify new quality improvement ideas that may arise while mapping the existing process;
- discusses the opportunity to visualize and document the ideal process.

Throughout the duration of the workshop the BPA sponsor
- attends the workshop as much as possible and invites other stakeholders;
- attempts to stay engaged throughout the workshop while remaining objective and impartial; and
- helps to lead a discussion on the process mission and scope to develop a one or two sentence mission statement.

At the conclusion of the workshop the BPA sponsor
- gives input into the discussion of next steps and the report to the stakeholders, but refrains from voting or accepting assignments other than arranging the meeting;
- informs the group that their work is important and does not end with the BPA and that they should look forward to continuing to work with each other on quality improvement teams, and their co-workers to help implement the measures they have recommended;
- concludes the workshop by thanking team members;
- administers feedback surveys on the workshop and presenters and solicits feedback on the sponsor's role.

4. Subsequent meeting with stakeholders—the BPA sponsor
- sets the stage for the report to the stakeholders by describing the state of the team and any concerns of the team members;
- reviews the objective of the presentation to share the results of the team's work and gain concurrence on the process flow, critical measures, and process ownership before proceeding;
- discusses the role of stakeholders at the presentation (i. e., be receptive and non-judgmental, suspend assumptions, don't dismiss the team's recommendations);
- discusses how the team's recommendations should be acknowledged; and
- decides how the team should be recognized for its efforts.

5. BPA team preparation for report to stakeholders—the BPA sponsor
- arranges a meeting for the team to report its results to the Operating Quality Service Council and other stakeholders;
- gives input into an agenda, timetable, spokesperson, and appropriate handouts;

- discusses the team's participation in developing critical measures, as a process advisory group, in helping to facilitate future BPA teams, or as a Quality Improvement Team (QIT);
- prepares opening and closing remarks for the presentation. Opening remarks should recap the team's task to map the existing process; recommend critical measures; recommend a process owner; and capture quality improvement team issues. Closing remarks should describe the team's wishes about further involvement; restate the actions left for the operating council and stakeholders; provide a date when the BPA team will hear back from the operating council and stakeholders; and thank the team for its efforts.
- restates the desired outcome of a decision from stakeholders on the:
  - map of the process;
  - critical measures;
  - process owner;
  - process for handling any QIT issues; and
  - further involvement of the BPA team.

6. BPA team report to stakeholders—the BPA sponsor

- welcomes the audience with the recap of the team's task and the purpose and desired outcome of the meeting;
- supports the team during its presentation; and
- concludes the presentation.

BPA WORKSHOP AGENDA AND THE ROLE OF THE FACILITATOR

SECTION 1: INTRODUCTION

In this session the BPA team sponsor will give the quality briefing to re-create the big picture of the quality effort and, in effect say "You are here" in the picture. Next, the sponsor will explain the scope and purpose of the work session, describing the final product of the BPA team and how it will be used to improve service to customers. The facilitator will lead a group discussion in which team members express their expectations and concerns for the BPA work sessions.

Section objectives. After participating in this session, team members will be able to

- explain how they and their BPA team fit into the quality service process
- recognize executive support for the team
- explain where the quality process will lead and how it ties with the company's vision, values, and strategic direction
- explain the role of QIT in improving business processes

Facilitator's notes

- describe the output of the work sessions and its value to the quality process (key output are measure points)
- discuss the individual and company benefits of participation in the quality effort

Rationale. If team members understand the big picture, their part in it, and the benefits of personal involvement and support, they will commit and take ownership for the outcome of the team.

The team sponsor should be the main presenter during the introduction, as a means of demonstrating ongoing support and advocacy for the team.

Activities

1. Introductions, scope, and purpose of the work session

The sponsors talk to the group about how they were picked for this BPA team. They should explain that the operating council decided that this process should be mapped and that they asked each department involved in the process to provide knowledgeable and respected people regarding the process. The sponsors should be asked to introduce themselves and tell a little about what they do.

The sponsors should explain that these sessions are work sessions. Team members will learn BPA by analyzing an actual process in which they each make current and significant contributions. The work sessions will continue as long as necessary to produce an accurate and detailed visual analysis of the target business process.

The final product of the work sessions will be an analysis reflecting the process as it is, not as it should be. Once completed, the analysis will reveal key measuring points and will be the pivotal tool for use in identifying process opportunities for improvement, glitches, disconnects, or problems. Special teams will be formed to solve the problems with the aim of improving the process of serving customers better.

The sponsors explain the role of QIT and encourage team members to develop a running list of QIT issues—issues that will come to light during the BPA process.

2. Big picture—"you are here"—The BPA sponsor

- gives the quality briefing or reviews this material if the group has already had a quality briefing;
- refers to the employee quality briefing to re-create the big picture and the rationale behind the quality effort and to help team members understand their role in the quality effort;

Note: The sponsor should do this in a participative way, evoking from team members their recollections and feelings from the quality briefing, then reinforce the feelings as necessary.

- describes how the quality service process is organized and how the BPA work sessions fit into it (refer to Figure 1).

3. Expectations and concerns
- The facilitator has each person write one expectation and one concern and drop in a box. Each person draws someone else's expectation and concern for discussion.
- Record the responses on the flip chart and post them on the wall for reference during the work sessions. Check them off the list as they are addressed (with participant agreement).

SECTION 2: TEAM DEVELOPMENT
During this session, team members will discuss group dynamics and learn how to become a high-performing team. They will work together in team building initiatives to build trust, loyalty, and *esprit de corps.* They will select a team recorder, discuss roles and responsibilities, and agree upon team norms and ground rules. Finally, they will work together to articulate their team mission and objectives.

Section objectives. After participating in this session, team members will be able to
- describe the characteristics of a high-performing team
- explain the phases of team development
- feel a bond of trust and *esprit de corps* among team members
- discuss the roles and responsibilities of the team liaison, team facilitator, secretary, and team sponsor
- articulate the team mission and objectives
- explain team norms and ground rules
- select a team recorder

Rationale. Team members must trust each other and understand the value of teamwork. They must know how teams develop and learn to perform at a high level. The activities in this session will help them achieve these important elements.

The team will select a recorder and team members must share a clear understanding of each member's roles and responsibilities, as well as how they will work together. The work on roles, responsibilities, and ground rules will provide the needed agreement and guidance.

Activities
1. The facilitator leads a discussion of what the group expects to get from working together as a team.
2. The facilitator builds team trust, loyalty, and *esprit de corps* by introducing and debriefing team building exercises.
3. Initial discussion are about team effectiveness. Simply and briefly explain that

teams always cycle through a predictable process of learning to work together effectively. The activities completed thus far will help the team short circuit the process and become productive more quickly. Throughout the project, the team will periodically discuss their effectiveness. *Note:* This is no more than a 5-minute discussion.

4. The facilitator leads a discussion to help the team develop ground rules. Use brainstorming and funneling (narrowing ideas by vote or by consensus after brainstorming) to develop the ground rules. The list of ground rules should define how the team will work together. The following are sample team norms:
   - start and end meetings on time
   - treat each other with respect and courtesy
   - fulfill all assignments—no excuses
   - allow each person, regardless of rank or level in the company, an equal say.

   The facilitator leads a discussion to select the team recorder, whose responsibility it will be to record issues on flip charts. The team should decide whether to select the recorder by democratic vote, consensus, or some other method.

SECTION 3: REVIEW PRE-WORK ASSIGNMENT
The BPA leader will distribute a handout listing the preferred responses to the glossary work sheets completed by participants as pre-work.

Section objectives. After participating in this session, team members will be able to confirm their learnings from pre-work, and to use their glossaries for reference.

Activities
1. Distribute glossary handout and conduct a five minute Q&A discussion.
2. The sponsor and BPA leader distribute mementos to acknowledge the team's pre-work.

SECTION 4: BUSINESS PROCESS SCOPE AND MISSION
This session will also help team members (1) define the parameters of their business process (where it starts, where it ends, and what are the steps in between); and (2) describe the mission of the process (its purpose, its output, what it is designed to do).

Section objectives. After participating in this session, team members will be able to
- define the scope of the target business process
- describe the mission of the process

Rationale. Before a BPA team is selected, the scope of the target process has been previously defined by the operating council. The resulting definition is the basis for selecting the team members for the BPA work sessions. Nevertheless, the team should repeat the scope definition exercise for at least two compelling reasons: (1) to verify the accuracy of the scope definition and (2) to give the team ownership of the definition.

The team should also understand the process mission as the basis for analyzing customer-supplier relationships, tasks and activities, and inputs and outputs. The process of articulating the mission will provide significant insight into the process.

Defining the process mission and scope constitute the first steps in the analysis and charting of the target process, which is the tangible output of this workshop.

Activities

1. Defining process mission
- The sponsor and BPA leader facilitate a brainstorming session to solicit ideas for a mission statement.
- They facilitate agreement on a mission statement at the end of the brainstorming session.

2. Defining process scope
- The sponsor and BPA leader facilitate a discussion on the scope.
- They have team members use the following questions as a guide to determine the scope of the targeted business process:
    - Where does the process start?
    - What does the process include?
    - What doesn't the process include?
    - Where does the process end?

SECTION 5: PROCESS ANALYSIS AND QUALITY IMPROVEMENT

In this session, team members will discuss the quality service cycle; process management tools; and process step, activity, and task. They will identify the activities and tasks of their process steps.

Section objectives. After participating in this session, team members will be able to
- define process, activity, and task and explain how they interrelate
- identify the activities and tasks of their particular process step

Rationale. Identifying the activities and tasks of each process follows defining the scope and mission when analyzing the target process.

Activities
1. The business process model
• The BPA leader reviews the BPA agenda.

BPA Agenda
1. Sub-groups list high level tasks and report back to the team.
2. Sub-groups identify inputs and outputs for tasks and report back to the team.
3. Sub-groups identify critical measure points and report back to team.
4. Each sub-group indicates critical measures it needs from other sub groups.
5. The teams finalize flows for report to stakeholders.

• The BPA leader presents a model of the BPA process to illustrate the big picture and introduce the team members to the model they will be learning during the work sessions. The model should be based on the process to be mapped. The BPA leader and sponsor should discuss the example to be used ahead of time.

2. The BPA leader divides team into sub-groups and
• discusses with the whole group what the major actions are in their process.
• leads discussion to decide among group who is best suited to define the process tasks for that function.

   Note: If there are any people in groups that have more than one functional responsibility, they should work in both sub-groups as floaters to ensure all steps are covered.

• informs groups that some will be finished sooner than others and these team members should discuss improvement ideas and circulate among other teams.

3. Identify all process activities and tasks
• Provide each team with a flip chart pad.
• Instruct each team to write the name of their particular activity at the top of a flip chart page.
• Instruct each team to list all the tasks of their activity on the flip chart page. Circulate among the working groups, offering assistance as they work through the analysis. Emphasize that tasks are actions.

4. Reporting
• Have each team present list to the entire group in sequence.
• After each presentation, lead a brief group discussion, encouraging team members to offer feedback, ask questions, and request clarification.

- The BPA leader and facilitator should discuss with the team the QIT issues that will surface and the necessity of capturing the issues but not resolving them during the session.
- Be alert for opportunities to take breaks if the team's energy is low.

SECTION 6: INPUTS AND SUPPLIERS, OUTPUTS AND CUSTOMERS, AND PROCESS FLOW

In this session team members will identify the inputs and suppliers and outputs and customers of their process steps and link their process step into the target process flow by identifying supplier–customer relationships.

Section objectives. After participating in this session, team members will be able to
- identify the inputs and suppliers and outputs and customers of their particular process step
- explain the concept of process flow
- identify supplier–customer relationships by linking the process steps of the target process

Rationale. Identifying inputs and suppliers and outputs and customers, and linking these customers and suppliers, are the next steps in the work of business process analysis.

Activities.
1. Inputs and suppliers, outputs and customers
- The BPA leader should refer back to the BPA agenda and model.
- Discuss the customer–supplier relationship and how value-added activities change input from suppliers into output for customers.
- Lead a brief group discussion to answer questions and clarify participant understanding.

2. Identify inputs and suppliers, and outputs and customers
- Divide team members into their process step work teams (same as activity 4, section 5).
- Instruct each team to list on a flip chart all the inputs and their suppliers, and all the outputs and their customers of their process step.

3. Reporting
- Have each team present its list of process step inputs and suppliers, outputs and customers to the entire participant group in sequence. Facilitate the reporting so the team does not repeat earlier discussion.
- After each presentation, lead a brief group discussion, encouraging team members to offer feedback, ask questions, and request clarification.
- Be alert for opportunities to take breaks.

Section 7: Identifying Key Measuring Points and Developing Useful Measures

In this session team members will identify the key measuring points in their assigned process steps. They will then develop measures of timeliness and accuracy for each key measuring point.

Section objectives. After participating in this session, team members will be able to
• define the terms *critical measuring point* and *measure*
• identify critical measuring points in their assigned process step
• develop useful measures for testing quality at key measuring points

Rationale. Identifying critical measuring points and developing useful measures are at the heart of the quality service process. From these measures, service goals are developed to measure progress toward improving quality service.

Activities.
1. The BPA leader introduces the concepts of critical measuring points and useful measures.
• Refer back to the BPA agenda and model
• Review elements of quality measures
  - accuracy service goal of 100 percent
  - timeliness viewed by the customer today
  - responsiveness
• Measures will be sampled where appropriate.
• Critical measuring points are process tasks that have tell-tale qualities. Critical measure points
  - are pivotal tasks because the accuracy and timeliness with which they are executed greatly affect the balance of the process
  - are visible to customers or affect them directly
  - have a disproportionately heavy impact on the quality of the final output of the process
  - cross departmental boundaries
• Once critical measuring points have been identified, it is then necessary to develop accuracy and timeliness measures.
• Following are the steps to take in developing the measures:
  a) determine whether the relevant measure is accuracy or timeliness and whether both are relevant
  b) define the measure in percentages and describe the relevant parameters
  c) identify the source of the measurement data
  d) determine whether a relevant measure is proposed or already exists

Additionally, the BPA leader must
- explain that the customer always has the final say in determining service goals. If the accuracy and timeliness of the process is not acceptable to customers, nothing else matters.
- explain how measures are summed into key measures.
- explain that actual performance measurements will be accomplished by employees with their supervisor.
- lead a brief group discussion to answer questions and clarify participant understanding.

2. Identify critical measuring points and measures
- Divide team members into their process step(s) work teams.
- Instruct each team to list on a flip chart all the key measuring points within their tasks using the criteria.
- Circulate among the groups, challenging them to identify critical measures that will cause the process to fail.

3. Reporting
- Have each team present its list of key measuring points to the entire participant group.
- After each presentation, lead a brief group discussion encouraging team members to offer feedback, ask questions, and request clarification.
- If necessary, give the process step teams some time to amend their lists of key measuring points based on the feedback they received.
- During the reporting sessions, challenge other teams to suggest measures critical to them as customers.
- Be alert for opportunities to take stretch breaks.

SECTION 8: COMPLETE AND PRESENT THE PROCESS ANALYSIS
In this session team members will finalize their flow chart, present it to the operating council, and make necessary modifications. *Note:* This work may be done in a session separate from the process analysis session, but should closely follow the work session.

Section objectives. After participating in this session, team members will be able to complete a draft of the visual analysis of the target process and prepare and deliver to the operating council and the team sponsor a one to one-and-one-half hour presentation of the target process analysis.

Rationale. The requirement to prepare and deliver a visual presentation of the analysis for the operating council or sponsor will lend importance and significance to the team's analysis, forcing team members to scrutinize their own work and developing in them a sense of ownership and commitment to the task. The flow of information in both directions in the presentation—team members presenting and audience responding and giving feedback—will enhance understanding of the process for all concerned. It will also provide important data and insights for refining the process analysis.

Activities
1. The BPA leader facilitates a discussion on the recommendation for the position of process owner.
   - The process owner has the most: resources, work, pain, and benefits
   - The process owner has the best chance of affecting positive change

2. BPA leader discusses objectives of the report and stakeholders.
   - Concurrence on process flow, critical measure, and process owner
   - Share QIT issues

3. Prepare to present the visual analysis to the operating council or team sponsor.
   a) Report to stakeholders format and structure
      - decide on meeting time and place
      - decide on agenda
      - decide on visual aids and handouts
      - decide who will do what
      - arrange rehearsal for presenters, if necessary

   b) Report to stakeholders possible agenda items
      - welcoming remarks
      - discussion of BPA
      - introduction of team
      - discussion of process mission and scope
      - walk through of process flow
      - discussion of critical measures
      - introduction of QIT issues
      - create a vision for the process
      - process owner recommendation
      - further involvement of the team
      - closing remarks

4. Finalize the process analysis.
   - Lead the group in finalizing the visual analysis.
   - Facilitate the arrangement of the flip chart data from previous exercises (scope and mission; process steps, activities and tasks; inputs and suppliers, customers and outputs; measures and standards; process flow) into a complete process analysis. Move them around on the wall until reaching consensus that the arrangement of the data describes the process.
   - Have the team work together to re-draft the complete analysis, if necessary.

5. Select a team liaison to arrange rehearsal meetings with the sponsor and lead team preparations.

THINGS TO WATCH FOR

Problems	Solutions
• Presenters not at rehearsals	• If you are one of the presenters, be sure to attend rehearsal(s)
• Too many presenters	• Limit number of presenters
• Too much detail on tasks	• Keep to major tasks
• Acronyms not understood by entire group	• Use titles whenever possible
• Questions held until the end don't encourage audience interaction	• Encourage questions during the presentation
• Presenters very serious	• Use humor where appropriate

6. Deliver and debrief the presentation
   - Make arrangements for a rehearsal, if necessary.
   - By pre-arrangement, have the team members make the presentation to the operating council and sponsor.

SECTION 9: WORKSHOP WRAP UP
   - Congratulate team members.
   - Refer to their lists of expectations and objectives and resolve any that are left.
   - Respond to final questions.
   - Obtain feedback about the BPA process and ideas for improvement.

Measuring Customer Satisfaction:
Linking Experience, Expectations, and Desires

The service industry has learned an important lesson the hard way. The number one reason customers fail to renew service contracts is not fees, convenience, or new products. The primary reason for shifting business is service. Customers take their business to companies who provide the best overall service because it is quality service that ultimately determines satisfaction.

The challenge facing thousands of organizations across America is how to enhance customer satisfaction amidst intense competition and an ever-changing business climate. Companies see increasing evidence that an investment in service pays large dividends in the forms of expanding industry reputation, elevating profits, and increasing employee morale. Top-rated companies are currently expending vast amounts of effort and resources to measure the factors that relate to customer satisfaction. With accurate data, they hope to re-order or re-structure their operations so as to provide the customer with exemplary service, and so avoid customer defection to the competition.

One central question confronts the managers behind these efforts: How does one measure this elusive, intangible abstraction called customer satisfaction? In this chapter, an approach to customer satisfaction measurement developed by Randall K. Stutman of Communication Research Associates (Valley Forge, Pennsylvania) based upon six working premises will be outlined. These premises serve as the bedrock for a self-teaching system for improving service satisfaction. In the following sections, these premises will be described and the major issues highlighted by each premise will be discussed. It should also be noted that Larry Gulledge of Elrick & Lavidge (Tucker, Georgia) has similarly developed a set of working premises used to tailor customer satisfaction surveys to specific corporate and customer profiles.

WORKING PREMISES

PREMISE ONE: SERVICE SATISFACTION IS FORMED AT THE INTERSECTION OF EXPERIENCE, EXPECTATION, AND DESIRE.

This premise, though somewhat unorthodox, makes a clear distinction between the measurement of (a) the service experience, (b) customer expectations about service, and (c) customer desires related to service. This distinction can serve as the building block for creating a customer measurement system which encourages and feeds strategies for service improvement. Each of these concepts are treated as distinct elements which form a crosscurrent of satisfaction.

Plainly stated, the service *experience* is the perceived quality of the service encounter based upon those features most salient to the customer. *Expectations* are anticipated actions in the service encounter. Most commonly, customers hold expectations about the nature of the service provider (gender, age, size, dress), the messages the service provider will use (sales pitch, technical information, instructions), the demeanor of the provider (friendly, professional, aloof), the step-by-step processes the service will follow, and the duration of the encounter. Customers form expectations based on previous experience, through media and other authority information, and by inference. *Desires,* on the other hand, are what customers would most like to see in the future. In other words, if the customer ran the show, without regard to cost or other constraints, how would they alter the service. Table 1 illustrates the differences between these concepts by stating fictitious customer beliefs across the constants of responsiveness and pleasantness.

It is important to distinguish between these three concepts during the measurement process. Consider the analogy of measuring customer satisfaction about dining at a local restaurant, a service event we can all identify with. Presume we wish to measure customer satisfaction with the entire encounter. The restaurant experience could be conceived as containing several parts: the meal (product), the host service (process), the delivery service (process), and the checkout service (process). We might begin by asking diners what they thought of this experience: Was the meal flavorful? Were the dishes hot? Were the serving portions filling? Did the hostess find a pleasing table? Was the waiter pleasant? Was the bill easy to understand? Did the cashier express appreciation for your business? The lines of inquiry are seemingly limitless, and are determined by the measurement view we hold about what is salient to the customer. If we apply a sound framework that encourages us to ask those questions of import to the customer, we will have a valid assessment of the service experience, and hence of satisfaction. Granted, this tells us very little about the factors that influence one's perceptions of this experience, but such questions and answers will capture the full range of perceptions which comprise the restaurant service encounter.

Measuring the factors which drive these perceptions is a different matter, one that is equally important but fundamentally distinct. We generally do not think of asking questions related to hunger, companionship, mood, financial well-being, day of the week, last meal eaten and the like when asked to assess the dining experience. The reason is simple. Intuitively we know that such factors shape but do not represent the experience. When one wants to know about satisfaction with the experience, one measures important elements of the process and product. When one wants to know how to influence this experience, one measures expectations and desires. At the heart of this distinction lies the difference between describing what customers see and describing the lens through which customers view reality. In the hands of a service practitioner, the former is a gauge, and the latter is a strategic device for change.

Table 1. Distinguishing between the key concepts of experience, expectation, and desire.

Concept	Example
Experience	The rep responded five hours after I made my service request.
Expectation	The rep will respond to service requests in the same day I make contact.
Desire	The rep should respond to my service request within two hours of contact
Experience	The rep was courteous and pleasanrt when talking to me.
Expectation	The rep will not make small talk when they first arrive.
Desire	The rep should introduce themselves in a formal greeting.

The point of this example is to illustrate the confusion over measuring other concepts peripherally related to service experience. Undoubtedly because of the litany of research evidence which shows that customer satisfaction is influenced by expectations, and to a lesser extent desire, there is a propensity on the part of investigators to measure expectations and desires as a reflection of, or substitute for, experience. By measuring experience directly, a company obtains an excellent gauge of current satisfaction. This is the best measure of how satisfied customers are with the service process. By measuring expectations, a company grasps the possibilities for dramatically improving service. One can quickly develop strategies for exceeding customer expectations. The measurement of desires gives one a larger idea of how to transform a service over time. This data enables planners to seize the next wave of new services and service-hybrids. Together, the three concepts give investigators and managers the best viewpoint from which to assess and enhance customer satisfaction. All too often, however, existing measurement systems combine these three concepts in their attempt to measure satisfaction. As a result, the parties neither obtain an accurate and reliable gauge of satisfaction, nor obtain a detailed picture of what customers think and feel. Just as importantly, such a misstep often leaves managers with an inability to provide service providers with useful feedback for improvement.

PREMISE TWO: TO MEASURE SATISFACTION, EXAMINE THE CRITICAL QUALITIES OF EXPERIENCE SHAPED BY EXPECTATIONS AND DESIRES.

In order to effectively measure satisfaction, it is necessary to look closely at the service experience from the viewpoint of the customer. The goal is to examine factors that are truly salient to the customer, not the measurement team. The key is to remember that the customer may rate the quality of the service based on any criteria that they wish. Perceived reality and the judgment criteria used to conceive of this reality are king and queen. Realizing that customers rarely formulate their opinions based on formal logic, it becomes clear that the only place to start is with an in-depth investigation of customer perceptions. Customers with recent service experiences can be recruited for focus groups, telephone interviews, in-home meetings. The point is to use a format where open ended questions allow customers to describe in detail why they are satisfied or dissatisfied with their most recent service encounter. Employ a format where customers can explain in their own words.

This data can then be used to create a model of satisfaction which reflects those attributes most important to customers. Models will vary from service to service, and company to company. Differences between key customer attributes for similar industries and companies in the same region is not unusual. While certain elements of service appear to be nearly universal in these models, such as responsiveness, the subtle distinctions of what they mean given a particular customer base and service context varies greatly.

Below is an example of a customer service model developed from a qualitative study with customers of a major utility company. Research conducted with a representative sample of residential customers found six dimensions directly related to the perception of quality of service. The six dimensions are: accessibility, pleasantness, responsiveness, powerlessness, control over the encounter; and favorability toward the company. While each dimension will be expanded upon in the following section, a summary of the dimensions can be found in Table 2.

Accessibility. Accessibility can be defined as the perception that service providers are available for contact and service. The customer should be able to determine, with a minimum of effort, where to go, or who to speak with, in order to solve the problem. Usually customers must rely on other employees of the company to transfer them to the appropriate department or individual, if the contact is made by telephone. Being shunted off to a person who cannot provide the proper service is a waste of time, and can lead to high frustration levels. For example, a customer in need of service, transferred to an employee that is not authorized to set up service appointments, will likely feel they are speaking to the wrong person. They have not managed to access the person who can, in a single contact, serve their need. Thus, availability is a function of the ease with which a customer can identify or contact the correct person who can assist them.

Table 2. Dimensions of service satisfaction for customers of a utility company.

Critical Dimension	Definition	Expanded Description	Customer Examples
Accessibility	The perceptions that service providers are available for contact and service.	When faced with a service need, a customer perceives that the appropriate person is available to assist them. In most cases, availability is a function of the ease with which a customer can identify the correct person, locate the appropriate telephone number or location, and actually make contact. The convenience of office location and hours may also influence a customer's perceptions of accessibility.	A customer did not find company accessible when her call was put on hold and transferred to different departments; a customer found the company extremely accessible in that they came out on Sunday.
Pleasantness	The overall quality of the service interaction.	When customers come in contact with a service provider, they form impressions about the quality of the encounter. Pleasantness refers to the character of this quality. In addition to other service factors, the customer's evaluation is influenced by the general attitude and demeanor of the representative. Service providers that express an appreciation and genuine caring for the customer are thought to be friendly and warm. As a rule, customers who feel they are treated in a courteous and respectful manner are more likely to evaluate an encounter as pleasant.	Customers reported that the company field and customer representatives were very polite, well mannered, very nice, considerate, and courteous; an office representative tactfully handled a customer complaint.
Responsiveness	The perception that service providers understand the customer's needs and will respond to them in a timely and accurate manner.	The responsiveness dimension reflects a customer's belief that their needs are attended to and resolved in an appropriate manner. In short, they feel that they receive individualized attention, that their needs are understood, and that these needs are met in a timely and accurate fashion. The extent to which a customer perceives a company as responsive is largely dependent upon the expectations they hold. For example, if a customer expects it to take 24 hours to get their heat turned-on but it takes three days for the service to be provided, the customer is likely to feel that the company is unresponsive to its customers' needs.	A customer questioned the company's responsiveness because her furnace is still not working; a customer felt that the customer service representative didn't take the time to understand what customer wanted so when field rep. came he couldn't help because he didn't have the right parts; a customer stated that whenever (he) had a problem the company responded promptly. A customer exclaimed that company service is fast and efficient.
Powerlessness	A negative feeling that the consumer is ultimately impotent in the face of a large and impersonal bureaucracy.	The extent to which a customer recognizes their right to choose influences the degree of power they possess. In industries like the utility industry, where there are few service providers, the customer's right to choose is limited and the degree of power they hold reduced. Customers feel threatened or powerless when they perceive that their concerns are not heard, when they have no control over rates, when no one is accountable for the quality of service, and when they have no recourse if a dispute is resolved against them. In such cases customers feel that they have no power over the quality and nature of the service provided.	Customers felt that they have no place to turn when the field service representative didn't fix yard or left pipes in the wall or when they are over-billed.
Control over the encounter	The perception that the customer maintains control over the human elements of the service encounter.	This dimension highlights the perception that customers desire to establish and control the nature of the service encounter. Specifically, customers desire to determine the best time to schedule service, the duration of a service encounter, as well as the social customs and rules that govern the nature of the interaction.	A customer reported feeling that he had no control over the service encounter, when the representative would not make a specific time for the service call.
Favorability toward the company	A customer's attitude toward the entire company.	In utility companies in particular, and in the service industry in general, consumers make global judgments about the caliber of a service company. In many cases these judgments create a halo-effect whereby general attitudes shape how customers perceive their current service contacts.	Customers speak highly of the company and the services they provide. One customer sums it up best by stating that it's good to know that when you have a problem that the company will come and fix it.

Pleasantness. Pleasantness is defined as the overall quality of the service interaction. As customers interact with service reps, they critique the interaction as it progresses, and at its conclusion have formed an opinion of the interaction as a whole. The service interaction will be viewed as more or less pleasant, depending on the customer's perception of the actual events. The attitude and behavior of the employee plays a large part in constructing this evaluation. Qualities such as politeness, respect, consideration, attentiveness, competence, warmth, friendliness, and tact are highly valued, and contribute to an overall impression of pleasantness. The higher the perceived level of pleasantness, the more satisfaction the customer experiences concerning the service contact.

Responsiveness. A perception of responsiveness is key to the development of satisfaction. Critical to this perception is not only what service providers do, but also how they do it. Service personnel must respond within a certain period of time to be considered responsive. This period varies, depending on the prior expectations held by the customer.

A service call that takes two days will be considered very timely by a customer who expects the call to take four days. In addition, customers want to feel that their service provider is accepting responsibility for the correction of the problem. This means the proper diagnosis of the situation, as well as an apparent commitment to see the operation through to its completion. Other than verbally stating such a commitment, a service provider can express this attitude by the way in which they deal with the customer. We can empathize with the person who complains that, "Talking with that guy was like talking to a brick wall!" Employees can demonstrate responsiveness by merely showing that they hear and understand what the customer is saying; this involves attending to nuances in the conversation, as well as hearing the needs of the customer and acknowledging them.

Basic listening skills are a prerequisite for establishing a reputation for responsiveness. Also highly valued is the service provider that demonstrates some degree of ingenuity and adaptation. A service provider who seems able to go beyond the book and utilize problem solving skills to help a customer is perceived as being very responsive and a pleasure to work with. Such an employee helps to build customer satisfaction in measurable ways.

Powerlessness. The degree of power one feels is often related to the amount of options one has. When a customer has few choices about where to go for service, power is limited by the ability to choose a different service provider if they are dissatisfied with the current provider. If a particular service provider is the only game in town, then their power over the consumer is almost absolute. This perception of nowhere else to turn is directly related to a customer's feeling of powerlessness.

Customers also experience powerlessness when they feel that they are unable to affect the service situation. Often customers will feel that the system is stacked against them. In each service interaction, they lose and the company wins—every time. They view the organization as monolithic and inflexible, maintained by minions who are themselves powerless in the face of company regulations. In such a scenario, each customer is treated as one of the herd, a truly dissatisfying position to be in. Given that many customers view large corporations in a manner similar to the one portrayed above, expectations for the service situation are generally low. A corporation that could provide employees who help the customer through such service quagmires would be positively disconfirming expectations, and thus contributing to strong customer satisfaction.

Control over the encounter. As a rule, people seek control over the events in their lives. A service situation is no exception. Controlling the human elements of the exchange is important to customers, for this affects the overall nature of the encounter. As mentioned above, customers often feel powerless in their dealings with a large organization, and this increases their desire to have some degree of impact on those aspects of the service situation that they *can* control. Their satisfaction level increases when they can call the shots.

This attempt at partial control is not designed to hinder the service call; it actually serves the purpose of individualizing the event to meet the needs of the customer. The customer may need to be away from the house in the morning, so needs the service representative to call in the afternoon. A customer may feel the need to supervise the work being done, or may ask that the employee not disturb her while she does something else. A customer may instruct the service person to enter the house at one particular door, and not another. Each of these actions helps the customer to remember that the service call is for their benefit, and not for the benefit of the company. This can lead to increased customer satisfaction.

Favorability toward the company. This dimension may be defined as the degree to which the customer has good feelings about the company in general, coupled with the extent to which this feeling carries over into the evaluation of a current service situation. This concept is sometimes referred to as the halo effect. Consumers tend to lump together judgments, rather than make a distinct determination about each discrete service area. These global judgments usually color the impressions customers have of their present service contract, as well as of the company in general. If these judgments are predominantly positive, a certain amount of goodwill about the company is generated. This is highly beneficial, as it will help to temper slightly unsatisfactory service experiences, and by the same token will reinforce and amplify pleasing experiences. For example, a customer who previously had strongly positive experiences with a company and a positive impression of that company as a whole, is quite likely to be patient and understanding with a service person who arrives at her house thirty minutes late. Conversely, a customer who previously had a very negative perception of the company might be outraged at this apparent lack of consideration.

PREMISE THREE: A RELIABLE GAUGE OF SATISFACTION ALLOWS A COMPANY TO ESTABLISH CLEAR BENCHMARKS.

Working from a sound model of service satisfaction, a measurement team can design a brief closed-ended instrument which accurately measures customer satisfaction. A two-to-three minute telephone interview can stand for an accurate gauge of customer satisfaction. This is a cost-effective method that can be used at any time to assess company or area performance. Periodic studies using the model-driven instrument can establish clear benchmarks for a company. The results of such studies provide managers with areas to emphasize in service strategies and training. In addition, companies can provide employees and service reps with valuable and timely feedback.

PREMISE FOUR: BY MEASURING THE BASIC EXPECTATIONS AND DESIRES CUSTOMERS HOLD, A COMPANY CAN DECIDE HOW TO STRATEGICALLY EXCEED EXPECTATIONS SO AS TO INFLUENCE SERVICE SATISFACTION.

In-depth interviews with customers that explore expectations and desires provide service managers with specific strategies for improvement. Improving satisfaction depends on the degree to which a service experience exceeds, falls short, or meets customer expectations. Existing expectations seen as a standard against which future service is judged. Research clearly shows that the service affects the expectations a customer holds in three ways: (1) expectations will be met or confirmed; (2) expectations will be exceeded; (3) the expectations will not be met. As common sense and the research literature on the subject indicates, not fulfilling expectations produces dissatisfaction, confirming expectations produces a neutral response, and exceeding expectations results in customer satisfaction. For instance, if you expect your water heater to be repaired in three days, and it ultimately takes five days, you will be dissatisfied and probably upset. With the same expectations, receiving repair service in one day will produce some measure of increased satisfaction.

The critical areas to study for this purpose are the customer's expectations concerning company representatives, service messages, the service encounter, the service product, and the service process. Information of this nature will enable the company to measure the full range of client expectations, and then design policies and procedures that will serve to exceed these expectations to a significant degree.

PREMISE FIVE: SATISFACTION BENCHMARKS ENABLE A COMPANY TO OBSERVE SHIFTS IN CUSTOMER SATISFACTION DUE TO STRATEGIC ACTIONS TAKEN BY THE COMPANY OR TO CHANGES IN THE MARKET ENVIRONMENT (POLITICAL, ECONOMIC, SOCIAL, ETC.)

By assessing customer satisfaction on a periodic basis, a company can establish clear benchmarks for service. Benchmarks can be used as indicators of quality performance or to establish the need for changes in company policies or actions. In times of uncertainty, a sound benchmark can also be used to assess the severity of a problem or to ascertain the current course of a company.

PREMISE SIX: THE EXACT EFFECTS OF STRATEGIES CAN BE ACCURATELY MEASURED BY OBSERVING SHIFTS IN THE SATISFACTION MEASURE.

With a reliable gauge of customer satisfaction, a company can track the effects of specific strategies and enhancements. As the adage goes, the proof is in the pudding. Guesswork is limited, if not eliminated. Strategies designed to improve service and customer satisfaction should meet the ultimate test. If changes in the satisfaction gauge can not be discerned over a specified period, the strategies have proven ineffective or unnecessary. Statistical analyses can provide managers with an assessment of the cost-effectiveness of those strategies which do have an impact. Large companies can test ideas before implementing them in the service process by judging their effect in a limited area or district.

Statistical Measurement Techniques for Service Operations

This chapter is devoted to statistically valid measurement techniques for service operations. Statistical quality control methodologies for manufacturing operations have received extensive coverage in texts and by the military for many years, and therefore will not be discussed here.

There is a growing appreciation for the fact that service functions involving individual customer contact or communication need to be assessed in a systematic manner. Functions such as computer generated invoices, customer service representatives' contacts, credit and collections staffs, purchase order preparation, and accounts payable operations need to be measured in order to create proactive attitudes toward problem identification, root cause analysis, and fast and effective corrective actions.

The information provided in this chapter is designed to aid operating managers in establishing appropriate sample sizes and sampling techniques for service quality measures.

SAMPLING TECHNIQUES

There are three types of sampling techniques that are applicable to service operations:

RANDOM SAMPLING

Through random sampling, each item in the population has an equal opportunity of being selected. This is done by assigning a sequential number to each item, then obtaining numbers from a random number table and selecting the corresponding item until the sample size is reached.

SYSTEMATIC SAMPLING

This method of sampling is most commonly used in connection with service operations. Items are selected at specific intervals in the sequence to provide a cross section. The interval is determined by dividing the population by the sample size. The result is rounded off and items are selected at this interval throughout the population until the sample size has been reached. For example, if the total population is 1,000 and the sample is 100, every tenth item would be selected

Stratified Random Sampling

Here, separate samples are taken for various components of a measure. For example, in an measure such as mortgage application processing, several sub-measurement items (i.e. approvals, declines, cancellations) would be calculated. Each sample is taken randomly or systematically. Individual results are weighted according to actual volumes processed in order to report the total result for the measure.

SAMPLING CONFIDENCE

It is not economically feasible nor necessary to require 100 percent reporting on all work performed. Where appropriate, computer generated data can provide 100 percent sampling; however, in other situations statistical sample is the only economically viable alternative. Appropriate sample sizes ensure a specified range of the sample results. That range is called the *confidence interval* which is made up of two elements: *confidence level* and *confidence limit*.

Confidence Level

The confidence level is the probability or likelihood that the reported results (i.e., average days or error rate) from the sample truly reflect the total population.

It is recommended that the minimum confidence level for service quality operations be set at 90 percent. This level appears to provide the best balance between precision and practical sample size. On an exceptions basis, problem areas can receive closer attention.

Confidence Limit

The confidence limit is the range around the reported result (i.e., average days or error rate) in which we can expect the total population to be. In other words, if all media for a particular measurement were sampled we could expect to find the result within this range.

Specification of confidence limits needs to be established. Typical examples for timeliness and accuracy measures follow:

Timeliness Measures

Range of Mean	Confidence Limits
0- 5 days	10% of the mean
6 - 10 days	0.5 days
over 10 days	5% of the mean

Confidence limits are based on range of error rates as follows:

Accuracy Measures

Range of Error Rate	Confidence Limits
0% - .59%	0.5%
0.6% - 4.99%	1%
5.0% - 19.99%	2%
20% and over	3%

CONFIDENCE INTERVAL

The following examples show how the above confidence level and limits are used:

Timeliness Example

- Our sample result	= 7 days
- Our confidence level	= 90%
- Our confidence limit	= +0.5 day

Therefore, we are 90% confident that the true performance of the total population falls between 6.5 and 7.5 days.

Accuracy Example

- Our sample result	= 10%
- Our confidence level	= 90
- Our confidence limit	= +2%

Therefore, we are 90% confident that the true performance of the total population falls between 8% and 12%.

SAMPLE SIZE

Sample sizes are calculated differently for timeliness, accuracy, and responsiveness. (Responsiveness is a measure of the customer's perception of the quality of service being provided. Criteria is developed to reflect customer perceptions of what constitutes quality service, and the criteria is then used as a standard against which actual performance is measured.) This section describes the statistical methods used for each. In instances where the media is sampled for timeliness as well as accuracy and responsiveness, it is left to management's discretion whether two different sample sizes will be calculated, or whether the accuracy and responsiveness sample size should be used for both measures. As a general rule, sample sizes are larger for accuracy and responsiveness and will, therefore, achieve the confidence intervals for timeliness as well.

SAMPLE SIZE TIMELINESS

Normally, a three month period of sampling should be adequate to determine the appropriate sample size for each measure. The sample size for the required confidence interval (as described in Section II) is calculated by using the mean and standard deviation.

Developing the mean (or average days). Using the example in Table 1, the following steps are taken to create the mean:

1. Column 1. List the range of days from 0 to the maximum result (highest turnaround time) in the sample.
2. Column 2. For each result, record how often they occur in the sample.
3. Column 3. Multiply column 1 by column 2 and record result.
4. Add the frequency column (2) to obtain the total sample size and record on total line.
5. Add the days column (3) to determine total days and record on total line.
6. Calculate mean (average days). Divide the total days by the total sample.

Table 1. Developing the mean.

1 Number of Days	2 Frequency in Sample	3 (Col. 1 X Col. 2) Days
0	1	0
1	2	2
2	3	6
3	4	12
4	6	24
5	4	20
6	3	18
7	2	14
8	1	8
--	--	--
Total =	26	104

$$\text{Mean} = \frac{\text{Total days}}{\text{sample size}} = \frac{104}{26} = 4 \left(\text{average days} \right)$$

Determining the standard deviation. Using Table 2, calculate the standard deviation through these steps.

1. Column 4 - Subtract the mean from column 1 and record result in column 4.

2. Column 5 - Square the result recorded in column 4.

3. Column 6 - Multiply the square (column 5) by the frequency (column 2).

4. Add column 6 and record on total line.

5. Calculate standard deviation:

$$\frac{\text{sum of frequency} \times \text{squares (column 6 total)}}{\text{total sample size less one}}$$

Table 2. Calculating standard deviation.

1 number of days	2 frequency in sample	3 (col. 1 x col. 2) days	4 col. 1 minus mean	5 col. 4 squared	6 (col. 2 x col. 5)
0	1	0	-4	16	16
1	2	2	-3	9	18
2	3	6	-2	4	12
3	4	12	-1	1	4
4	6	24	0	0	0
5	4	20	1	1	4
6	3	18	2	4	12
7	2	14	3	9	18
8	1	8	4	16	16
Total =	26	104	Sum of frequency x squares =		100

$$\text{Mean} = \frac{104}{26} = 4 \text{ (average days)}$$

$$S = \text{Standard deviation} = \sqrt{\frac{100}{26-1}} = \sqrt{4} = 2$$

Sample size calculation. To determine the sample size for timeliness (average days) measures, the following formula is used:

Formula:
$$\frac{\left(1.65\left(\text{std}.\,\text{deviation}\right)\right)^2}{\text{confidence limit}}$$

The minimum sample size for any measure is 100 items, even if the calculation results in a sample size of less than the amount.

If the calculation results in a sample size greater than the monthly volume of work measured, or the monthly volume is less than 100, then 100% of all media is to be sampled:

Example:

Mean (average days)	= 4
Confidence limits (10% of mean)	= .4
Standard deviation	= 2
T = 1.65	= Given

Formula:
$$\frac{\left(1.65\left(\text{std}.\,\text{deviation}\right)\right)^2}{.4} = \frac{\left(3.3\right)^2}{.4} = \left(8.25\right)^2 = 68$$

Substituting values:

$$\frac{\left(1.65\left(2\right)\right)^2}{.4} = \frac{\left(3.3\right)^2}{.4} = \left(8.25\right)^2 = 68$$

SAMPLE SIZE FOR ACCURACY AND RESPONSIVENESS MEASURES

Accuracy and responsiveness measures are proportions expressed in terms of error rate. Normally, a three month period of sampling should be adequate to estimate the error rate and determine the appropriate sample size.

There are two steps required in determining the sample size for proportion measures. First, determine the estimated sample size, then correct the estimate for monthly volumes.

Determining the estimated sample size. To obtain the initial sample size, Table 3 provides a wide range of error rates and confidence limits. Based on your sampling, if your results fall within the chart ranges, the estimated sample size can be obtained by referring to the column and row appropriate to your results.

For example, assume that your sample results reflect an 8% error rate. The first column on the chart is the error rate. Next you must determine the appropriate confidence limit. As shown earlier in this chapter, having an 8% error rate, the confidence limit is 2%. Moving along the 8% row you would select the 2% confidence limit column. Your estimated sample size is 501.

If the sample results do not fall within the ranges provided in the chart, it is necessary to calculate the estimated sample size. The formula below requires an error rate from your sampled work and the associated confidence limit.

Formula: $S = \dfrac{(1.65)2 \times RQ}{C^2}$

where: S = Estimated sample size
      1.65 = Given
      R = Error rate
      Q = 100 minus error rate (R)
      C = Confidence limit (%)

Note: The error rate (R), 100-R (Q), and the confidence limit (C) may be expressed as whole numbers or as percentages. Whatever method you choose, it must be consistently used.

Example: 1) Whole numbers

$$S = \dfrac{(1.65)^2(8)(92)}{2^2}$$

2) Percentages

$$S = \dfrac{(1.65)^2(0.8)(92)}{(.02)^2}$$

Not

$$S = \dfrac{(1.65)^2(8)(92)}{(.02)^2}$$

Correcting estimated sample size for monthly volumes. This step must be performed whether the estimated sample size is calculated or taken from the chart:

Formula: $V = \dfrac{S}{1 + \dfrac{(S-1)}{N}}$

where: V = sample size
      S = Estimated sample size
      N = Monthly volume

Example #1

Utilizing Table 3 for estimated sample size and correcting for monthly volume,

Error rate   = 1%
Confidence limit   = 1%
Monthly volume   = 12,000

Formula: $V = \dfrac{S}{1+\dfrac{(S-1)}{N}}$

Substituting values:

$$V = \frac{270}{1+\dfrac{(270-1)}{12{,}000}} = \frac{270}{1+.0244} = 264$$

Example #2
Calculating estimated sample size and correcting for monthly volume,

- Determining estimated sample size
  Error rate = 5%
  Confidence limit = 1%

Formula: $S = \dfrac{(1.65)2(R)(Q)}{C^2}$

Substituting values:

$$S = \frac{(1.65)2(5)(95)}{1} = \frac{(2.72)(475)}{1} = 1292$$

- Correcting sample size for monthly volume
  monthly volume = 15,000

Formula: $V = \dfrac{S}{1+\dfrac{(S-1)}{N}}$

Substituting values:

$$V = \frac{1292}{1+\dfrac{(1292-1)}{15{,}000}} = \frac{1292}{1+.086} = 1190$$

Table 3. Error rate sample size chart.
Confidence level 90%   t = 1.65

Proportion of error rate (R)	Confidence Limits (C)					
	0.5	**1**	**2**	**3**	**4**	**5**
0.5	542	135	34	15	8	5
1	1078	270	67	30	17	11
2	2143	534	133	59	33	21
3	3169	792	198	88	50	32
4	4182	1045	261	116	65	42
5	5173	1293	323	144	81	52
6	6142	1535	384	171	96	61
7	7089	1772	443	197	111	71
8	8015	2004	501	223	125	80
9	8919	2230	557	248	139	89
10	9801	2450	613	272	153	98
15	13885	3471	868	386	217	139
20	17424	4356	1089	484	272	174
25	20419	5105	1276	567	319	204
30	22869	5717	1429	635	357	229
35	24775	6194	1548	688	387	248
40	26136	6534	1634	726	408	261
45	26953	6738	1685	749	421	270
50	27225	6806	1702	756	425	272

Part II

Case Studies of Quality Management in Leading Companies

William L. Rammes
Vice President-Corporate Human Resources
and
Lee J. Waltemade
Vice President-Labor Relations

Anheuser-Busch: The Strength of Tradition, the Power of People

U.S. business faces tremendous challenges today, and those challenges come at us from all sides—from a changing marketplace, both here and abroad, from our shareholders and from our customers. Anheuser-Busch is no exception. But we have always believed that the toughest challenge we face comes from within. It is a challenge that has been summed up very well by our chairman of the board and president, August A. Busch III:

> Anheuser-Busch has built its business and its reputation on a heritage of quality. Through the years our strict adherence to uncompromising quality standards has been the cornerstone of our success. Competitive pressures have changed. Industry challenges have changed. The social environment has changed. But our commitment to quality has never changed and it never will. (Anheuser-Busch Companies 1989 *Annual Report*)

No matter where our other challenges come from, there is one that we set for ourselves—the quality challenge. And it is one we gladly accept, because a clear focus on that one self-imposed challenge gives us a true competitive edge in meeting the many challenges that are thrust upon us. What we would like to do here is describe the philosophy of quality that has enabled us to grow and prosper through the years. Then we would like to discuss the way we apply the concept of quality not just to our product, but to our people. We believe that only by providing a superior internal environment are we able to continue producing a superior product.

But as much as we have grown and changed over the years, the real key to our success lies in some things that have not changed—our uncompromising commitment to quality, a dedication to maintain our company's traditions, a desire to build for the long term. Those words we quoted earlier from our chairman, August Busch III, echo some words written more than a century ago by Adolphus Busch, our company's founder. Adolphus once said in a letter to his son: "Keep on making good beer, the very best you can, as our whole salvation lies in that. People are beginning to appreciate our beers more and more every day. Our name is becoming more famous daily and our popularity is rising, so that in a few years we will have the finest and most independent business in the world."

This 19th-century approach to our business is central to our company—to what we are, who we are and where we are going. This approach, this philosophy of quality, is best understood in the context of three central ideas.

First, we are a company that looks at the future from the vantage point of 140 years of history. We know the earnings we report next quarter are important, but we also know that steady growth over the years and decades is even more vital.

Second, in the words of Adolphus Busch, "making friends is our business." That means we recognize that, without our customers, we are nothing. We can never take our customers for granted. But as we will soon point out, the people who buy our beer—or visit our theme parks, or purchase our bread—are not the only customers we serve.

Third, we are firmly anchored in our basic craft of brewing. Even though today we are involved in food products, family entertainment and a variety of other ventures, our craftsman's pride puts its stamp on everything we do. This idea is worth dwelling on for a moment. At Anheuser-Busch, we believe that there is a right way and a wrong way to do things. And we settle for nothing less than the right way.

Some critics of American industry have claimed that our nation's competitive position suffers because too many corporations are headed by people who are not grounded in the production process. As with many generalizations, this one has been overblown, but it contains a grain of truth. Companies tend to be most successful when they keep their eye on their basic business. And chief executives who are well-grounded in the essential production process have a tendency to do that. Our chairman is a certified brewmaster, and his strong orientation to brewing quality has shaped our entire company. While we will always remain open to technical innovation, we will never consider production short-cuts that risk the integrity of our products.

Quality control in our business begins with the brewmaster's senses. Does the beer taste and smell as it should? Is the barley malt the right color? How do the hop blossoms feel between the fingers? In short, quality control has everything to do with the right way to do things.

For example, all of our beers undergo an extra fermentation step in which beechwood chips are spread in the bottom of the lagering tank. The chips provide extra surface area for the fermenting action of the brewer's yeast.

It's an old-fashioned technique called beechwood aging and we do it to mature the flavor of the beer and to provide natural carbonation.

We are the only brewer in the world to use this traditional process to age and carbonate our beers. Is it the most efficient way to make beer? No. Is it the most cost-effective way? No. On the contrary, it's the most costly way. But the point is, at Anheuser-Busch we feel it is the right way.

Just as we believe there is a right way to make beer, we also believe there is a right way to lead and motivate people. That is why we put a great deal of effort into providing a superior workplace. We have a long tradition of being an excellent company to work for, and we see it as a key management responsibility to ensure that we continue to provide a high-quality work environment for our employees.

We firmly believe that if we go the extra mile for our employees, they will go the extra mile for the company and our products. For example, our people take a lot of pride in what they do, and they feel a great deal of responsibility for our product, even after it leaves the brewery. Our beer cans and bottles all carry a date code that indicates where and when the beer was made. A great many of our employees know how to read this code. And if they go to a store or restaurant and get a can or bottle that's not fresh, they'll bring it to our marketing department's attention for follow-up. You don't see that kind of pride in people who feel they are just drawing a paycheck. That sense of responsibility and ownership is part of knowing that you have more than just a job—you are a member of a team.

People work hard and they are proud of what they do when they feel they have a stake in the business. That's why we provide plenty of opportunity for employees to share in the success of the company. About three quarters of our eligible employees participate in our 401(K) plans. Through the plan, they own more than 13 million shares of Anheuser-Busch stock. Employees have contributed more than $340 million to this savings plan since April 1, 1976, and the company has matched those contributions with about $124 million in stock. In 1991, the market value of those contributions was close to $800 million. About 8.5 percent of Anheuser-Busch's total shares are owned by employees. We also have been pushing our stock option plans down the management chain. We offered stock options to seven hundred executives last year; that's more manager-level employees than are offered options at most companies our size.

Because our employees have such a big stake in our success, they deserve to be kept up-to-date on the state of the company. We see to it that they get that information firsthand by doing an annual round of employee communications meetings. We get the top management of the company, including the chairman, out into our plant cities for face-to-face meetings with all our employees. And we put just as much preparation and thought into these meetings as we do into our annual shareholder's meeting. We have to, because our employees are important shareholders and significant contributors to shareholder value.

These are two-way meetings. And our employees are not shy about telling us what they think. They ask tough questions. During a recent round of meetings, one employee asked what the company was doing to avoid further excise tax increases. Another expressed concern that he was not being used to his potential, that he could use some cross-training to make him more productive.

Employees ask about new products, they ask about environmental issues, they ask about international marketing strategy and political issues. These meetings are useful for the information our employees receive from them. But they are just as useful in reminding us that our employees are smart, they are articulate, and they pay attention to what's going on in the business.

We put a lot of effort into other channels of communication, too. In addition to our grievance process for bargaining unit employees, we have an ombudsman program that salaried employees can use to seek fair solutions to job-related conflicts and problems.

We also have an employee suggestion program that encourages employees to propose more cost-effective ways of doing things. This program rewards employees for cost-saving ideas. We emphasize recognition over cash, though we do give cash awards. Employees whose suggestions save the company $25,000 or more are invited to St. Louis for dinner and a ball game with top executives.

One of our best channels of upward employee communication is the annual employee attitude research done by our human resources department. We poll about six thousand employees each year, and some additional surveys are done by other staff groups around the corporation. Our surveys give us a lot of good data on how people feel about a wide range of issues—pay and benefits, management style, opportunities for advancement, employee autonomy, fair treatment, and so forth. Our employees get an effective way to express their concerns anonymously, while we in management get some solid data on what we're doing right, and where we need to improve.

One thing we have learned over the years is that people like working for a company they respect. One of the things Anheuser-Busch employees respect about their company is the fact that we are a responsible corporate citizen. We support a great many community activities, and we encourage our employees to do likewise. For instance, we encourage our employees to support educational institutions by matching their contributions up to $5,000 per donor per year. Within certain limits, we also contribute money to charitable organizations for which our employees do volunteer work.

We also believe employees like working for a company that's actively committed to protecting and preserving the environment. As part of our long-standing commitment to the environment, Anheuser-Busch has been an industry leader in the use of environmentally sound packaging, and in the reclamation and reuse of brewing and manufacturing by-products. Our recycling subsidiary, Anheuser-Busch Recycling, has grown to be the nation's largest recycler of aluminum beverage cans. We have also provided major support for a wide range of environmental efforts, from solid waste disposal and community beautification to wildlife conservation and habitat preservation.

We encourage employees to share this commitment. For example, we initiated a paper recycling program at our St. Louis headquarters. We estimate that the program keeps fifty-five tons of paper a month from winding up in landfills. Similar activities are underway or planned at other Anheuser-Busch facilities around the country.

We've also communicated a tough message to all our employees about how serious we are about ensuring compliance with environmental regulations that affect our operations. We've distributed to all employees an environmental policy manual that makes it very clear that we will not tolerate any carelessness when it comes to keeping our operations environmentally sound.

We believe you have to work at being a good workplace. And we're working especially hard at it now, because our industry is extremely competitive. We, like most companies, are under a lot of outside pressure to manage our business for the short-term, from quarter to quarter. But we do not look just at the next quarter, we also look at the long term. Our ability to succeed long-term depends, obviously, on how well we continue to provide quality products to our customers. But our success is also linked to how well we maintain the commitment and the enthusiasm of our employees.

We referred above to our founder's slogan, "Making friends is our business." As we noted, it's a saying we do not just apply to our customers. We can not maintain the goodwill and trust of our customers unless we work at maintaining the goodwill and trust of our employees.

When you earn trust, you also earn loyalty. Our employees show a lot of loyalty to Anheuser-Busch. They tend to stay with us. Maybe that's because so many people come to Anheuser-Busch for more than just a job. They see the company as a place where they can build a career. But that doesn't happen by accident; we do a number of things to encourage people to feel that way.

We offer the best wages in our industry, and our operations—wherever they are — tend to be among the better-paying employers within their local and regional markets. We add to that a superior package of benefits. We offer an excellent health insurance package and, in the vast majority of cases, the company pays the premiums. We have an excellent vacation policy, up to six weeks for salaried, and eight weeks for hourly employees, based on seniority. Our pension plan is very competitive within the consumer goods industry and other companies our size.

In the increasingly important area of family benefits, we have had flexible work schedules in some of our field locations for some time and we have started to implement them at our St. Louis headquarters. We offer pre-tax spending accounts to help employees with dependent care and medical expenses, and we pick up the tab for employees' use of local referral services to find suitable day care. Because we recognize that employees sometimes need to stay home with a sick child or other family member, we allow them to use sick days for that purpose. In more serious cases, we allow extended family-related leave under our personal leave of absence policy.

We are especially proud of our employee assistance program, which we have offered since 1978. The program has provided help to employees at every level of the company, from production workers to senior management levels. It's run very confidentially and we have generated a high level of employee awareness and trust, as evidenced by the fact that the program has a self-referral rate of better than ninety percent. That means employees have gained confidence in the program, because they are seeking help without their manager's urging them to do so.

We believe our employees would give us high marks for standing by them when they need special support. Whether it's a leave of absence to take care of a family problem or help through the employee assistance program, we want to give our employees extra help during tough times. That is only fair when you consider the years of service the company will receive from an employee. It is also a good investment. But most important, it's the right way to do things. We run our business for the long term and we invest in our people for the long term, too.

One way we manage for the long term is by working hard to provide employment stability. We noted earlier that Anheuser-Busch has a strong sense of history. You might say we are a company with a long memory, and one thing we remember all too well is Prohibition. During Prohibition, when other brewers were simply closing their doors, we bent over backwards to keep our work force intact. We made ice cream, trucks, refrigeration equipment, soft drinks—we worked hard to keep people working.

And we still work hard at it. In our production areas, we monitor hiring and retirements very closely so we can minimize lay-offs due to seasonal fluctuations or plant modernization projects. If we can take action now to avoid a lay-off down the road, we do it. But sometimes we can't avoid cuts. On most occasions when we have to idle employees, we extend their medical insurance coverage and other benefits to ease the strain on their families. A few years ago, when we shut down one of our smaller businesses, we had to let approximately ninety people go. It took some effort, but we were able to place more than two-thirds of them elsewhere in Anheuser-Busch. The others were given help in finding jobs outside the company.

Another reason people stay with us is the fact that we have a strong policy of promoting from within. In support of that policy, we encourage people to develop their skills, both at work and outside of work. We have an extensive management development program. We do a great deal of operational training; this has been especially important over the past few years as we've modernized our plants and added more high-tech equipment. We also offer salaried employees tuition assistance for higher education, picking up 75 percent of the cost of books, tuition, and fees.

Then there are the things we do just to help people feel more a part of the family. We have annual service award banquets for employees who have been with us twenty-five years or longer. Anyone who retires in a given year is also invited to one of these banquets, which are attended by our top management. It's a tribute to the kind of longevity we have in our work force that we invited 550 employees or recent retirees to last year's St. Louis banquet.

Each brewery has an employee activity budget; how it is used in each location is largely determined by the employees themselves. In some cases it is spent on sports activities, in other cases it goes to fund wellness programs or employee social activities. Most of our facilities have an annual family event—a picnic, a barbecue, or a special day at a local theme park.

All our breweries annually compete in our Reach for Excellence program. Each year we recognize one or more breweries as the plants of the year based on safety performance, production cost control, and support for the community. This friendly competition has done a lot to reinforce team spirit and pride at our various locations. We try to help our employees feel like part of a big family. In some cases, though, we are *literally* a family company. We have current employees who represent the third generation of their family to work for us. It is also not unusual for several members of the same family to work in various parts of the company. We know some companies discourage that, but we do not, assuming there are no business conflicts or superior-subordinate relationships that are not approved by our business practices committee.

What it comes down to is this: Anheuser-Busch has had the good fortune to become a very stable and successful company. We owe a great deal of that success to the fact that we have set out to attract and retain good people by offering them an exceptional work environment. We believe most people want to work for company where a strong spirit prevails, where they have the opportunity to be a valued member of a team. We work hard to offer people that opportunity and they pay us back by keeping us successful. We strive to empower our employees to do work they can be proud of. And they in turn empower Anheuser-Busch to meet our quality challenge.

Fred L. Thompson
Director, Total Quality

Monsanto: Employee Empowerment through Total Quality Management

The Chemical Group of Monsanto has developed a total quality improvement process that is helping to ensure continuous improvement in its many administrative, business, manufacturing, and service processes. This case study will focus on that process and how it is empowering employees to help improve business results.

As a result of rising standards being created and met by global competition, consumers have become more aware of quality and its importance. Every time they receive the features and performance they look for in a product, consumers become less tolerant of poorly made items. In fact, a 1988 survey conducted by the Gallup Group for the American Society for Quality Control indicated that Americans are willing to pay a substantial premium to get high quality products rather than average quality products.

Consumers, for example, indicated that they were willing to pay twenty percent more for high quality automobiles, sixty-seven percent more for premium televisions, and seventy-two percent more for high quality sofas. Granted, Monsanto does not manufacture these products, but it does produce a number of different materials that go into them, such as *Lustran* plastics, thermoplastic elastomers, and *Wear-Dated* fabric fibers. Our entire product portfolio consists of high-performance materials that add quality and value to our customer's products: quality that the end-user is looking for.

The foreign car market offers one example. Japanese and German car manufacturers have taken a large share of the American automotive market by providing what the consumer is looking for: better gas mileage, quality, and styling.

In response to this loss of market share, the American auto industry—firms like Ford, Goodyear, Armstrong, and others—initiated aggressive campaigns to improve the quality of their products. They also approached their suppliers, including Monsanto Chemical Group, and asked us to join them in their efforts to improve the quality of their goods and services.

Not surprisingly, Monsanto elected to work with them as did its competitors: Dow, DuPont, General Electric, and Borg Warner. These companies recognized that those who did not play—and play well—would be replaced by someone else. The journey toward total quality had begun.

About the same time, quality consultants and individual companies, recognized as leaders in quality management, determined that internal inefficiencies in most American firms represent twenty-to-thirty percent of revenues. That figure represented several hundred million dollars for companies the size of Monsanto Chemical.

Finally, the consultants and leaders showed us that by eliminating inefficiencies and the hassles that go with them, employees would become motivated, and their productivity and pride in their work would increase.

MONSANTO'S APPROACH TO QUALITY IMPROVEMENT

Monsanto defines quality as consistency in meeting agreed upon requirements with goods and services that add value, i. e., product purity, just-in-time delivery, or invoice accuracy. To deliver quality, we worked with SRI International to develop the total quality improvement process. Total quality involves a systematic process designed to change the culture of a company to make it more effective and efficient in meeting customer requirements. Hallmarks of this process include a strong customer focus and a commitment to continuous improvement.

Monsanto's process encourages employees (1) to meet with their customers (internal or external) to agree on the requirements or factors most important to the customer and (2) to use systematic procedures to create opportunities that will reduce waste and improve customer satisfaction. Quality improvement teams, typically multifunctional and multilevel, are used extensively to address opportunities to improve quality. Monsanto is committed to continuous improvement; the target is perfection.

Three guiding principles describe the total quality process at Monsanto.
1. focusing on the customer
2. constantly striving to improve everything we do with perfection as our goal
3. involving every person in the process

Monsanto focuses on the customer by:
• meeting agreed-upon requirements
• understanding how our products and services add value for customers
• collaborating with customers to develop new products
• continuously seeking objective feedback on our performance

We continuously improve by:
• viewing all work as a process
• making all processes effective, efficient and adaptable
• controlling with in-process measures
• maintaining constructive dissatisfaction with the present level of performance

- eliminating activities that do not add value to the customer
- holding gains and incorporating lessons learned

And finally, all employees view their job as part of a process that can be systematically improved. They

- recognize people as the major source of all process improvement
- understand our customer's needs and expectations
- realize that every level in the organization must be actively involved to assure long-term success
- reward those employees who practice and apply these concepts in their pursuit of customer-focused continuous improvement

EMPOWERMENT

Total quality was introduced company-wide in 1986. Since then, extensive training has been conducted. Essentially, all fifteen thousand Chemical Group employees have completed a one-day course that introduces quality improvement concepts.

From the very beginning, much time and effort was put into training employees in the tools and techniques of quality management. It was our belief that this is the only way employees can truly become empowered to make improvements in our many work processes. We say an individual is empowered as a result of being provided with the necessary authority, resources, training, direction, and freedom to contribute to improving work processes.

The following two courses and workshop are examples of the type of quality management training available to employees so that they have the necessary tools and techniques for continuously improving customer satisfaction and our work processes:

Principles of Continuous Improvement is a workshop intended for all employees. Entire teams are encouraged to go through the workshop together to work on improving specific processes. Participants are exposed to basic total quality concepts, as well as the definitions of quality and customer-supplier partnerships. They learn how to apply our ten-step process to continuous improvement and simple statistical process control tools and techniques. Upon completion of this course participants will have:

- learned the elements of customer-focused continuous improvement;
- learned how to effectively participate on teams; and
- learned the importance of properly defining a project in terms of measures, process flow, customer requirements and process ownership.

Total Quality Team Leaders is a course intended for employees who are Quality Improvement Team Leaders or any employee who is a Group Leader. The course is done in a workshop style. Its primary emphasis is on understanding the group dynamics process and how a group of people can become an effective team producing significant results. Upon completion, participants will be able to successfully lead a team; know how to use effective group dynamics and meeting skills tools; and get a team to effectively use our ten-step process to continuous improvement.

Team Facilitator is a course intended for individuals that want to help teams become more effective. Participants are exposed to task oriented team models, stages of group development, group behavior, maintenance behavior, individualistic behavior, meeting standards, consensus building, intervention techniques and consultation models. Upon completion, participants will understand how to apply group process; understand how to apply the task oriented team model to improve team effectiveness; and, understand how the group process supports problem solving.

Courses in basic statistical control techniques are available to all employees. Participants learn how to apply simple statistical tools for monitoring and controlling key product and process variables; how to identify and prioritize systems that need improvement; and how to develop appropriate sampling techniques. Advanced training in designed experiments is offered on a more select basis to help employees eliminate special causes of process variation.

EMPLOYEE INVOLVEMENT

As previously mentioned, employees focusing on improving our many work processes is one of the hallmarks of our total quality improvement effort. Teams are used extensively and are a valued part of the Chemical Group's culture.

In the next several pages we will describe three case studies involving various teams within the Chemicals Group:

The MERIT Communication Team

Monsanto Emergency Response Information Team (MERIT) is our system for communicating with and responding to a chemical emergency incident site outside of plant boundaries. The MERIT system often interacts with the Chemical Manufacturers Association's Chemtrec system. This system had proven effective with no obvious problems; however, a team of Monsanto employees decided to apply the total quality improvement process to the MERIT system. The team's objective was to reduce the time required for Monsanto's response to requests for assistance during outside emergency incidents.

Figure 1 shows the results of the team's continuous improvement efforts. The average MERIT response time was reduced by nearly sixty percent from 1987 to 1991. The techniques this team used are text book examples of the continuous improvement process.

First this team validated their project's objectives by holding discussions with several metropolitan St. Louis emergency response organizations. (These are the customers in the quality context.) The MERIT response communications system is complex. To ensure that all improvement possibilities were reviewed, a flow diagram of the communications process was developed and is illustrated in Figure

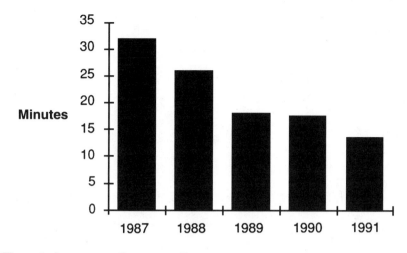

Figure 1. Average merit response time.

2. After defining the process, a cause-and-effect diagram known as a fishbone or Ishikawa diagram was developed (see Figure 3). This tool records and shows relationships between potential causes of an effect such as improved response time. Usually it's produced by brainstorming, organizing, and diagramming potential causes into categories. The diagram then serves as a focal point to discuss such topics as what the most probable causes are and what data should be collected to verify these cause-and effect relationships.

The MERIT Communications Team then designed a survey instrument to collect detailed categorized data on all incidents. The causes of delays in communications were identified, and corrective action on the systemic causes of these delays was developed and implemented. One solution was to improve the system for selection and training of MERIT personnel. The MERIT team's work is typical; many other teams are currently pursuing improvements in virtually every process we use to serve our customers, employees, communities, and stockholders.

Greenwood Machine Shop Team

Plant of the 90s is a slogan that originated in the Fibers Division that is used to describe a state of being after a plant has achieved a certain level of improvements in productivity and automation. The cornerstone of the Plant of the 90s challenge Fibers Division was to achieve a step change improvement in productivity. For a plant support function like the Greenwood Machine Shop Team, this meant stepping outside the traditional mode of doing the best you can with what you have. It meant totally changing the business philosophy and applying the talents, teamwork, and brain power of the team to achieve significant bottom-line results. If the Greenwood Plant was to be a player in the 1990s, teams

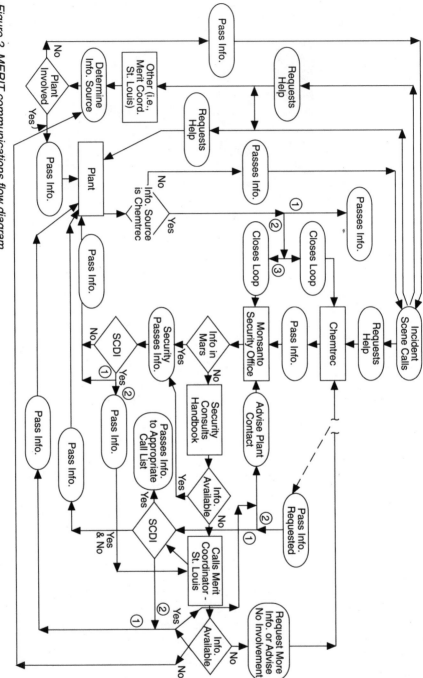

Figure 2. MERIT communications flow diagram.

MERIT COMMUNICATIONS PERCEIVED OBSTACLES

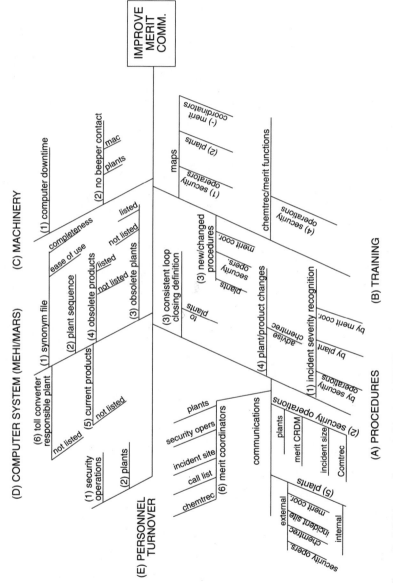

Figure 3. A fishbone diagram showing MERIT communications perceived obstacles.

like this one would have to deliver! Deliver they have. The Machine Shop Team has been a premier example of innovation, focus on the internal customer, team dynamics, and continuous improvement in productivity through cost reduction.

Measuring productivity in a maintenance function can be a little tricky. Costs can be reduced, but service, on-stream time, and quality cannot be sacrificed. Over the past five years, the Machine Shop Team has achieved documented cost reductions of over $1.3 million. This has been accomplished not by reducing resources or services, but through innovation. Collectively, the team has well over two hundred years of maintenance experience. The most significant change in how this group has functioned has been the shift from the job of just running shop machinery, to the job of solving problems in plant operations. In this way, the team has expanded its horizons and not only reduced costs, but actually improved quality, process efficiency, and safety. Certainly this team has been a key part of the overall Greenwood success story.

Machine shop innovations generally start with the internal customer, where the problem is identified and discussed team member-to-team member. Designs are put on paper, prototypes built and tested, economics developed, and actual fabrication or modification work done in the plant shop. Over the past several years, thirty innovative projects have resulted in the following savings:

1987	$164K
1988	$409K
1989	$218K
1990	$291K
1991	$238K

A few of the more significant projects include redesign of clutches on drawjet texturing machines, redesign and fabrication of all spinning drive roll bearing housings, and major redesign and renovation of type G spinning winder assemblies. Other major projects include reclamation of most expendable mechanical parts of thirty-seven drawjet texturizers, installation of a gasket die-cutting machine, and modification of precision parts on air compressors and polymer transfer pumps.

Quality Improvement Teams at La Salle, Canada Plant

In early 1990, the LaSalle Plant was already realizing the effects of the Canada and United States Free Trade Accord and the imminent global recession. As a small plant we did not have the economy of scale to be competitive in the world market. Without tariff barriers to protect us, our survival was at stake. Both management and the union at LaSalle knew things had to change.

Our project goal was to create a world class manufacturing operation with ISO 9001 registration to produce specialized, value-added performance products. We also knew that we had considerable distance to go. The plant used total quality management principles, tools, and techniques to achieve step change improvement in overall results. The following is the LaSalle Plant story.

BUSINESS RESULTS

Quality: Although becoming the first Monsanto operation to achieve ISO 9001 registration is the most obvious, there are over thirty other significant achievements of which we are proud.

- GE Appliances (CAMCO) - Preferred Quality Supplier plaque (1989). We won one-hundred percent of this large appliance manufacturer's long term business.
- DuPont - Crystal Trophy for Quality (1989). Monsanto LaSalle was the world's first recipient of this award.
- Agriculture Canada - Scored highest overall on their Preferred Quality Award Rating audit rating (1990).
- Other preferred supplier awards include those from Northern Telecom, Uniroyal-Goodrich, Michelin Tire, PPG, Valspar, MSB Plastics/ABC Group, and General Polymers.

Profitability: Annualized gross profit contribution at LaSalle has increased by $3.0 million over the last 2 years due to improved output, a 10 percent reduction in staff, elimination of one whole layer of management, and product cost reductions were realized.

Product specialization: The most significant result of the LaSalle project, one which will help ensure the ongoing value of this facility, is our two new world mandates.

- World Mandate - Scripset (1990-91): Capacity was doubled to 24 million pounds annually. These new production levels were achieved in only 10 months, 44 percent faster than normal, with no disruptions in regular supply and without the addition of personnel. As a result, the product unit cost decreased by almost 20 percent.
- World Mandate - Triax 2000 (1991): Full production was reached in less than 9 months. Color lead times have been reduced by 50 percent to 3 weeks and product cost reduced by 20 percent. No product quality complaints, and only one service complaint (attributable to the carrier) were registered in 1991.

SAFETY RESULTS

In 1991 we reached 376 days in a row without an injury. LaSalle is also one of the first plants in the world to be registered for Industrial Hygiene and Safety under ISO 9001.

- CPI - Outstanding Performance Award for Safety (1991). First recipient ever.

	1991	1986-90 (Avg.)
MIIR	0.92	1.5
$ Incidents	Approx. $100,000	$400,000

ENVIRONMENTAL RESULTS

Our plant goal is zero waste. To that end, we are well on the way to converting much of our manufacturing and distribution into closed loop processes.

- Scripset manufacturing is approaching the closed loop state. Effluent has been reduced by 90 percent, saving 40,000 pounds of Xylene annually from disposal, and resulting in the reduction of Xylene purchases by $10,000.
- A QIT implemented a closed loop returnable container system for agricultural products in Canada, which included designing a new container seal. The system not only eliminates the disposal of 16,000 containers and 40,000 gallons of rinse water, but saves $250,000 annually in government tax on the containers.
- A project to remove and resell the settleable solids from one waste stream was initiated by a QIT. The project redirected 400,000 pounds of previously landfilled waste into gross annual profit of $80,000.
- Other projects include cardboard and paper recycling and returnable pallets for plastic resins.

COMMUNITY AND GOVERNMENTAL RESULTS

Community: The LaSalle Plant has progressed from being about as welcome as most chemical plants in a community to recognition as a favorite corporate citizen. This change in profile has been brought about through numerous programs, from training the local fire department to hosting the annual Hazardous Household Waste Collection Day for the City of LaSalle.

• Best Corporate Citizen Award - City of LaSalle (1992)

• Enterprise of the Month - LaSalle Informateur (March 1992)

Governmental: The 1990 Agriculture Canada audit of the LaSalle Plant was so favorable that we were enlisted to help write their new regulations governing pesticide formulation in Canada.

CONTRIBUTION TO CULTURAL CHANGE

Monsanto LaSalle's success has been built on full participation in every major plant initiative by our complete pool of employees. Every single QIT is multi-level and multi-functional. This empowerment of our employees has demonstrated its value way beyond our expectations. A continual stream of new ideas from our hourly staff has resulted, for example, in increasing inventory accuracy from not quite 75 percent to greater than 99 percent. The transformation has been so significant that the Conference Boards of Canada and the United States asked us to conduct two meetings in 1991—the key speakers were our union leaders.

Not only has the way we work with each other at LaSalle changed, but our world mandates have increased our contact with Monsanto worldwide. A good example of which was our assistance on the certification of Triax 2000 with GM, Ford, and Chrysler.

EMPLOYEE RECOGNITION

Experience has shown that there is a direct correlation between the recognition given employees for their contributions and the rate of quality improvement they achieve. Employee recognition within the Chemical Group takes many forms. It ranges from casual words of encouragement from the Boss to presentations before large audiences of peers and senior management at our Conference of Champions.

Here are some examples of the various forms and types of recognition provided to employees of Monsanto:

When a quality improvement team is established, it is not uncommon for the sponsor of the team to present to each member an inexpensive memento, such as a coffee mug, key chain, or mechanical pencil, as a token of appreciation for their willingness to serve on the team.

Once a team completes its project and the recommendations for corrective action have proven successful, management generally will present the team with various recognition options, such as tickets for each team member and their spouse to a local sporting event, the theatre, or dinner. Quite often teams will be asked to present their project to senior management. This has proven to be a very effective way of keeping senior management informed and involved with leading the total quality process. Also, as a result of senior management's participation in multiple team reviews, cross-pollination of team results and experiences is achieved.

To promote the sharing of team results and provide recognition for those involved in quality improvement, many of our locations, sales offices, and staff units hold Total Quality Days. The agenda for many of these events include team presentations, poster presentations, customer and supplier presentations, and remarks by members of senior management. Some of our locations will include a plant picnic or dinner for all team members and their spouses at a local restaurant.

Each year we celebrate the accomplishments from our many quality improvement teams at an event we call the Conference of Champions. This event is roughly equivalent to Oscar night for the motion picture industry. It is designed to provide recognition, motivation, and education for Monsanto's Chemical Group employees through the sharing of success stores, as well as learning from industry leaders in quality. Employees from around the world gather in St. Louis to celebrate and share successes achieved through the use of customer focused continuous improvement. Similar events are held by the various divisions and units, but not as frequently. Future plans are to alternate between the company-wide conference and division and unit conference each year.

As our total quality process has matured, so have we matured in our ability to recognize and reward greater than expected team performance. This is accomplished through the implementation of gainsharing on an individual business unit, plant, or staff group basis. We define gainsharing as the process of allowing the employees of a particular team, staff unit, plant or business group to develop a methodology whereby they can collectively benefit financially from the success they achieve in surpassing established goals for the unit. The gainsharing initiative has proven to be very complimentary to our total quality process. We have decided to encourage the expansion of this reward process across the Chemical Group on an individual business unit and staff group basis. This is designed to encourage maximum contributions from each employee to the continuous improvement of the work unit.

Sam Endy
Senior Vice President Quality, Service
and Technology Management
Chief Service Officer

Centex Telemanagement: Improving Client Service through Leadership

A long standing business axiom is that the quality of service a customer receives is directly proportional to the revenue that customer generates. This has been especially true in the telecommunications industry where a small business does not have the revenue potential and professional telecommunications staff and expertise to demand the same service, priority, and attention to its needs as a larger business receives. Telephone companies, long distance carriers, and other telecommunications vendors devote extraordinary attention to their major customers. The small business is generally left to fend for itself.

Historically small businesses in America received their telecommunications services from a combination of equipment vendors, the local telephone company, and AT&T. Although the service quality of the telephone call, itself, was excellent, customer service for the small business was mediocre. Telecommunications providers paid a lot of attention to their largest customers but customer service for small businesses was sorely lacking.

Competition in the long distance communications industry, which led to the breakup of AT&T, concentrated more on price than customer service. Indeed, the price of a typical long distance call fell more than forty percent over the last ten years, but there has been little change in the customer service attention a small business receives. Additionally, as local telephone companies also strive to improve their economics under the nudge of state regulatory commissions, the pricing for telephone calls carried by these local companies is also declining; but once again there is no significant improvement in customer service attention to small businesses. Worse, although competition brought many new developments in services and functions (e.g. voice mail, telephone call detail, and 800 service) smaller businesses were losing out on obtaining the benefits of these developments.

With the 1984 breakup of AT&T, Centex Telemanagement, Inc. sensed that the provision of high quality, cost effective, outsourced telecommunications management, backed by superior customer service, could provide value to these neglected small businesses and form the basis for a viable business opportunity.

In turn that outsourced telecommunications management would result in reduction of business costs or greater market access by expanding the use of telecommunications services, and increased customer service from all telecommunications vendors. To meet this demand, Centex embarked on building a corporate culture that has client satisfaction as its dominant theme.

CLIENT SERVICE STARTS AT THE TOP
In 1985 Centex recruited Chief Executive Officer, Peter A. Howley, because of his reputation for delivering customer service coupled with a tight-fisted approach to achieving the bottom line. If Centex was to succeed, both were imperative. Howley set as his goal the mission statement in Figure 1.

He introduced the following three guiding principles:

- *Associates (he placed everyone on an equal footing) have to feel strongly that client service is the key to success.* To do that they have to feel part of the business. Accordingly, all associates are provided with stock options in the company.
- *Controlling costs is a client service.* Ultimately the client pays for the service, so the higher the costs become the higher the prices must be to cover those costs. Since small businesses are very price conscious, increased costs will erode the opportunity to provide those client services.
- *In client service style does count.* Building a client service reputation is as much conveying a sense of concern and hard work on the client's behalf as is the pure level of service itself.

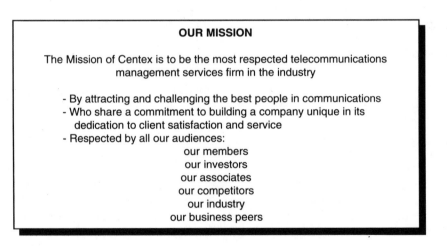

OUR MISSION

The Mission of Centex is to be the most respected telecommunications management services firm in the industry

- By attracting and challenging the best people in communications
- Who share a commitment to building a company unique in its
    dedication to client satisfaction and service
- Respected by all our audiences:
    our members
    our investors
    our associates
    our competitors
    our industry
    our business peers

Figure 1.Centex Telemanagement mission statement.

LEADERSHIP

As the CEO, Howley sets the example for client service. Centex does not have secretaries. There are no perks that separate officers from other associates. All associates, including Mr. Howley, answer their own telephones and take ownership of the client's needs. Howley invites clients to call him directly at the office or at home. They do...at all hours of the day...and he owns the issue until it is resolved.

At associate meetings Howley always puts client service on the agenda. He uses this as a vehicle to communicate service values and recognize success stories.

Howley sends out memos and messages with examples of client service excellence to every associate in the company. His intent is to educate associates on the philosophy and techniques of client service and to set high expectations.

Howley also sets the example for cost control. He travels frugally and the stories of his concern for using the clients' billings wisely are legend. An often repeated tale is when he took a bus, instead of a taxi, in New York to a meeting of Wall Street analysts and almost missed the meeting. These stories permeate the company and help all associates deal with and support the tight cost controls that, in turn, permit resources to be devoted to the company's client service mission.

Information: A Key Service Indices (KSI) report provides a thumbnail sketch of every field location concerning business data and service quality—from client billings to numbers of trouble reports. It serves as a management information vehicle for tracking the business, client satisfaction, and cost control.

Human resources: Much attention is paid to associate motivation.
- Attitude and dedication to serving clients counts as much as technical skills.
- Associates are encouraged to become involved in all phases of the business. Everyone is addressed by their first name. Ideas are sought after and success is roundly recognized.
- Besides the initial stock options grant upon hiring, special year-end stock option awards are widely given for exceptional success.
- President's Circle Winners—typically reserved for sales people in most companies—comprises associates from all functions. Success at serving their customers, whether internal or external, is the prime criteria.
- Promotions are made from within whenever possible.

QUALITY ASSURANCE OF PRODUCTS AND SERVICES
- A Member Assistance Center was established where clients can call any time (day or night) for help or advice on any issue regarding their telecommunications needs.
- Personal account managers were established to maintain contact with our clients. Traditionally telecommunications customers are socialized to call only when something breaks or they have a question concerning their bill. Centex is committed to helping its small business clients grow their businesses; so

clients are encouraged to call for any reason. If the client does not call Centex, Centex calls the client.

- Since ensuring high quality telephone calls is a basic tenet, Centex chooses high quality services for its clients. With the recognition that all long distance companies experience network problems, there are at least two long distance carriers—one prime and one backup—for Centex's clients (a reliability standard found typically in only the largest companies).

CLIENT SATISFACTION

Client service is what the client says it is. Early on Howley established a brief report card that was sent to each client. All the returned report cards were reviewed personally by Howley and actions taken where the client was dissatisfied. Since excellent customer service in the telecommunications industry to small businesses was a new phenomenon, many clients responded by writing unsolicited letters relating stories how Centex associates went the extra mile. These stories vividly reinforced the corporate culture and the wisdom of the saying style does count. The letters were framed and hung on the office walls. They quickly covered the walls and became an inspiration to all associates.

THE BOTTOM LINE

This period, 1984-1987, proved that the concept was correct and that, if vigorously executed, it could form the foundation for a successful business. Clients valued and were willing to pay a fair price to receive high quality telecommunications management services and superior customer service. In the fourth quarter of 1987 Centex became profitable. This could not have been possible without satisfying the Centex clients and controlling costs.

BUILDING THE BUSINESS

Having proved the concept, Centex now focused on building the business. Centex created the position of Chief Service Officer to serve as the focal point for building the client service reputation.

STRATEGIC QUALITY PLANNING

Two very substantial efforts were undertaken to improve client satisfaction during this period.

- Centex clients' expectations increased with their knowledge of telecommunications. To meet these needs Centex beefed up its strategic marketing department and managed the development, in conjunction with clients and high quality vendors, of a series of business productivity management services for its clients. These included Centex managed services for voice mail, access to databases, credit check service, 800 service, and a calling card with abuse protection. A telemarketing function was established within Centex to contact all clients and advise them of these new management services.
- A special need requested by Centex clients was main number retention. Basically, a small business cannot afford to change its main business telephone

number. Centex clients wanted a way to have their main number appear within the local telephone company CENTREX that Centex Telemanagement clients share. Centex devoted substantial time, effort, and expense in representing this need to the telephone companies and state regulatory agencies and urging them to provide this service. Today, seven out of nine telephone companies providing local service to Centex Telemanagement clients now provide this service.

QUALITY ASSURANCE OF PRODUCTS AND SERVICES

A substantial review of all clients who left Centex during the first half of 1989 was performed. Each of these former clients was contacted concerning their reason for leaving. Several major findings and actions resulted from this study.

- Clients wanted further improvements in the reactive and proactive response to their service needs; yet they also wanted the costs to provide these services kept under control. A process review of the field service function was subsequently completed in order to improve our management and reduce costs. This resulted in the design and implementation of a more efficient field service architecture to meet client requirements, both reactively and proactively.
- Clients wanted increased demonstration of value. Sales presentations and ongoing client contacts were further enhanced to sell and explain the value of Centex management to the small business as opposed to only the cost for those services.
- Clients wanted to be kept informed. An increased array of client communications in the form of report card evaluations, newsletters, and crisis management communications were initiated. Among the latter were the 1990 San Francisco earthquake, the 1990 major local telephone company central office failure in Stamford, Connecticut, the 1992 Chicago flooding caused by the Chicago river breaking into the Loop, and the 1992 Los Angeles riot. Thousands of Centex small business clients were affected by these crises. In each case, the proactive, supportive response of Centex Telemanagement demonstrated a customer service positioning unheard of in the telecommunications industry.

CLIENT SATISFACTION

Client satisfaction, as demonstrated by declining client defections during the period, increased. Word of mouth and value of product permitted Centex to continue its growth even during the recession of 1991-1992. In fact, Centex experienced a record sales quarter during the fourth quarter of 1991, followed by a new record in the first quarter of 1992.

BUILDING A REPUTATION

Centex Telemanagement is now focusing on building, as a management services company, a solid reputation for client satisfaction, unassailable in the industry. Centex has embarked on an extensive Total Client Satisfaction Program under the sponsorship of the chief service officer, but with the active involvement of all associates. This program focuses on three key areas: process improvement, human resources, and communications.

PROCESS IMPROVEMENT

With the mutually supporting objectives of improved client satisfaction and cost control, Centex has embarked on a long term effort to review and improve work processes. Although all process will be eventually reviewed the initial effort is focused on three areas.

Member assistance center—An 800 number has been established where clients call for help, advice, or information. The increasing demand by clients for this function requires streamlining and increased attention to improved client satisfaction. Working with the associates in the Member Assistance Center the entire work flow process has been flow charted and redesigned. A new process is now under test.

Order administration—Orders for most telephone company products and services are processed at field locations. The large increase in orders and the standardized nature of many of the tasks led to a process review to evaluate centralization of these order administration functions. Working with associates in the field the entire order flow process has been flow charted and redesigned resulting in a major part of it becoming centralized.

Proactive client service—As a result of client demand, Centex is experimenting with the concept of having a cadre of field associates completely dedicated to proactively and regularly working with clients at their place of business. The test is being conducted with all 1,200 small business clients in the largest Centex field office location. The focus of the test is to assist clients in managing and using telecommunications to grow their businesses. The full test began in January 1992 and the clients are responding very positively. The next phase has already begun at another field location with over 1,000 small business clients. Seventy percent of Centex clients are now under the program with further expansion planned in 1993.

Many other process reviews will be conducted with both cost control and internal and external customer satisfaction as the objectives.

HUMAN RESOURCES

Centex has embarked upon a massive training program for all associates that will take about one and one-half years to complete. Designed with Zenger-Miller, Inc. of San Jose, California, the program uses Zenger-Miller trained and certified Centex associates to provide an integrated training program of management skills for managers, skills for non-managers, and quality improvement skills for all. Instructor training and certification have been completed and training began in April 1992. The training modules are in Figure 2.

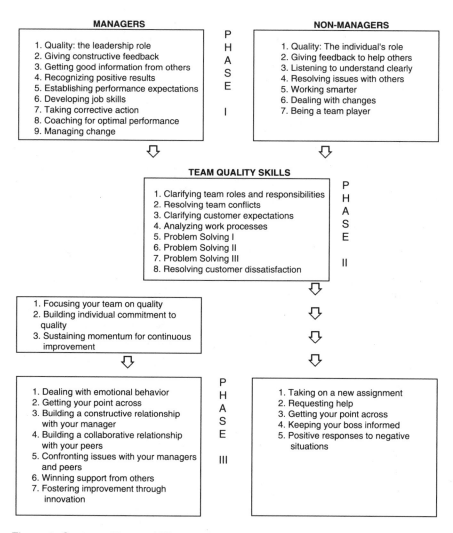

MANAGERS

P
H
A
S
E

I

1. Quality: the leadership role
2. Giving constructive feedback
3. Getting good information from others
4. Recognizing positive results
5. Establishing performance expectations
6. Developing job skills
7. Taking corrective action
8. Coaching for optimal performance
9. Managing change

NON-MANAGERS

1. Quality: The individual's role
2. Giving feedback to help others
3. Listening to understand clearly
4. Resolving issues with others
5. Working smarter
6. Dealing with changes
7. Being a team player

TEAM QUALITY SKILLS

P
H
A
S
E

II

1. Clarifying team roles and responsibilities
2. Resolving team conflicts
3. Clarifying customer expectations
4. Analyzing work processes
5. Problem Solving I
6. Problem Solving II
7. Problem Solving III
8. Resolving customer dissatisfaction

1. Focusing your team on quality
2. Building individual commitment to quality
3. Sustaining momentum for continuous improvement

P
H
A
S
E

III

1. Dealing with emotional behavior
2. Getting your point across
3. Building a constructive relationship with your manager
4. Building a collaborative relationship with your peers
5. Confronting issues with your managers and peers
6. Winning support from others
7. Fostering improvement through innovation

1. Taking on a new assignment
2. Requesting help
3. Getting your point across
4. Keeping your boss informed
5. Positive responses to negative situations

Figure 2. Centex—Zenger-Miller training program.

Various other human resource initiatives are underway. For example, the traits of Centex client service stars were identified and these were used to profile field positions. Interview question sets with interview training was conducted for hiring managers to facilitate the identification and hiring of client focused associates. other efforts include a new performance appraisal focusing equally on production, teaming and client satisfaction, and an improved recognition and reward program and a suggestion program. All of these will be supportive of the cost control and client satisfaction objectives.

Client satisfaction measurement. The client report card discussed earlier has been expanded to a series of satisfaction measurements from calling the client after service installation to follow-up on report cards during the client's anniversaries. Centex has also worked with an external customer survey company to develop a survey instrument that was sent to all clients in April 1992. This has two purposes: first, to set a baseline measurement of client satisfaction as Centex begins this long term program; and second, to respond to individual client needs which were missed by other methods.

COMMUNICATIONS

Centex has begun an extensive program to further improve communications with its clients. A consultant has reviewed existing communications vehicles and provided advice on methods and language. Written communications and verbal responses to clients' queries are being crafted so that the message they carry is consistent and understood.

SUMMARY

Centex Telemanagement has demonstrated that high quality, cost effective telecommunications management services, backed by superior client service can form the foundation for a very successful business. Achieving such service levels does not come easily. Leadership, a clear mission and strategy, dedicated people, a bias for the client, and a strong focus on execution—every day—is the prescription for success. Centex will continue to strive to achieve its mission to be the most respected telecommunications management services firm in the industry.

Beth Ann Moore

Octel Communications Corporation: Putting Metrics in Motion

"I never had time for things that broke or fell apart," begins Bob Cohn, founder and chairman of Octel Communications Corporation, "and my experience with a 1970 Chrysler Barracuda taught me a lot about the importance of product quality and customer satisfaction.

"I ordered this car loaded. But when it arrived there were problems with almost everything. The steering pump, air conditioning, radio and tape player, speedometer, adjustable seats, the console, and the glove compartment all had problems—even the paint was damaged. Everything except the main engine and transmission had to be replaced or fixed at least once. This required many drives to the dealership where I bought the car, which was difficult because it was far away and I was a student at the time. The back-and-forth repair process dragged on for several months. Finally, I called Chrysler and asked for the president. His secretary put me through to Eugene A. Cafiero, group vice president—U.S. and Canadian Automotive. He listened as I explained the problems I'd been having with the car and he immediately got the regional manager on the phone. 'I don't care what you have to do, but fix this guy's car,' is what Cafiero told him. He assured me that Chrysler would fix the car, at a local dealership, and told me to let him know what happened. So I drove it to the local garage where it seemed as if everyone there was waiting for me. The line of cars parted—'Mr. Cohn, please drive your car up here to the front'—they gave me a loaner, and they fixed the Barracuda. They finally got everything right. But from that experience, the importance of doing things right the first time was burned into my mind."

Almost ten years later, Cohn met a kindred spirit whose philosophy of doing things right matched his own. In 1980, Peter Olson was hired to consult on a project at Acurex Corporation, a manufacturer of microprocessor-based measurement and control systems, where Cohn held a marketing position. "From a marketing standpoint, we had one of the most successful products of this type in the world," recounts Cohn. "But they were dropping dead like flies, and our engineers were at a loss as to how to fix the problem. Peter was brought in and said he could fix it. His fee was high, particularly for those days, but we had no choice—this was critical to our survival. He spent four days and nights and fixed the problem. He also pointed out that while it was fixed, this solution also resulted in extremely high product manufacturing costs. For another sizable sum, he would re-engineer it. Which he did. In less than three months he re-engineered the product, dropped the manufacturing cost 25%, and tripled its performance."

Cohn and Olson were both interested in starting a company. Cohn was searching for a technical partner and Olson was looking for a president—someone to find startup money, get the company started, and grow it to a large size. The fortuitous combination of Cohn's business experience and Olson's technical experience resulted in the founding of Octel Communications Corporation in 1982. Their shared passion for quality led to the articulation of Octel core values—six principles that guide the company's business practices.

OCTEL CORE VALUES
Octel core values (shown in Figure 1) formalized Cohn's and Olson's approach to business. They didn't want to be simply a product manufacturing company. "We set high expectation levels in the company," says Cohn. "They're based on dignity, respect, authority, and responsibility, and from the beginning we've hired people who care about making things that work as much as we do."

Octel core values laid the foundation for the company's successful first decade. While today they help set employee attitudes and expectations, they also play an integral role in the development of Octel's quality programs. Together with feedback from the 1990 and 1991 Baldrige Award applications, core values provide the framework and guiding spirit for the implementation of Total Quality Improvement (TQI) processes and metrics as the company moves forward into its second decade.

"The Baldrige scoring summary characterized Octel as a company that has made considerable progress in our total quality program even though we're in the early stages," explains Douglas Chance, Octel CEO and president. "We value the Baldrige criteria for several key reasons. First, it gives us a way to recognize people internally. Second, it also helps certify us to our customers. We've always believed in a quality approach and the Baldrige criteria make us more aware of the specific issues to address. We're focusing on TQI because we want to keep getting better."

THE PROGRESS...AND THE POTENTIAL
From Chance's perspective, Octel's processes fall into two areas—production processes and knowledge worker processes. "We've received high marks in production processes," he notes. "Progress in the design and introduction of quality products, quality control, continuous improvement, and ensuring supplier quality is strong."

PROGRESS IN PRODUCTION
Octel systems have the highest rate of system availability in the industry—99.98%. "Our systems must be available at all times," explains Steve Ciesinski, executive vice president, operations. "Like telephone company switching equipment, they simply have to work. One way to achieve this level of reliability is to

We work to maximize the value of our shareholders' investments in Octel over the long term.
• We strive to be the best in our industry.
• We concentrate on building a company that produces a consistent record of excellent
 financial results.

We drive ourselves to meet customers' needs in everything we do.
• Each employee has a customer.
• We provide our customers with dependable service and reliable products of lasting value.
• We expect our products and services to meet our customers' needs.

We set high-quality standards, live up to them, and focus on continuous process improve-
ment.
• We are obsessed with quality.
• Continuously improving everything we do is the way we maintain high quality.
• Meeting our commitments on time, dependably, and accurately is an important ingredient of
 quality.

We plan our moves carefully.
• Goals are aggressive.
• We grow because we take risks.
• Structure follows strategy.

We care about our people and help them grow.
• The individual worth of each employee is highly valued.
• We want people to grow and develop.
• We value results and recognize that results come through a combination of hard work,
 personal initiative, creativity, and teamwork.
• Making mistakes can help people grow.
• We succeed together.

We respect our ethical obligations.
• As a company and as individuals we will apply the highest standards of honesty and
 integrity to all our relationships with individuals, groups, and our community.
• Winning is only acceptable if we win fairly and honestly.

Figure 1. Octel core values.

design and manufacture it in. And in Octel's manufacturing process, three key
fundamentals have to be in place to get us to this level of reliability—and then take
us beyond it to our goal of 99.99% in two years."

The first fundamental is Octel people. "It begins with our hiring practices,"
continues Ciesinski. "We especially look for honesty and integrity because
working at Octel is more than just a job. Everyone is expected to act as if this is
their company. People in manufacturing are empowered to take initiative.
Anyone in manufacturing can shut down the production line if they see a problem,
or form a team to resolve a manufacturing issue. For example, a team was recently
formed to figure out how to increase the yield of a circuit board on the first pass."

Not only are employees empowered, but they are also recognized publicly for their efforts. Manufacturing managers are responsible for seeking out employees who go above and beyond the normal call of duty. Selected employees' pictures and summaries of their achievements grace the Manufacturing Wall of Fame recognition board.

Achievements fall into one of three categories.

- Efforts that improve quality. For example, improved quality could be a process to increase the number of defect-free boards or produce higher quality work.
- Efforts that increase productivity. Increased productivity may include getting work done faster, making data more available, or being more efficient.
- Creativity on the job. Creativity includes new ways of solving problems or developing new processes.

Empowered employees will do amazing things on their own initiative. For example, a customer called late one Friday afternoon with a system problem that he needed to have fixed before business reopened on Monday. Several Octel engineers and manufacturing employees voluntarily worked with the customer to resolve the issue and build a backup system at the same time—just in case. On Sunday afternoon, the backup system sat on the dock, ready to be air-shipped for business the next day if necessary. The issue was handled with no involvement from executive-level managers. That's empowerment.

Ensuring supplier quality is the second prerequisite for high system availability. "It took two to three years to develop our core suppliers," says Ciesinski. "We surveyed all potential suppliers, visited each one, met with their engineering departments, and checked references. Today we work with as few vendors as possible and develop relationships with the leaders of these companies to understand their long-term strategies, management philosophies, and ideas about quality. We hold an annual vendor fair to update them on Octel's business goals and to select a vendor of the year. We don't believe in just sending in purchase orders, we believe in building relationships."

Octel's manufacturing process is the third fundamental. Procedurally, Octel manufacturing is a tight ship. Metrics are in place to measure almost every aspect of the manufacturing process including inventory turns, attrition, percent uptime in the field, and manufacturing yields on drives, boards, and systems. Manufacturing issues are addressed as far back in the process as possible—back to product design if necessary. "We perform extensive up-front planning and testing to eliminate scrap and rework down the line," continues Ciesinski. "And we hire people who think this way too. Quality manufacturing depends as much on attitude and values as production line equipment."

THE POTENTIAL

While the operation and production areas most clearly demonstrate Octel's results in instituting quality processes, Chance sees the biggest potential for quality improvement in knowledge worker processes. American industry studies have shown that while there have been real increases in United States manufacturing productivity, areas such as marketing, sales, research and development, and finance have shown little improvement.

"We have approximately 55 production workers as opposed to 1,150 knowledge workers," he explains. "So the potential for improvement is great. But knowledge worker processes are different than production processes for several key reasons.

- Knowledge worker processes are interrupt-driven—we juggle several tasks simultaneously and are constantly interrupted by phone calls, meetings, and crises.
- Increasing demands on limited resources leave people hurried, overwhelmed, and frustrated.
- Communication is nonstop, with approximately 80 percent of it internal to the company—callers need to obtain information, ask questions, get answers, or impart information hundreds of times daily.
- Because knowledge workers bounce from process to process, there is a lot of scrap and rework involved in office work. It's harder to do things right the first time and it's difficult to distinguish mere activity from accomplishment.

If we could focus on one thing at a time, our productivity could increase drastically. But now knowledge workers time-slice through numerous tasks while working on multiple processes."

It's a pretty fair description of most large organizations' environments these days. So how does one even begin to attempt to identify and improve discrete knowledge worker processes?

"First we must identify and characterize knowledge worker processes, then we have to allow people to focus on them. Our business is improving knowledge worker productivity—Octel voice processing products enable people to become more productive and efficient in their communications. By storing real-time information until a person is ready to use it, our products allow them to access the information they need when it doesn't interrupt their process."

One of Octel's breakthrough objectives for fiscal year 1993 is to institutionalize TQI practices in all functions—especially in knowledge worker processes. And, successful examples of TQI are already appearing in a number of administrative processes.

For example, a cross-functional Credit Memo CPI team convened to reduce the number of pricing error credit memos being generated. Participants from order administration, logistics, and accounting, successfully

1. identified various types of pricing error credit memos such as:
   - incorrect pricing
   - discounts given to customers but not communicated by sales representatives
   - marketing program promotional discount errors
   - duplicate billings
   - service parts warranty errors

2. assigned a code to each credit memo, identifying it by type.
3. collected data via credit memo checkpoints (i.e., manager sign-off, etc.).
4. ran monthly reports and used Pareto charts to identify the three most frequently types of credit memos.
5. solved the top three problems by:
   - developing procedures for applying discounts
   - training users on the order entry computer system
   - establishing a channel for sales discount communication

After applying TQI principles, the Credit Memo CPI team was able to generate more accurate customer invoices, lower receivables, and reduce overhead cost in processing errors. This translated into a 75 percent reduction in the number of credit memos issued over nine months, and a 90 percent reduction in dollars!

MEETING CUSTOMER NEEDS

While customer satisfaction is the primary focus in every Octel department, it's the corporate mission for two areas in particular. The Customer Support Group (CSG) supports Octel customers with a wide range of innovative, high-quality service, support, and training programs. The Octel Customer User Groups department holds an annual Executive Advisory Committee meeting to seek executive-level feedback from ten top customers.

From field service engineers, to the regional response centers and corporate-based applications consultants, Octel CSG employees not only respond to customer calls for assistance 24 hours a day, seven days a week, but they also closely track and seek out customer feedback. Beginning in 1988, CSG developed a customer satisfaction market research survey, and in 1990 and 1991, further improved it with the assistance of a third-party consulting firm. Conducted annually, it has successfully documented Octel customer satisfaction in areas such as overall system satisfaction, installation processes, maintenance and support, system uptime, PBX integration, administrative and technical training, and documentation.

Says Ed Ang, vice president, customer support group, "Customer satisfaction in each of these areas improved from 1988 to 1991 due to concerted efforts in up-front analysis and planning. Because these metrics yield such valuable information, we're now surveying our customers twice a year, instead of annually, and are able to more closely monitor customer satisfaction trends."

In addition to a third-party survey, Octel has internal metrics in place to measure both quantitative and qualitative aspects of customer support and service. For example, service calls are analyzed by
- call volume and reason for each call
- average time to close service calls
- audits conducted for each call to ensure complete customer satisfaction with the service provided

From the beginning of the 1992 fiscal year to the end of the year, call volume has steadily decreased while the average amount of time required to close a service call has dropped from nine days to less than five. The ultimate goal is to resolve over 95 percent of all service issues in the first call, and gain agreement from the customer that their issue has been resolved satisfactorily before closing the call. Fewer reasons to call and shorter resolution times result in more satisfied customers. Qualitative measurements also include measuring customer feedback—both positive and negative— via letters received. Customer letters are routed to CSG where they are collected and analyzed to discover service process defects. If a breakdown in the process is discovered, the sales and CSG support team work together to resolve the issue and change the process to improve delivery of services.

But what happens when a crisis situation unexpectedly erupts? How is it escalated and resolved? That's the true test of quality processes. Just such a situation occurred early in 1992, and Octel's response demonstrated both the determination to proactively meet customer needs as well as the power of their voice information processing technology.

On Saturday, February 29, a date-related software inconsistency was reported on several Octel systems in Australia. This would seem to be relatively inconsequential, but because this happened to be a leap year, all date-related system functions would be off by one day and could seriously disrupt business on Monday morning. The report came over the phone into Octel's western Technical Assistance Center (TAC) at noon on Saturday from Octel's Australian distributor. Using Octel voice processing capabilities, the TAC placed an urgent outcall to product technical support and engineering staff members. A technical support and engineering team met to tackle the problem. Using the remote diagnostic capabilities of the voice processing system, they were able to isolate the problem to a certain hardware and software configuration. By early Saturday evening, the team had developed a software configuration which they verified in Octel's lab. Now with the six to nine hour North American time difference to their advantage, CSG on-call employees turned their attention to similar platform configurations located at accounts in North America and Europe. By midnight, they had communicated the problem to all Octel support organizations and implemented the alternative configuration to over 95 percent of the affected systems—before customers knew of the problem. On Monday morning, customers who had been affected by the change were impressed by CSG's proactive action over the weekend.

"Fortunately, these situations are extremely rare, " smiles Ang. "But we take this proactive attitude in every area of customer service and support. We're streamlining information and procedures and putting appropriate metrics in place to more accurately track our efforts and measure results."

For example:

- Octel Customer Support Specialists (CSS) provide pre- and post-sale customer support. Each CSS is assigned to specific accounts and is asked to call every account semi-annually. Proactive communication with customers enables CSS to discover potential service issues before they become problems, provides a vehicle for updating customers on new products and services, and often helps uncover new sales opportunities. With semi-annual calling schedules, CSG can accurately track the number and type of customer calls made to each Octel customer.

- The CSG employee of the month program encourages innovative process improvement by seeking out and recognizing employees who have made major contributions in furthering the department's goals. For example, one employee created the CSG *Product Manual*—a tool that streamlined CSG service and support programs and provided better access to information about CSG programs, products, policies, and pricing. Each employee of the month receives a plaque and a dinner, and each is publicly recognized on a bulletin board and in a voice mail memo distributed to all CSG employees.

- The CSG recently assigned an account team to document and communicate CSG's escalation process. As a result, they have clearly documented the escalation path for service issues and streamlined the process of obtaining customer feedback via voice mailboxes.

- All CSG employees will be trained in TQI processes by the end of fiscal year 1992.

- Regional operations managers now make regular, scheduled visits to Octel distributors to listen to customer issues and obtain customer feedback.

Combining powerful technology and performance metrics with a positive, proactive attitude is why Octel customer satisfaction levels consistently rank above the industry average.

CUSTOMERS TELL IT LIKE THEY SEE IT

Octel user groups provide Octel with customer feedback through regular meetings and the annual wish list. Approximately thirty-one customer user groups meet regularly around the country to share information about Octel voice information processing systems and programs. Customers form these groups themselves—Octel contributes speakers and topics for their agendas. In return, the groups act as sounding boards for new Octel product and program ideas and offer suggestions through their wish lists. Wish lists are submitted annually by regional user groups and they contain comments or requests for future features and capabilities relating to:
- user features
- system management capabilities
- software and hardware features and enhancements
- Octel administrative procedures
- Octel account support

After wish lists are received, they are analyzed by user group and product management staff. Trends and frequently-appearing comments are noted, responses are developed, and Octel's position on each is communicated back to each group. User groups are updated on Octel's progress through their regular meetings.

One of the most influential Octel user groups is the Octel Executive Advisory Council (EAC). A vice president and one operational person from approximately ten of Octel's largest customers comprise the EAC. Council members attend an annual three-day meeting, where they meet with Octel's executive staff to conduct executive-level dialog, discuss current business issues, brainstorm about voice and information processing applications, and speculate about the direction of voice information processing. Participants rotate from year to year so that feedback and insight can be obtained from a wide range of industries.

In many cases, specific customer needs and requests have helped shape Octel's product and program direction. General Electric, Inc. is one of Octel's largest customers utilizing 170 Octel voice information processing systems worldwide, serving 95,000 subscribers in 2,000 sites. Connie Kelly, manager of applications development at General Electric, recounts two examples of how information shared between GE and Octel at the EAC meetings resulted in enhancements to Octel systems.

"We had a special concern about mailbox security, and we particularly wanted to protect our mailboxes from hackers," she explains. "When mailboxes are created, the system assigns an initial password to each mailbox before the user initializes it. Usually, the password is the same as the telephone extension to which the mailbox is connected, making it easy for hackers to obtain unauthorized access. Octel worked with us and addressed this security issue by adding a random number generator to our system software. Now it's virtually impossible for an unauthorized user to guess the system-assigned password and control an uninitialized mailbox.

"Over twelve hundred GE field engineers receive their dispatch orders via Octel voice mailboxes. Service call dispatches are placed in the appropriate engineer's dispatch mailbox, where they are retrieved regularly throughout the day. However, when a field engineer is ill or on vacation, messages would accumulate in the mailbox and service calls would go unanswered. Octel created a new type of mailbox that allows system managers to share dispatch mailbox access with field engineers. Now when a field engineer is ill or out of town, the mailbox can be checked and service calls re-routed to ensure maximum field engineer coverage and better customer service."

In striving to meet their customers' needs, Octel has often found that important product and service enhancements result from customers saying "we need this," and then working with them to make it happen.

CRITICAL NEXT STEPS

While there are a number of important measurement processes already in place, and several examples of quality measurement in knowledge worker areas, the trick lies in growing successfully from a small company to a large one. "We're not a four-seat Cessna 172 anymore," grins Cohn. "We're more like a 737 and getting bigger. When a system isn't well-aligned in a large vehicle, the potential consequences of error become much larger. That's why we're taking several critical steps to implement telemetry."

OCTEL EXECUTIVE QUALITY COMMITTEE

The first critical step being taken is the formation of the Octel Executive Quality Committee (EQC). Octel senior executives are each assigned responsibility for one area of the Baldrige Award criteria as seen in the table below.

Senior Executive Leadership	Doug Chance, President and CEO
Information and Analysis	Gary Wetsel, Vice President and CFO
Strategic Quality Planning	Walter Bell, Director, Corporate Quality Assurance
Human Resource Development and Management	John Viera, Vice President, Human Resources
Management of Process Quality	Steve Ciesinski, Executive Vice President, Operations
Quality and Operational Results	Don Campodonico, Vice President, Manufacturing
Customer Focus and Satisfaction	Mike West, Executive Vice President, Sales and Service

Octel's balanced scorecard approach measures key performance areas from five perspectives.

1. Financial perspective—how is Octel meeting its financial goals?
2. Customer perspective—how well is Octel addressing and meeting customer needs?
3. Internal business process perspective—how well do the internal business planning and implementation processes further performance goals?
4. Innovation and learning perspective—do performance goals encourage continual innovation and willingness to learn?
5. Octel employee perspective—how does Octel look to its employees?

Each functional area will develop measures applicable to its responsibilities and aligned with Octel corporate goals. Corporate measures will be compared to external benchmarks to ascertain how Octel's practices compare with those of other successful companies. Over time, the scorecard will be refined as needed. The end result will be a performance measurement process that aligns the company with our stated goals.

John F. Cooney
Chief Quality Officer

Xerox: A Leadership Approach to Total Customer Satisfaction

LEADERSHIP

Xerox senior executives create and sustain a clear and visible quality value system along with a supporting management system to guide all activities of the company.

Senior executives at Xerox have been the driving force behind the company's total quality strategy, Leadership Through Quality, since the early 1980s. Senior management first recognized the need for a quality effort at Xerox, developed the plans, benchmarked Xerox performance against other world-class companies, and created the quality environment that has made Xerox one of the few American companies to halt market erosion by the Japanese.

Total quality control at Xerox began with benchmarking our performance against that of our very successful Japanese affiliate, Fuji Xerox, in 1980. Results showed a need for dramatic improvement. Our eight percent per year productivity improvement lagged far behind the eighteen percent we would need to catch up with competition. Even worse, our production costs were similar to their selling costs. It took us twice as long to introduce products, and their manufacturing product quality was about twice as good. Benchmarking against other companies also revealed performance gaps. Clearly, sweeping changes were necessary in the way Xerox did business.

In September 1982, the Corporate Management Committee, approved the concept of a total quality process for Xerox. Senior management decided policy, objectives, and the desired future state of the company. In 1983 senior management appointed the company's first corporate vice president of quality, a quality implementation team of senior managers, and a supporting quality training task force. Xerox also consulted well-known quality experts for their guidance in creating the most effective quality strategy possible.

LEADERSHIP THROUGH QUALITY RESTS ON THE XEROX QUALITY POLICY

Since 1983, the leadership through quality effort has continued to be driven from the top. Xerox senior management sets our top priority: customer satisfaction. They continually assess our growth, survey employees to receive employee input about quality, and institute the changes necessary to continuously improve quality. In addition, senior managers participate on quality teams and act as quality role models.

Leadership through quality is supported by our management system. Objectives based on our quality priorities and on the Xerox quality policy are developed at the corporate level and then deployed throughout the company, becoming more specific at each level. The objectives are translated into action by managers, by quality improvement teams, and by the efforts of individuals. At Xerox, an important precept is that quality is everyone's job.

The Xerox relationship with the Amalgamated Clothing and Textile Workers' Union (ACTWU) is recognized as a national role model for employee involvement. Since 1980, the contract between Xerox and the ACTWU has included clauses supporting joint quality efforts. In 1991, a joint team negotiated the contract using the quality principles and tools.

Our quality strategy has been shared with the outside community by senior executives who often make presentations about quality to other companies and to governmental agencies. In addition, other companies come to us. Through our Corporate Quality Day and Xerox Quality Forum we have shared our quality story with thousands of customers. Xerox also shares its quality achievements through annual teamwork events, attended by employees, customers, suppliers, community representatives, academic and government leaders, and the media. Xerox employees further serve the community through the Xerox Social Service Leave Program, which grants leaves of absence at full pay to employees who want to work in community projects of their choice.

PLANNING FOR QUALITY

Leadership through quality has changed the ways in which Xerox plans for the future. We have shifted our planning focus from a primarily financial orientation to one in which planning for quality, defined as fully satisfying customer requirements, is foremost. Our belief is that if we deliver world-class products and services that fully satisfy customer requirements, we will also reach our business goals.

Both long- and short-term quality planning begin with defining customer requirements. To do this, we use information-gathering systems, including market research studies. Project teams have goals and targets based on customer requirements. We know that what our customers value most is copy quality, reliability, productivity, and operability.

At every stage, new-product plans and performance are checked, not only against customer requirements and short-term targets, but also against the performance of competitors' products and services. This is benchmarking, defined as the continuous process of measuring our products, services, and practices against our toughest competitors, or those recognized as world leaders. Benchmarking can lead to changes in a product's design or scheduling.

We measure ourselves against the industry average (the mean performance of companies in our industry), against the competitive benchmark (the best performance in our industry), and against the world-class benchmark (the best performance in any industry). We analyze all this data, by the numbers, to learn how we're doing, and by processes to learn how other companies have achieved success. Our benchmarking with Cummins Engine, for instance, resulted in a Xerox daily schedule improvement of 75 percent.

All Xerox planning rests on clear priorities. Our number one priority is customer satisfaction, which has improved significantly over the last six years. Our quality priorities focus on providing continuous price and value improvement for our customers. All of our plans center on concentrating Xerox' resources—time, money, and personnel—on what our customers want most.

CUSTOMER SATISFACTION

Xerox' knowledge of our customers, overall customer service systems, responsiveness, and our ability to meet customer requirements and expectations drive the total quality process.

We listen to our customers. Information about customer requirements is collected in a number of ways: from data that details the needs of different market segments; through market research; through our customer satisfaction measurement system (CSMS); from information collected at various points in the product development process; from benchmarking; from product user groups, and from data collected by the sales, service, and administration personnel who daily come in contact with Xerox customers. Analysis of this data is the basis for management decisions regarding continuous customer satisfaction improvement.

Six strategies integrate data about customers with management action. These are (1) customer obsession, a focus on making customer satisfaction our number one priority; (2) field partnerships which increase cross-functional focus on common goals related to customer satisfaction; (3) information technology strategy to bring quality related information to the field partnerships; (4) business simplification, to make it easier for customers to do business with Xerox; (5) customer-focus marketing, to address the differing needs of various market segments; and (6) empowerment, to use all the talents and expertise of every Xerox employee.

We make it easy for customers to make their needs known to Xerox via toll-free numbers, hot lines, extensive follow-ups, and customer contact employees who have received additional empowerments to resolve customer issues. Examples of such empowerments include self-managing service work groups, and sale reversal authority at the district level. Customer-contact employees are supported by extensive technology, including automated systems that can provide nearly any piece of information required about a product, a process, or even an individual machine.

When customer-contact systems need upgrading, the problem solving process and the quality improvement process is used. Standards for customer-contact employees, such as time spent in applications support or problem-resolution time, are set nationally to ensure consistency, then customized at the field level to reflect customer needs. The customer satisfaction management system verifies how well standards are being met. The standards are continuously reviewed and, as necessary, raised to reflect our customers' expectations.

Aspects of Xerox performance important to customers are our warranties and guarantees. Because our customers' needs vary widely, we offer a broad and comprehensive range of service contracts from which they can choose, including the maximum flexibility of negotiated procurement contracts. We have further improved our commitments to our customers through such changes as a three-year warranty, unique in the industry; our total customer satisfaction guarantee; trade-in and fleet upgrade changes; and increased after-hours service.

Our customers' voice let us know how well we are honoring our commitments to them. One example is the ninety-nine percent rating our customers give the professionalism of our service personnel. Customer satisfaction with sales telephone follow-up is also ninety-nine percent. Telephone waiting time has shown a three-year improvement of twenty-eight percent and is now sixteen percent better than industry standard. Billing transaction quality has improved thirty-five percent. Again, the major means for achieving these successes has been leadership through quality processes.

When customers do have complaints, every effort is made to resolve them. Customer relations groups use an eight-step, closed-loop process supported by the customer resolution information system, and follow up on negative comments on surveys. The current target is to resolve ninety-five percent of all customer complaints within two days, and one-hundred percent within five days.

Complaints are reviewed monthly at all levels to identify root causes and devise solutions. The number of complaints received by the Office of the Chairman has dropped by over sixty percent.

Our major method for assessing customer satisfaction has been the customer satisfaction management system. Each month 55,000 surveys are mailed to customers, asking them to rate Xerox equipment, sales, service, and customer administration performance.

The resulting data are segmented into nine categories and through the use of statistical and root cause analysis we identify and implement successful countermeasures. Short-term concerns are referred to the district for resolution. Monthly reviews at the district, regional, and national levels focus on countermeasures for continuous improvement.

Annual comprehensive reviews set the next year's customer satisfaction targets by product category. These are then incorporated into the organizations' operating plans.

Customer satisfaction trends have shown continuous improvement over the last five years. Customer satisfaction has improved forty-two percent. Xerox is the current industry benchmark in customer satisfaction. Outside research companies confirm this: Buyers Lab has awarded Xerox their Best Product Line of the Year award consecutively for the last two years.

While customer satisfaction has been increasing, adverse indicators of customer dissatisfaction, such as sales returns and accommodation adjustments, have both declined.

Perhaps the best indicator of customer satisfaction is customers who stay with Xerox. Our customer retention over the past five years has remained consistently above industry standards and correlates with our overall improvement in customer satisfaction. We determine customer retention by measuring our customer base in three ways: numbers of locations, machines, and copiers produced. Targets for all three customer-gains measurements are set at the start of each planning process and strategies are put in place to reach them. Customer losses are carefully analyzed for root causes in order to develop preventive strategies.

VISION OF THE FUTURE

Xerox believes that quality alone is not enough. We must become very proficient at quality and then add our own inherent qualities: entrepreneurism, innovation, autonomy, and diversity.

As we move toward the year 2000 we have concluded that quality is the entry card in the race for global competitiveness. We won't be able to compete without it. However, it may not be enough. The challenge for Xerox and other like-minded American companies is to move forward and find ways to leverage our inherent competitive advantage—the American worker and the American work culture.

We're focusing on making Xerox one of the most productive companies in the world. This new productivity is defined as one which creates value and helps our customers become more productive. We are focusing on five areas to keep growing and improving.

First, bust up the bureaucracy. Take out layers of management. Streamline processes. Improve clock-speed. Push decision-making, responsibility and accountability down to the people closest to the problems or to the customer. Empower our workers.

Second, we must leverage diversity. We must fully appreciate the implications of the work force in the year 2000. Our companies and our country cannot compete and succeed unless all our people are productive. But there's also another side of the diversity coin—one that we are just beginning to understand. Diversity in its broadest sense—diversity of race and religion, diversity of gender and genius, diversity of ideas and innovation—are a competitive advantage. There is value in diversity. The whole is always greater than the sum of the parts— particularly when the parts are truly diverse.

Third, we are building what we call communities of practice. These are small, entrepreneurial units that have capacity to manage themselves. They raise the concept of total quality management to new heights. Each individual and each team has the freedom to act, the security to be bold, the motivation to succeed, and the opportunity to contribute.

Fourth, we are building a learning organization. This is an environment in which learning is pervasive and second nature. We are trying to create an environment in which failures are seen as opportunities; successes are studied with an eye to improvement; new ideas are cherished, nurtured and implemented, and where learning is defined as doing things differently.

Fifth, we are enhancing the use of information technology. To pull this off, people need the right information at the right time. They need to combine information with experience to act quickly and decisively.

We must create new organizations that *build* things; organizations that take these little pieces and put them together. We are coming to believe in the value of bringing things together to create work units or teams responsible for a whole set of activities. This concept, of course, rests on faith in the human spirit and intellect. It assumes that a diverse group of people—using their own creativity, innovation, judgment, intuition and brain power—can do a better job in today's world of constant change than any set of procedures, methods, or controls administered by a remote, centralized management. It assumes that group learning is possible and that the group social mind is more than the sum of the individuals.

The key is in people—helping them do what they can do, what they want to do, what they inherently know is the right thing to do. We must lead, set clear direction, provide the right training and tools—and get out of the way!

In summary, our focus on leadership through quality has enabled Xerox to become a world-class company, competing effectively on a worldwide basis. Our vision of the future leverages the innovation and creativity of the American worker. Coupled with quality tools and practices this makes a powerful combination for business success and, most important, will enable highly satisfied customers.

Roy Bauer, Retired
Director, Market-Driven Quality

IBM Rochester:
Market-Driven Quality

IBM Rochester has worldwide development and United States manufacturing responsibility for the AS/400 computer system and hard disk storage devices. The AS/400 system software is translated into 28 national language versions to support the over 60 percent of AS/400 systems that are installed outside the United States. The storage devices produced in Rochester include hard disk drives for the AS/400 and RS/6000 systems, and the PS/2 computer. Rochester also provides hard disk drives to other computer equipment manufacturers.

ROCHESTER'S HERITAGE
The cornerstones of the IBM culture are the IBM basic beliefs of respect for the individual, the best customer service, and pursuit of excellence. These fundamental cornerstones of the business have remained unchanged for 75 years.

Corporate Policy Letters and Corporate Instructions (CIs) provide guidance for implementing these basic beliefs. For example, CI 101 requires that all business processes, product and nonproduct, improve continually to make them more efficient, effective, and adaptable. CI 105 states that each new product must be superior in quality to previous products (both IBM's and competitors'). Before announcing a product, each IBM development lab must demonstrate to the corporate quality organization and other line executives that it is complying with CI 105.

Goals and market-driven quality principles are developed from the Corporate Policy Letters and Instructions. IBM's Market-Driven Quality Principles are: make the customer the final arbiter, understand our markets, commit to leadership in the markets we choose to serve, and deliver excellence in execution across our enterprise.

Rochester's quality journey began in 1981 with the People Responsibly Involved in Developing Excellence (PRIDE) initiative, which focused on improving product reliability. In 1984 the quality journey was expanded to include process efficiency and effectiveness, and manufacturing cycle-time improvements. In 1986 the quality journey continued with planning and development cycle process improvements and integrating suppliers and customers into development and production processes. In 1989 Rochester's quality journey led to embracing market-driven customer satisfaction goals, focusing on total cycle time to the market, and extending customer involvement even further.

THE MARKET-DRIVEN QUALITY

Meeting customer needs is the foundation of the entire development process. The market-driven quality cycle (see Figure 1) integrates the six critical success factors Rochester identified into a closed-loop strategy and process. Those factors are:

- enhance total product strategy and plans
- improve the requirements definition process
- implement Six-Sigma defect-level quality strategy
- create and deploy an excellence in education plan
- enhance and enable employee involvement
- develop and implement reductions in total cycle time

In working toward Six-Sigma quality goals, IBM Rochester has reduced development, manufacturing, and service rework by ensuring that processes produce correct results the first time. Improving education and employee involvement has increased productivity and reduced cycle times.

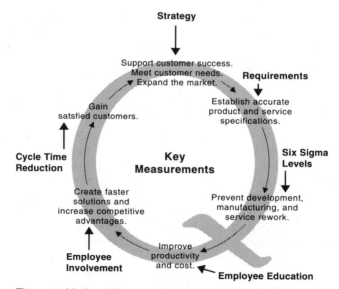

Figure 1. Market-driven quality cycle.

THE CUSTOMER VIEW

Throughout its total enterprise--marketing, product development, manufacturing, and service--IBM's objective is to provide total customer solutions. Market-driven quality begins with understanding what is important to customers, considering all aspects of their relationship with IBM and its business partners, from products to support and after-sale service. Satisfying customers requires the ability to provide superior and reliable solutions; administrative excellence; marketing and sales support; and delivery, maintenance, and service performance.

STRATEGIC PLANNING FOR QUALITY

Each year, a five-year strategic plan is developed, using information from market analysis, competitive and industry data, and evolving technology (see Figure 2). This plan describes the long-term business and quality goals set by the IBM Corporation.

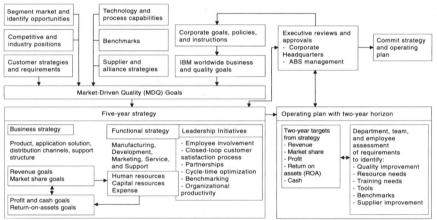

Figure 2. Five-year strategic plan.

Customers are included in the strategic planning process, providing product direction and suppliers assist in the product sourcing strategy. Teams of employees develop a business strategy that includes product and business goals. Manufacturing, development, marketing, service, and support teams develop functional strategies that contain the quality improvement plans required to achieve the business strategy. Functional strategies describe the resources, capital, and expenses required to achieve the quality priorities and the business strategy.

Resources and associated expenses are compared to the revenue and profit goals to balance the strategic plan. Once this strategic plan is approved, an annual operating plan is developed with a two-year horizon. The operating plan is a detailed description of how to implement the strategy. It is also the vehicle used to commit resources to quality improvement.

The strategy and the operating plan owners ensure that the plan process is continually reviewed and improved. A cross-functional executive team reviews and approves the Rochester strategy and operating plans.

PRODUCT PROCESS

Rochester's customer-driven product process is organized into four phases; planning, development, manufacturing, and marketing and service. These phases are tightly linked to each other and to the customer. Cross-functional teams jointly shape the strategies and plans for the process. The planning process identifies customer needs and converts them into specifications. The development process takes the specifications through a rigorous series of design stages and verification activities, involving both manufacturing and customer evaluations. The manufacturing process engages suppliers and the product development team through joint decision making activities early in the cycle. The marketing and service process tailors solutions to the customer's needs and represents the voice of the customer in defining new requirements.

MARKET ANALYSIS AND SEGMENTATION

IBM Rochester begins its global market analysis and segmentation process by gathering data from sources in all geographic markets, such as consultant reports, government demographics, economic forecasts, university studies, and user group feedback. Each geographical area is segmented into small, medium, and large enterprises and establishments. These enterprises and establishments are further segmented into industry, sub-industry, and application opportunity market segments. For example, the distribution industry can be segmented into wholesale, specialty, and retail; retail sub-industries can be segmented into drug stores, auto parts, and hard-goods application opportunity market segments.

PRODUCT QUALITY AND SERVICE FEATURES EVALUATION

IBM Rochester performs detailed analyses of targeted markets to identify customer quality features and requirements. Tools like Conjoint Analysis are used to evaluate items within four strategic categories: product, applications, service, and channels. Each item is ranked for its importance within each category.

Product quality features and requirements are weighed against the resources (both people and expenses) needed to achieve those requirements. To balance the plan, the items are prioritized into short-term (two year) and long-term (five year) projects. This plan is validated through customer councils and marketplace feedback and is adjusted as required.

DEFECT PREVENTION STRATEGY

PROCESS IMPROVEMENT

Removing defects early in design improves cycle times. Defects are removed by continuously improving design tools and techniques. Design quality is improved and cycles are shortened by eliminating manual operations and errors in interpreting specifications.

On-line systems provide the data used in root cause analysis. This analysis is based on a fundamental ability to trace information back to its source. For example, information collected by the Manufacturing Control System can be analyzed to assess changes in new designs or to track a problem back through the process parameters of a particular operation.

If a process upset occurs, IBM Rochester follows a disciplined approach to find the precise cause of the upset. This approach consists of the following steps: confirming the details of the problem, probing for any related information, analyzing the data to review frequency and initial trends, correlating the information with recent actions or changes in the processes or materials, and isolating the causes through statistical techniques and controlled experiments (see Figure 3). This method uncovers the root cause of a problem, identifies required improvements for products or processes, and expands existing knowledge of the complex interrelationships involved in satisfying customer needs.

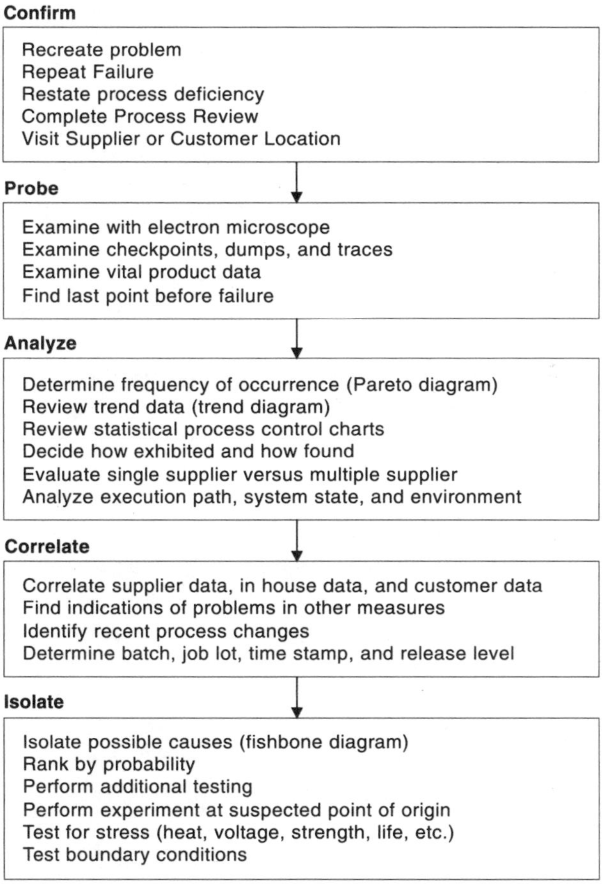

Confirm

Recreate problem
Repeat Failure
Restate process deficiency
Complete Process Review
Visit Supplier or Customer Location

Probe

Examine with electron microscope
Examine checkpoints, dumps, and traces
Examine vital product data
Find last point before failure

Analyze

Determine frequency of occurrence (Pareto diagram)
Review trend data (trend diagram)
Review statistical process control charts
Decide how exhibited and how found
Evaluate single supplier versus multiple supplier
Analyze execution path, system state, and environment

Correlate

Correlate supplier data, in house data, and customer data
Find indications of problems in other measures
Identify recent process changes
Determine batch, job lot, time stamp, and release level

Isolate

Isolate possible causes (fishbone diagram)
Rank by probability
Perform additional testing
Perform experiment at suspected point of origin
Test for stress (heat, voltage, strength, life, etc.)
Test boundary conditions

Figure 3. Root cause analysis.

IMPROVEMENT TEAMS

Producing high-quality products requires effective and efficient quality processes and excellent cross-functional teamwork. Process owners are responsible for ensuring high quality levels. Process improvement teams are used extensively to simplify processes, create new defect prevention methods, and reduce cycle times in product and nonproduct processes.

For example, a quality improvement team, the process owner, and a line manager successfully completed the engineering change process transformation from the traditional printed copy method to an efficient on-line environment. Working very closely with customers from across the site, the team began by modeling the process to identify bottlenecks and process inhibitors. By performing root cause analysis, the team determined the cause of the process upsets. The process flow was restructured and unnecessary steps were removed. To implement the new process, education and support were provided to customers across the Rochester site. Business gains have been realized in product cycle time, efficiency, and communication as a result of these improvements.

DEFECT REMOVAL MODELING

Historical data is used in the software development process to build a defect removal profile. With this profile, a model is established to track development and accurately predict the number of defects to be removed at each step in the process.

VERIFICATION TESTS

Before manufacturing begins, products are subjected to a series of verification tests that confirm both the product characteristics and the integrity of the development process. These verification tests serve as development checkpoints and are coordinated with the design of the manufacturing processes. An independent assurance organization certifies readiness at each checkpoint and verifies adherence to government regulations, industry standards, and corporate instructions.

PROCESS MANAGEMENT

One major reason for IBM Rochester's quality results to date, and the key activity for achieving its future critical success factors, is process management. Process owners define their processes and identify their customers and suppliers. Each owner's objective is to continuously improve quality and reduce cycle times. Managing processes effectively has resulted in significant cycle time improvements for computer systems and hard disk development and manufacturing. The serial processes for producing the System/36 and the System/38 have been transformed to a parallel, continuous flow system for producing the AS/400 system. Simulation, early manufacturing involvement, software component development, and parallel system tests have contributed to a forty percent reduction in the development cycle time.

DEVELOPMENT PROCESS

IBM Rochester's prevention-based design approach uses process management and simulation tools to remove defects before fabricating hardware and integrating software (see Figure 4).

Early manufacturing involvement teams, work out details of product introduction, software installation, and distribution logistics. These involvement teams begin working in the early design stages to improve the manufacturing processes, enabling rapid, high-volume production capability. Manufacturing teams build the machines used throughout the development cycle. Suppliers also participate on EMI teams.

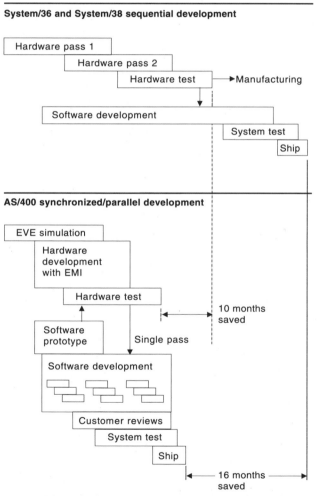

Figure 4. Comparing system/3X with AS/400.

CUSTOMER INVOLVEMENT

To ensure that market and customer needs are continually satisfied, customers and business partners are involved throughout the total product cycle, from planning requirements through support and feedback.

Customers play a major role in clarifying requirements and ensuring that products meet their wants and needs. An iterative software development process is used to involve customers. Customers are asked to validate the development decisions. If changes are needed, they are made in subsequent iterations of the development cycle.

Innovative new techniques established by IBM Rochester integrate customers into the development process. For example, customer and business partner councils bring together customers worldwide to review future product plans. Customers visit an executive briefing center at IBM Rochester daily. This briefing center is supported by development and manufacturing teams. An independent user group, COMMON, comprised of over 6,000 customers worldwide, meets regularly to provide AS/400 requirements to development and manufacturing departments.

The Software Partner Lab provides an opportunity for customers and business partners to jointly develop solutions for future product releases. Customers validate that their requirements are being met and that their application programs will operate effectively on newly designed systems. Customers participate regularly in the usability testing center to verify that Rochester's products meet their operational requirements.

In addition, an extensive early availability program provides AS/400 systems to select customers before they are available to the general public. These systems are monitored closely to ensure that customers are satisfied with the latest development-level products, services, and order and delivery systems. Customer support procedures are also evaluated during this program.

Customers are surveyed frequently to maintain an awareness of their satisfaction. They are contacted by IBM ninety days after receiving an AS/400 system. They are thanked for being an IBM customer and asked about their satisfaction with their new system.

INFORMATION AND ANALYSIS

Information systems support effective communication among employees and with customers throughout the entire product cycle. IBM Rochester has comprehensive, world-class global information and analysis systems available, as needed, to all employees.

ON-LINE TOOLS

IBM Rochester's electronic office system links employees worldwide, allowing real-time communication. On-line systems ensure that accurate and consistent data is available for quality improvement and root cause analysis. Rapid communication with sales representatives, systems engineers, and field engineers aid in problem solving and communicating opportunities for improvement.

MANUFACTURING PROCESS

The process of moving a product from development to manufacturing is highly automated. IBM Rochester translates design data into on-line manufacturing controls to improve the quality of manufactured parts. The central control point of the manufacturing processes is the Manufacturing Control System (MCS).

On-line information is important to the quality of the manufacturing process. Customer orders are automatically transmitted from the branch office to the MCS and fed directly to the manufacturing assembly line.

All production is controlled by the customer order. Product design data is automatically translated into manufacturing process control information. Assembly and sub-assembly areas provide process information to the MCS for analysis and review by cross-functional teams for root cause analysis and future improvements. On-line systems provide timely and consistent design information to worldwide manufacturing locations.

The automatic translation of information eliminates opportunities for error injection and reduces process steps and time.

CONTINUOUS FLOW MANUFACTURING

Being flexible and responsive is a key to excellence in manufacturing processes. IBM Rochester has implemented Continuous Flow Manufacturing (CFM), integrating all elements of its production and nonproduction support processes to achieve reduced cycle time, reduced cost, and continuous focus on defect prevention

CFM begins with an examination of the total process, from a customer order to raw material gathering through manufacturing and customer installation. Order sizes, improvements in tooling, and changes to process flow are some of the factors affecting CFM cycle time reduction. Cross-functional teams use process management techniques to evaluate and remove steps from the process. Employees are empowered to provide input to improve their jobs. Cooperative projects with suppliers, including CFM training, improve cycle time throughout the total process and improve business results for IBM its and suppliers.

STATISTICAL PROCESS CONTROL

Statistical Process Control is used in critical operations throughout the Rochester site and its suppliers' sites. Teams work with development engineers to identify critical parts, parameters, or process steps that require continuous control through statistical monitoring techniques. Hard disk drive manufacturing lines are monitored using on-line process control. Operators and engineers continuously monitor production operations, observe the process capability at which the operations are performing, and assess the operation by comparing the last twenty-four hours of data with the established specification limits.

ORDER CONFIGURATION SYSTEM

An on-line order process electronically links customers to the AS/400 production process. A customer orders a system by working with a marketing representative to define the system configuration that meets the customer's needs. As the data are entered at a branch office, the system validates the order configuration and data accuracy, preventing order errors. The validated order is then transmitted directly into the plant MCS where a build order and assembly sequence control information is generated and sent to the plant floor. Process steps and opportunities for translation problems are eliminated.

CUSTOMER RELATIONSHIP MANAGEMENT

Customer satisfaction processes not only ensure that customers are satisfied but also provide feedback to the development process on product quality and service requirements. The customer partnership call process is used to thank customers for purchasing an AS/400 system. The call is made ninety days after a system is shipped from the Rochester site, and it seeks the customer's likes and dislikes, as well as any comments they may have. These comments are placed in a database, analyzed, and distributed regularly to engineering, programming, marketing, manufacturing, and service teams for evaluation.

Dissatisfied customers or customers with concerns are contacted to understand their concerns in more detail. The Customer Satisfaction Project Office receives notification of the results of the customer contact. Thirty days later, the same customers are called back to ensure they are satisfied. Other methods to ensure leadership in customer satisfaction include customer satisfaction surveys, independent consultant reviews, and industry-accepted reports.

ELECTRONIC CUSTOMER SUPPORT

Customer communication with IBM is enhanced by Electronic Customer Support, which is provided with every AS/400 system. This service provides an electronic connection to IBM for access to question and answer databases and IBM documentation. It also provides automatic problem identification, service requests, problem management, and software fixes and distribution. Electronic Customer Support provides a real-time, closed-loop capability for IBM and its customers to communicate.

COMPLAINT MANAGEMENT PROCESS

To achieve the goal of being the undisputed leader in customer satisfaction, IBM Rochester has established a complaint management process that tightly links marketing and service teams to development and manufacturing teams. Complaints are managed by the Customer Satisfaction Management Team working with the branch office closest to that customer. An investigator is assigned to investigate and understand the specific details of the complaint, which must be resolved within two weeks. Feedback from the complaint is sent to the team where it is recorded, assimilated with other information, and correlated for use in reports to the Customer Satisfaction Council, resulting in product and service quality improvements.

ROCHESTER IBM EMPLOYEES

Rochester employees have continuously had very high morale—the highest among IBM sites—as measured by annual opinion surveys. Employees' pride in their work fosters a desire to be the best in everything they do. Rochester's safety record is sixty percent better than the industry average and its turnover rate is significantly below the industry average.

INTEGRATION OF PEOPLE INTO QUALITY AND BUSINESS PLANS

Quality objectives are integrated into employee performance plans and agreed on by both the manager and the employee. This process fosters employee participation and empowerment. Each element of quality improvement builds a solid foundation for achieving Rochester's business objectives.

Achieving market-driven quality goals depends on enabled, empowered, excited, and rewarded employees. IBM Rochester's human resources strategy strives to bring about a cultural shift from a product-driven quality focus to a market-driven quality focus and consists of three initiatives: formal education, on-the-job customer contact, and participation. Morale, buy-in, participation, and productivity are measured to ensure these human resource initiatives are continuously improved.

IBM Rochester has continually increased its participation in technical vitality initiatives. Technical vitality and innovation are measured by employee participation in categories such as writing articles in professional journals, patent applications, and inventions.

CUSTOMER CONTACT

All employees from senior managers to production are given opportunities to have regular contact with customers. The on-the-job, market-driven experience program advocates

- temporary assignments in sales
- telemarketing assignments (contacting customers for satisfaction information)
- customer partnership call assignments (thanking customers for purchasing AS/400 systems)
- executive assistance to marketing (site senior managers assigned to support marketing areas)
- installation assessment team (teams from the factory that participate in a customer installation)

EDUCATION AND COMMUNICATIONS

IBM Rochester is continually training employees and developing their skills—expenditures for education are five times the national average. Individual discussion between employees and managers is the most common and important communication channel. Other avenues used to deploy Rochester's vision and goals are shown in Table 1.

Table 1. Employee training at IBM Rochester.

Education Partnership	Education and Training	Management Development	Communications
• Faculty loan	• Quality education	• Quality training	• Employee-manager discussions
• Cooperative education program	• Manufacturing skills integration	• Management College	• Regular department meetings
• Technical interchange with universities	• Voluntary education	• Shadow program	• Functional meetings
• Greater Rochester Area University Center	• Technical vitality	• Mentor program	• IBM TV network
	• Graduate work study	• Technical assistant assignments	• Bulletin board notices
	• Supplier education	• Cross-functional assignments	

COMMUNITY AND SOCIAL RESPONSIBILITIES

IBM Rochester's involvement in the community ensures that its external assistance meets the needs of the communities where it conducts business. Employees respond to a wide variety of social, cultural, and educational needs in our society. These initiatives support IBM's stated principle: "We serve our interest best when we serve the public interest." Worldwide, IBM contributions of cash, equipment, and other resources to social, cultural, and educational programs amounted to 135 million dollars in 1989. IBM Rochester is a major contributor to the local United Way agency through both cash donations and employee volunteers.

Community involvement. IBM's community involvement works in conjunction with local organizations such as the education system. It was through the school district that an organization called Building Equality Together (BET) was formed. The group includes the Rochester Mayor, the Police Chief, and representatives from IBM, the Mayo Clinic, and area churches. Two IBM employees are active participants on the board of BET. The group was formed in an effort to examine the social and economic impact of cultural diversity on the future of Rochester. Also, the group will explore practical solutions to assure that diversity will be a positive aspect of the rapidly growing community. The primary focus of the group is on youth. By working through the educational system, the group involves youth members and adults.

Patrice Johnson
Vice President
Corporate Communications and Marketing

Intelligent Electronics, Inc.: Building a Corporate Culture of Service Quality Excellence

Since its founding in 1982, Intelligent Electronics, Inc., has become a multi-billion dollar company and a leader in its field. Between 1987 when the company went public and 1991 when it completed its ninth fiscal year, Intelligent achieved a compound annual growth rate of 120 percent in revenue and 104 percent in earnings. Its network of approximately 1600 franchised and affiliated business centers and 100 large-format BizMart supercenters provides a complete range of products for offices, large and small, nationwide.

As a result of three back-to-back acquisitions and sky-rocketing growth, Intelligent became the recognized leader in its field. Most importantly, however, the company became known for its service to customers, for setting new standards of excellence in exceeding customers' expectations. In every level of the organization employees stay close to their customers and focus on enhancing the company's relationship with them.

World class service has been achieved, in part, through management's focus on building the organization's corporate culture, a culture characterized by a passionate commitment to customer satisfaction and systems in which key performance measurements are regularly reported and rewarded. The following pages discuss some of the strategies and tactics Intelligent has pursued in order to build a culture committed to quality and excellence.

CULTURE

No doubt a company's products and services play a critical role in its development. But it is the spirit and determination embedded in a company's core culture that ultimately determines its success or failure. This culture, though not easily quantifiable, is often cited as a key contributing factor to the long-term successes of most industry-leading corporations. Such is the case with Intelligent Electronics.

The intense commitment to customers on which Intelligent was founded a decade ago is the company's driving force today. It enables Intelligent to leverage its strengths, take calculated risks, embrace change, and ultimately maintain its position in the computer retail and wholesale marketplaces. In general, Intelligent's cultural strategy may be summarized as follows.

THEMES BUILD FOCUS

Intelligent's fundamental commitment to quality has generated a variety of customer oriented programs. The importance of treating customers with the utmost respect and priority permeates the culture of the business. Franchisees are referred to as "customers," and every employee from the chairman to the receptionist is focused on earning the customer's business every day. Pay stubs read, Brought to you by the customer, and quality tips called Thoughts for the Week are sent over electronic mail to employees. Posters depict the 7 Rules for Customer Satisfaction, and a Commitment to Customer award program recognizes employees each month for their outstanding service to customers. Framed drawings of pink hearts with the names of individual customers inscribed on them decorate the corridors of the Franchise Division in Denver, Colorado.

Recognizing that the company's enormous size warranted the formation of a department to ensure the company's continuing achievement of world class service to its customers, Intelligent's board of directors created a senior level position specifically responsible for the company's continued maintenance and achievement of quality service standards.

DISCIPLINE BUILDS HABITS

Employees are committed to enhancing Intelligent Electronics' position as a world class service provider, and the highest level of service quality is implemented down to every detail of the business.

Intelligent Electronics and IBM Corporation jointly developed an IE/IBM Six Sigma Program, which provides a foundation for expediting the resolution of customer issues. Many of the elements of the six sigma program play a key role in measuring the performance and improving systems throughout the company.

Phones are answered in less than two rings, and if a message is taken, a return call must be made within two hours. All written communications, both internal and external, are error free, or employees are charged one dollar per error. People quickly learn to attend meetings on time, as one dollar fines are good-naturedly levied for each minute a person is late.

Although rules and regulations may initially seem schoolish, the resulting habits create continuity in high quality performance and self-imposed standards with long-term effects.

PROGRAMS CREATE RESULTS

Customers play a key role in the decision making process in all divisions within Intelligent Electronics. As a result of these feedback and support systems, Intelligent is able to identify issues within its distribution system and quickly implement solutions.

Formal programs ensure the delivery of high quality service. The fundamentals of talking to customers, listening to their suggestions, and acting upon what they say lies at the heart of management's practices. The chairman of the company personally visits more than 300 franchisee customers each year. An executive visitation program encourages managers to meet with customers on a regular basis. Several customer-based committees focus on specific issues such as marketing, product planning, and profitability. National and regional conferences are held each year to provide communications forums to share information, to educate, and to listen and learn from customers.

DISTRIBUTION PROGRAMS

In order to measure the improvement process, a direct response system known as the Focus Program was put in place, tracking accuracy levels of all shipments. A 3 Right survey card is placed in each outgoing shipment asking customers if they received the right product, at the right time, in the right place.

This customer-oriented theme is reinforced throughout the organization. The chairman visits warehouse facilities, discussing issues with receiving clerks and inspecting boxes for shipment defects. All employees who have an impact on distribution performance are empowered to make changes and improvements and are given a bonus each month based on the results of other improvements. At the programs' inception in late 1989, performance from the customer's perspective was reported at a 75 percent average attainment level. By early 1991 the satisfaction rate rose to 99 percent, where it consistently registers today.

TELEMARKETING PROGRAMS

Intelligent's 122 telemarketing representatives receive ongoing in-house training on sales, systems, procedures, products, services, customer service and customer satisfaction. Hands-on supervision, controls, and quantifiable performance measurements enable telemarketers and their managers to monitor and improve their service to customers continually. All systems focus on enhancing the company's relationship with its customers and maximizing the customers' perceptions of value for the services they receive.

CUSTOMER TRAINING, TECHNICAL SUPPORT, AND CONFIGURATION PROGRAMS

As an ongoing segment of Intelligent's franchisee support program, the company operates a 3,000 square foot training facility in Denver in which four classes may be conducted simultaneously. Vendor authorized technical training includes a wide array of vendors and platforms.

Twenty-four experienced technical support specialists are on hand to support end users and franchisees' total product support needs. Configuration services with a total quality management focus support TQM guidelines. Configuration services reinforce Intelligent's partnership with its vendors and enhance the company's service to its customers.

SALES, MARKETING, AND FINANCING PROGRAMS

Sales, marketing and financing programs have all become more effective through customer involvement. For example, in response to improved communications, a marketing support tool known as PromoLine conducts bi-weekly mailings and provides franchisee customers with an update on all current promotions and programs related to their businesses.

Dealer feedback also assists Intelligent in fine-tuning the financial programs offered to its customer base. A lease program provides Intelligent's resellers with a cost effective financing solution for their customers. The financial support Intelligent offers its franchisee customers is further enhanced through a focus on developing inventory financing programs with most vendors. In negotiating some of the most competitive rates in the industry, Intelligent offers its customers a solid inventory financing solution.

Programs such as these illustrate the company's commitment to providing service excellence at all levels. As a reflection of this commitment, the company's customer base enjoys continued health. This health, in turn, contributes to Intelligent's own financial performance.

CUSTOMERS ARE #1

Customers are valued as such a critical element of the business, that no major decisions are made without their input. Various committees, representing a diverse range of business sizes and locations, meet regularly to discuss issues of importance to their businesses. The committees assist in the selection of new vendors, products, and programs. They also suggest ways the business may improve the quality of its delivery of products and services to customers.

VENDORS ARE KEY

As the industry continues to mature, prices have declined, products have become more abundant, and competition has intensified. Intelligent recognizes that establishing and growing the correct vendor relationships is critical, and the company views its vendors as strategic partners. Intelligent participates in planning sessions with its vendors as new products and programs are designed. Manufacturers and Intelligent share quality feedback on product offerings. As a result, the challenge of bringing products to market is addressed according to the interests of all parties involved. Executive briefings involving customers, Intelligent's executives, and key vendor executives occur several times each year, ensuring the integrity and effectiveness of the planning process.

INNOVATION CREATES LEADERSHIP

Another characteristic which distinguishes Intelligent from its competition is its thirst for innovation. The company's ability to recognize change and embrace opportunities plays an integral role in its continued success. Intelligent's management pays keen attention to market dynamics, identifying the best opportunities, then designing and implementing strategies to address them most effectively.

As an example, in 1991, Intelligent Electronics led the name-brand computer industry into the superstore business through its acquisition of the BizMart superstores. Large-format computer retailing was in its infancy at the time, as Intelligent partnered with key customers and vendors to develop an innovative approach to office productivity retailing. Through the BizMart acquisition, the company created a hybrid category of supercenters, in effect, combining the concept of an office products superstore and a computer superstore under one roof. In focusing on the vision that the office products industry and the computer industry would converge, Intelligent essentially made its vision a reality. Approximately one year into the process, BizMart's office productivity supercenters were delivering record-breaking revenue growth, once again reaffirming Intelligent's ability to envision, implement, and effect change in its industry.

Nearly eight years ago, Intelligent Electronics pioneered a new business strategy that eventually changed the computer franchising playing field. In lieu of burdensome royalty fees levied by all other computer franchisers at the time, Intelligent launched a revolutionary cost-plus pricing system which charged franchisees a mark-up on only those products they purchased from Intelligent. The cost plus program, in effect, transferred the burden of performance to the franchiser, off the backs of its franchisees. Initially the cost plus method of computer dealer franchising was difficult for the industry to accept, but it has since become the industry standard.

Additionally, rather than selling franchises to inexperienced hobbyists, as was typical at the time, Intelligent focused on recruiting experienced office equipment dealers who knew how to run a business and served a loyal customer base. Instead of training its franchisees how to run a business, Intelligent provided the assistance its experienced dealers needed to extend their product lines to include top-brand computer technologies. Additionally, the company targeted dealers in secondary and tertiary markets, unlike larger competitors whose strategy was to grow in the major metropolitan markets.

Intelligent's cost plus and recruitment innovations combined to become key competitive advantages, fueling the company's growth. Over time, these advantages helped displace Intelligent's competitors and put the company in the number one leadership position in its industry. Based on this heritage, innovation is encouraged and advocated at Intelligent. A phrase originated by the chairman and repeated frequently throughout the company is, "Be careful not to fall in love with your own ideas." Intelligent recognizes that as good as ideas may seem at the time, smooth and flexible change in the fast-paced, rapid-fire computer industry is not only important, it is imperative. Those who execute the wisest changes with the smoothest transitions will be the ultimate winners who lead their companies into the 21st century.

RELATIONSHIPS BUILD LOYALTY

Since the company's inception, management has recognized the long-term importance of strategic business relationships. Managers focus on building alliances with top-flight individuals and companies. It might be said Intelligent took its core commitment to providing exceptional value to its customers and extended it to include employees, vendors, investors and other constituencies.

Despite intense pressures to the contrary, management has successfully negotiated some of the company's most critical turning points by deciding in favor of partnership over isolation, or sharing over greed. Generous programs grant employees and franchisees stock options, bonuses, and other incentives. The company's open door policy, its franchising of BizMart computer departments, and its overall win-win approach to negotiations work to build a foundation of loyalty and trust among Intelligent and its strategic partners.

Examples of extraordinary employee commitment are plentiful, ranging from the mail room clerk returning during the middle of the night to be sure he activated the security alarm, to a distribution center manager driving a truckload of product personally to a customer's site to ensure its safe and timely delivery.

This type of loyalty characterizes Intelligent's relationships with all its constituencies. Customers, employees, vendors, and investors alike are treated as personal guests. In turn it is not uncommon for them to perform acts of exceptional loyalty and commitment.

COMMUNICATIONS PROVIDE VALUE

The company's involvement in the technology industry has proven to be a significant advantage, enabling management and staff to identify and deploy the latest, most advanced technologies to improve communications and reduce human error. Electronic mail, extensive databases for tracking customer needs and measuring key performance indicators, teleconferencing, desktop publishing, graphics capabilities, and distribution systems continually push cycle times downward and reinforce the company's commitment to each and every customer. Additionally, electronic mail systems, telephone and mail surveys, and hot lines make it convenient for customers to have regular and frequent input into the organization.

KEY MEASUREMENTS DRIVE PERFORMANCE

Because of the company's closeness to its customers, it is a relatively straightforward task to identify the key performance issues affecting customer satisfaction. Management and staff simply ask customers what is important to them, document their responses, and follow up with meticulous attention to detail.

Management approaches its service offerings in much the same way Abraham Maslow, the renowned psychologist, approached the concept of human need, i.e., through a hierarchical pyramid. In other words, Intelligent focuses on developing and maintaining its services according to the needs and priorities of its customers. Key here is the principle that unless the customer's critical needs for survival are first met, all other services—regardless of their quality—will be extraneous. Just as human beings must have oxygen, water, food, and shelter before they may focus on higher levels of need, Intelligent recognizes its customers must have the right product delivered to them at the right time at the right price before they will be interested in the company's marketing, training, product repair, or communications programs.

CULTURE PERPETUATES LEADERSHIP

It can be concluded that Intelligent's commitment to quality and innovation during its formative years has grown to become the foundation of some of its most decisive competitive advantages today. As an example, Intelligent's commitment to building quality relationships attracts some of the most highly talented franchisees, managers, employees, investors, and vendors in the industry.

Looking to the future, management plans to continue to nurture the company's quality focused culture to maintain the company's leadership position and its rapid pace of profitable growth.

Larry J. Hoecherl
*Vice President, Quality and
Customer Satisfaction*

Novell, Inc.:
Customer Driven and Loving It!

INTRODUCTION

Novell, Inc., is an operating system software company and the developer of network services and specialized and general purpose operating system software products. Novell's network computing products manage and control the sharing of services, data, and applications among computer work groups, departmental networks, and across business-wide information systems.

Networks allow personal computer terminals to share resources such as files, printers, memory, and software applications. Networks are effective in offices as simple as two terminals or as complex as thousands of terminals located throughout the world connecting mainframe computers, minicomputers, DOS terminals, Macintosh terminals, UNIX terminals, and OS/2 terminals.

Novell's corporate values include:

Our Mission: To accelerate the growth of the network computing industry
Our Vision: Responsible leadership
Our Products: Software, systems, service, and support
Our Priorities: Customers first, employees second, shareholders third
Our Commitment: Two years ahead and gaining
Our Theme: Customer driven and loving it!

The Malcolm Baldrige National Quality Award criteria are weighted most heavily toward the category of customer focus and satisfaction. Novell, Inc. was founded on the principles that put our customers first. I have arranged my presentation to highlight some of the customer-first actions we have taken over the years. More than a history or an academic reading, I hope our experiences can be a sounding board or a guide to other companies who are experiencing problems or who are at a crossroads. Although not every category neatly fits my format, I have listed a customer-responsive action Novell has taken, why we took that action, how our customers felt about it at the time, how we dealt with customer sentiments, what the customer's perspective is now regarding that action, what worked and what did not work, and what we would do differently if we could go back and take that action again.

To help our segment of the market grow faster with us than it would without us—this has been Novell's corporate philosophy ever since 1983. This conviction is one of many key ingredients that have come together to form Novell. This statement emphasizes growth from a customer's point of view, and an accent more on the network computing industry than on Novell. It focuses employees' minds on the inescapable fact that if we accelerate the growth of the market, we also will grow. Striving only for market share does not necessarily serve customers nor ensure growth (you could have 100 percent of the buggy whip business or the slide rule business).

A company must possess at least the following attributes to grow a market: customer driven, technology, and vision. For the remainder of this presentation I will detail Novell's focus on our customers. I will present, in roughly chronological order, sixteen major events that have helped form Novell and have demonstrated our customer commitment.

1. In January of 1983 Ray Noorda was asked to help with turnaround efforts for Novell Data Systems, Inc., a company that had seen its size shrink from a high of 150 employees to 14 employees. We were a hardware and software company, producing CP/M network software as well as terminals and printers. The contemporary wisdom was that Apple and Tandy desktop systems would be much more successful than IBM whose PC had entered the market eighteen months earlier and had attained only a three to four percent market share. Mr. Noorda thought the IBM PC would become the standard, and people could be more productive if these PC's were linked together into networks. Mr. Noorda asked the hard questions, "How can we be of greatest service to our customers? What do we do best? What unique capabilities do we have that will accelerate the growth of our segment of the market?"

From this perspective Novell discontinued manufacturing some of their hardware, discontinued CP/M software development, and focused on a new technology of file server hardware and software.

Why did we take this step?
With limited resources and a mission to grow the industry, we had to focus our efforts on our unique talents. Our abilities with software and the vision of how networks could revolutionize the industry pointed our direction toward Local Area Networks (LAN) and away from non-strategic hardware and software.

What were the customer sentiments?
At this time we did not have a huge customer base, probably in the hundreds of users. To achieve our vision we knew we needed to refocus. We sought new directions and new customers while being careful not to abandon our existing customers. We don't recall any discontent, but these were smaller installations with simpler needs and limited interfacing.

How did we deal with those sentiments?

Because our interface with our customers was a one-on-one without an extensive distribution system, we were able to be and required to be much closer to all our customers. Given this intimacy we counseled with customers, explained our reasons for our new directions, and helped with any conversion as needed.

What is the customer's perspective now?

The strategy appears to have been correct, and the growth and market acceptance speaks for itself. Having obtained our current stature in the industry, our biggest challenges are to continue to grow the market, drive the technology, and retain the closeness and responsiveness we had with our customers when we were small and they took a chance on us and our new technology.

What worked and what did not work?

Everything went fine, but we were stretched very thin. We did not have the need for nor the luxury of a technical support team. If a customer had a technical problem, a knowledgeable person from manufacturing would talk with the customer. Then we received an average of one call each day requesting technical support; now our technical support group receives more than five thousand calls each day.

One thing that worked then and continues to be our overriding objective is to do what we can for our customers. We tried to always be customer advocates and see and feel things from their perspective.

What would we do differently?

We had the usual problems of a startup company, however we were extremely fortunate in that Ray Noorda had a strong strategic plan. That plan was communicated to his direct reports, but it sometimes did not flow to the entire company. The combination of resource limitations and lack of tactical plans sometimes got us into tight spots. For example, the sales department would sometimes commit to delivery on products that did not exist (and were not even in development). This made for some frantic times as we tried to make good on those promises while discouraging such future statements. It's too easy to look back and say we should have been more organized or more communicative, but it does seem like we could have done a little better.

2. We provided service and support for non-Novell products. In February of 1984 there were a couple of other companies selling competing hardware and software network products. If a company had Novell hardware, they had to purchase Novell software to run on it. Our hardware, while very good, was not the total solution—there were advantages and disadvantages depending on the situation. In order to give our customers a freedom of choice, we modified the NetWare Operating System (NOS) to run on non-Novell hardware. Then we purchased that hardware from our competitors, bundled it with the appropriate modified NOS, and offered the package to the market. We were able to provide a complete networking solution from sales through technical support. The NOS was also modified to run on five other non-Novell hardware products. This was a new concept, to purchase from a competitor and resell and support the product.

Why did we take this step?
We were in a unique position to accelerate the growth of the network computing industry. If we removed as many of the customer concerns as we could, the choice to network would be easier.

What were the customer sentiments?
The customers preferred buying both hardware and software from one place and knowing it would be supported. In 1985 and 1986 Novell really started growing. We were able to provide a complete solution, including technical support.

How did we deal with those sentiments?
We strove to provide the best technical support possible to our customers. We were very familiar with the base NetWare OS—that was the common link. We rapidly came up to speed on the variant NetWare Operating Systems and could quickly resolve most hardware problems we encountered. This was a new concept that customers readily accepted.

What is the customer's perspective now?
The concept of one company supporting all products on a network is so universally accepted that it is now expected and taken for granted. Customer satisfaction surveys taken in 1989, 1991, and 1992 show that customers are pleased with our technical knowledge, follow through, and courtesy. Greatly improved but still needing work are the response time and resolution time of the technical support staff.

What worked and what did not work?
Customers really dislike paying for technical support. There was no charge for technical support until September of 1986 when we established our 800 LANSWER number, but we have always encouraged customers to work through our resellers for the support they need. Listed below are the reasons we feel Novell's support policy benefits the end user.
- Novell has an extremely strong distribution channel. The customer benefits from this strong channel and we want to do all we can to support this strength.
- Because of a customer base of approximately twenty million Novell users on one-and-one-quarter-million networks and because tens of thousands of new networks are shipped each month, we do not have the resources to encourage customers to call us for technical support.
- Since there are hundreds or thousands of NetWare Operating System installations worldwide, the technical questions customers have are more detailed and generally involve much more time to answer than application software questions might take.

- NetWare OS installations can range from a two-connection network to a worldwide, multi-vendor, multi-protocol network. Picture yourself as a technical support engineer trying to address a customer's question and relate the answer at the appropriate technical level—neither too technical for the novice user nor too elementary for the sophisticated user. The best use of everyone's time is a mechanism to screen out the elementary questions and get them quickly resolved (the resellers job) and use Novell's knowledge to work on the more difficult questions.
- Authorized Resellers, Gold Resellers, and Platinum Resellers are capable of answering ninety percent of the questions their customers have. Gold and Platinum resellers can place free technical support calls to Novell. If the resellers don't know the answer to a question, Novell is ready to help. With Novell working through the reseller, that knowledge is leveraged so that the next time a customer has that question the reseller can answer it. If Novell answered directly to the end user, the reseller would have no knowledge of the answer and would be unable to help with any succeeding queries on the same topic.
- If end users are not comfortable with their reseller, we can provide the names of other resellers in the end user's geographic area. We are also very active in de-authorizing resellers who do not live up to expected levels of service and customer support.
- We have stratified our support so Novell personnel are available and trained to quickly answer the most difficult questions, while empowering resellers to answer easier questions and allowing resellers to call Novell for free answers to questions they can't answer.
- If we offered free support customers would probably call Novell rather than calling their reseller. This number of calls would increase and the response and resolution time for every call would deteriorate. It would take longer to get an answer to all questions.
- If customers called Novell instead of their reseller, the closeness and familiarity between reseller and end user would suffer. Resellers do much more than just collect margins on the sale of products. We expect resellers to be familiar with their customers, the customer's network configuration, the peculiarities of the customer's business, new products (Novell or others) which will help the customer in their business, enhancements or upgrades to existing products the customer has installed, and any other aspect of being a resource and an aid to the customer. A critical element of this familiarity is being aware of network problems or questions the customer is encountering with installation, continued operation, enhancements, additions, capabilities, limitations, optimizations, etc. If Novell provides this information to end users, we are not really serving them to the best interests of all involved.

These are some of the main reasons for the structure of our technical support and why we feel so strongly about the way it is set up. The support philosophy goes to the core of and is tightly integrated with Novell's channel distribution.

We have worked hard to ensure that a number of different avenues for obtaining technical support are available to our customers. Given the absolute necessity of providing top notch support, Novell has tried to make technical information commonly available and easily accessible to a variety of different customers. All customers are encouraged to work closely with their resellers. For those who would like to have additional personal expertise there are education and training classes and course curriculum leading to a Certified NetWare Engineer (CNE) status. If none of the above options work, end users can telephone Novell directly for technical support.

Larger installations may consider an annual support agreement that allows unlimited calls to technical support. Support can also be purchased on a per incident basis. (An incident is defined as one problem, taken through resolution, regardless of how difficult the problem is or how long it takes to resolve.) Incidents can be pre-purchased and used as needed or they can be purchased at the time of need.

There are many aspects of our technical support that have worked very well.

- We have a very extensive real-time data base that we use to open incidents, track progress, escalate if more technical expertise is needed, and close incidents.
- Our telephone system allows customers to place one call and receive support for all of Novell's products. Each call is routed to an available technician.
- Each month we survey more than four hundred customers who have had incidents resolved within the previous thirty days. Referencing their most recent call, we ask them to give our technical support a letter grade (A, B, C, D, or F) in the areas of response time, resolution time, courtesy, knowledge, and follow-up. Since July 1989 when we began the Novell Service Report Card, our overall grade point has risen from a B- (2.94) to an A- (3.82). This is a continuous improvement rated by our customers where we ask how we are doing, make improvements based on the responses, then ask again how we are doing.
- Technical support employee training and incentives are based on a combination of individual and team grades.

The design and implementation of the above support options, processes, and measurements has been a direct result of our responsiveness to the varied needs of our customers. We think our support process is working well. There will, of course, be more changes as we become aware of our evolving customer's needs.

What would we do differently?

A few years ago Novell had a reputation of providing poor technical support. Over the past two or three years this issue has been addressed and support has greatly improved, as measured by our customers (we still need to and will continue to make improvement changes). If we could have been more perceptive and worked toward a resolution of this concern before it became a problem for customers, we would have been much better off. This would have involved earlier leveraging of the sales channels, stratification of the levels of support, and education and training of these third party sources. Technical support is not trivial. It is perhaps the most difficult, varying, and changing challenge we face.

3. For a period of time, we sold our competitor's products, at our cost, to help grow the market.

Why did we take this step?
We did this because Novell did not manufacture a total LAN solution. We had networking software, servers, and work stations, but our customers also needed the network interface cards (NICs) manufactured by our competitors. To make it easy for customers to select and use a LAN, we bundled competitor's NICs with our products and provided a complete solution to our customers.

What were the customer sentiments?
Being an emerging industry, customers were somewhat hesitant to purchase LANs. If we added to that hesitancy a requirement to configure the system from several different (and small) companies, the hesitancy grew into reluctance. By providing a total solution (incorporating both Novell and non-Novell products) we took some of the stress out of the customer decision. We sold and supported the total solution.

The resellers did not seem to care whether or not we sold competing products. However, one competitor (and major supplier) concerned over the amount of their business that Novell represented, discontinued selling to us.

How did we deal with those sentiments?
Since our customers needed the hardware and our former source would no longer sell to us, we decided to produce the hardware ourselves. We always tried to make it easy for the end user to do business with us. We tried to see things from a customer perspective and make sure our short- and long-term directions aligned with customer needs.

What is the customer's perspective now?
Our customers are still reaping the benefits of the seeds that were sown. Within the bounds of the law, we have formed strategic and technical alliances with companies that were once viewed as competition. In fact, some of our alliance partners are still competitors or have competing divisions. Examples of these alliances are the Novell Labs and the Technical Support Alliance. Each of these areas are widely applauded by our customers. Customers and the industry benefit as barriers are knocked down and companies cooperate in serving customers.

What worked and what did not work?
The concept and actualization of providing a total solution to our customers worked very well by helping to drive and mature the industry. This also helped to establish a feeling of trust and concern with our customers.

What did not work but was probably out of our control was the degree of cooperation we received from others in the industry. Some couldn't see our vision of cooperative competition and thought the relationship had to be 100 percent one way or the other. We felt there had to be a fine balance between competition (required by law and required for industry growth) and cooperation (required to establish and grow an emerging industry).

What would we do differently?

We don't see any glaring errors in the way we designed or administered the concept. There were probably some little things we would do differently, but we are satisfied with the results and the contribution we think we have made to help the market mature.

4. We designed and developed hardware with a specific purpose to keep the cost to the end users as low as possible and thereby make network computing a more attractive alternative. This helped to grow the industry and protect the customer's LAN investment.

The model is: Keep the core business in-house. Conceive and nourish enabling ventures in-house, then spin them off to trusted third parties as soon as they are strong enough to support themselves.

Why did we take this step?

Our customers needed NICs and our former supplier (who was also a competitor) decided not to sell to us anymore. Of the many options we had open, we decided to design and build our own NICs.

Novell acquired Santa Clara Systems, a desktop hardware company, so we could further influence the total solution we would deliver to our customers. Local area networking using distributed processing and intelligent terminals was competing against mainframe and minicomputers using centralized processing with dumb terminals. We felt a successful industry-growing strategy would be to drive the work station hardware (where the biggest costs reside) costs as low as possible. At that time, one package of NetWare OS could support up to 100 work stations. If the workstations and NICs were very costly, it wouldn't take long before LANs would not be viable alternatives. To preserve and mature the industry, the cost of hardware had to come down.

What were the customer sentiments?

Our customers were happy to see the work station and NIC prices go down.

How did we deal with those sentiments?

We continued (even through today) to do all we could within the bounds of the law to lower the cost of network hardware.

What is the customer's perspective now?

The networking hardware and software industry is growing, indicating there are both needs and business opportunities.

What worked and what did not work?

What did not work was the problems we had with hardware manufactured offshore. Although we tried to do a good job of managing our offshore production, we did not.

There were problems on both sides of the Pacific Ocean. We did not have anyone reside at the manufacturing facility, we did not have any strong ties with the facility, and we had very little leverage over them. On this side of the ocean, we had very little experience in managing a long-distance relationship, the manufacturing process was not fully in control before we turned it over to them, and the hardware management direction was a little out of synchrony with our corporate direction. All of these complications led to products that were not up to the quality standards we demand now.

What worked was the accomplishment of presenting a vision to the industry of what the LAN model might be—commodity hardware with optimized software. The quality of the hardware hurt Novell, but the episode was very beneficial to the networking industry.

What would we do differently?

We would try to be more prepared going into such an arrangement and exercise more control over the quality of the products.

5. Novell spun off hardware connectivity and commodity items to companies who could produce them more efficiently, allowing Novell to concentrate on software and strategic, enabling hardware. As this hardware gains acceptance and widespread use, it too, will be spun off to companies who are more efficient at manufacturing and promoting hardware commodities. This allows Novell to continue our focus on our core software and strategic, enabling hardware.

Why did we take this step?

In the early days of networking, hardware and software produced by different vendors were not as compatible as they are today. As a young LAN provider our customers almost compelled us to provide a complete system comprised of software, servers, and hardware peripherals. As the industry began to mature we found that the majority of our hardware evolved into commodity items, while our software remained our key product and was definitely not a commodity item. Even though there was still a very strong market for Novell hardware (about forty percent of our revenue), we thought we could grow the market more by concentrating on software development and let the mass production houses manufacture the hardware.

We did not completely leave the hardware business, just the commodity items. We still designed, developed, and marketed new hardware products. As soon as the hardware products gained acceptance and another manufacturer could add more value to the process or we could add more value to the industry by spinning the product off, we were quick to strike manufacturing and royalty agreements with capable, aware, and quality conscious third party manufacturers.

An example of this was the Ethernet topology, a key to the widespread use of LANs. Existing Ethernet interface cards (which are housed inside file servers and work stations and allow communication over the LAN) were selling for $795. We thought this price excessive, so we designed and built our own Ethernet interface card and sold it for $395. After providing and proving the design, growing the market, and selling nearly one million Ethernet cards, we sold the rights to manufacture this card to a third party manufacturing company. We had taken the card from an enabling product to a commodity product, and now it was time to follow our model and turn our attention to other enabling hardware products. Later on we developed and sold a diskless terminal with a built in Ethernet card, specifically designed to be used as a LAN work station. We sold this entire product for $795—a greatly increased value from our initial entry point of $795 for the Ethernet interface card alone.

What were the customer sentiments?

Our customers were concerned that without Novell hardware, there would be finger pointing whenever problems arose. The potential existed for a hardware vendor to tell a customer with a non-functioning system, "That's not our problem, our hardware works. Go get help from Novell." Novell could then tell the customer the same story, "That's not our problem, our software works. Go get help from the hardware vendor." This was a very real concern and something that could easily happen if we did not have the proper preventative measures in place.

How did we deal with those sentiments?

The resolution of this customer concern was the beginning of two important Novell programs that will be discussed later—Novell Labs (Independent Manufacturer Support Program, IMSP) and the Technical Support Alliance (TSA). Our IMSP tests and approves third party hardware on various versions of the NetWare OS. We allow these vendors to use "Novell Labs Tested and Approved" logos in their advertising. This allows compatibility to be determined before hardware and software are purchased.

The TSA concept takes IMSP one step further by forming an alliance with other hardware and software vendors. If a customer has a problem with any network that contains products represented by a TSA member, the customer can request technical assistance from any TSA member and that member will retain ownership of the problem until it is resolved. There is no passing customers on to other vendors for a resolution—with one call ownership is taken and an intra-TSA resolution is made.

What is the customer's perspective now?

Customers and vendors have realized the benefits of the spinning off of hardware, the IMSP, and the TSA. The NetWare OS has become a multi-platform operating system that supports DOS, OS/2, UNIX, and Macintosh. This would have been more difficult if we had kept our own hardware. Novell also protects customer's information services investment. As companies grow and needs grow, Novell software grows with the company. This too would have been difficult if we had not made a decision to be hardware-independent.

Customers seek out hardware and software solutions that have been tested and approved by Novell. They know there is a greatly reduced chance of a problem occurring, and if a problem does occur it will be quickly resolved.

What worked and what did not work?

Things went pretty well except for some initial customer perceptions. Some customers felt like they had bought into a dead line; they trusted Novell and bought our hardware products, then we discontinued manufacturing the hardware. They felt they were going to be deserted, and we had to make sure that did not happen.

What would we do differently?

We should have gotten out of the hardware business earlier. At a time when we should have been moving away from hardware, we got in deeper with more products and offshore production. The difficulty in managing the manufacturing aspects from thousands of miles away hurt the quality of the products and slightly tarnished Novell's reputation. It would have been easier on our customers and on us if we had moved away from hardware more aggressively.

We were frustrated by wanting to hand off our hardware to a trusted and competent party, knowing the attributes this party had to possess to produce a quality product, and yet having difficulty finding such a party. We had two manufacturers in Korea. Despite many trips of many Novell people going to Korea and many trips of their people coming to Novell, the process and the communication was not reliable. We hired a full-time Korean national to perform source inspections and we performed receiving inspections, but we still were unable to produce a product of consistent quality. Because of our lack of confidence in the hardware produced, we had to abandon our offshore efforts, even though it was economically attractive.

We later were very successful in developing fully competent hardware partners in the United States. The secret was not that the partners are United States, although differences in language and culture make communication much more difficult. The main benefit was that of geographic closeness. We were able to spend much more profitable time with these partners, making sure that our philosophies, values, and customer attitudes were in synchrony. We were also able to monitor their processes in real-time and in person. Any potential problems were cleared up before a questionable product could be manufactured. We had to be fully comfortable with the product our customers were going to receive.

Even with all the advance preparation, the hand off from Novell to the third party manufacturers could have gone smoother. This is a very critical aspect of technology transfer and great pains must be taken to prevent any slip-ups. We sacrificed some time for the sake of quality. With better planning we could have had the quality and saved some time. Even with the most detailed planning, problems will occur, but you will have better control of your resources to deal with these unexpected obstacles if they are the exception and not the rule.

6. In 1985 there were no networking trade shows, and it was difficult for networking to get attention at the existing PC and electronics trade shows. If the industry was going to grow it would need more publicity. In 1986, Novell started NetWorld, a trade show specifically focused on the networking industry. The show fulfilled the following three needs:
- It educated customers on the capabilities and versatility of networking. In addition to vendor displays there was a complement of seminars, instructions, and demonstrations.
- It identified the networking industry as an important subset of the PC and electronics industry.
- It gave network software developers equal footing and display capabilities.

Why did we take this step?
The establishment of a networking trade show was an important step to help grow the industry, to show the viability of network computing, to provide a forum in which all network developers could participate, to educate attendees, and to identify and help establish networking as an industry.

What were the customer sentiments?
NetWorld was a success from the first show. This event is built around the attendees and is supported by seminars, tutorials, and vendor displays. With every show there has been a large, functioning local area network. With our first show the network involved all the displaying vendor's products, demonstrating to the attendees that networks were viable, functional, and easy to use. After a few shows we did not have to prove the viability of networks to attendees, so the network contained a variety of new hardware and software products, allowing attendees to "test drive" combinations of networking products.

How did we deal with those sentiments?
We continue to closely monitor attendee interests through surveys and provide what is needed. There is a NetWorld Advisory Board made up of one-third high end (power) networkers, one-third editors of major industry publications, and one-third consultants and systems integrators. This board decides the topics of seminars and tutorials. (A seminar is a panel or vendor's perspective on a technology. A tutorial teaches from a college perspective. A tutorial is the theory or education whereas a seminar is a vendor biased application of the theory.)

What is the customer's perspective now?
Customers are delighted with the NetWorlds, which have grown into a major show in the industry. Networking is a new concept to one third of the attendees at each NetWorld show. Education classes are 25 percent to 30 percent beginners topics (What is a network? How do you set up a network? How do you get a network approved? etc.), 30 percent detailed networking topics, and the balance is troubleshooting and optimization techniques. There is a Spring NetWorld in Boston, a Fall NetWorld in Dallas, a NetWorld Europe, and a NetWorld Japan.

What worked and what did not work?

The first NetWorld was a Novell event. The second year Banyan (one of our competitors) wanted to participate. After some consideration and a review of our long-term goal to grow the industry, we admitted Banyan and anyone else who was associated with networking. This establishing of NetWorld as an industry trade show and not a Novell trade show worked extremely well. Even though we sponsored and produced the show, we encouraged competitors to participate. We tried to keep everyone and everything associated with the show at "arm's length" from Novell. Within Novell this concept was at first met with some difficulty, but the view of market growth prevailed, and we were able to initiate an important industry forum.

Another important factor in the success of NetWorld was the following of the Novell model. We started and ran NetWorld for a couple of years, then passed it off to someone who could more efficiently handle it. Along with the hand-off there were some very rigid restrictions to maintain the focus on networking and help ensure NetWorld would still serve and grow the industry.

What would we do differently?

If we had the vision or forethought, we would have had more seminars and tutorials the first two years. We always think we are offering too many of these, but they continue to be the most popular aspect of NetWorld. User groups (Microsoft, Banyan, NetWare Users International, etc.) have been a tremendous benefit in helping NetWorld achieve recognition both through invitations to their members and by supplying presenters at the seminars. If these groups had been strong enough, we should have had them more involved earlier.

7. Novell helped form a users group, NetWare Users International (NUI). NUI is the largest computer user group in the world with more than 200 chapters worldwide and over 80,000 members.

Why did we take this step?

In the summer of 1984 at PC Expo, several Novell customers asked Novell to form a user group. The initial benefit customers expected would be twofold. First, Novell employees could hear firsthand the concerns and frustrations of users, as well as provide immediate feedback to questions asked. (Local Novell employees attend the NUI chapter meetings.) Second, customers would be able to participate in and influence the product development cycle. (NUI conducts an annual survey of their membership. The top ten issues are presented to Novell for inclusion in product designs and process improvements.)

What were the customer sentiments?

Since NUI was formed in direct response to customer requests, it was very well received by customers and Novell alike as a means to bring users and employees closer together, allowing Novell to align our products and services with customer needs.

How did we deal with those sentiments?

We tried to support NUI in any way we could, realizing the importance of impartiality and autonomy if this group was to be effective.

What is the customer's perspective now?

We are thrilled with the tremendous success of this group. Although NUI is governed and administrated separately from Novell, we work hard to contribute to the success of NUI. Novell contributes about $1 million and some internal services each year to NUI, but this direct Novell support is decreasing.

NUI is continuously increasing in autonomy and independence, and thereby increasing in strength and value to end users. This is the course the group has chartered for themselves. The initial benefits of having a pipeline into Novell for product design, process improvement, and feedback are still very prevalent, and some additional advantages to NUI members have evolved as they grow the NUI vision to its full potential.

There is a wealth of knowledge and experience embodied in the membership of each NUI chapter. First hand answers to questions regarding configurations, hardware, and application software are provided at each meeting.

Chapter meetings provide a structured forum for presentations by complementary hardware and software vendors. While not endorsing any of the presenters, NUI facilitates a free flow of ideas among its members.

Seventy percent of those in attendance at chapter meetings are not NetWare OS users. They are people looking for solutions by investigating networking. The independence of NUI helps to keep chapter meetings impartial and informative. Most chapters have a novice session before each monthly meeting. Questions such as "What is a network?" and "What are the relative benefits of each topology?" are answered. NUI meetings are excellent at informing and educating all levels of network users or potential network users.

What worked and what did not work?

Initially, NUI was strongly coupled with Novell. For NUI to be all that end users and Novell wanted it to be, it would have to be more independent and operated by Novell at arm's length. This concept fit the same model we have already discussed—nurture it until it can stand on its own, then encourage it to have a life of its own. With its own charter, logo, and board of directors, there is no doubt that NUI thrives on independence.

There were some things that went well from the launching of NUI.
1. The end user feedback directly to Novell was beneficial and well received from the beginning. The first list of the top ten concerns NUI compiled was welcomed by Novell, and every concern on the list was resolved within six months. The top ten list continues to be an important input mechanism for both parties.
2. Another successful area benefiting from NUI's increasing independence is the production of NUI conferences. These conferences are an annual event in 12 cities domestically and 6 cities internationally, with attendance ranging from

400 to 1300 at each conference. Originally started by Novell and now completely taken over by NUI, these conferences are a huge success.

3. A NetWare OS users magazine, *NetWare Connection,* was initially produced by Novell with heavy input from the user groups. Now this magazine is published by NUI and is distributed to 180,000 users worldwide. The magazine contains news, tips, informative articles, and paid advertising from Novell and other vendors.

What would we do differently?

At the inception of NUI, we had a vision of the important role this organization could have in advancing network computing. Instead of letting the NUI foundation and infrastructure evolve naturally, we tried to hurry the development. As is often the case when anyone is teaching something new to someone else, the tendency exists to do it yourself. This however, is almost always a mistake. Trying to do it ourselves would have certainly resulted in a critical loss of creativity, diversity, and independence that is so crucial to the success NUI has realized.

8. Novell was a leader if not the leader in requiring service through the reseller channels. Other network providers gave special incentives to their resellers who would take extra service training, but Novell was the first to require the additional support training as a condition to selling our products.

Why did we take this step?

Our end users were not getting consistent quality of service. The industry was young enough that resellers were asked to configure, install, and service networks, but in general, they lacked the depth of knowledge to provide quality support. Novell tried to help the industry grow by requiring our resellers to have technical people on staff and requiring completion of a technical training curriculum. Resellers either had to successfully complete the training or cease to sell our products. It was a bold step, but one we felt was needed for the benefit of our end users and the continued growth of the industry. For four years we were the only network provider that required training as a prerequisite to selling.

What were the customer sentiments?

Novell has many different types of customers, but generally they can be classed as resellers (distributors, dealers, OEMs, VARs, system integrators, consultants, etc.), end users, and developers. Our resellers were upset when we took this direction.

They viewed this as just one more requirement and generally failed to see the importance of the step. Our end users were skeptically positive about this approach. Positive because of the enhanced support and knowledge that would be available, but skeptical of how fully the resellers would actually participate.

How did we deal with those sentiments?

We spent a lot of time with our resellers, evangelizing the long term benefits of increased knowledge and skills. We encouraged our resellers to differentiate themselves on the basis of their technical abilities. This differentiation allowed a premium price for goods and services or the ability to serve a premium market. This long term perspective separated the solution providers from the product sellers and gave our end users more confidence, more support, and more choices, while accelerating the growth of the industry.

Our end users skepticism faded with the strengthening of our resellers. It was purely a results oriented action. The end users put their trust in Novell, and we put our trust in our resellers. There was risk involved, but we felt justifiably confident with the capabilities and vision of our resellers.

What is the customer's perspective now?

The majority of our resellers are very qualified service providers. Especially over the past two years, customers have noted a dramatic improvement in our technical support. Novell's requirement for rigorous training has made our resellers stronger, even though some of them felt at first like they were at risk of losing their business.

There is always more that can be done, and we are actively and continuously looking at ways we can improve the level of support given to our end users. A reseller network and customer base as extensive as ours requires detailed attention. Novell is constantly involved in training, retraining, and updating conscientious resellers while de-authorizing substandard or the occasional unscrupulous resellers. We do our best to ensure competent support is available to all our customers.

One concern that is frequently raised by customers is our lack of free technical support. Some other software companies provide free technical support, although a majority do not. Below are some of the reasons we feel we serve our customers best by not providing free technical support:

- End users derive more total benefit by working with knowledgeable resellers who:
  - are in close proximity to the end user.
  - are more familiar with the end user's equipment, configurations, business, and requirements.
  - are familiar with the customer's current configuration and can keep the customer current with upgrades and enhancements from Novell and all other networking hardware and software providers.
  - are involved with the end user's total networking experience from specification through configuration, purchase, installation, support, and upgrades.

- The large installed base of NetWare Operating Systems and the complexity of allowable connections and configurations prohibits us from doing an adequate job of centralized technical support.

- This allows a more efficient match of customer needs and Novell capabilities. Easier questions can be answered by the resellers, and more difficult questions can be forwarded to Novell.

Customer satisfaction surveys taken in 1991 and 1992 show that our customers who receive support from a source other than Novell express mild concern with the support provider's technical follow-up. The customers are overjoyed with the support provider's courtesy (they say they receive more than is necessary), and although improving, the level of knowledge of these technical support staffs, the call response time, and the call resolution time provided by non-Novell technical support is not up to customer standards.

What worked and what did not work?
The training and educating worked well because of a feeling of exclusivity on the part of resellers. There were requirements for authorized resellers and more stringent requirements for Gold authorized resellers. This differentiation and market edge was enough to cause the resellers to invest in the process and make it work. There were no major failures. We spent a lot of time with the resellers and customers during the design stage. We took pains to enhance the relationship and mold the process to the needs and perspectives of all parties involved. There was less likelihood for major failures because we changed the program frequently as the need arose. We did not let minor irritants or inconsistencies fester into major problems. Although some resellers claim our many changes was a problem in itself, we felt that change was a must due to the defining and groundbreaking support program we were implementing.

What would we do differently?
It is difficult to identify anything that we would do differently. As mentioned above, we tried different approaches, each representing our deepest thoughts and best efforts. But, as we realized a method would not work, we felt no obligation to stay with that approach—our only unchangeable constant was service to our customers and we thought this could best be achieved by strengthening our reseller support.

9. One major roadblock to acceptance and use of networks was the lack of public familiarity and knowledge. Education and training on networking was not available, because the market was still too new and there were too few sources qualified to instruct others. To serve our customers better, Novell established Novell Education Centers (NECs) at many of our company-owned NetWare Centers around the world. We developed the curriculum and the courseware, and provided the instructors and the classrooms. As the success of the NECs grew, we established Novell Authorized Education Centers (NAECs). These centers were third party instructors authorized to teach the same classes the NECs taught.

Why did we take this step?

There were a number of reasons why the NAECs were established.

- The customer needs and requests for training were increasing beyond our resource capabilities.
- There were requests for training in cities in which we did not have NECs. Authorizing NAECs would allow the training to grow where the market needed it, not where we had NetWare Centers. There was a customer need to make the training more widely available.
- Although we feel we are good at training, education is not our main thrust. We felt that if we could do a good job at regulating and authorizing third party trainers, those trainers could train and educate at least as well as we could. Outside trainers could also add a fresh perspective to the network industry.
- We felt this would help spawn a profitable industry centered around networking education. This would be one more element of the critical mass that would help grow the industry, encourage competition, and protect the customer's networking investment.

What were the customer sentiments?

Our end users fully embraced the added class locations, but were concerned whether third parties would provide the same quality instruction as Novell.

The resellers had mixed feelings. Some were upset about changes. Even though we did not require anyone to become an NAEC, they perceived that they would somehow be at a disadvantage if they did not certify as an NAEC. Others were happy about the change, enthusiastic about the number of choices Novell offered, and excited about the prospects of becoming an NAEC.

How did we deal with those sentiments?

To help overcome end user concerns we offered a full tuition refund if a student was not completely satisfied with the course. This refund clause was a requirement we placed in the NAEC agreement, and it provided an economic incentive for NAECs to advertise and teach conscientiously and professionally. It also helped Novell to monitor the NAECs and insist on improvements when violations occurred. Our current policy as stated in our education catalog is presented below.

CUSTOMER SATISFACTION GUARANTEED

NAECs and Novell, Inc., guarantee* complete customer satisfaction on all Novell courses listed in this catalog when the course is taught:

- With original Novell course materials.
- In the recommended time frame.
- At an authorized NAEC facility.
- By a Certified NetWare Instructor (CNI).

* At Novell's discretion, a customer may receive money back or have the opportunity to retake the course at no charge if he or she believes the defined course objectives were not met.

What is the customer's perspective now?

End users, resellers, and NAECs are happy with what has happened. There are, of course, many customer suggestions of how we could improve the process. Some suggestions have limited application or limited appeal; most suggestions, however, would result in benefit to the overall network industry. We are always looking for ways to improve. Customer satisfaction surveys taken in 1989, 1991, and 1992 show that our education customers are pleased with the classroom environments, the organization and planning of the courses offered, the geographic locations of the courses offered, the course content, and the current topics of the courses offered. There is mild concern over the relevance of the instruction to individual needs and the cost of the courses. We are continuously monitoring customer feedback and making improvement changes.

In addition to educating our customers, Novell feels strongly about educating our employees. At no cost to the individual, Novell has regularly scheduled courses on quality, management, change, customer relationships, time management, stress management, and wellness seminars; classes on word processing, spreadsheets, and DOS; courses leading to certifications and refresher courses in NetWare Engineering, network management, and software programming. Novell places a heavy emphasis on internal and external education.

What worked and what did not work?

It was beneficial at first to work with a limited number of NAECs. This allowed us to respond more quickly to program needs or oversights as our infant started to grow.

What worked and what did not work?

It was easier to establish and monitor our standards and authorizations with a smaller group of NAECs, and having worked closely with them, we had assurance that these NAECs would be good educational representatives of the networking community. It was critical to the confidence of the industry that the rollout go as smoothly as possible.

What would we do differently?

It would have been better to increase the number of NAECs more quickly. For four years we held our NAEC ranks to the initial starting members. We wanted to do all we could to ensure the program success, but looking back, we probably did not allow it to grow as rapidly as it should have. We should have opened up the program after two years instead of four years. There are no ill effects now as a result of this concern, but the market could have advanced faster and our customers would probably have been better served if we had allowed a quicker progression through the infancy stage of the process.

10. The NetWare Operating System was originally designed to run on IBM and IBM-clone personal computers. In 1988 Novell began designing revisions to the NetWare OS to allow interfacing between Macintosh computers and PCs. This was the beginning of a multi-protocol, multi-platform NetWare Operating System.

Why did we take this step?
A NetWare Operating System that worked only with DOS served a large portion of our market, but we began to see a customer need for a system that would allow communication between different operating systems. This need was notable both with companies that were growing and needed extra capabilities and small companies with unusually diverse network requirements. Customers were requesting operability with Macintosh, and we felt like UNIX requirements would also arise.

What were the customer sentiments?
Our customers were excited about the concept of one network being able to communicate with different operating systems. This further protected their existing investment in hardware, software, and personnel training and proficiency. Employees could each work on the work stations they were used to with the software that was best suited to them while optimizing individual efficiency and allowing inter-group communication.

How did we deal with those sentiments?
We kept on improving the NetWare OS interoperability through customer input, increased familiarity with other operating systems, and strategic alliances with other vendors.

What is the customer's perspective now?
We are now in our sixth release of Macintosh interoperability with a product that networks Macintosh products better than Apple networking products. In 1991 we released our first UNIX-compatible NetWare OS, and in February of 1992 we updated that release. The NetWare OS now allows communication and sharing of files and resources among DOS, Macintosh, UNIX, OS/2, and Windows operating systems. Novell networks can be as small as two terminals or as complex as multiple networks involving any combination of all the operating systems listed above, minicomputers, and mainframe computers.

What worked and what did not work?
Our first release of a Macintosh-compatible NetWare OS had some functionality problems. Because of differences in the structure and foundations of the two operating systems, we had to make some assumptions of the most user-friendly way to merge the two while ensuring each maintained its own look and feel. (Some of the differences include the file structures, Macintosh has three security parameters while the NetWare OS has eleven, DOS allows eight characters for file names while Macintosh allows 32 characters and spaces, and a host of other large and small differences.) Although we did a lot of research and talked with a lot of customers, our first offering needed some help.

What worked and what did not work can be summed up in our first release of our Macintosh compatible NetWare OS—our customers were excited about the capability of connecting DOS and Macintosh networks but were annoyed with some of the functions.

What would we do differently?

The Macintosh NetWare OS took longer to perfect than we thought it would. Our initial approach was to use Novell's DOS design knowledge and hire some Macintosh designers with the expected outcome of Macintosh networking capability. This effort was not fully successful because our design team did not have enough knowledge of Macintosh networking and the designers that had Macintosh knowledge did not know the NetWare OS very well. We also had some parts of the software developed via a third party contract. This did not work as well as we wanted either.

In 1989 we merged with Excelan, and their Macintosh group (formerly the Kinetics Company) was one of the top companies outside of Apple who knew how to network Macintosh. Having both DOS and Macintosh expertise in the same company provided us the capability to spend a lot of time exchanging information, allowing both sides to understand the intricacies of both systems. The design that resulted from this collaboration is a tremendous success.

We saw the same success when we merged Excelan's UNIX expertise with Novell's networking mastery to produce NetWare NFS (networking communication between UNIX networks and DOS networks).

There are a few other things we would do differently.

- realize the differences and capabilities of designs performed by third parties, by hiring to design, and by acquiring to design
- build internal expertise sooner that understands both environments and both architectures
- develop an overall integration architecture at the beginning, instead of looking at each individual project on an ad hoc basis
- involve all product development resources to build and adhere to an integration architecture to support multi-client environments concurrently.

11. Novell established an industry publication, *LANTIMES,* which provided a LAN voice, view, and education.

Why did we take this step?

In 1984 we could not get network attention in any of the PC publications. We realized that network computing would never be accepted unless it had exposure. *LANTIMES* was started to help provide this exposure and to be a local area networking voice.

What were the customer sentiments?

The *LANTIMES* was well received by the industry. Although it was a Novell publication, it was viewed by many readers as an industry publication. This put added responsibility on us to treat the contents of each edition as objectively as possible. We actively encouraged articles on LAN industry issues and included press releases of interest to the networking community.

How did we deal with those sentiments?
We actively promoted competition in LAN publications to help grow the industry. Any industry or business without competition tends toward stagnation and lacks the incentive necessary to fully benefit the industry it serves.

What is the customer's perspective now?
Despite the advertising revenues, *LANTIMES* was only profitable the last six months before it was sold to McGraw-Hill in 1989. It was designed to be a LAN voice, not necessarily a self-sustaining publication. It's eventual financial independence and the acquisition of it by McGraw-Hill indicates customer acceptance.

The *LANTIMES* project followed the model presented earlier. There was a need in the industry for this type of publication. Novell took the responsibility to get the publication going and nurture it through its infancy. When the publication was self sufficient and strong enough to stand on its own (when there was sufficient competition to help it grow), it was spun off to someone else in the industry. The company it was spun off to was experienced in the industry and could take advantages of economies of scale and industry familiarity to help the product grow even more. Even the fact that the publication is now completely independent of Novell cannot help but give some added growth potential to the *LANTIMES*. Having transferred this responsibility, Novell now has more resources to concentrate on our core business.

What worked and what did not work?
To further promote the acceptance of *LANTIMES* as an industry voice, advertising space was available to everyone—even our competitors. There was also an Open Forum section that encouraged views on the industry. While the criticism was sometimes about Novell and sometimes stinging, the input was essential in perfecting processes and growing the market. The adherence to this openness was critical in the industry acceptance of this publication.

What would we do differently?
We feel that bringing *LANTIMES* from inception to independence took too long. We would try to speed up the process by more actively focusing and guiding the evolution to independence rather than letting it happen naturally. There is a trade off and a fine line between being too aggressive and being too lax, but we think we should have been more aggressive in influencing the independence.

12. In an age of industrial espionage, trade secrets, and intellectual property right protection, there have been many times when Novell has openly shared technological information with its competitors. Novell has made available to other companies the design of some of the data transport software, interface software, network monitoring and diagnostic software, and even operating system software (LAN drivers, IPX stacks, shells, disk drivers, backup products, routers, network management, and Portable NetWare for minicomputers).

Why did we take this step?
Sharing of technology allows other vendors in the industry to provide and sell Novell compatible products. Interfacing with Novell during product design and development allows for more thorough and reliable products. Complementary products perform better, making networking an easier choice and grows the market.

We are at our best and the market is best served when there is flourishing competition. Most industries or markets that are dominated by one player are stagnant. This is why Novell actively works at tearing down traditional proprietary walls, opening up the operating system to everyone, and creating an industry where all can participate.

What were the customer sentiments?
Although they were the primary beneficiaries of the technology exchanges, our customers generally were unaware that it was happening.

How did we deal with those sentiments?
We worked closely with Microsoft, one of our major competitors, to make Windows (a Microsoft product) and the NetWare OS more compatible. This was in direct response to some of our prime customers, including a delivery service company and two east coast banks. This cooperation with a competitor on issues for large customers benefited all users by the development of more compatible NetWare OS and Windows.

What is the customer's perspective now?
Customers are becoming more aware of Novell's interaction with other vendors to improve network computing. Novell Labs, the Technical Support Alliance, and many other strategic relations all publicize the coming together of diverse products, capabilities, ideas, and concepts to serve customers and grow the industry.

A 1991 Novell national advertising campaign featured messages aimed at making the public aware of our industry cooperation. One ad showed a 1960s style spy briefcase complete with tie tack camera and martini olive microphone. The caption read, "There Used To Be Only One Way To Get Information From The Competition." Another ad made mild fun of notions that promote monopolies rather than growing industries. The overriding theme of both advertisements was that industry, companies, and customers are all best served by competition with products and cooperation with developing and guiding concepts.

A competitor's recent press release said they were going to begin designing their products to be more NetWare OS compatible. Our president and CEO, Ray Noorda, called them on the telephone, identified himself, referred to their press release, and said, "Good, we'd like to help you!"

What worked and what did not work?

What was not productive for us was membership in standards bodies. For some reason, participation in these huge committees, formed from vendors and users in the industry and chartered with developing a networking or communication standard, was too slow for Novell. The groups seemed too committee oriented (surprise). Rather than try to mandate a standard, we choose to solve customer problems and work toward becoming the *de facto* standard.

One area that went well was our sharing code, specifications, and information. With the first few companies we shared this information, our actions were somewhat reactionary as we determined what they would need, then find it, write it, or clean it up. Further into the process we knew what would be required and we had the information available and ready to explain and hand over in a more professional manner. This organizing information for others required us to be more organized in our internal development, education, and communication of all products, not just those that would be shared with other vendors.

What would we do differently?

We should have taken a more integrated and planned approach to developer support and offerings. Novell does not develop any software applications. We develop the operating system and encourage third parties to produce applications to run on our NetWare OS. Although we have software developers kits, a professional developer's program, and a software testing program, we feel like we could be more proactive in the design stage so that writing applications for the NetWare OS is easier. We are taking steps in this direction.

13. In November of 1988, Novell formed a Customer Satisfaction Department (CSD). This six person department originally reported to the vice president of technical support, but in January of 1989 their report was changed to the president and CEO of Novell.

Why did we take this step?

In the five years Novell had been in existence, we had merged with at least four other companies, and our growth was phenomenal. We wanted to make sure we weren't growing at the expense of alienated customers. Although we had strong and unwavering strategic directions, we were breaking new ground in many areas and the implementation of the strategy was sometimes cumbersome. More than providing customer service, the customer satisfaction department was established to be a customer advocate and a customer liaison within Novell. The CSD responds to customer (end users, resellers, OEMs, etc.) telephone calls and letters and works within the framework of Novell worldwide and with any Novell department to resolve the customer concern. If a customer has a unique, legitimate problem with a Novell policy or practice, the CSD can usually work out a solution that is fair and agreeable to all parties—the customer, Novell, and the thousands of other customers who are abiding by the policy. The CSD is the ear and the heart of Novell, constantly looking at how Novell can change to serve our customers better.

What were the customer sentiments?

There was no grand announcement or press release concerning the formation of the CSD, so customers were not immediately aware. Thousands of customers have taken advantage of this service Novell offers. Over the past 12 months, less than nine percent of the customers CSD has helped have been dissatisfied with the solution. This is an impressive number considering that nearly one hundred percent were dissatisfied when they first contacted the CSD.

Almost as important as us helping customers is the information we receive back from our customers; information on what policies should be changed and how to change them and what we can do to make Novell easier doing business with. This input has been valuable as we mold Novell's policies to fit customer's needs.

How did we deal with those sentiments?

The CSD goes as far as it can for every customer, and considers each call on its own individual circumstances. Sometimes the only way we could give a customer what is wanted would be at the expense of hundreds or thousands of other customers—we cannot do that. We cannot make an exception for no good reason; we cannot do it just because we are big. With each call, we try to view the concern from an empathic, customer-oriented perspective. We actively investigate customer claims of Novell misleading or misrepresenting through advertising, sales, marketing, product information, technical support, or any other source. Our first action is to make it right with our customer, then enact whatever additional training, education, or clarification is necessary to help prevent the misinterpretation from happening to other customers.

What is the customer's perspective now?

In the first quarter of 1989 the CSD received 91 calls, in the fourth quarter of 1992, 1686 calls were received. We attribute this steady increase in the number of calls to increased awareness of the department. The CSD is not viewed by customers as a "way to get around policies you don't like," rather an empowered, sympathetic ear for our customers. A customer satisfaction survey taken in 1992 showed that customers were content with the courtesy of the CSD and felt like the representative listened to them and understood their concerns. Needing improvement were the areas of timely response, timely resolution, knowledge, providing status, and resolving concerns to the customer's satisfaction.

In addition to resolving customer concerns, the CSD further promotes the customer by performing yearly Customer Satisfaction Surveys, asking customers how Novell is doing and how we can improve in the areas of strategy, general support, technical support (Novell and non-Novell), product quality, telephone communications, product price, customer documentation, advertising and promotion, sales (Novell and non-Novell), presale information, education, product shipments (Novell and non-Novell), order entry, credit policy, and customer satisfaction.

These surveys are administered by diskette. The customers select the areas which they have interfaced with Novell during the previous twelve months, and the survey self-programs to ask questions from only those areas. Close-ended questions allow comparison and correlation between surveys taken at different times, and open-ended questions pinpoint the areas that need the most improvement. Every question asked by a customer in the open-ended section receives a personal response from Novell. We are currently in the process of putting this survey information and much other customer information in an on-line database so every employee in the company can receive firsthand customer feedback on how customers would like Novell to change. We want this information to be a constant guide to performance in all areas of Novell from shipping to sales, education, product development, or any other way we influence our customers.

The CSD also conducts the following activities:

- total quality management process training and administration.
- monthly report cards to technical support personnel containing customer's ratings of Novell's support in the areas of response time, resolution time, courtesy, knowledge, and follow-up.
- a yearly customer month, placing a special focus on customers through presentations, rallies, awareness, and other special events.
- yearly in-touch week where directors and above spend a four hour session meeting with customers with whom they normally do not interact. This provides executive empathy for and review of the policies and processes within which front line employees must work. It also provides an immediate feedback from customers of how friendly our processes are.
- monthly silver service award for one person in the company who has a history of providing sterling service to our customers (internal or external customers), and does one specific act that goes above and beyond the call of duty in providing service to a customer.
- administers the distribution of all customer comment cards received from our customers. It is impressive that every one of these cards is personally answered. Customer comments are an invaluable and continuous source of areas considered for improvement changes.
- guiding Novell in our Malcolm Baldrige National Quality Award application.

What worked and what did not work?

A hard concept to get through is that Novell cannot always give the customer exactly what they want. The people in CSD have to be intelligent, technical, and knowledgeable enough to provide what is needed. Occasionally customers ask us to provide something that goes against the strategy or basic philosophy of our company. This we can not provide. The CSD talks with customers and almost always comes to a mutually acceptable agreement. This is a harsh reality to be a customer advocate and have a customer curse at you because you would not do what is wanted. What did not work is pleasing 100 percent of the customers who call the CSD. What does work is trying to please 100 percent of the customers, while realizing that a very small percentage may not be fully satisfied.

In the last four months of 1992 less than two percent of the customers calling the CSD were dissatisfied with their resolution. We hope that through proper education, excellent product and service delivery, empowered and knowledgeable employees, and setting proper expectations for our customers, we can significantly reduce the number of dissatisfied customers. The CSD wants to work itself out of a job.

What would we do differently?

We should have been more aggressive in embracing and promoting total quality management and in being a resource to help empower employees. More than resolving the customer concern, the CSD should have more quickly and aggressively helped other departments to see the types of concerns encountered by customers, then aid in revising the practices, policies, or programs to be more customer friendly.

14. Through its Independent Manufacturer Support Program (IMSP), Novell works with third party manufacturers to test and certify hardware components designed to interoperate with the NetWare Operating System. Novell publishes these test results to inform our customers about products that have formally demonstrated NetWare OS compatibility. In effect, IMSP certification programs help vendors market their products through Novell's distribution channels.

The primary goal of IMSP is to foster working relationships between Novell and strategic third party hardware manufacturers. Secondary goals include promoting certified hardware to industry resellers and working with vendors to codevelop critical network hardware components.

Why did we take this step?

As Novell moved further away from being a hardware provider, our customers became more concerned that there would be compatibility problems between our software and other vendor's hardware. With no total vendorship of both the hardware and the software, there were two main customer apprehensions:

• How would customers know which hardware and software products were compatible?
• Would either vendor take ownership of problems encountered during installation or during operation?

The IMSP program was established in 1987 to put our customer's minds at ease regarding these two issues. Our testing of products with various NetWare OS configurations gives customers confidence with their initial purchase. Our testing also weeds out any problems customers might have during normal operation, thus making for a more reliable network.

What were the customer sentiments?

Our customers were relieved to see us assume this responsibility. This was one more activity that took some guesswork out of buying a Novell product; it made it easier for customers to make the decision we wanted them to make. The hardware vendors were also excited about the extra marketing capabilities that "Novell tested and certified" would mean for their products.

How did we deal with those sentiments?
We had to be very careful that the products were tested under real life operational conditions, and that a Novell certification really meant something. It was really a responsibility not to betray the trust of a customer, a vendor, or an industry.

What is the customer's perspective now?
There has been widespread industry acceptance of our IMSP process. As of early 1992, we have worked with more than 400 vendors, certified more than 1900 products, and continue to certify 40-50 products each month. Given the amount of testing each product must undergo and the credibility that a Novell certification has in the industry, this is a tremendous effort.

What worked and what did not work?
What has worked well is the concept of two vendors working together at an engineering level to produce a more user-friendly product. This synergistic relationship allows the working out of bugs and problem resolution before the products hit the street. The IMSP labs test alpha code (pre-release versions) from eighteen different companies which cover ninety percent of our major marketplace. The IMSP program puts customers first by giving them a higher level of assurance in the products they purchase and it allows them freedom of choice with literally thousands of configurations to choose from.

What would we do differently?
With early versions of the NetWare OS, there were few drivers (software controllers of interface cards, disk drives, etc., which are specific to a particular vendor, protocol, or convention) that needed to be included with the NetWare OS to allow configuration of a network. However, as many more vendors began participating in networking and as the scope and capabilities of networking increased, the number of drivers needed to configure a network grew almost exponentially. With early NetWare OS versions, Novell provided in-house development of the required drivers, but as networking grew it became impossible for Novell to develop all the needed drivers to assure operation of all valid configurations. For reasons of control, testing, and reliability, we felt it was necessary to ship with the NetWare OS only those drivers which had been developed in house, and require customers to purchase from a third party those non-Novell drivers that were needed to configure their network. Although our intent was to be socially responsible by only shipping software that we could support one hundred percent we inadvertently left our customers in a predicament over which peripheral products to use and which had reliable interfaces to the NetWare OS.

In retrospect we could have and probably should have worked more closely with these vendors. Under nondisclosure we could have given them specifications on NetWare OS revisions before they were released, we could have encouraged vendors to design and test (with IMSP help, if requested) with these specifications in mind, and at first customer ship, we could have the confidence in the drivers to include them as a part of the NetWare OS package we shipped. This would have made it easier for our customers and it would have helped grow the market.

15. In May of 1991, Novell and eleven other vendors announced the Technical Support Alliance (TSA). The TSA, a result of six months of active planning, coordinating, and refining, was established as a means to provide better technical support to our customers. All vendors within the TSA produce hardware or software that runs on or with our NetWare Operating System. The organization is customer-focused and provides technical support for common networking configurations. If a customer encounters a problem with a TSA vendor's product, the customer will try to isolate the problem and call that vendor. One call to a TSA vendor is all that is needed—that vendor will take ownership of the problem and use the TSA resources to expedite the problem resolution. TSA members will confer and resolve the problem rather than the customer having to prove their case to each vendor connected to the network.

Why did we take this step?
This innovative alliance was formed to eliminate frustration by customers and vendors over support problems and to help grow the industry. Customers were frustrated by vendors who said, "That's not our problem. Our product has been tested and it works. Call the other vendors." Vendors who wanted to provide good service to their customers were frustrated by having no established procedure of working with other vendors to resolve a customer concern. The TSA was a bold concept that looked like it would help to resolve these concerns. The cover of a TSA brochure sums up the reasons for the alliance:

> "Sounds like hardware. Let me transfer you."
> "Sounds like software. Let me transfer you."
> "On second thought, let's put our heads together."
> TSA Ends the Multivendor Support Runaround!

The TSA is more than an agreement to resolve customer concerns. It involves Novell trading products with other TSA members so each vendor can have a fully configured network and see first hand how the system interacts with other hardware and software on the network. Having the identical network a customer has is critical to duplicating and resolving the customer problem. Technical support people at each TSA company receive intensive training and yearly refreshers at Novell, and we receive the same training from each of the TSA members. Although this is a tremendous investment and takes a lot of time, it is necessary as any TSA member may receive a call from a customer involving a problem with any TSA product. There is no requirement for TSA members to cross train each other, but Novell is taking a leadership position in establishing the forum, becoming familiar with other vendor's products, and helping other vendors to become familiar with Novell's products. This brings companies closer together to help customers, resulting in an expanding of the industry.

What were the customer sentiments?

Since the TSA was a direct answer to customer frustration, customers were elated that the alliance was formed. Our customers are disappointed with companies who will not become part of the TSA. As of the end of 1992, there were thirty-five member companies and a list of one hundred more companies who would like to become part of the alliance.

Vendors also readily accepted the concept of support alliances, and some other major non-Novell alliances have been established.

How did we deal with those sentiments?

We need to limit TSA membership to those vendors for which we receive a lot of support calls. Because of manpower constraints there is a limited number of members we can accommodate in the TSA. Some companies want to use TSA as a sales tool, but we have to put that issue aside and make membership a matter of support needs. This is difficult for some vendors to understand.

The TSA is a service involving many vendors, not a product of one vendor. As such, it was difficult to deliver full capabilities on the first day of operation. Although the alliance is going very well, there are more supportive and less supportive members of the TSA. We are working to continually enhance the value of the TSA and always provide excellent service to our customers.

What is the customer's perspective now?

Our customers recognize the advantages of the TSA and are experiencing quicker resolution on TSA-related issues. Some of the TSA partners are IBM, NEC, Digital Equipment Corporation, Compaq, Unisys, Hewlett Packard, Intel, Borland, Ungermann-Bass, Lotus, Microsoft, Dell, and Apple. With these vendors and other members of the TSA, we cover a large portion of the network computing industry. Additional members may be added based on service needs.

What worked and what did not work?

One aspect that caught us off guard was the amount of overhead needed to administer the TSA. Even though this is a TSA and not a Novell TSA, there is a tremendous amount of coordination needed to assure its success. We have a full time TSA Program Manager dedicated to making sure the alliance works and is responsive to our customers.

A new TSA member is not authorized until we have a contact at their company, we have trained on their products and them on ours, and we have exchanged products. This practice gives the alliance a much greater chance of success by getting it started on the right foot. We want to do all we can to ensure each link of the chain is as strong as possible.

What would we do differently?

It has been less than one year since the announcement of the TSA, and we have no major concerns. We have future plans for the internationalization of the TSA. We wish we would have trademarked TSA. While we welcome other groups of companies using the TSA concept to provide better, more integrated service to their customers, we would not like to see our TSA "brand name" become generic. We have no control over the operation of other TSA type alliances, yet our TSA name will suffer if the support provided is not on a level with our support.

16. Novell is investigating the submission of an application for the Malcolm Baldrige National Quality Award (MBNQA).

Why did we take this step?

The Malcolm Baldrige National Quality Award is a nation-wide yardstick to measure the quality management of companies. Our ultimate goal is unequaled service to our customers, and the award criteria could point out some of our deficiencies. This award would not be our destination, rather a marker helping us to achieve our destination.

What were the customer sentiments?

Our customers are not aware we are investigating this award. The public has generally looked very favorably on companies that are awarded the MBNQA, however, what customers really want to know is "How will this affect me? Will the award help Novell serve me better? Will Novell be more responsive to my needs?"

The award is valued to Novell only to the extent that working toward it results in noticeable and tangible improvements to our customers.

How did we deal with those sentiments?

We consulted with some former award winners regarding our desire to change for customer improvement, not just to satisfy the requirements of an award. All the winners felt that any changes made were for the betterment of their company not for the benefit of a committee. The Cadillac Motor Car Division of General Motors, a 1990 winner, said there were some suggestions made by the MBNQA examiners that Cadillac could not see the justification for and consequently did not incorporate. It was with that same spirit we wanted to keep our eyes focused on our customers, while assessing progress by whatever measure that can help us; in this case the Malcolm Baldrige National Quality Award. Former award winners recommended an internal self assessment as a first step toward submitting an award application. In January of 1992 Novell conducted an internal questionnaire surveying employee perceptions of the seven Malcolm Baldrige National Quality Award criteria: leadership, information and analysis, strategic quality planning, human resource development and management, management of process quality, quality and operational results, and customer focus and satisfaction.

What is the customer's perspective now?
What worked and what did not work?
What would we do differently?

I cannot speak from a historical perspective on these issues, because we are living them now. The analysis of the survey revealed, as expected, that Novell's performance (as measured by employee perceptions, not MBNQA examiners) could be improved in each of the seven areas measured. Although we bettered the data base score (the average of all other companies that had taken the same survey) in six of the seven areas, we were still shy of the average scores of the MBNQA-winning companies in each category. We will work on improving the deficiencies and investigate further our chances of winning the coveted Malcolm Baldrige National Quality Award.

Frederick W. Smith
Chairman, President, and CEO

Malcolm Baldrige
**National
Quality
Award**
1990
Winner

Federal Express: The MBNQA is Our License to Practice

Since we were awarded the Malcolm Baldrige National Quality Award, I have been asked many times if this means we have now achieved the ultimate level of quality. My answer is that the receipt of this award is simply our "'license to practice." We have recognized since the beginning of this company that the key to our ultimate success would be quality service. What set us apart from the very earliest days was an absolutely zealous approach to quality and customer satisfaction. Customers chose us for that reason in 1973, they choose us for that reason today.

AN EVOLUTION IN SERVICE IMPROVEMENT

Admittedly, in this seventeen-year period our approach to quality has become more sophisticated. The formal quality program was begun as Q=P (quality = productivity) management. As we have grown, it has become crucial to adopt a common language of quality. That is what led us a few years ago to begin training all employees in the concepts of the Quality Improvement Process (QIP). The fact that first-line, customer-contact employees usually have the best sense of what customers really need led us to pursue the concept of Quality Action Teams (QATs). This has enabled us to provide a structure that best utilizes the ideas of every employee, from courier to billing agent to vice president; from secretary to operations manager to senior vice president.

We have also refined our measruement techniques over the years. From the old Hierarchy of Horrors to its descendant the Service Quality Indicators, we have long sought to measure service delivery from the *customer's* point of view. This SQI index has helped us make extraordinary improvements in actual service. And there is no questions that we measure service with a more reliable and more timely process than any of our competitors.

The SQI index has also helped us change our thinking, from looking at service quality as a *percentage* of on-time deliveries, to looking at it as the *actual* number of service failures that occur on a given day. I believe this change in thinking has made a profound difference in our own perceptions of how we are performing, and as a result we have radically improved our delivery of service to the customer.

THE NEXT CHAPTER IN QUALITY MANAGEMENT

I believe that another profound series of improvements lie ahead. One that can use the same principles of QATs, root cause identification, and the other experience gained in improving the SQI. Recently, we achieved our highest recorded daily service level, 99.7 percent. Just as significantly, on that same day we had our lowest cost per package *ever*. Imaging, the very best service and the lowest cost!

Our challenge is to find ways to continue delivering the highest quality service at increasingly lower costs. I believe we can do this and all evidence proves it can be done using these quality management tools.

Recently I was asked what additional incentives could be provided to find these cost savings. I think the incentives we have in place are more than adequate rewards for doing this. The ultimate incentive is to achieve a cost structure that keeps Federal Express competitive throughout the 1990s and into the next century.

I am extremely proud of the thousands of individual efforts that led to our designation as the first service company to receive the Malcolm Baldrige National Quality Award. While there may not be a similar award for reducing costs and operating more efficiently, I think we can all benefit from the effects that continuing quality efforts will have in the competitive arena. Competitively priced services, a continued reputation as the standard for quality service, and improving profitability are ultimately the greatest trophies to acknowledge your determination, enthusiasm, and creativity.

WHY WE APPLIED FOR THE NATIONAL QUALITY AWARD

"Our number one managerial task is to improve the quality of our services. Therefore, not to have competed for the Malcolm Baldrige National Quality Award (MBNQA) would have been to relegate our quality focus to a secondary status," according to Chief Executive Officer Frederick W. Smith.

Applying for the MBNQA is a major undertaking but it is an incredibly valuable experience. The process of completing the 75-page application provided us the opportunity to pinpoint our strengths and weaknesses in the area of quality improvement. Assessing areas that need improvement will help us develop future improvement plans—the biggest benefit gained by applying for the award.

Benefits of winning the MBNQA, in addition to self-assessment, include:
- credibility
- accomplishment
- validation
- leadership
- national recognition of our quality efforts and performance

FEDERAL EXPRESS' APPLICATION PROCESS

The following is a brief overview of how Federal Express approached the Malcolm Baldrige National Quality Award application process. Our winning the Award does not indicate that our approach is the best. Every applicant should determine the best approach for their company.

1. Each of Fed Ex's twelve divisions was asked to complete and evaluate their own quality processes. Every division appointed a team leader for each one of the seven categories of the application. Time frames were set for the completion of the application by each division.
2. The division reports were then submitted to a Malcolm Baldrige task force and merged, with one team leader and one writer for each of the seven categories. In other words, twelve reports for each of the seven categories had to be reduced to less than eight pages in order not to exceed the seventy-five page application limit.
3. After being selected for a site visit, Federal Express brought in consultants to prepare for that step of the application process. The consultants conducted a mock site visit and summarized our strengths and weaknesses.
4. Our employee communications department produced a live television broadcast describing how the site visit would occur and how every work group could prepare for it. Follow-up materials were distributed.
5. Seven trained evaluators and one supervisor from the Department of Commerce visited Federal Express for one week. Some of the evaluators were statistical experts, others were complaint handling experts, and some represented previous Malcolm Baldrige National Quality Award winners.

THE SITE VISIT

The following questions and answers were developed for Federal Express employees in preparation of a site visit by the Malcolm Baldrige National Quality Award examiners.

Q. How does the MBNQA judging process work from the time an application is submitted?
A. After the 75-page application is submitted, it is given to a team of examiners who independently score the application. Next, the applications and comments are given to a senior examiner who's primary role is to develop a consensus score on the application. If the score is low, the application is assigned to one examiner who finalizes the report and provides the company with feedback. If the score is high, the examiners get together in a consensus building process to resolve any differences in scores on the application. Once a consensus score is developed, the scores are compared by nine judges on the board of examiners. Then, the judges decide who warrants a site visit.

Q. What is the purpose of a site visit?
A. Site visits allow companies the opportunity to expand insights and information beyond those described in the application. The visit is designed to verify firsthand, through observation and interviews, the information presented in the application. Examiners verify data, interview employees and inspect facilities. Examiners will

be able to dig a little deeper for clarification. For example, there may be a document referenced in the application, but because of the 75-page limit there might not be as much information provided as they would like to have. During a site visit, examiners have an opportunity to take a look at the documents, ask some questions, verify information and get that little bit more they may need to better understand.

Q. Which locations will be selected? What are the most likely choices?
A. Locations are selected at random. The main determinant in selecting a site is information in the application that may cause them to want to get more information that can be obtained from a visit. A good guess is that they will visit corporate headquarters to talk to executive management, a staff group, a major operation such as a hub or metroplex, and a facility outside of corporate headquarters. Selected sites will be notified three-to-four weeks prior to the scheduled visits.

Q. How long will the visit to each site last?
A. Visits at each site will last three to five days.

Q. What will the examiners be looking for?
A The examiners will want to see how pervasive the quality improvement process is throughout the corporation—deployment needs to be uniform across the corporation. Companies will be expected to have excellent measurement systems in place to provide information and data in support of claims for quality improvement. There should be evidence that there is a prevention-based approach that has come about through some kind of training or education. Other things they may want to see are:
- If a process is being evaluated, what does the analysis look like? What's the data look like?
- Use of some common quality terminology that came about from training/ education.
- How do you/your employees determine if something really is a problem? What did you do to resolve it? Are you fighting fires or making improvements? How do you/they know?

Q. What kind of written documentation or data will the site inspectors want to see?
A. Measures of both internal (service and operations-oriented) and external (customer or supplier-oriented) quality are expected. For external or customer satisfaction data, the examiners may request direct customer input. Typical things that show evidence that there is quality involvement are training materials, policy and procedure manuals, the company's philosophy and mission, etc. All of these materials should be readily accessible.

Q. Who will they want to talk to? What will they want to see? Is there anything they should not see?

A. During the site visits, examiners will talk to management and non-management employees at various locations about quality improvement. They will want to know what process is used for improvement when employees deal with customers. It is highly desirable to get a diagonal slice across divisions and the top of the organization to lower levels. There's a strong possibility that new employees will be interviewed. By interviewing new employees examiners can determine how well a company trains and orients new hires. The answers would be typical of what's experienced by all. Employees should be open and honest and there's nothing that they should not be able to see.

Q. What type of questions will they ask?

A. The examiners will ask employees generic questions regardless of where they are located in the company or the job they hold. Examples of questions that may be asked:

- To what degree are you involved in the quality process?
- How do you spend your time?
- How much time do you spend making improvements?
- What education and training have you received? Are you using it? To what degree?
- How does your improvement effort relate to others in your work group?
- How do you manage that interface?
- Do you feel empowered to make decisions beyond current service standards in the interest of customer satisfaction?
- To what degree do you feel you can suggest improvements to management? Are your suggestions acted upon?

Q. Will management and non-management interviews be different?

A. Questions for managers may be a little more expansive regarding the areas they manage but they will not be much different than what non-management employees will be asked. The examiners should be introduced to each area by management.

Q. Does management need to prepare formal presentations with slides and overheads for the visits?

A. No. The assumption is that the information requested will be readily available if it exists.

Q. Will employees be asked to stop working at random? Or, will managers be able to schedule time off for the employees?

A The examiners will get together and propose an agenda to the management in the quality improvement department. The preference will be to talk to employees while they are on break, this allows more flexibility. Impromptu interviews are desired. For time sensitive positions like couriers or customer service agents, they may pre-schedule someone off work or sit next to a courier in a van or customer service agent at a phone station.

Q. Are they going to monitor customer calls?
A. Maybe. If they chose to do so, more than likely this will be scheduled. Here, they will want to know what is the process used for improvement when employees are dealing with customers.

Q. Are they going to want to observe job functions or see teams in progress?
A. They will observe employees working. Also, they will be interested in the degree to which people are involved individually in quality improvement as well as in quality action teams and what the teams are working on. It should be noted that the examiners will not expect all employees interviewed to be on a team. There's a number of ways people can be involved in quality improvement without having to be on a formal team—and this will be looked at.

Q. How many people will be in the visit and who are they?
A. There will be four to six people visiting the sites—two or more examiners, one senior examiner, and an observer from the National Institute of Standards and Technology. The Board of Examiners are made up of experts from various fields who were certified in three different categories (judge, examiner, senior examiner) based upon their qualifications and degree of experience.

Q. Will we get feedback from the visit? If so, to what extent?
A. All applicants receive a written report from the board of examiners giving them feedback on how their applications were scored, including information about their standing relative to other applicants. Additionally, the examiners comment about each applicant's strengths and weaknesses. Like the written application, the feedback reports are treated confidentially.

FIVE POINT STRATEGY
CEO Frederick W. Smith's five-point strategy for achieving our number one objective—improving the quality of service we offer—is listed below.

1. Use the quality improvement process to improve service levels to 100 percent and lower our costs at the same time—in short, Q=P (quality equals productivity) management.
2. Use information and information systems as strategic weapons to achieve Q=P goals.
3. Recognize that Federal Express must become a truly global company.
4. Get closer to our customers.
5. Continue to emphasize our people-first philosophy by investing in our employees.

Federal Express' criteria for improving quality:
1. Establish clear quality goals;
2. Measure accurately what we are doing;
3. Identify the critical points in the value chain—such as final sort points—and manage flawlessly;
4. Demonstrate discipline in our operations; and,
5. Provide immediate and accurate feedback to our employees.

QUALITY IMPROVEMENT AT FEDERAL EXPRESS

Although Federal Express is the acknowledged leader in the express transportation industry and the quality of our service has yet to be matched, a formal quality improvement process (QIP) has been implemented throughout the entire corporation to continue meeting the needs of our customers. The objectives of the QIP are:

- to achieve a 100 percent service level;
- increase profits; and,
- make Federal Express a better place to work by focusing everyone's attention on doing right things right and catching and fixing problems when they happen.

Our corporate mission supports the philosophy that Quality must be a part of the way we do business. Themes such as "Do it right the first time," "Make the first time you do it the only time anyone has to," "Fedexcellence" and "Q=P" have always been a part of our culture. Even our People/Service/Profit philosophy is an expression of our commitment to quality. Now, in light of intense competition and expansion into global markets, quality must become more than a slogan at Federal Express—it must become the normal way of life.

Experts say that in an organization committed to quality as a way of life, the following three things happen.

- The level of customer satisfaction increases and satisfied customers bring more business which ensures the financial health of the corporation and continued job security for us.
- Profits increase because time and money are not wasted correcting mistakes.
- The quality of work life is improved because we have fewer customer complaints, less hassle, and less rework to deal with.

Quality improvement means meeting the needs of our internal and external customers. While it is easy to recognize the ultimate customer, we also must recognize that we have many customer-supplier relationships with other Federal Express employees. Quality improvement activities are critical to the continued success of Federal Express. Constantly striving to improve the system and finding better ways of doing things will make it possible for us to keep our leadership position in the industry as we move into the global marketplace. The competition will continue to get tougher and customers will continue to demand the best quality of service available for the price they pay. We must meet all of these challenges and do so better than anyone else can.

DOING RIGHT THINGS RIGHT

Quality means doing right things right. We have to look at our work from two perspectives: What we do and how we do it.

It is possible to do the right thing the wrong way and it's also possible to do the wrong thing in the right way. Whenever we do not Do Right Things Right we are wasting money and resources that could be used in other, more productive ways.

1-10-100 RULE

The 1-10-100 rule shows that if a problem is not fixed when it happens, it will only become more expensive to fix later. If a problem is caught and fixed as soon as it occurs, the cost is one dollar or one hour. If the mistake is caught downstream in another department or location, it may cost 10 times as much to fix. If the customer catches the mistake or is impacted by it, it can cost 100 times as much to fix.

CONTINUOUS IMPROVEMENT

Quality improvement requires us to continuously develop ways to do better work. Continuous improvement means "Fix it now!," "Prevent problems before they happen," and "Look for new ways to meet customer needs." The theory of If it ain't broke, don't fix it" has no place in a quality organization. Instead, our approach needs to be *"If it ain't broke, improve it."*

SATISFYING OUR INTERNAL AND EXTERNAL CUSTOMERS

Quality begins and ends with the customer. The customer tells us what the right thing to do is and then we have to find the right way to do it. As the supplier of a service, Federal Express is famous for doing whatever it takes to satisfy the customer. We all recognize who the ultimate customers are and know how important it is to meet their needs. However, we also need to recognize and meet the needs of our internal customers—other Federal Express employees with whom we exchange information, products, and services every day. All of us have people who depend on us for products or services to do their jobs and each of us depends on services or products from others in order to do our jobs.

To make the work process flow smoothly and deliver a quality product to our external customers, we need to build positive working relationships with our internal customers. We can accomplish this by asking them three questions:
- What do you need from me?
- What do you do with what I give you?
- Are there any gaps between what I give you and what you need?

The answers to these questions are the key to doing right things right.

QUALITY ACTION TEAMS

In a quality organization everyone, not just management, must be committed to improving both quality and productivity. Everyone must share responsibility for achieving corporate goals. Quality Action Teams (QATs) get employees involved in designing the work process for maximum quality at minimum cost. Teams are generally more effective than individuals in solving problems or improving the way things are done.

MEASUREMENT SYSTEMS

Our service standard is 100 percent customer satisfaction. Our Service Quality Indicators (SQI Index), which measures in absolute numbers, tells us where we are in achieving this goal.

SERVICE QUALITY INDICATORS (SQI)

Federal Express established the Service Quality Indicators (SQI) to determine what the main areas of the customers' perception of service are and how we are meeting them. *The purpose of the SQI to identify and eliminate causes, not to place blame.*

The SQI has twelve components weighted to reflect the customers' view of our performance by placing greater weight on those SQI categories that have the greatest impact on the customers' perception of service received. The number of average daily failure points for each component is calculated by multiplying the number of daily occurrences for that component by its assigned importance weight. Factors such as abandoned calls are included in order to measure internal performance that can significantly affect external customer service. SQI categories are expanded and adjusted, as necessary.

The SQI is the sum of the average daily failure points for all twelve components and is tracked and reported on a weekly basis with monthly summaries.

The service goal will always be 100 percent failure-free performance with the emphasis on finding the root causes of failure and implementing solutions which *prevent* the failures rather than simply fix the consequences of failures. For example, if courier mislabeled packages are a major cause of wrong day late failures, the SQI team would focus on creating effective new solutions to prevent courier miscoding at the source, rather than perfecting the expensive expediting system. Effective quality improvement programs and teamwork such as this are essential to achieving the SQI goal. Knowing what makes a customer unhappy is important, but it is even more important to understand it and solve it through a concerted effort by several areas. Goal congruence, improved methods, contingency plans, and teamwork are vital parts of the total commitment to service.

Our measurable people goal is the continuous improvement of our management leadership index score, which we track through our annual Survey-Feedback-Action (SFA) program.

SURVEY-FEEDBACK-ACTION PROGRAM

From the beginning Federal Express has lived by a corporate philosophy People-Service-Profit. We measure continuous leadership improvement with one of our most effective quality program tools which is the SFA or Survey-Feedback-Action program. The SFA program is comprised of the following:

1. Survey: An anonymous survey completed by all employees.
2. Feedback: A feedback session in which the employees in each work group use quality improvement techniques to identify solutions to problems identified in the survey.
3. Action: An action plan which may serve as an ongoing quality improvement plan for the people issues identified by the work group during the feedback session.

The survey instrument consists of a set of carefully developed questions about leadership (both corporate and local management), about the employee's identification with Federal Express, about reward systems, about work group cooperation, and about job conditions. Survey results are provided as part of the continuous improvement process within Federal Express. Employees completing the survey are ensured individual anonymity. A representative of the personnel division administers the survey and forwards the completed surveys to the human resource analysis department. Survey are analyzed electronically and work group or composite results are provided to the manager. This report provides the basis for discussion for the work group during the feedback session. For work groups with fewer than three members, work group results are not provided. After each survey, managers must meet with their staff, as a group, within six weeks after survey results are distributed to discuss any problems identified, and are required to come up with a plan of action to resolve them. Survey results tell us where our leadership's strengths and weaknesses lie. Every year, SFA is used to diagnose corporate-wide leadership improvements needed.

The action phase of our annual employee attitude survey is a vital tool for helping managers surface potential work group problems. Some of these action plans have resulted in programs that have been implemented company wide. For example, we added a professional incentive compensation to our established management incentive program and a performance improvement program was initiated.

We have found that in an open environment, people are more apt to take part, offer suggestions for improvement, question decisions, and express concerns. The Guaranteed Fair Treatment Procedure (GFT), our in-house avenue for alarming grievances, is one way we listen to our people. Every week the CEO, Executive VP, Chief Personnel Officer and two senior vice presidents, on a rotating basis, review grievances under Step 3 of the GFTP.

GUARANTEED FAIR TREATMENT PROCEDURE

The Guaranteed Fair Treatment Procedure affirms your right to appeal any eligible issue through a process of systematic review by progressively higher levels of management. Though the outcome is not assured to be in your favor, your right to participate within the guidelines of the process is guaranteed.

The Guaranteed Fair Treatment procedure is a three-step process which requires specific actions to be performed by specific individuals within a designated time. The steps are identified as follows:

1. Management Review
   - Complainant
     - Submits written complaint to a member of management (manager, senior manager, or managing director) within seven calendar days of occurrence of the eligible issue.

   - Manager, senior manager and managing director
     - Review all relevant information
     - Hold a telephone conference and meeting with the complainant
     - Make decision to either uphold, modify, or overturn management's action
     - Communicate their decision in writing to complainant and personnel matrix

2. Officer Review
   - Complainant
     - Submits written complaint to an officer (vice president or senior vice president) of the division within seven calendar days of Step 1 decision.

   - Vice president and senior vice president
     - Review all relevant information
     - Conduct additional investigation, when necessary
     - Make decision to either uphold, overturn, modify management's action, or initiate a board of review
     - Communicate their decision in writing to complainant with copy to personnel matrix and the complainant's management

3. Executive Review
   - Complainant
     - Submits written complaint within seven calendar days of the Step 2 decision to the employee relations department who investigates and prepares the GFTP case file for appeals board review.

   - Appeals board
     - Reviews all relevant information
     - Makes decision to either uphold, overturn or initiate a board of review, or take other appropriate action
     - Responds in writing to complainant within three calendar days of the decision with copy to personnel matrix and the complainant's chain of command.

SUMMARY

Quality improvement activities are critical to the continued success of Federal Express. The competition will continue to get tougher and the customer will continue to demand the best quality of service available for the prices paid. We must meet all of these challenges and do so better than anyone else can.

The objectives of the quality improvement process are to achieve 100 percent service level, increase profits, and make Federal Express a better place to work by focusing everyone's attention on doing right things right and fixing problems when they happen.

Quality improvement means meeting the needs of our internal and external customers. While it is easy to recognize the external customer, we must also recognize that we have many customer-supplier relationships with other Federal Express employees. Constantly striving to improve the system and finding better ways of doing things will make it possible for us to keep our leadership position in the industry as we move into the global marketplace.

Carmen Hegge-Kleiser
Vice President, Human Resources

American Express Travel Related Services: A Human Resources Approach to Managing Quality

In a service company, the quality of service and customer satisfaction are directly linked to the quality of employees and their satisfaction. Travelers Check Group's (TCG) total quality approach is based on three quality ordinals:

1. Prevention-based work processes and data systems, with identifiable standards, targets and continually improving results;
2. Commitment to participatively manage, train and reinforce its employees, who are empowered to improve service, improve systems, and stop errors before they happen;
3. Commitment to customer satisfaction, backed by a leadership which allocates the time and resources to shape the integration of processes and people to deliver the best products and services.

In the TCG, it is our people, through their daily actions, who have enabled us to achieve the product and service quality leadership we enjoy today. Since 1983, accuracy of telephone service in our claims processing group has increased from 69.9 percent to 99.7 percent and accuracy of encashment assistance service has increased from 76.2 percent to 99.9 percent. Not coincidentally, within that same time period, employee turnover in our operating center which accounts for over 80 percent of our employees decreased from 24 percent to under 9 percent while employee perception about the company increased from 68 percent favorable to 85 percent favorable.

We achieved these results by instituting a human resource strategy of Becoming the Best Place to Work. It embodies the fundamental concepts of the TCG quality ordinals by:

- treating employees as customers;
- using employee input and a fact-based approach for decision-making in the design and implementation of human resources policies, programs, and processes;

- measuring employee satisfaction and trying to continuously improve the workplace environment; and
- benchmarking and incorporating best practices.

Becoming the best place to work is not a one time human resources program or a catchy slogan. Rather, it's an on-going long-term business strategy for the creation of programs and processes designed to raise employee satisfaction. To achieve this strategy, TCG developed an integrated employee survey program to monitor the health of the employee franchise by assessing organizational performance in terms of living the values (values index), increasing employee satisfaction (satisfaction index) and achieving a total quality culture (quality index). The makeup of each survey is illustrated in Figure 1.

VALUES INDEX	SATISFACTION INDEX	QUALITY INDEX
Core Survey 11 questions	**Core Survey** 25 questions (TBD)*	**Core Survey** 12 questions
Full Survey 83 questions	**Full Survey** 65 questions	**Full Survey** 47 questions
• 10 dimensions • 3 longitudinal data points	• 13 dimensions • 4 longitudinal data points	• 6 dimensions • 1 data point
1989 1991 1992	1984 1986 1990 1992	1992
*Will be finalized based on correlation analysis.		

Figure 1. Makeup of the Employee Survey Program.

SATISFACTION INDEX

In 1984, a traditional employee attitude survey consisting of over 150 questions grouped into 16 dimensions was developed. The vendor selected to design and process the survey also provided access to a normative data base of world class companies with a strong representation of financial services organizations.

The survey has been refined and administered to all TCG employees every two years since 1984 except in 1988 when American Express introduced the values survey. The response rate to the survey has consistently exceeded 80 percent. Until 1990, only financial industry normative comparisons were used. Since TCG's results matched the norm in all categories and significantly exceeded it in half the categories, in 1990 a high performance norm was developed with the vendor which included companies with superior financial performance and employee satisfaction scores, regardless of industry. To ensure that the survey addresses the topics of greatest interest to TCG employees, employee focus groups are conducted and the survey tested with a pilot group before each administration.

Over the years, the survey has been condensed and the dimensions consolidated. The percentage of questions linked to high performance norms has also increased from 44 percent to 92 percent. The TCG standard is to score in the 75th percentile for each dimension compared with other companies in the high performance norm. This has been incorporated into the TCG long-term strategic plan.

VALUES INDEX

While employee satisfaction is important, having a consensus as to the values of the organization and living those values is equally important to realizing the vision of becoming the best place to work. For more than a century, quality has been imbedded in the company culture. Like many other progressive companies, American Express over the years had also valued the importance of the customer, employee, and community. In 1988 when the financial services industry was undergoing tremendous change and ethical issues within the industry were front page headlines, American Express through a series of focus groups with employees and interviews with senior management developed a values survey.

However, the company went beyond just issuing the traditional values statement. It utilized employee input to identify the behaviors associated with living these values. In other words, what are the daily behaviors that either reinforce or undermine the values of the desired organizational culture? The employees were then asked to indicate their satisfaction level with these behaviors and the degree of change they felt was needed to fully realize the values. The organizational values survey results then became another measure or index of TCG's efforts in becoming the best place to work, and senior management's compensation was tied to improving the results. The values survey consisted of eighty three questions grouped into the following ten dimensions:

- quality
- customers
- integrity
- people
- teamwork

- management
- meritocracy
- overall satisfaction
- career development and job satisfaction
- citizenship

It has been administered within the TCG on an alternating year basis since 1989. The eleven core questions which correlated highest with the overall dimension results from the values survey were incorporated with the full satisfaction survey administered in 1992 to provide an annual values indicator. Since normative comparisons are not applicable for this type of survey, TCG management has set a standard of no less than 65 percent favorable for every value dimension. This standard has been incorporated into management's individual goals and the TCG long range strategic plan. After three years, each value dimension's favorable score has increased from 6-16 percent to the point where four value dimensions have favorable scores between 60-70 percent, two dimensions have scores in excess of 70 percent favorable and no dimension has less than 55 percent favorable. These results were achieved in the midst of an economic downturn and organizational restructuring.

The individual leadership of senior management in living and supporting the values is critical to our overall quality effort. When reviewing organizational values data, management can find it tempting to view areas with low scores as someone else's issue. To increase senior management's awareness of their behavior and personal contribution to the organization's overall values survey results, an individual leadership survey was developed to be completed by peers and subordinates. As illustrated in Figure 2, individual behaviors have been identified for each value.

Starting at the very top of the organization, every level of executive from presidents to directors is required to survey their peers and staff, receive confidential aggregate feedback, attend a training session to improve their leadership skills and implement a personal action plan addressing areas for improvement. By 1992, the TCG president and vice presidents had been through two feedback cycles, the directors had completed one cycle, and the managers were just starting the process. To further reinforce the learning process, the president helped teach the leadership course to the directors and the vice presidents serve as faculty for the leadership course for the managers. While external feedback counselors were used and an individual's data was processed by an external vendor, aggregate TCG data by level was collected and shared with participants so they could see how their top ten and bottom ten scores compared with the aggregate scores of their peer group and more senior levels of management. This aggregate data was also used by the TCG human resources staff for organizational development purposes and in identifying training needs for specific skill areas, e.g., coaching, empowering, giving feedback.

While the upward feedback from the values survey is *not* incorporated into the appraisal process, the recipient is required to share his or her areas for improvement and action plan with his or her manager.

QUALITY INDEX

When TCG applied for the Baldrige Award in 1991, it developed its own survey to assess employee knowledge of quality concepts and understanding of quality tools within the organization. While the survey provided a rudimentary internal evaluation of the quality communications and training effort, it did not afford comparison with other companies. Management wanted to chart its progress in

- **Clients**
  Strives to maintain a competitive advantage
  Ensures honest reporting of business data. (i.e., projections, results and measures)
  Is willing to incur short-term costs to achieve long-term profitability
  Keeps crises and setbacks from interfering with strategic focus
  Deals with customer concerns in a timely manner
  Encourages and acts on suggestions for increasing profitability
  Is more committed to the customers' long-term satisfaction than short-term results
  Makes realistic commitments to customers (avoids over-committing)
  Encourages and listens to input from customers (rather than assuming a knowledge of their needs)
  Takes personal responsibility for achieving customer satisfaction

- **Quality**
  Treats quality as top priority
  Effectively balances work load demands and quality performance
  Presents self in an effective and persuasive manner
  Has a command of the technical/functional skills needed to do the job
  Is looked to for effective thought leadership
  Balances profitability and people issues
  Avoids compromising quality standards
  Makes it clear that quality is everyone's work
  Dedicates sufficient energy to the job
  Is more concerned with identifying causes of mistakes than assessing blame
  Focuses on continuous quality improvement
  Assumes personal responsibility for the achievement of quality
  Is willing to rock the boat in trying new ideas performance
  Recognizes and rewards creativity and innovation
  Clearly communicates quality standards

- **Integrity**
  Confronts and deals with integrity problems
  Knows which decisions to make and acts on them appropriately
  Levels with people on what is not negotiable
  Allows you to stand up for what you believe
  Gives others appropriate credit for accomplishments
  Is a role model for the values of the company
  Demonstrates honest, ethical behavior in business transactions
  Challenges higher management when appropriate (stands up for beliefs)
  Practices what he/she preaches
  Admits mistakes readily
  Lets others know where they stand (no hidden agendas)
  Shows a high degree of personal integrity in dealing with others

- **People**
  Demonstrates commitment to the development of others
  Gives people the freedom they need to do their job well
  Encourages others to take as much responsibility as they can handle
  Involves people in decisions which affect their work
  Demonstrates the best way to do the task
  Effectively deals with performance problems
  Avoids talking down to others
  Manages change in an effective manner
  Has the respect of direct reports
  Provides effective orientation to people on new tasks
  Provides effective coaching when needed
  Provides regular developmental feedback and coaching
  Asks people what they need to do their job better
  Allows mistakes
  Demonstrates effective interpersonal skill
  Supports people of all backgrounds to reach their full potential (regardless of race, sex, etc.)
  Helps people work towards their long term career goals
  Supports employees' attendance at training programs
  Has the respect of peers and superiors
  Consistently treats people with respect and dignity
  Demonstrates an appropriate sense of humor
  Rewards and recognizes excellent performance
  Gives clear and specific directions
  Conducts fair, objective performance reviews

- **Teamwork**
  Treats others in the company as colleagues, not competitors
  Encourages the communication of bad news
  Proactively supports One Enterprise goals
  Works to eliminate unnecessary expense
  Encourages and accepts constructive criticism (responds to upward feedback)
  Avoids sarcasm and cynicism about work or the organization
  Takes risks in letting others make decisions
  Discourages destructive comments about others
  Removes barriers to improved teamwork
  Collaborates with people in setting objectives and plans
  Encourages two way communication about roles and responsibilities
  Sets clear goals and objectives with individuals
  Encourages individuals to work together as a team
  Avoids playing favorites
  Supports agreed-upon decisions
  Communicates and supports the company's mission

- **Good Citizenship**
  Represents American Express in a positive manner when dealing with external constituencies
  Recognizes others for their involvement in community affairs
  Actively works to help the community
  Demonstrates a personal concern for the betterment of the community

Figure 2. Desired leadership behavior.

becoming a world class total quality company from the viewpoint of its employees and be able to compare this with similar data from other companies. To achieve this goal, TCG developed a Quality Survey with the assistance of an external vendor. The survey consists of forty-seven questions grouped into the following six dimensions:

- commitment to quality
- quality training
- measurement of quality
- communication of quality
- evaluating quality
- employee involvement

The normative data base for this survey is being built. The first survey was administered in 1992. The results coupled with periodic assessments utilizing Baldrige criteria will be used to improve and advance TCG's Quality Plan.

DEMOGRAPHIC TRENDS

In addition to the three indices of the health of the employee franchise, TCG is continuously monitoring the demographic profile of its work force as well as demographic trends in the external labor pool.

In 1986, American Express conducted an internal work force profile survey followed by a work and family survey in 1989. These surveys were designed to assess the impact of child care, elder care and work and family demands on our employees. The data was used to identify areas of need. In addition, the activities of other progressive companies in responding to similar needs was benchmarked. Based on these findings, a series of highly successful initiatives were launched including the following:

- an expanded employee assistance program
- a childcare resource and referral service
- adoption assistance
- health care and dependent care reimbursement plans
- family leave
- family sick days
- kids cheque, a child care subsidy program
- family cheque, a dependent care subsidy program
- flexible returns
- sabbaticals
- improved part-time employee benefits
- spousal job search assistance as part of relocation
- workplace flexibility initiatives including job-sharing, flexplace, flextime scheduling
- flexible benefits

Employee reaction to these programs within TCG has been very favorable.

LESSONS LEARNED

Over the years of utilizing this fact-based approach to becoming the best place to work, the following lessons have been learned:

- Define the most critical factors driving survey results using representative employee focus groups. Total quality management problem solving techniques such as Pareto analysis, root cause analysis, and force field analysis are essential in this process and should be understood by employees and used in discussing potential action plans.

- Refine and cross validate results for key employee segments by correlating values surveys with full census attitude surveys. There is a strong link between the two even though they are targeting different types of data.

- With employee input, brainstorm action plan to respond to critical, causal factors. Implement highest impact items with greatest halo effect, e.g., communication issues also impact management and integrity categories. If you don't focus on critical, causal factors, you can have a lot of activity, but little progress.

- Stagger implementation over a period of time. Better to have a sustained effort with series of small, but meaningful actions than a one-time big program launch immediately after the survey that is forgotten by the next survey. Also understand the key segments of your employee population and how their needs differ. Career development issues, for example, are different for managers and associates (non-exempt). The sequence of actions can also send important signals.

- Little things make a difference. For example, a PC benefits planner on a local area network had minimal cost, but tremendous positive impact in introducing flexible benefits, because each employee could input their own scenarios and get a printed summary to use in making the best choice.

- Give the greatest share of voice in survey communications to actions not plans. Position every action as a response to the survey and a step toward becoming the best place to work. This should be specifically stated and not taken for granted.

- Have immediate, quantitative employee evaluation of every action. Publicly celebrate successes. Correct mistakes. Measure progress. This increases employee involvement and emphasizes that improvement, not perfection, is the goal.

- The business or function head must personally take responsibility and provide leadership. The entire organization evaluates the level of commitment by the leader's actions.

- Position employee satisfaction as a business issue on par with customer satisfaction, not a human resources issue. Make it part of the business operating plan and require each function to support the best place to work strategy.

- Make the entire management team personally accountable for improving results—at least twenty to twenty-five percent of the goal rating of each VP and director should be based on employee satisfaction.

- Make employees accountable for part of the solution as well as management, e.g., career development.
- Give an annual report of action steps taken since the last survey.

Finally, it is important to understand that as an organization evolves in its utilization of employee surveys to design and deliver employee programs, employee expectations rise. An activity that was viewed as a breakthrough in response to this year's survey becomes the perceived standard that has to be exceeded for incremental improvements in the next survey.

By understanding the linkage of employee satisfaction to customer satisfaction and actively tracking and continuously improving both dimensions, a service company can achieve an unassailable quality advantage.

Rob Davis
Vice President and Chief Quality Officer

AT&T Universal Card Services: The Center of the Universe

Walk into the lobby of AT&T Universal Card Services' (UCS) headquarters in Jacksonville, Florida, and you will see these words engraved on the wall: "Customers Are the Center of Our Universe." The words set the tone for everything that happens at UCS; they summarize a philosophy that drives our business.

At UCS, Paul Kahn, President and Chief Executive Officer, and his team had the unique opportunity to build a credit-card operation from scratch. Kahn brought to that endeavor a vision of consistent, world-class customer service and value, achieved through long-term investment in our customers, people, and technologies.

Kahn had very definite ideas on how the ideal credit-card company would operate. He was convinced that there was room in the business to give something back to the customer. This commitment to customers and value resulted in a charter membership that included:

- variable interest rates linked to the prime rate[1]
- no annual fee (free for life, as long as the cardmember used the card at least once a year)
- an unconditional service guarantee
- customer service available 24 hours a day, seven days a week, from anywhere in the world
- commitment to act as customers' advocate in billing disputes, which are handled quickly and efficiently, by phone[2]
- combination credit card and calling card, with a 10 percent discount on calls

---

1. Having the annual percentage rate tied to the prime rate resulted in four drops in interest rate in one twelve-month period in 1991-1992.

2. When one customer called UCS' executive response center to complain that a Caribbean hotel had put $200 in unauthorized charges on his bill and had refused to remove them, Gretchen Cuyler, who took the call, got in touch with the hotel and its headquarters organization (it was part of a chain). When she had finished her work, the $200 in unauthorized charges had been deducted from the customer's bill, and she had negotiated with the hotel to give the customer a free vacation to compensate for his inconvenience.

- standard cards with the same features usually associated with gold cards
- applications completed over the phone in less than four minutes

Building on our AT&T heritage, UCS established its business with the express purpose of becoming the standard for world-class service.

To measure their progress, Kahn and his team members personally participated in the creation of a long-term executive incentive plan unique among Fortune 500 companies. The plan is based on the results of UCS' quality management and customer delight efforts, as well as financial results.

BEGIN AT THE BEGINNING

Before launching the AT&T Universal Card, quality values were established to guide the business. To bring to life the vision and the company values for all associates, UCS created a special threshold experience for associates called Passport to Excellence. One of UCS's vice presidents attends every session to emphasize quality values, answer questions, and listen to associate concerns.

One year after launch at the annual strategic quality planning session, the corporate values were redefined based on suggestions made by associates. Those values, which form the framework for empowering associates to respond to customer needs, are:

- Customer delight: delight our customers by exceeding their expectations.
- Teamwork: teams make things happen when everyone's voice is heard.
- Mutual respect: everyone at UCS deserves to be treated with dignity.
- Commitment: UCS people will deliver what they promise to each other and to customers.
- Continuous improvement: each day, we should seek to get a little bit better since small improvements, added up, bring us closer to our goals.
- Sense of urgency: we will move quickly to accomplish our goals, meet our commitments, and delight our customers.
- Trust and integrity: we will trust one another to accomplish what we say we will accomplish. We will conduct ourselves—in dealings with customers and colleagues—with integrity always.

A comprehensive communications plan was developed and executed to bring these values to life. As a part of this plan, business leaders met with their associates to discuss the values. Our public relations team ran special articles in UCS' internal publications and created a values logo that was used on posters, tent cards, lapel pins, wallet cards, and T-shirts. The posters and tent-cards are displayed in all buildings, in the cafeteria, and in conference rooms. The UCS values are the basis of many of our recognition programs. These values are fundamental to UCS and today are well entrenched in the fiber of the business.

IT STARTS AT THE TOP

The direction, the character, and what might be called the personality of any organization is set at the top. Independently and collectively, Paul Kahn and his team members use cross-functional forums to review quality plans and performance. For example:

- Every day, Fred Winkler, Executive Vice President-Customer Services, and Bob Golitz, Senior Vice President and Chief Information Officer, lead reviews of the previous day's quality results in their areas of responsibility. Key suppliers attend these daily meetings, and with UCS managers, they focus on quality performance trends and corrective actions.
- Monthly, Alan Schultheis, Executive Vice President-Marketing, leads a similar review for the program management process, the process we use to develop and introduce new programs and products.
- In their bi-weekly meetings, Kahn and his team regularly review UCS quality results.
- The business leaders invest a day each month analyzing and acting on quality results including:
    - customer-satisfaction surveys
    - customer-contact surveys
    - customer-attrition results
    - key measurements
    - program-management process
    - Ten Most Wanted quality improvements (a list that is constantly revised)
    - daily process measurements
    - customer behavior
    - associate-opinion surveys
    - supplier performance
    - key initiatives

Rewards and recognition are a crucial part of our quality drive, and business leaders personally present many of the awards that motivate associates to strive for excellence, such as

- Associate of the Month
- Service Excellence Award
- Team awards; the business team recognizes the accomplishments of continuous improvement teams, and the teams make presentations on their work.
- The President's Circle Award; Kahn selects and recognizes three percent of the associate body who exemplify the UCS values. This is UCS' most prestigious award; winners are recognized before their peers and receive a trip hosted by business leaders. A smaller group chosen from the winners serves as a board of advisors, meeting with Kahn and his team throughout the year following their selection.

OUTSIDE INTEREST

AT&T Universal Card Services efforts to build quality values into a high-growth organization have attracted interest outside the company. Representatives from a number of organizations have visited our headquarters, including: Federal Express, Milliken, IBM, Johnson & Johnson, First Union Bank, Marriott Hotels,

Xerox, Mayo Clinic, and Barnett Banks. We encourage visitors to share their viewpoint with us; to facilitate an exchange of ideas, UCS established the Universal Quality Forum. The Forum encourages other businesses to learn about quality and customer focus at UCS and to share what works in their own businesses.

MANAGING FOR QUALITY

The quality focus at UCS is based on the Baldrige template. That is not unique—many companies have found the Baldrige guidelines highly effective. UCS is unusual, however, in that we did not impose a quality process on a functioning organization but, rather, built it in from inception.

Our quality process includes a strong focus on customers coupled with extensive use of measurements and an emphasis on continuous improvement. The plan aligns individual and team efforts with the strategic direction of the company (see Figure 1).

We use the Baldrige criteria to evaluate our total quality management (TQM) system with an eye on continuous improvement. In the past two years, we have conducted three Baldrige self-assessments. The most recent assessment identified more than 100 gaps; each of those gaps was assigned to an owner with a (high, medium, or low) priority and a time frame for action.

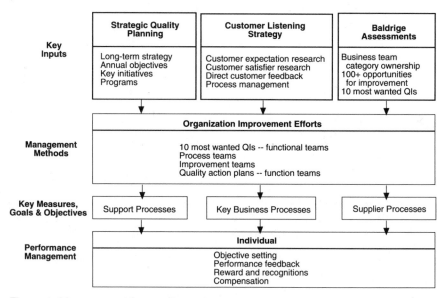

Figure 1. Management for quality system.

The business has designated the ten gaps with the highest priority as the business's Ten Most Wanted quality improvements list. These are worked with a sense of urgency. In addition, each functional area has a Ten Most Wanted quality improvement list. Each item on the lists has an owner and, if necessary, an improvement team that includes associates from all levels. As improvements are implemented, those items are eliminated from the list in a celebration ceremony, and other items take their place. There are specific criteria for selecting the items that go on these lists, such as customer impact and cycle-time reduction.

THE CUSTOMER IS ALWAYS RIGHT

Since the customer is the center of our universe, our measurements are designed to determine if our customers are receiving the quality service they want and we promise to deliver.

Our strategy for building and maintaining relationships with customers is based on:
• determining the requirements and expectations of customers.
• formulating and modifying our products and services based on the requirements and expectations we identify; and
• evaluating and improving the business processes that affect customers.

UCS' strategy is illustrated in Figure 2 and includes four key customer listening categories:
• customer expectation and needs research
• performance research
• direct customer feedback
• process management

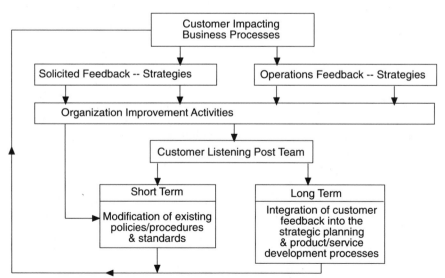

Figure 2. Customer relationship management strategies.

A cross-functional team—the Customer Listening Post Team—aggregates the customer data and uses it as the basis for decisions. This team meets every month and addresses existing policy and procedural matters that affect customers and long-term strategic-planning efforts. This keeps the customer at the center of our universe.

DETERMINING CUSTOMER DELIGHT

Customers' needs and expectations are dynamic, so in January 1991, we initiated an on-going research program that provides insight into factors that determine customer delight, account retention, and use. Our customers have identified 8 primary, 18 secondary, and more than 100 tertiary satisfiers.

These factors are central to the management of our customer relationships; to help us understand them, we've developed a customer-value tree. As we examine the branches of the tree, we are able to identify what drives the quality of a contact between a customer and one of our customer-contact associates.

Through telephone interviews with 200 UCS customers and 400 competitors' (prospective) customers each month, we obtain ratings on a scale of 1 to 10 that allows us to detect shifts in customer perception of UCS and our competitors. Data has also been accumulated from more than forty focus groups and from analyzing customer commendations and complaints.

We also survey our customers every month to gauge their perceptions of our service delivery processes. These event-specific surveys assess the performance of our customer contact associates and include competitive comparisons. Currently we conduct over 4000 surveys every month which provide actionable data for fourteen different customer contact points.

This customer feedback is enhanced by internal measures. We collect and analyze the results of more than 100 daily measurements, which are linked directly to our customer satisfiers; the results are shared with our customer-contact associates.

THE PEOPLE WHO MAKE IT HAPPEN

Quality: Take it Personally is more than a catch phrase at UCS. Our associates do take quality personally; they have been hired and trained—and are rewarded—to do just that.

Following an orientation workshop attended by all new hires, telephone customer-contact associates attend an eight-week training program with two facets—emphasis on customer delight and proficiency training on the equipment they will use.

A specific career path for customer service associates intensifies the focus on customers. The career path offers guidance and development opportunities for telephone associates. UCS offers training that complements this process. Customer-contact associates develop proficiency in a variety of job assignments and are rewarded through certification that leads to a higher-level position within the career path.

THE UCS COMMITMENT TO CUSTOMERS

The UCS commitment to providing customers with the greatest value is embodied in the fundamentals of our offering. Features of our product—our free for life offer and the card's variable interest rate and calling card discounts—reflect our commitment to the customer.

Another important commitment is our explicit Service Quality Warranty which represents a unique commitment to the needs of our customers. Our customers can expect UCS to

- treat them as trustworthy and respected individuals.
- regard their problems as legitimate and their point of view as valuable.
- provide 100 percent error-free service.
- be available when they need us. Our service staff is just a toll-free phone call away, 365 days a year, and we will always tell customers if they have to wait longer than a minute for service.
- act quickly to protect their interests. Any problem with a transaction made with the AT&T Universal Card can be solved with just a call, and we will take immediate action to protect our customers' billing rights.
- be more than just plastic. If an AT&T Universal Card is lost or stolen, in most cases we will replace it in 24 hours anywhere in the domestic U.S. (and most worldwide locations). In addition, we will provide emergency charge capacity, access to cash, and calling-card capability until the new card is received.

To back up our warranty, we offer an unconditional service guarantee: if at any time a customer is unhappy with the service provided, we will correct the problem and send a $10 service-guarantee certificate that can be applied to the customer's bill. It's our way of saying, "Sorry for the inconvenience." We encourage associates to use the service guarantee as a way of managing customer relationships.

Another commitment to customers is our privacy guarantee. In 1991, we discontinued telemarketing and direct-mail offerings of new products and services to customers who informed us they did not care to receive promotional material. But we did not wait for them to contact us; we contacted them and asked their preference. In addition, our internal list of customers is proprietary; these lists are not shared or sold for profit.

In two short years, UCS has grown to become the third largest issuer of credit cards in the United States. UCS leads competitors in the satisfiers customers say are most important. By making customers the center of our universe, they continue to use the AT&T Universal Card.

Carl Arendt
Manager, Communications

Westinghouse: TQM Targets the Bottom Line

Recent magazine articles and letters to the editor have been grumbling about a perceived lack of results from total quality management initiatives in many American businesses. These firms, claim the critics, simply install activity for activity's sake and never count the cash or demand concrete results.

Westinghouse people blink in surprise when they hear such claims, because measured results have been a feature of activities at this firm since the early 1980s. Diagnosis and measurement of performance improvement efforts largely result from a Westinghouse technique called cost-time profiling.

Westinghouse total quality practitioners use the cost-time profiling method to drive the radical changes needed for business success today. Profiling even overhauls operating areas not yet touched by other improvement methods. And the cost-time technique models and measures the performance aspects of the business—the ones American firms must tackle to become and remain world class competitors.

Cost-time profiling also provides a measurable link between grass-roots team driven process improvements and the profit-and-loss statement of a total business. This case study will show how the cost-time method works and illustrate the technique using the example of the 1988 Malcolm Baldrige National Quality Award winner, the Westinghouse Commercial Nuclear Fuel Division.

SHOW YOUR PROFILE

The cost-time profiling method starts with a simple idea: any set of business activities (a process) can be defined as a buildup of costs over time (illustrated in Figure 1). The process can be as basic as machining a component or responding to a customer complaint; or as complex as deciding product development and manufacturing strategies for an entire business entity.

Any process, however complicated, can be mapped and analyzed, and its cost and time dimensions charted on a cost-time profile.

As Figure 2 explains, *vertical lines* on the Profile represent purchased materials and services. In a factory, they are raw materials; in the office—supplies, outside services, and information.

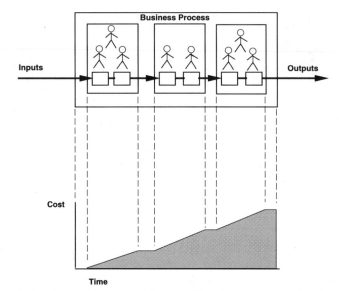

Figure 1. At its simplest level, cost-time profiling is a way to understand business processes and identify ways to improve them. A process (top) consists of people receiving inputs, adding value, and delivering outputs. The profile (below) describes those activities in the context of the total elapsed time (or cycle time) required to perform one iteration of the process. The vertical axis represents the costs of materials, purchased services, and overhead; the horizontal axis represents cycle time—the total elapsed time required to perform one cycle of the process.

Cost-Time Profile Components

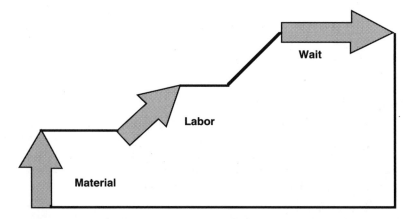

Figure 2. Every cost-time profile, however complex, has three components. The vertical lines represent purchased materials and services, including information. The diagonal lines are labor, or work performed. The horizontal lines are wait times.

Horizontal lines are wait times when nothing is happening to the process, but time is going by. In factories, the material sits in storerooms or in the aisles. In offices, the information resides at in-baskets or electronically inside computers. Reducing wait times, which can approach ninety-five percent of elapsed cycle time, offers the most immediate opportunities for improvement efforts.

Diagonal lines represent work—dollars per hour of cost added over time. The slope of the diagonal line depends on the workers' pay rates and how long the work takes.

Using analysis and the profile, teams of managers and other employees can find ways to shrink the profile—reducing both the cost and time required to perform the process.

Any process can be mapped and profiled to identify and prioritize opportunities for improving the process most effectively. We usually start with an objective of fifty percent reduction in cycle time for the process—looking to get the same results in half the time. Costs come down as a result of time reduction and quality improvement. In general, costs diminish by some 20-30 percent of the percentage cycle time reduction achieved. In other words, when we reduce a process's cycle time by 50 percent, we expect a corresponding 10-15 percent reduction in process costs.

The area under the curve of a factory cost-time profile is inventory (Figure 3). Shrinking the profile in effect shrinks inventories. You do it by improving the process, and the new, smaller profile measures the change.

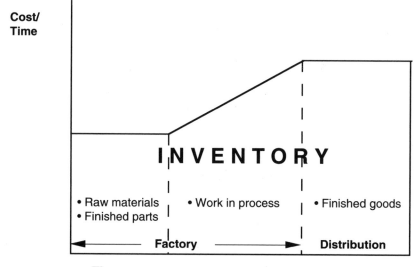

Figure 3. The area beneath a cost-time profile represents cash invested in the process being profiled. For a manufacturing operation, the area is inventory—either raw materials and finished parts, work in process, or finished goods inventories. Reducing inventory levels is therefore synonymous with shrinking the cost-time profile of the process.

One Westinghouse division that makes electrical components for the construction industry used the cost-time technique to cut manufacturing cycle time by 70 percent, from 70 days to 21 days. Scrap, a big cost of waste, was reduced by 33 percent and inventories also went down by one-third.

Between 1983 and 1991 Westinghouse permanently cut the need for inventories throughout our operations by over one-third—nearly $1 billion—using cost-time methods to improve manufacturing processes and eliminate waits.

LOOK AT THE TOTAL BUSINESS PROFILE

The next step is to extend the cost-time methodology to cover the total operations of a business.

Traditionally, we have approached financial evaluation using the income statement (Figure 4). This cost perspective aggregates the total cost of sales including factory costs and office costs—managed, strategic, committed, and so on. The difference between sales billed and the total cost of sales is operating profit, the bottom line.

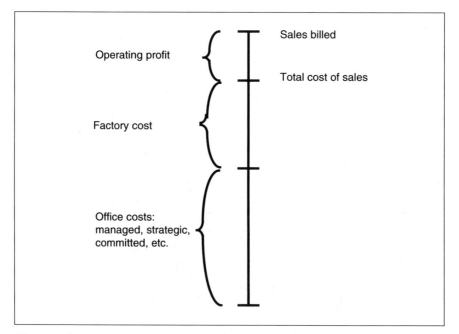

Figure 4. Elements of the income statement.

Constructing a macro cost-time profile of the total business (Figure 5) adds the dimension of time to that of cost. The macro profile provides a true view of the cash component of the dynamic investment in the business. In this total business profile, the vertical axis reflects the traditional elements of the income statement. The profile adds a horizontal-axis time dimension—reflecting elements of the balance sheet—so that the area under the curve is the shareholder investment required to operate the total business.

This macro profile illustrates the way costs build up over time as products or services pass through their entire cycle in the business operation. The profile is developed from a flow model of all business processes—from initial product concept through negotiations with customers to collecting receivables (Figure 6).

The cost-time area in the non-manufacturing part of the profile includes processes like research and development, customer contact and negotiations, engineering drawing and specification, purchasing, manufacturing planning and scheduling, distribution, billing, and payment. These areas include the informa-

Macro Cost-Time Profile Segment

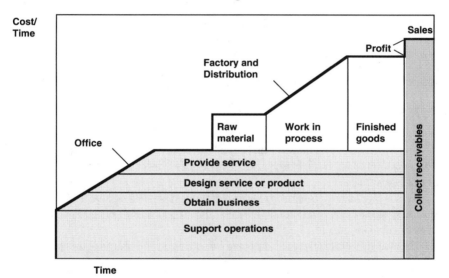

Figure 5. The entire business process can be described with a macro cost-time profile. The profile includes factory and distribution processes involving raw materials, work in process and finished goods. The profile also includes the office (white-collar) functions of R&D, negotiation and sales, as well as pre-manufacturing processes such as order entry, manufacturing information and control, and the like. And it includes receivables. The differential between the total cost (highest point of the factory profile) and the total sales represents operating profit for the business. This macro profile can be used to analyze and prioritize opportunities for dramatic improvement in all business operations.

MACRO PROFILE QUANTIFIES THE FLOW MODEL

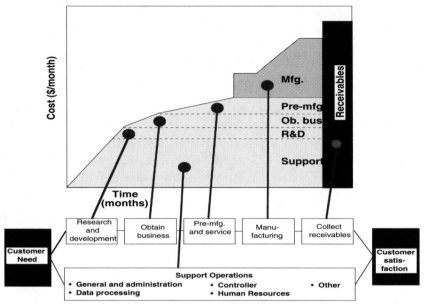

Figure 6. Macro profile quantifies the flow model.

tion and knowledge needed to perform all the non-manufacturing activities and services required to move from product concept to order receipt to delivery of a product or service.

This is the invisible inventory for the total business. We believe it offers a very large and significant opportunity to raise the productivity and quality levels of American businesses.

Used at this macro level, the profile becomes a management decision tool. It provides a model for selecting the most effective improvement activities in terms of their overall effect on the business.

Shrinking the profile relative to sales results in higher operating profit margin and more turns of a smaller investment—true measures of performance and value creation. This kind of process improvement results in higher-quality performance and increased responsiveness to customer needs.

COST-TIME IN STRATEGIC PLANNING

The most recent development in Westinghouse cost-time methods, called cash conversion analysis, extends the cost-time perspective into strategic decision processes. The analysis is used for such decisions as selecting the best strategy for increasing shareholder value; determining which businesses should grow, be divested or be acquired; determining how much cash is required to run and grow the business; and establishing acceptable profit levels for each component of the business.

In this analysis the business is viewed as a cash-conversion machine. You put in shareholder cash, turn the crank (operate the business), and out comes operating profit. Performance can be measured by the efficiency of the relationship of input to output—how efficiently you convert shareholder cash to operating profit.

Input and output, both expressed as percentages of sales, are charted as shown in Figure 7. Management's performance goal—return on the operating investment—is shown as a diagonal performance line. Each business which falls on or near this line is considered equally valuable—it's the ratio which counts. Each business on or near the line is generating the same operating profit percentage return on shareholder cash.

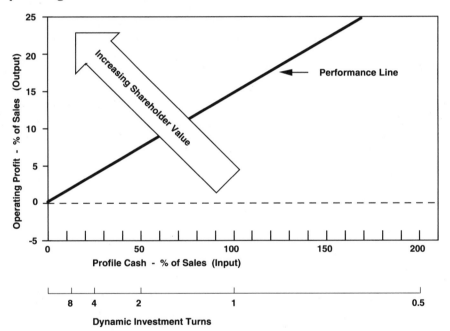

Figure 7. Cash-conversion efficiency uses the area of an operation's macro profile to gauge its performance relative to its operating profit. Profile cash as a percentage of sales is plotted versus operating profit as a percentage of sales. This diagrams the relationship of cash input to profit output for each individual product-line or divisional component of a business. The Increasing Sharehoulder Value arrow points to the northwest—the desired direction for all units of a business. The diagonal performance line represents management's financial goal—businesses on the same diagonal line are equally valuable regardless of the magnitude of their cash and profit positions.

Shrinking the cost-time profile of each component of the business—reducing cycle time and lowering cost—will improve the investment turnover and the operating profit percentage of sales. Further, it will move the performance line northwest and, by definition, increase the shareholder value of the business.

For Westinghouse, the cash-conversion methodology adds the element of time and the invisible inventory dimension to our strong value based strategic management methodologies. It also links strategic considerations directly with day-to-day operations and processes in each segment of the business.

PUTTING IT ALL TOGETHER: A BALDRIGE-WINNING PERFORMANCE

The cost-time perspective, in its fullest application, is used to select specific improvement projects and to quantify their effect on operating profit and cash turns. By using micro and macro profiles, as well as the cash-conversion efficiency plane, a management team can measure, evaluate, rank and select options to attain its goals.

To illustrate the full process, here's how one Westinghouse division used this methodology as an integral part of their total quality planning. The Westinghouse Commercial Nuclear Fuel Division (CNFD), used the cost-time technique as their primary management tool for business improvement from 1983 onward.

By 1987, after making TQM progress for several years featuring steady growth and margin improvement, the division management observed that market forces were beginning to adversely impact their operating profit margins. By 1990, they reckoned, the situation would be deteriorating as shown in Figure 8.

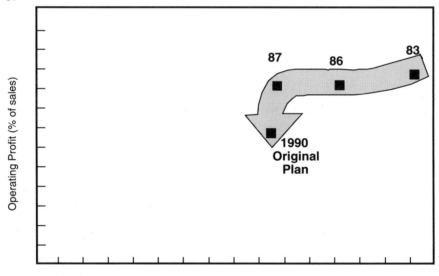

Figure 8. Westinghouse Commercial Nuclear Fuel Division cash-conversion efficiency.

General Manager Mead D'Amore was unwilling to accept this situation—even though the forecasted 1990 operating profit margin would still have been outstanding by corporate standards. Instead, the GM demanded an improved 1990 objective. The issue clearly was how to get there.

The division's first step was to construct a forecasted 1990 macro cost-time profile (Figure 9), showing the anticipated operation in 1990 if present operations were simply extended for three years. In other words, if nothing changed, the operation's profile would look like Figure 9.

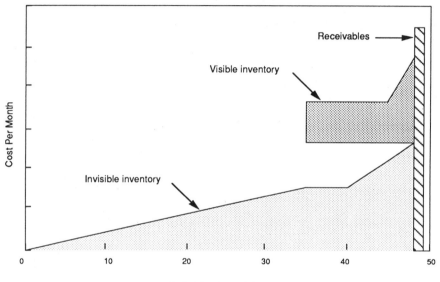

Figure 9. The original 1990 Cost-Time Profile from the CNFD strategic plan.

Then the GM and staff conducted a multi-functional, interdepartmental workshop, examining sixty value-enhancement opportunities. Each opportunity represented a process-improvement project aimed at shrinking the cost-time profile relative to sales.

The leadership team then distilled these sixty opportunities into the twelve highest potential projects (Figure 10). They analyzed and quantified each of the dozen chosen projects for its impact on cost and cycle time. Then they displayed each in stand-alone fashion on a cash conversion efficiency plane (Figure 11). The black square represented the forecasted position of the division if nothing changed. The numbers refer to the projects listed in Figure 10, each plotted without reference to any other project.

Figure 12 shows the cumulative impact which would result if all twelve projects were performed and met their target objectives. At this point, the team knew that the General Manager's 1990 goal was attainable.

Total Quality Improvement Projects

Number	Type	Description
2	Cost	Improve product efficiency
6	Cost	Reduce assessments, G&A, and other fixed costs
7	Price	Achieve price increase
8	Volume	Increase manufacturing volume
14	Cost	Reduce DM & PFE costs
17	Time	Reduce engineering development cycle time
18	Time	Reduce pre-manufacturing engineering cycle time
19	Price	Reduce raw material holding time
21	Time	Reduce manufacturing cycle time
26	Cost	Reduce finished parts costs
29	Cost	Reduce engineering costs
54	Volume	Increase engineering service and technology transfer sales

Figure 10. The top twelve value-enhancement opportunities at CNFD.

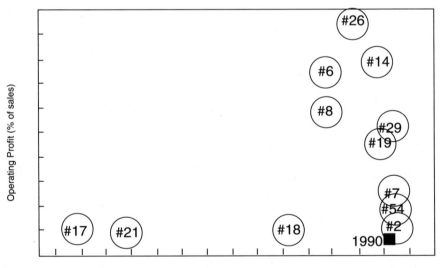

Figure 11. Impact of individual projects on cash and operating profit.

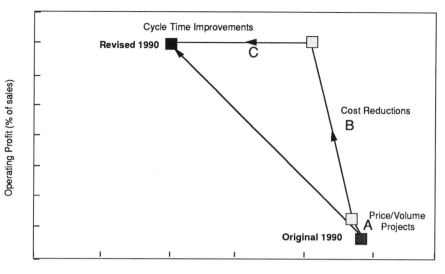

Figure 12. Cash-conversion efficiency impact of selected improvement projects.

Figure 13 shows both the original, forecasted 1990 profile and the projected, shrunken 1990 profile which assumed that all twelve projects would be successfully implemented. At this point, the division management team had a clear, quantitative road map to achieving their three-year strategic plan—and they had calculated the direct linkage between individual improvement projects and their contributions to achieving over-all financial goals.

1990 GOAL: SHRINK THE COST-TIME PROFILE

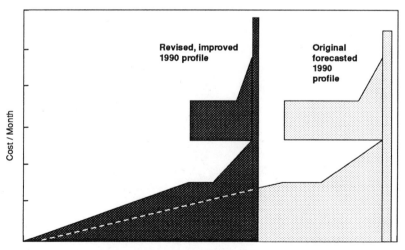

Figure 13. Effects of cost-time analysis on projected operations improvement.

This example, drawn from an award-winning operation, clearly illustrates a simple process for connecting financial results with total quality improvement projects, large or small. It puts to rest the question of whether total quality initiatives actually achieve measurable financial results!

Cash Conversion Efficiency

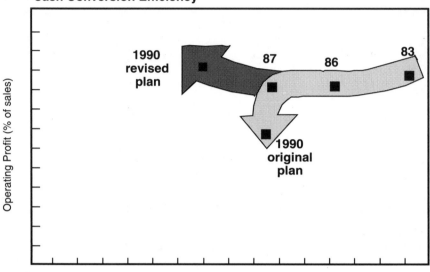

Profile Cash (% of sales)

Figure 14. Effects of cost-time analysis on 1990 planning targets at CNFD.

Robert E. Bartley
Vice President, Corporate Quality

Whirlpool Corporation: Leadership is the Critical Success Factor in a Quality Initiative

Whirlpool Corporation was founded in 1911 in Benton Harbor, Michigan to manufacture washing machines. In the early history of the company it sold 100 washing machines with defective cast-iron gears but promptly replaced the defective gears in every machine with cut-steel gears because it was the right thing to do. This customer satisfaction philosophy was implemented over 80 years ago but is still a model for Whirlpool customer focused actions today.

In the early fifties Whirlpool had a special task force on quality made up of the top representatives of major functions. The basic concept was that the ultimate judge of quality was not the engineering laboratory or an inspector, but rather the customer's satisfaction with the product after it was purchased and used over a period of time. The slogan was "Customer Satisfaction After the Sale". The customer satisfaction criteria was measured by an outside research firm.

In 1967 Whirlpool pioneered a consumer nationwide toll-free telephone service to enhance customer satisfaction long before 800 numbers became commonplace. The Cool Line started on a small scale, largely providing information on where an individual could find qualified service. In 1976, 150,000 calls were received; in 1991, 1,700,000 calls were received and 3,000,000 calls are projected for 1992 on the 24 hour a day, seven days a week toll free lines. Today most calls are for assistance.

In the late 1970s Whirlpool Corporation began the transfer of production quality responsibility from quality control departments to manufacturing with elimination of the plant quality control director's position in the 1980s.

IMPLEMENTING QUALITY WITHOUT A CRISIS

Many companies launch a quality initiative due to loss of market share, foreign competition, or poor operational performance. A review of several of the Malcolm Baldrige Award winners reveals that when domestic markets are threatened by offshore producers, major changes are required to remain competitive. This often results in moving to a Total Quality Management (TQM) approach to business.

While other sectors of American industry were battling foreign competitors manufacturing in the United States, appliance industry participants were locked in their own competitive survival struggle with each other. This forced an emphasis on plant productivity and efficiency and product improvement.

The appliance consumer receives a tremendous value in terms of price paid for appliances in the decade of the nineties compared to the price paid in the sixties, seventies or eighties relative to automobiles, housing and some other consumer durables. Customers pay little more for a major appliance today than was paid in the previous three decades. The product has been continuously improved and the price has remained fairly constant.

The nature of the industry has also discouraged the shipment of offshore product into the United States due to competitive margins, shipment costs, and aggressive industry players. People drive automobiles with foreign names, have televisions and other products from Far East manufacturers, but purchase United States manufactured refrigerators, washers, dryers, dishwashers, and ranges.

A LEADERSHIP DRIVEN QUALITY INITIATIVE

Within this context, the challenge for Whirlpool was how to motivate and launch a TQM approach when it was not immediately threatened by imports and by most measurements has been a successful company. The future threat of foreign competitors was a factor in driving senior leadership to acknowledge that changes were required. A CEO driven TQM initiative was the answer. Anything less than CEO David Whitwam's leadership, in the absence of a crisis, would probably not succeed. The CEO and Executive Committee are the quality champions, leaders and motivators and they view the quality initiative as both an offensive and defensive management strategy.

THE JOURNEY BEGINS

In December 1989, twenty-five members of the North American Appliance Group led by Executive Vice President Bill Marohn, boarded a bus for a two and one-half hour journey east to The University of Michigan in Ann Arbor for a three day seminar on total quality. The seminar, developed for Whirlpool, was conducted by then Associate Dean and Professor of Business Administration, B. Joseph White, Robert E. Cole, then Professor of Sociology and Business Administration, and Ed Rothman, Professor of Statistics.

While attending the seminar the Whirlpool group realized that they had omitted several key leaders from the trip, such as human resource representatives, controllers, sales and plant managers who are all necessary for a total approach to quality. In January 1990, Professors Cole, White, and Rothman were brought to the corporate headquarters in Benton Harbor to conduct follow-up seminar workshops with the entire senior leadership from all functional areas. In March a similar workshop was again held for all Whirlpool officers including the senior leadership from Whirlpool International Europe.

The major impact of the seminars was that Whirlpool realized that its approach to quality was traditional, product based and lacking in strategic implications. Quality was quickly redefined by Whirlpool leadership as follows: "Quality is earning the trust of all customers and consumers by exceeding their expectations in everything we do."

CORPORATE QUALITY FUNCTION ESTABLISHED

In April 1990, a Corporate Quality office was established and the CEO named a Vice President, Corporate Quality. Initially the function was planned as a small, focused organization with three to four members. The organization, in fact, consists of two staff people, a vice president and director. The primary reason for only two staff people in the Corporate Quality function is to drive quality leadership responsibility and ownership into the line and staff units. The units are accepting this responsibility and as a result are the owners of the quality initiative. The corporate staff role is to provide structure, ensure a common global approach, act as a focal point, and facilitate and guide the implementation. Other corporate quality philosophies included integrating quality into existing structures and using non-bureaucratic approaches. The principle of line ownership is a critical success factor in implementing a quality initiative. This philosophy begins with the CEO and executive committee and extends into the organization through the elected officers and senior leaders.

In chartering the corporate quality function and launching the quality initiative, the CEO established two basic principles:

1. Everything in the quality initiative would focus on the customer.
2. A common one-company global approach to quality would be implemented.

Major business group and staff functional areas also designate individuals who have quality as their primary focus. These individuals are either one person functions or have staffs of up to six people to facilitate and guide the quality initiative in their business unit or functional area. There are currently seven total quality organizations operating below the corporate level. A Quality Implementation Council consisting of the professional quality leaders is used to ensure a one-company approach and provide a structure for implementation.

An Executive Committee Quality Council was formed in 1990 similar to the model recommended by Dr. J. M. Juran. This council adopted a charter for the top leadership—to be the champions of the global quality agenda, promoting continuous improvement in all that we do.

SENIOR LEADERSHIP EDUCATION

It was recognized early that if senior leadership was to lead the quality initiative, extensive education was necessary to equip them to be the most knowledgeable people in the company on quality.

During 1990 and 1991 peer learning trips were made to recognized IBM, Westinghouse, and Xerox quality leader companies. These visits were structured exclusively for Whirlpool to learn from CEOs, former CEOs, senior officers, and experienced quality professionals.

To increase quality education and awareness, groups of senior leaders were formed in major company areas. The North American Appliance Group (NAAG) formed The Group of Fifty consisting of the fifty top leaders of NAAG. Similar groups were formed at the Corporate Center and in Technology and Procurement. Senior leader groups like these met on a periodic basis (normally quarterly) for up to one and one half days of workshops dealing with quality topics. In addition, speakers were brought into elected officer meetings to expand the knowledge of this group on quality topics.

Through these various forums, Whirlpool leadership listened to experts on topics such as the role of leadership in customer satisfaction, re-energizing the mature organization, empowerment, measurement, re-engineering processes, quality awards, QFD, Taguchi methods, 1OX and Six-Sigma and a multitude of other quality topics. It was determined that before quality could be cascaded down through the organization, senior leadership would learn and then teach.

STRUCTURES FOR ACHIEVEMENT
A number of structures for achieving quality were identified through the assistance of Professors Cole and White (Figure 1). These structures were analyzed and plans were developed to ensure implementation.

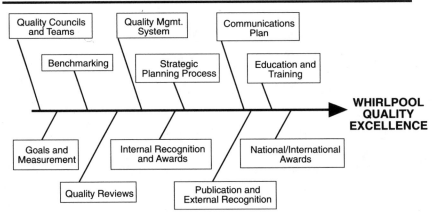

STRUCTURES FOR ACHIEVEMENT

Figure 1. Structures for achievement.

Quality councils and teams were established to provide leadership. The councils were formed for major business units and functional staffs and were designed to focus attention on quality during the implementation phase. As the quality initiative progresses, they will merge into regular staff meeting agendas. Education and training was increased with a substantial number of quality courses added to the existing curriculum in North America and Europe. A quality communication plan was developed through a partnership approach between corporate communications and corporate quality. The strategic planning process and annual budget planning process were studied to improve the process and incorporate quality planning into strategic plans.

A new global management measurement and reporting system was launched to focus on the four value creating objectives which were developed to drive shareholder value: customer satisfaction, total quality, people commitment, and growth. This system was developed by a global team and is used by the company around the world with summary reporting on a single page.

Quality reviews were launched in Europe under the umbrella of Internal Diagnostic Teams. These teams, led by those with functional responsibilities for a given product or function, are designed to promote the deployment of the quality initiative, with their activities being reviewed and guided by senior management officials. Similar teams have been formed in the United States.

A quality award process was developed in 1991 to recognize teams for quality achievement. In North America, 236 teams representing 1906 people applied for the award in 1991. In 1992 this effort will be expanded with executive officer sponsorship and leadership.

A one week educational course was developed to train facilitators to work with cross functional teams to improve business processes. This education was developed with the assistance of The American Supplier Institute and representatives from the University of Michigan. All functions have responsibility to identify and improve key processes using a disciplined systematic approach.

Starting in 1989 a Quality Day was held concurrently with the October National Quality Day telecast. The day was expanded in 1990 and again in 1991 when Whirlpool video-telecasted a Whirlpool Quality Day celebration to twelve hundred employees in Michigan, Arkansas, Indiana, Ohio, and Canada. The Quality Day was led by senior leadership and a key event was presenting quality awards to teams.

INTERNAL QUALITY ASSESSMENT

Whirlpool established the philosophy that the quality initiative was being initiated to better satisfy customers and improve performance. It was not being done to win an award. If Whirlpool does win a Malcolm Baldrige National Quality Award or European Foundation for Quality Management Award, or other national or state awards, it will be rewarding; however winning an award is not the primary objective.

The North American Appliance Group (NAAG) performed an internal quality self-assessment in 1990 using the Malcolm Baldrige criteria. The assessment was completed and scored by two Malcolm Baldrige examiners. It provided a baseline and was an outstanding learning experience. The strengths and areas for improvement provided a roadmap for future objectives and action plans.

In addition, a quality assessment of the executive committee was requested by the CEO to benchmark its status, educate the executive officers on the assessment process, and provide a leadership example to the corporation. It was assessed against The Whirlpool Worldwide Excellence System (an internal quality system modeled after Baldrige) using the Westinghouse Fitness Review process. A Westinghouse Malcolm Baldrige examiner assisted in this effort and it was followed by a chairman's office quality assessment, again modeled after the Westinghouse approach.

During 1991, internal assessments were conducted in all Whirlpool functions. To accomplish this over six hundred Whirlpool people were trained in the quality assessment process. Now organizations are performing internal self-assessments. These assessments provide a valuable learning experience in addition to highlighting organization strengths and areas for improvement.

GLOBAL QUALITY SYSTEM
In the United States a quality system, Total Quality Assurance (TQA) to ensure product quality was in place. European operations were using The Philips Company-Wide Quality Control System (CWQC) and moving toward ISO 9000 implementation. The need for a common quality system for the new global Whirlpool surfaced early.

A global team, consisting of senior line and quality people from the United States, Europe, Canada, Mexico and Brazil were chartered to develop a one-company total quality continuous improvement system with education, training, and communications plans.

The team outlined the following requirements for the quality system:
- common core beliefs and principles
- common world-wide system
- emphasis on customer satisfaction
- emphasis on continuous improvement
- emphasis on management involvement and leadership
- central element in all business activities versus separate
- endurance ... management system versus program
- address all functions versus product
- emphasis on involvement at all levels
- emphasis on human side of quality

Visits were made to several companies such as 3M, IBM, Olivetti and Westinghouse to learn about approaches taken to develop a quality system. All of the companies visited had praise for the Malcolm Baldrige Award criteria as the basis for a quality system. However, in reviewing the Baldrige criteria it was evident that both the Whirlpool TQA system and Whirlpool Europe quality systems had more focus and detail on product quality so it was decided to use Malcolm Baldrige criteria as a base but incorporate TQA and ISO 9000 into a more Whirlpool specific and user friendly system.

The Malcolm Baldrige Award criteria includes areas not addressed by the previous company quality systems and ISO 9000 such as leadership, human resources, strategic planning, and customer satisfaction. The Baldrige criteria were rewritten to include TQA and ISO 9000 and published in two employee handbooks: an overview booklet in an abbreviated 5" x 7" format for communication and orientation requirements, and a detailed 8-1/2" x 11" booklet with the full system and several appendices.

The system was titled Worldwide Excellence and quickly became known as WES (Worldwide Excellence System). The categories and appendices are as follows:

Categories: Leadership
Fact-based Management
Strategic Planning
Whirlpool People
Quality of Processes and Products
Measurement and Results
Customer Satisfaction
Appendices: Business Process Improvement
Product Delivery System
Design Assurance
Manufacturing Quality Planning
Process and Quality Control
Supplier Quality Assurance
Product Distribution, Installation and
After-sale Servicing

During the development of the system the initial approach was eighty percent technical with twenty percent focusing on the human side of quality. It was determined that the correct ratio should be an eighty percent emphasis on the human side of quality.

Fourteen focus groups around the world were exposed to the system prior to finalization and publication. Extensive graphics and white space was used to improve the booklet's ease of use and provide space for foreign translations. At this date versions in English, Spanish, German, Italian, French, and Swedish are in print. Worldwide Excellence is a standard, a management tool, a planning tool, a communications and educational vehicle, and a one-company script.

Communication and education has been by and through line management beginning with senior leadership. Internal quality professionals are available to facilitate with slides, booklets, and other materials but the responsibility for communication clearly rests with line management.

A three-day event attended by 275 Whirlpool senior NAAG managers was conducted in May of 1990 as the launch vehicle for Worldwide Excellence. The meeting was led by the senior leaders of North American operations with the objective of preparing the next two levels of leadership to communicate the new quality system.

POLICY DEPLOYMENT

During the period in which the quality initiative was being launched it became apparent that quality planning had not been effectively integrated with strategic planning. The company had both quality and strategic plans.

Each year since 1990 more integration is in evidence with major improvements being made in the strategic planning process. The strategic plan now focuses on the four value creating objectives: customer satisfaction, total quality, people commitment, and growth. Five year strategic plans include projections in implementation and assessment scores of the Worldwide Excellence System as well as projected measures in all of the value creation categories.

With the Whirlpool approach to total quality developed and largely in place, the major emphasis is currently on deployment. This phase of the quality initiative is equally critical and requires continued strong leadership to sustain and totally deploy the quality initiative.

The primary success in implementing the approach was due to senior management educating itself and leading the initiative. The same dedication to quality leadership is necessary for continued success.

LEADERSHIP LESSONS LEARNED

The key lesson learned by Whirlpool is that the critical success factor is the strong and active role of senior leadership. One of the two most powerful events in this process was the peer learning that occurred as the result of the CEO and senior leaders visiting and learning from senior leaders of other companies. The role of leadership in the internal assessment process also continues to be a key success factor. In summary, leadership is the critical success factor in any quality initiative.

Robert Woods
Vice President, Quality Assurance

Springs Industries, Inc.:
Quality through Improved
Use of Human Resources

Anniversaries are a time for taking stock of yourself, for looking at where you have been and where you would like to go. So it was with Springs Industries, Inc. in 1988 when it celebrated its 100th birthday.

Springs had many reasons to be proud. One of the nation's largest manufacturers of home furnishings and finished industrial fabrics, the company had clearly established itself as a survivor in the highly competitive textile industry. It had invested heavily in modern technology, reduced manufacturing costs, divested unprofitable business lines, and acquired other companies offering good product and market compatibility.

A period of introspection following its 100th anniversary, however, led Springs management to take a second look at its approach to quality and to human resource utilization. While Springs was a recognized leader in the textile industry, management saw untapped potential for improved profitability and growth and enhanced work life for all Springs people.

THE QUALITY PROCESS IS BORN

The Springs quality process was created in 1989 as a result of this period of introspection. While this process would require a massive training effort involving all of Springs' 20,000 people, the company embraced the quality process as the best vehicle for taking the company to new levels of achievement in the 1990s and beyond. By the end of 1992, nearly all Springs associates had been trained in the process, and associates at all levels were participating through quality teams and offering thousands of new ideas for improvements.

The corporate purchasing department created a more effective working relationship with the plants by assigning each plant their own personal purchasing representative; new procedures in corporate accounting produced a savings of two million pages of computer paper a year; associates were given a role in interviewing and hiring new associates at some plants; and thousands of dollars were being saved throughout the company as a result of innovative ideas for product and process improvements.

Throughout Springs, the company has improved its utilization of people by creating a new sense of ownership at all levels. The major components of the quality process include training in the importance of continuous quality improvement and in team participation, creation of associate-led quality teams at each location, opportunities for associates to implement improved methods, and ongoing recognition for superior achievement.

Perhaps the best way to understand how the quality process has changed Springs Industries is to take a close look at a plant that has been involved in the process since 1990.

SPRINGS PLANT EMBRACES QUALITY PROCESS

Katherine Plant, located in Chester, South Carolina, is one of Springs' most modern weaving facilities. This plant opened in 1968 and has been continually expanded and upgraded over the years. During recent years, the pace of change has been greatly accelerated with the installation of high-speed, computerized looms and a large influx of associates from nearby older plants, some of which were being closed.

While Katherine Plant was meeting general expectations for quality and productivity, management felt the facility had reached a plateau and could do better. Whenever new ideas to motivate the work force to new levels of achievement were tried, the results were lackluster. Plant management decided that creation of a new culture at Katherine Plant was the only way it would reach its full potential and become the kind of work environment they wanted for themselves and their associates. Management saw the quality process as one of the answers.

In the summer of 1990, Katherine Plant began a multi-faceted program of continuous quality improvement emphasizing improved human resource utilization. Both hourly and salaried associates were involved in encouraging all associates to work in teams. They empowered associates to identify and solve problems, encouraged personal growth, created an environment supportive of creativity, reduced associate turnover and absenteeism, and improved safety, quality, and productivity.

TRAINING PROVIDES THE CORNERSTONE

Training has been the cornerstone for the success of the quality process at Katherine Plant. Hourly and management associates have been fully oriented in continuous quality improvement. They have learned to be team leaders and team members, and they have learned to solve problems and present new ideas to management.

Meeting the training needs of nearly eight hundred associates was a tremendous undertaking. In July of 1991, the plant made an unprecedented move by stopping production so that every associate could take part in quality process training at an off-site location, and this commitment to training continues today. Salaried associates at the plant received 3,688 hours of quality and development training in 1991 when only 1,200 were required.

One of the newest training efforts is a train the trainer program begun in early 1992. This program, which is an effort to hone team member skills even further, involves ten associates—five hourly and five management. This group of associates attended an intensive school in team member responsibilities and skills at the University of South Carolina where they were certified as instructors for this program. After completing their training, they shared the course with associates in the plant through a special eight-hour school.

In addition to core training activities related to the quality process, the plant has undertaken specialized training activities that support improved human resource utilization. For example, the plant's safety teams discovered soon after their creation that they were facing technical issues beyond their expertise. As a result, a consulting firm was brought in to provide eight hours of safety training. Selected associates have also received training in statistical process control. This training helps them better understand how standards and conditions are set and gives them the background they need to have an input in setting control.

A number of educational efforts at the plant are also aimed at giving associates the opportunity to improve their general educational backgrounds. A room at Katherine Plant is designated for continuing education, with materials available for high school equivalency testing and basic skills improvement.

The plant has also given sixty of its clerical and potential clerical associates the opportunity to have their skills evaluated by a temporary employment agency. Clerical positions offer a route for advancement within the company, and these assessments are used to identify additional training needs.

To encourage greater awareness of the importance of education, the plant has adopted a nearby middle school. This program includes letters of recognition sent to honor students, a teacher's day at the plant, tours for teachers and counselors, and financial support through a Partners In Education program. The plant has also donated equipment to the local career center.

Finally, management is continuously looking for new training programs. When programs of potential value to the plant are identified, associates attend and report back to the plant concerning potential use. Programs found to be of value are offered to other associates.

KATHERINE PLANT INTRODUCES SELF-DIRECTED TEAMS

Training has been critically important to Katherine Plant because it has become a team-oriented work environment. Quality teams exist for each of five shifts and for a number of special purposes, including safety, wellness, plant tours, human resources, and the plant newsletter. Quality teams are responsible for responding to suggestions from other associates, as well as initiating their own activities.

The plant's safety teams were the first ones created because safety is an area that has an impact on the entire plant and because management had been unable to make safety a team effort with hourly associates. Seven safety teams address everything from accident investigation and housekeeping to safety inspections, audits and fire and emergency plans.

Whenever an accident occurs, a safety team investigates and recommends an action to prevent a recurrence, including additional associate training or changes in machinery or processes. In addition, associates designated as safety contacts meet individually with other associates each month to talk about safety concerns, a role that used to be carried out by supervisors.

Associates have also developed their own housekeeping criteria and audit every department monthly. Problems are documented and corrective actions recommended.

Fire brigades have been created by a safety team for every shift. Fire brigades are comprised of associates who are trained to extinguish fires, handle hoses and know when to call for assistance from the fire department.

Another safety team audits hazardous chemicals labeling, while still another team is responsible for creating employee awareness through posters, slogans and contests. In fact, safety team members are responsible for all aspects of safety at the plant except OSHA requirements.

As a result of safety team activities, Katherine Plant moved from thirty-eighth to third among all Springs plants in its safety performance and rose to first in its division. Workers' compensation claims were cut by three-fourths between 1990 and 1991. (Springs Industries, meanwhile, topped the textile industry's safety performance list for 1991.)

Another of the important teams at the plant is the Attitude Survey Team. Associate attitude surveys have been used for many years, but with the introduction of the quality process, hourly associates have been given an expanded role. They're now responsible for distributing attitude surveys, collecting them and communicating results. This approach has resulted in an eight percent increase in the return rate, and has encouraged greater openness and candor, reflected in increased written comments.

Katherine Plant has several other special teams. The new associate team orients new Springs people, a role that had been played by salaried associates. Orientation by peers is more effective in bringing people into the quality process.

Teams of wage and hour associates conduct plant tours for Springs customers and civic and community groups. The result has been greater participation by wage and hour associates, who make extremely credible tour guides.

Hourly associates are responsible for publication of the quarterly plant newsletter, and a Wellness Team has taken a pro-active approach to associate health at the plant.

The Wellness Team created a quarter-mile walking trail, which they designed and have promoted. This team has sponsored associate health screenings, reaching 650 associates for blood pressure screening, 670 for body fat composition measurement, 160 women for mammograms from a mobile unit, and 58 men screened for testicular cancer.

In addition to on-going team member training, the plant has created a group of four team coaches who have received intense training in team member and team leadership skills. Coaches regularly sit in on team meetings and offer detailed critiques on how associates are functioning as a team and how they can improve.

TEAMS RESPOND TO SPECIAL NEEDS

While the majority of teams at Katherine Plant are on-going, the plant also has what are known as SWATs, or Springs Working Achievement Teams. SWATs are created as needed to address special concerns.

One team was created specifically to reduce the cost of hearing protection, while also improving associate compliance in wearing ear plugs. Katherine Plant uses 49,000 pairs of ear plugs a year, or forty-nine pairs per associate, at an annual cost of $9,000.

The ear plug SWAT team reduced ear plug expenditures by one half in 1992 through an associate awareness and education campaign. Their campaign included a number of activities, including a new procedure for issuing ear plugs. The ear plugs are now issued one pair at a time, not by the box, which emphasizes that ear plugs should not be a disposable item.

Another SWAT team was created to address the issue of early replacement of warps on looms; warps are large spools that contain thread used for weaving. Standard practice in the weave room had been to pull warps early to avoid a situation where several might run out at the same time and cause loom downtime.

While this approach benefited the weave room, it meant that departments that prepare warps saw a greater portion of their production going to waste. The result of this team's work has been a more balanced approach to warp replacement, weighing the needs of the weave room against its impact on the production of other departments.

The plant has also determined that one SWAT each year should concentrate on reducing the cost of a specific overhead item. While ear plugs were the focus in 1992, this team will look at other cost items in the future and determine how the plant can reduce these costs.

JOB IMPROVEMENT CARDS ASSURE WIDE PARTICIPATION

While teams provide one of the most effective means for associate involvement in the quality process, Job Improvement Cards have opened the process to all associates. Any associate can suggest a change or cite a problem. The card begins with the quality team leader, who can respond to the card or forward it to a quality team. The quality team has the option of addressing the card itself or creating a special purpose team.

Every card must be resolved according to predetermined time limits. These cards have opened up communications and encouraged input from all associates, with nearly 200 cards submitted between July 1991 and March 1992 with 73 percent of those implemented.

Many of the suggestions submitted are addressed immediately. These suggestions often represent details concerning day-to-day operations that might be left unresolved if there were not a mechanism for capturing, tracking and addressing them.

Many other suggestions represent more involved improvements for quality and cost reduction. For example, an associate suggested that instead of using chemicals to kill bacteria in air handlers, an electrical device could be installed that would be just as effective, but much less costly.

Other suggestions have resulted in the installation of a new type of wheel on carts so they roll more easily, a new type of hand release added to looms for safety and increased cross-training of technicians to improve the availability of trouble-shooters.

COMMUNICATIONS PROVIDES THE GLUE

The glue holding the quality process together at Katherine Plant is improved two-way communications, and the most important means of communications at the plant actually began with other goals in mind.

When Katherine Plant began implementing the quality process, it was clear that turnover levels that had been running as high as fifteen percent would sabotage the process. What good would it do to train employees to work in a team-oriented environment, only to see them leave the company for other jobs?

The approach management selected to stabilize the work force was based on a new system of monthly associate evaluations. Under this program, shift supervisors evaluate hourly associates every month, providing associates with comments on their attendance, attitude, participation in the quality process, personal goals, and areas needing improvement. These evaluations also include an opportunity for hourly associates to evaluate their supervisors. (Actually, the title "supervisor" was replaced by the title "quality team leader" in 1991. Supervisors suggested this change in their own titles as a way of demonstrating their commitment to the quality process and as a way of highlighting their changing role at the plant.)

Monthly performance evaluations between quality team leaders and hourly associates have provided two benefits. As was management's original intent, the program has stabilized the work force. Because of more open communication, problems are addressed early and the turnover rate dropped to about 6.5 percent in 1991.

But, just as importantly, these monthly evaluations have improved communications throughout the plant. It has created an on-going dialogue between hourly and management associates and established a customer orientation. Associates ask, "What can I do better for you?" Supervisors ask, "What can I do to make your job more successful?"

In addition to monthly appraisals for hourly associates, a new system has been put into place for salaried associate evaluations which has also improved communications. Salaried associates write their own appraisals on one side of a form and their managers write their appraisal of the associate on the other. The dialogue that results from this process has meant improved performance.

Communications at the plant is being enhanced in several other ways. Straight Talk is a weekly closed circuit television program featuring the plant manager, quality teams, or associates addressing various quality process issues.

"We're listening," on the other hand, is a program that provides associates the opportunity to submit written questions to Springs CEO Walter Elisha, who provides a personal, written response.

Associates gain a better perspective of other areas of the plant through two other communications-oriented programs. Hourly associates spend a day with a quality team leader in an effort to bridge the gap between hourly and salaried associates. Since this effort was implemented, one associate in each department on each shift has been spending a day each month with a quality team leader.

Cross training of managers is also encouraged, and regular transfers between departments occur. The goal is to improve management's understanding of different areas of the plant, which also leads to improved teamwork.

RECOGNITION OF OUTSTANDING ACHIEVEMENT

Monthly and annual appraisals are only one vehicle for recognizing outstanding associate achievement. More visible are recognition activities throughout the plant.

While Katherine Plant has historically used a wide array of statistical measures to evaluate quality, productivity, and cost performance, this effort has been intensified as a result of the quality process. These measures are widely communicated on tracking boards on virtually every wall of the plant. Boards are updated weekly by associates, providing recognition that's immediate and on-going.

A number of specific awards are presented for outstanding performance. Associates select two Top Achievers of the Month based on criteria they establish. The Top Gun Program recognizes slasher operators who have achieved quality performance of at least ninety-eight percent. (Slashing is the process of adding starch to yarn before weaving.) The top Warp Crew of the Month is also recognized. Warp crews install thread carrying warps on looms, and teams are evaluated on speed and quality.

One of the most creative approaches to associate recognition was a Super Bowl competition in 1992. One of the weaving departments awarded "yards" for specific quality and productivity performance. Associates gaining the most yards won Super Bowl recognition.

Katherine Plant also presents service awards during parties held monthly for employees who joined the company during that month in years past. Recognition begins at the five-year level.

Finally, Katherine Plant recognizes personal and family achievements. Brag Boards are reserved for associates to brag about their children, families, or personal accomplishments. A son or daughter making the honor role, a wedding or a new baby are examples of Brag Board items.

INNOVATION RESULTS FROM THE QUALITY PROCESS

Among the most exciting aspects of the quality process at Katherine Plant are the peer review process and the Star program.

Peer review is a new way for resolving conflicts that arise at the plant between hourly associates and management. Whenever a conflict occurs, an hourly associate can submit the conflict to peer review by completing a peer review form. This form documents the associate's problem and the resolution. The associate's supervisor and department manager review the form and respond in writing. Unsatisfied associates have the option of submitting a request to the manufacturing manager or to a peer review panel.

Peer review panels, selected at random, consist of three hourly associates and two salaried associates. These panels review management personnel decisions in terms of consistency and fairness in the application of company policy. Peer review panel decisions are final.

Since the program began in January 1991, there have been twelve cases submitted to peer review, with eight going all the way to a peer review panel. Out of those eight cases, five management decisions were upheld, while in three other cases part or all of a management decision was overturned.

Peer review panels have been extremely diligent and objective. The three cases decided in favor of associates were cases of disputed terminations and in each the peer review panel's decision showed a balanced approach.

One terminated associate who appealed to a peer review panel was reinstated, but instructed to enter the employee assistance program to deal with a personal problem. Another associate was reinstated, but given a three-day suspension due to violation of company policy. A third associate was reinstated unconditionally because the panel felt management had not been consistent in following its own policies concerning terminations. Policies were ultimately modified as a result of this case.

Another of the innovative approaches to human resource management at Katherine Plant was created by the carding and spinning departments. These departments have implemented a Star program with excellent results.

Under the program, five teams, representing five points on a star, have been created—human resources, process control and maintenance, waste management, carding department quality, and spinning department quality. Associates volunteer for the team of their choice and are regularly rotated from one team to another to give them a better overall picture of the department.

The human resource team interviews potential new associates, considers transfers and cross training requests, coordinates transfers, posts jobs, schedules vacations, projects overtime, and forecasts labor needs. Team members regularly visit each shift to counsel underperforming associates.

The process control and maintenance team is responsible for keeping production in balance between the carding department, which prepares fibers for spinning, and the spinning department, which spins fibers into thread for weaving. They also assist with monthly inventories, monitor preventive maintenance, and address process problems. Team members regularly work with underperforming technicians to raise their skill levels.

The waste management team is responsible for materials that can be reworked into the production process, as well as recyclable wastes. One of their efforts has been a project in which the department's most waste-conscious operators work individually with operators having difficulties.

The carding department and spinning quality teams are responsible for quality in their departments, monitoring performance against goals, posting and updating results, and addressing problems. These teams meet each week to review problems and brainstorm new ideas.

Results from these teams have been gratifying. Associate turnover has been reduced to less than one percent, waste that was running five percent over budget has been reduced to seven percent below budget, yarn variations have been reduced by eight percent, yarn defects are down by fifteen percent, and overall loom stops have been reduced by seventeen-and-one-half percent, which, in part, reflects a higher quality of yarn production.

RESULTS ARE MEASURED IN FINANCIAL AND HUMAN TERMS

Katherine Plant's experience with expanded human resource utilization has proven that the key elements for success are active participation by associates at all levels; empowering associates to identify and solve problems; open, candid communication; education and training in team activities; recognition of the importance of total associate well being; and immediate and on-going recognition.

The quality process, with its emphasis on improved human resource utilization, has resulted in specific financial and human dividends.

- Absenteeism has been reduced, falling from 2 percent in 1989 to 1.67 percent in 1990 and to 1.39 percent in 1991.
- Turnover has been slashed, falling from more than 15 percent in 1989 to 14.6 percent in 1990 and to 6.58 percent in 1991.
- Quality has improved, rising from just under 98 percent finished first quality to more than 99 percent during 1991.
- Productivity is up, with loom stops reduced by 17.5 percent.
- The plant's safety record improved.
- The overall work environment is much more positive. People find their work lives more enjoyable, as documented by the following employee attitude survey results:

From May 1989 until August 1991, pride in company increased 3.4 percent; feelings of security were up by 4 percent; feelings toward top management increased from 18 to 33.9 percent; feelings toward supervision were up 7.7 percent; feelings toward the job improved by 4.8 percent; perceptions of overall treatment were more positive by 12.3 percent; and advancement opportunities were seen as better by 21.7 percent.

Changes that have taken place at Katherine Plant and throughout Springs since the quality process began have not been easy; it has required risk taking, new ways of thinking and an open, creative process. Associates at Katherine Plant and throughout the company, however, can imagine no other way of operating today.

During a recent department managers' meeting at Katherine Plant, the Wellness Team requested time on the agenda. Their item of business was simple—a surprise of coffee and ham biscuits and a heart-felt thanks to management for supporting the team and its efforts to improve the well-being of all associates.

"We just wanted to say thank you," wellness team leader Shirley Brooks told the plant management group. "We couldn't have done all we did during the last year without your help."

"And, we want to thank you," plant manger David Burns responded. "You've done a terrific job and we really appreciate it."

In that moment, the success of the quality process was summed up nicely— hourly and management associates working together as a team that's supportive, caring, innovative, and proud. The culture of this plant has been changed fundamentally, opening up new levels of achievement. Springs Industries and Katherine Plant will never be the same again.

Christin H. Buzanis
Director, Quality Assurance

Hyatt Hotels and Resorts: Achieving Quality through Employee and Guest Feedback Mechanisms

Hyatt Hotels Corporation, founded in 1957, is one of the leading hotel companies in the United States. By the late 1960s, Hyatt had become recognized for distinctive architecture, as exemplified by innovative vaulted atriums and glass elevators. As competitors copied the design breakthroughs, the amenity packages, and the club floor concept, we increasingly focused on providing the highest quality service.

During the early growth stages, Hyatt delivered an atmosphere of informal sophistication. This atmosphere was derived from our early west coast beginnings and entrepreneurial management founders. As the company grew we realized that we needed to formalize some of this cultural atmosphere and began to look in the mirror as opposed to looking out the window. Much of what was happening was our competitors trying to out-shine Hyatt. We needed to ensure that all of our new employees could deliver the quality service to which the guest became accustomed.

The process by which senior management has committed to service quality is through our In Touch initiative. Darryl Hartley-Leonard, President of Hyatt Hotels Corporation, is personally involved in responding directly to customer comments and presenting employee service awards for excellent guest service. Service is a vital part of our employee orientation and ongoing training throughout the company.

Our quality emphasis has always derived from the conviction that employee participation is an integral part of superior service. Management will use several strategies for quality through employee involvement. Extensive employee recognition systems to reward and encourage service quality throughout Hyatt exists in each hotel. Since 1980, our employees have voiced their ideas on service at regular employee roundtable discussions with hotel management; and since 1984, a regular survey assessing employee attitudes toward our company and local management has represented a major component in manager evaluation.

© *1992 Hyatt Hotels Corporation.*

Advanced technology is a primary factor in our services. Recently, we have increased our automation capabilities with a focus on improving productivity and guest service simultaneously. We now have an extensive customer database for local and national guest history and fully automated reservations and hotel accounting systems.

Hyatt has focused on customer feedback mechanisms as tools to assess customer satisfaction. Hotel management interacts frequently with guests for direct input on our quality performance. Customer panels and targeted customer questionnaires are used to shape new products or operating decisions. Many innovations emerged from customer suggestions and travel research projects, such as off-premise check-in that eliminates lines at check-in; a daily entertainment program for children and teens; and healthy, tasty foods for the health-conscious traveler.

In 1989, a strong commitment to customers and employees was developed through Hyatt's annual In Touch Day. All executives and staff in the Chicago corporate offices disperse to hotels across the country to work in direct service and customer contact jobs, such as bellperson, housekeeper, and waitperson. Similarly, managers at many individual hotels also work as direct service employees. The purpose of this day is for all corporate employees to experience front-line and back-of-the-house positions and for senior management (who have been out of the field for several years) to get back in touch with employees.

The tourism market has experienced dramatic changes in the past few years—options have increased and expectations have risen. Few industries experience the varied management challenges as does the hotel industry. Staying competitive today is a very different challenge than it was a few years ago.

In the 1960s, location was the key to success. The traveler often selected a hotel or motel based upon convenience and proximity. The biggest key to success in the 70s was to impress the guest. Construction budgets soared as the industry tried to win guests with impressive and expensive facilities. Amenities were added in the 80s to spoil the guests. As guests became accustomed to magnificent facilities they began to expect the little things that made them feel special.

In the 90s, quality will determine success. Location, top-notch facilities and a room filled with amenities are expected and even commonplace. The industry has taught the guest to want more. They have come to expect superior quality service and will settle for nothing less.

Faced with issues surrounding a plethora of circumstances and events, which includes the variable of guest perceptions and expectations, assuring quality service is a continuing challenge. For example, an average Hyatt Hotel will check-in 96,800 guests during 1992. In other words, that hotel has 96,800 opportunities to error at check-in—only one of the many points of contact that a guest will experience during a stay. Approximately eighty-five percent of these customers will eat in our restaurants, order room service or participate in a catering function. They may use our business center, laundry services, transportation services, the children and teen programs, spas or sports facilities. Because we are so many varied businesses in one, it is easy to see that achieving and maintaining our goal to be the best service provider within our industry is both complicated and exciting. Our In Touch 100 Quality Assurance Process addresses these issues.

HYATT'S IN TOUCH 100 QUALITY ASSURANCE PROCESS

In Touch 100 provides a framework for our philosophy that quality is an integral part of the way we do business. Quality at Hyatt means consistently delivering products and services 100 percent of the time. It is setting high standards through guest and employee feedback and working to achieve those standards every day.

The following seven components outline Hyatt's process:

- standards
- technology
- training
- measurement
- recognition
- communication
- continuous improvement

Each hotel and resort is committed to maintaining the quality assurance process. Because we are a highly decentralized organization, variations in individual hotel implementation is appropriate. The corporate office supports hotel efforts by communicating a universal strategy and developing and updating minimum standards and skeleton programs to function as a blueprint for hotel quality assurance programs. In addition, the corporate office measures, rewards, and communicates quality progress. The many programs which fall within the components constantly change and evolve to reinvigorate and energize the quality process.

STANDARDS

The American Hotel and Motel Association defines quality assurance as "a management system which ensures the consistent delivery of products and services," and consistency only happens through standardization. Listening closely to our guest feedback, we saw a need to get back to basics. Fast check-in, friendly, helpful service, and cleanliness were some guest concerns. We became so efficient at inventorying glassware and stamping our logo onto the ash urns, it was time to refocus on viewing our products and services through our customers' eyes. Therefore, we integrated guest feedback, employee concerns and operational issues to develop twenty-eight quality standards (see Figure 1). The standards are applicable to all Hyatt Hotels.

In support of our quality standards, all Hyatt Hotels must also adhere to specific operational basics, Americans with Disabilities Act (ADA) standards and Hyatt's frequent traveller program standards.

1. Guest satisfaction is every employee's number one priority.
2. When a guest approaches in any area of the hotel, employees acknowledge and greet the guest (by name whenever possible) in a friendly, professional manner.
3. Guest interactions are efficient, expedient, and personalized.
4. All guest requests for information or services are followed through until guest satisfaction is achieved.
5. Employees at all levels demonstrate initiative and follow through in satisfying guests.
6. Employees anticipate guest needs by suggesting or offering services.
7. Employees make consistent efforts to thank every guest and extend an invitation to return.
8. When dealing with guest complaints, employees portray an attitude of concern, acknowledge inconvenience, and offer alternatives.
9. Telephone interactions are handled utilizing proper telephone etiquette.
10. Proper announcement of name and department are given prior to entering a guest room.
11. Guests are notified in advance of unavailable services and products, closed facilities, and delays.
12. Guest feedback is actively solicited by employees at all levels.
13. Guest privacy is respected at all times.
14. All information provided to guests is factual and accurate.
15. Pricing policies reflect concern for providing guests with value for dollars spent.
16. Employees are surrounded by a safe and supportive work environment.
17. Employee input and suggestions are actively encouraged and utilized.
18. Employees are selected based on adherence to Hyatt standards and hiring practices.
19. Employees have completed Hyatt orientation and received appropriate departmental training prior to having guest contact.
20. Employees are in proper uniform and meet Hyatt grooming standards.
21. Communication systems are provided and frequently updated to keep all employees well informed.
22. Employee efforts are recognized and rewarded on a consistent, regular basis.
23. Management provides an empowered atmosphere for employees.
24. All employees are knowledgeable about hotel information, hours of operation, facilities, and established guidelines of special programs and promotions.
25. All employees are aware of department procedures and guidelines for ensuring guest satisfaction.
26. All facilities and equipment are maintained in proper working condition.
27. Exterior facilities and landscaping are attractively maintained.
28. Responsibility is taken by all employees to ensure cleanliness is maintained in all guest and work areas of the hotel.

Figure 1. Hyatt's quality standards.

TECHNOLOGY

The use of advanced technology enables us to not only improve our transaction processing; but more important, improves our guest contact interactions at the front line. Hyatt's property management system, which includes guest history, also allows one-minute check in and remote check in. Spirit is our centralized reservations system, and our revenue management process helps hotels determine an optimal mix of inventory and demand. Hyatt's human resource information system automates our human resource function by eliminating manual tracking for employee records. These technical systems provide tools to support employee efforts in serving our customers.

TRAINING

Our training programs include quality concepts, managing diversity, senior management development, employee relations, skill building, and language courses. We most often add guest experiences to our orientation training—an overnight stay or dining in one of our restaurants—so that our new employees will identify Hyatt's customer service goals with their training experience. Leadership and management fundamentals, communications, motivation, team building, time management, and conflict resolution workshops provides management staff with the necessary tools and knowledge needed to produce firm business results.

MEASUREMENT

A guest feedback scoring system whereby every hotel is held accountable in reaching a year-end goal is in place. This goal continually elevates toward 100 percent perfect service each year (see Figure 2). It *would* be *easy* to rationalize that, because of the thousands of guest contacts that take place within the hotels each day, it is impossible to reach the goal of 100 percent perfect service.

The following is an example of why we feel it is so important that our goal be 100 percent. Let's look at ten categories: reservation, front desk, food and beverage, housekeeping, personnel, engineering, accounting, the frequent traveller program, transportation, and wake-up calls. If each area is operating at ninety percent, then one in every ten contacts, or ten transactions, will be incorrect. It would be convenient to have the capability of allocating all ten errors to one guest, thereby losing only one customer!

Unfortunately, we cannot control the error distribution. Therefore, it is possible that each of our guests could experience an error. Not all of those ten guests would switch brands, but, depending on the severity of the error, we could certainly count on losing three or four of them. Because it costs five times more to acquire a new customer than it costs to keep a customer who we have already sold, these numbers are significant. If you translate a ninety percent satisfactory goal into the possibility of every guest experiencing an error, it is easy to

In Touch Score					
	1st Qtr. Actual	Year End 1991	Var. 1992 vs. 1991	Year End 1992 Goal	Var. 1992 Goal
Hotel A	97.9	95.6	2.3	97.4	0.5
Hotel B	98.6	96.0	2.6	97.6	1.0
Hotel C	97.0	95.8	1.2	97.5	-0.5
Hotel D	97.7	96.9	0.8	98.1	-0.4
Hotel E	98.5	97.2	1.3	98.3	0.2
Hotel F	98.9	98.1	0.8	98.9	0.0
Hotel G	96.6	95.0	1.6	97.0	-0.4
Hotel H	95.9	94.2	1.7	96.5	-0.6
Total Region	97.6	96.1	1.5	97.7	-0.1

Figure 2. Letters and phone contacts, region 3, first quarter variance—1992.

understand why 100 percent can be our only acceptable goal. Because of Hyatt's commitment to the quality standards and the overall quality process, complaints have dropped dramatically as shown by our letter and phone tracking system (see Figure 3).

Additional measurement vehicles such as our secret shopper program, comment card system, customer focus group meetings, guest surveys, and confidential employee opinion surveys drive Hyatt's continuous improvement process. Only with this knowledge can we update our standards at the rapid pace needed to remain competitive.

RECOGNITION

We have an employee recognition program for outstanding customer service whereby employees receive letters and certificates from our president. We recognize hotels for percentage of improvement and zero escalated complaints to the corporate office. Each hotel gives employee of the month and employee of the year awards at an annual awards banquet in recognition of outstanding employees.

COMMUNICATION

Examples of communication vehicles such as In Touch Day, video newsletters, employee focus groups and quality circles, bulletin boards, and a suggestion box

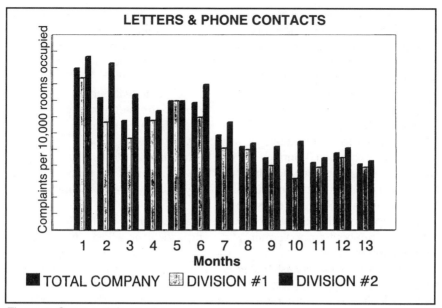

Figure 3. Guest satisfaction improvement.

system all serve to strengthen the relationship between management and employees to ensure a cohesive environment within Hyatt.

CONTINUOUS IMPROVEMENT

Regional quality assurance teams assist the hotels in maintaining Hyatt standards consistently throughout the company and improving service by:

- using the twenty-eight quality standards and operational basics as guidelines for assuring overall quality;
- reviewing specific cost areas related to adherence of the standards to supplement the subjective review with quantitative support; and
- monitoring the status of training, recognition, and communication programs.

During a site visit the teams will evaluate total hotel issues and will recognize strengths as well as opportunities.

The team training consisted of two phases. Phase one of the training focused on defining quality, integrating the twenty-eight standards into the inspection process, interviewing employees, presenting information to management and facilitating the action planning process. During the training emphasis was placed on finding out why mistakes are made rather than who made them; how to prevent errors; training as an investment rather than an expense; measuring to uncover opportunities for improvement; leadership responsibilities of management; customer satisfaction; and welcoming rather than resisting change.

Phase two of training was an on-site test visit. The teams put their new skills into action and refined their approach in evaluating the hotel.

Once the test visit was completed, the teams scheduled the hotels in their region for a site visit. The visit opens with an executive committee briefing. The team introduces the process and asks the executive committee if there are specific areas in the hotel where they should concentrate their evaluation.

Next are the departmental visits, when the teams interview managers and employees throughout the hotel. For example, the fourth standard states, "All guest requests for information or services are followed through until guest satisfaction is achieved." During their visit the teams would test the guest request system by requesting housekeeping items. They also might ask employees how they would handle a late check-out request or what they would do if they did not know the answer to a guest question.

Examples of other questions the team may ask which relate directly to the standards are about empowerment, handling difficult situations, and the hotel recognition programs.

The teams might also ask managers about specific actions they have taken to encourage employee input and suggestions, what criteria they use for selecting new employees, and communication between departments. The teams will also talk to guests in the lobby. Most of the information presented during the recap is from these interviews.

The team also gathers data to supplement the subjective quality reviews with quantitative information. These areas include reviewing the adequacy of staffing levels, checking recipe cards to ensure the published product is consistent and priced appropriately, reviewing purchasing practices as established by corporate office specifications, and checking energy management practices to ensure the guest's environmental comforts.

The team will also evaluate the cost of sub-standard quality expenses to decrease costs and improve the guest experience. This analysis might include rebates, amenities guest relocations, inviting a guest back or complimentary food and beverage in recompense for less than satisfactory service.

The executive committee recap closes the site visit. The team communicates their findings by presenting the top five standards that are strengths and the top five standards most in need of improvement. The team facilitates the action planning process by involving all members of the executive committee to solve hotel-wide issues.

Following a site visit, the team will track their hotel action plans and schedule follow-up visits. Each hotel is evaluated annually. If necessary, the teams return for a follow-up visit in as soon as three months. Individual hotel issues drive the scheduling. The Corporate Quality Assurance Department tracks the status of the team site visits and schedules, and reviews hotel action plans. Measurable improvement is visible as shown on the guest feedback tracking vehicles (Figures 2 and 3).

The reaction to this process has been very positive. The teams are excited and comfortable with the approach and their coaching role. Executive committee members like the communication and interaction and forming action plans with their own ideas. Employees appreciate the interest and concern displayed by the team. And guests are impressed with the teams' initiative and the concept of the process.

The benefits resulting from our quality assurance process are threefold. First, improved customer satisfaction by designing products and services that meet customers' needs will attract new customers. Also, we will reduce complaint-handling costs.

Secondly, organizational effectiveness has improved through teamwork, communication, and inter-department cooperation. Increased employee involvement lowers employee turnover. (Employee turnover within the hospitality industry averages between 100 percent and 150 percent. Hyatt's' employee turnover has been running below 40 percent.)

Last, profitability and competitiveness has improved by producing more with the resources at hand, and by improving and streamlining work processes to eliminate errors.

Loyalty among customers is very fragile. Through guest feedback mechanisms we have learned that at least fifty percent of all travellers are floating guests. They have no loyalty to a specific brand because they experience mishandled situations at every stay. This fact presents many opportunities

We view each guest experience as an opportunity. Most customers in today's service-oriented market prefer to do business with organizations who focus on providing quality experiences, and they want to know how that quality service will be provided. During the 90s, survival will come to those companies who are able to differentiate *how* they deliver their service from the competition.

James A. Moyer
Senior Vice President,
Total Quality Management

Marriott Corporation: Improved Customer Satisfaction through Real Time Complaint Feedback and Resolution

From the start, Marriott Corporation has had one motto: "Take care of your employees and they will take care of your customers." Both Bill Marriott Sr. and his son Bill Marriott Jr. have consistently believed and practiced this philosophy. Throughout the company, examples of this theme hold the fabric of our culture firmly in place.

A primary technique used in Marriott Hotels and Resorts to obtain customer feedback is the Office of Consumer Affairs. The primary purpose of the office, which was established in 1979, remains the same today: "to foster and maintain the integrity of the Marriott Corporation in its dealings with consumers; and to encourage and promote effective communication and understanding between all Marriott employees and consumers, whether those consumers be present or potential customers."

In 1990, a new customer service strategy was developed to further enhance customer service. This case study offers insight into how the organization researched, piloted, and implemented the service strategy it uses today.

THE CUSTOMER SERVICE STRATEGY

The new Customer Service Strategy was developed to improve Marriott Hotels and Resort's ability to respond quickly and effectively to every guest concern and to provide an effective method of measuring our success and in eliminating the problem that the guest encountered.

A task force was formed in mid-1989 to identify how we capture and respond to guest feedback and what should be done to achieve total customer satisfaction. The task force believed that our guests are not telling us what goes wrong; the guests depart the hotel feeling the frustrations and disappointment of unmet expectations. Task force participants identified that the guests either do not know how to complain, do not know who to talk to, or feel threatened or intimidated for letting us know of our problems.

The task force felt the existing guest services index system needed to be improved:

- The comment cards placed in the rooms were not a customer response system, but a flawed survey system.
- Processing of the cards was a slow method by which to respond to guest issues and delayed the opportunity for problem resolution.
- Customer input was not going directly to the property and placed Headquarters in the position of watchdog.

The task force also recognized the confusion our guests experience when they want to communicate with us. They have several areas to choose from, including the properties, the Marriott Reservation Center, and the Office of Consumer Affairs.

Based on the recommendations of the task force, three division-wide initiatives were developed:

1. A customer rapid response system to be executed on the property during and after the customer's stay. This system supports guest issues at the property. The objectives of this element of the service strategy are:
   - increased volume of customer input at property
   - customer concerns resolved before departure
   - customer input used in identifying root causes and in decreasing repeated problems
   - total customer satisfaction and customer loyalty gained through effective implementation
2. Uniform on-property customer service provided by a guest relations manager who initiates immediate resolution of customer problems
3. Customer survey system executed by mail after the customer's visit. This system provides the statistical data for the measurement of service quality.

PILOT STUDY

A group of seven hotels in the Washington, D.C. area were invited to participate in a pilot study of the new customer service strategy which incorporates the rapid response system, property guest relations manager, and customer survey system. The pilot kick-off was February 1, 1990. The objective of the pilot was to test the conclusions of the task force and determine the best methods to implement those conclusions.

This presentation details the components of the service strategy which combine on-property customer problem resolution and customer survey information.

PILOT RESULTS

All general managers of the pilot properties enthusiastically supported the new customer service strategy pilot study. They used individual approaches to implement the task force recommendations. In five of the properties, the guest relations manager was located in a prominent place in the lobby with a desk and a direct line. Six of the seven hotels within the pilot group deployed a dedicated guest relations person.

We identified three measurements to validate the success of the Washington area pilots:

1. Increased volume of guest feedback. During the six weeks that we monitored the pilot properties, those properties with a guest relations person in the lobby realized significant contact through walk-up visits.

All pilot properties experienced a high volume of calls on the direct line to the general manager where there was minimal use of the hot line in the past. Those properties, with a highly visible guest relations manager and a strong marketing campaign, experienced a higher volume of calls versus rapid response forms placed in the drop box.

Feedback from the folio remained higher than the rapid response form (generally greater than fifty percent). We feel that, in the long term, check-out folio volume will decrease as we improve resolution of guest concerns while guests are still at the property. Figure 1 illustrates feedback volumes for the seven properties participating in the pilot study.

Hotel	Line 55 Calls*	Rapid Response	Folio Piece	Walk Up
Guest Feedback Volumes				
February 1 - April 20, 1990				
Bethesda	93	25	54	Not Avail
Dulles	30	25	71	285
Crystal Gateway	100	342	208	151
Greenbelt	122	21	33	0
Key Bridge	96	39	84	25**
Tysons Corner	183	12	41	1,180
Washington	89	25	98	1,140
Grand Totals	713	489	589	2,781

* All properties receive more calls, however, simple requests (i.e., "What time does the restaurant close?") are not documented.
** No lobby desk.

Figure 1.

2. Improved resolution of guest concerns while at the property. Figure 2 compares division's and pilot property's abilities to resolve guest concerns while still on the property. Survey scores should eventually reflect markedly improved customer satisfaction. However, it would be difficult to realize significant immediate changes.

Quarter	Division Average of Guest Concerns Raised & Resolved at Property	Pilot Property Avg. of Guest Concerns Raised & Resolved at Property *
1	57%	65%
2	56%	65%
* Pilot properties with Guest Relations Manager.		

Figure 2. Comparison of resolved guest concerns at property.

3. Positive feedback from pilot participants. All general managers emphatically support the new customer service strategy. The customer service strategy provides the general manager with immediate customer feedback on the services provided through multiple collateral pieces. One resource should be responsible for gathering the feedback from guests and hotel associates, coordinating the resolution of issues prior to the guest's departure, and consolidating the data for implementation of service improvements.

GUEST RELATIONS MANAGER

The guest relations manager is the designated and responsible person who is focused on customer needs and concerns. This position is key in that it creates ownership of the strategy and accountability for resolution of guest issues.

The guest relations manager is an active part of the operation. With one person responsible for attention to guest issues, patterns emerge and can be resolved through joint effort of the guest relations manager and department managers. The pilot group recommended that the service provided by the guest relations manager be consistent throughout the hotels or the guest may be confused.

Training requirements. Presentations to all departments on the role and responsibilities of the guest relations manager are essential to guarantee success. Immediate resolution will be achieved through effective teamwork when all departments are aware of the responsibility of the guest relations manager. We must reinforce to associates that this strategy supports the quality improvement process while providing immediate service to the guest.

The guest relations manager requires expertise in the following areas:

- dealing with difficult people through anger diffusion
- letter writing skills
- communications
- stress management
- corporate and division organizations and responsibilities
- credit and accounting policies
- honored guest awards and programs.

This expertise can be acquired through previous property experience, current on-property training modules, and proposed new training programs.

IN-ROOM RAPID RESPONSE FORM

The In-Room Rapid Response Form is a major marketing element of the new Customer Service Strategy. It educates our guests on how to communicate with management. This form is placed in every guest room and in other high visibility areas.

We provide two or three options for communication:

- Dial 55 to speak directly to the guest relations manager.
- Dial 56 to leave a recorded message (optional)
- Answer the questions on the inside of the card and place in a drop box at the front desk.

Line 56 provides the guest with the opportunity to leave a recorded message rather than speaking directly with hotel staff. We recommend it be made available whenever possible.

CHECK-OUT FOLIO

The folio jacket has been redesigned as a feedback mechanism. Mr. Marriott's presence and concern for customer satisfaction have been continued in this piece, with a personal statement of his commitment to meet guest expectations. We ask three questions:

- Did you have any problems or concerns during your stay with us?
- Were any of our associates especially courteous or helpful?
- What are your suggestions for improved service?

This is an additional opportunity to gather guest feedback. The comment page separates from the sleeve for mailing. The document returns directly back to the hotel to expedite a response to guest comments. The guest relations manager will respond to the guest and resolve any outstanding issues. All issues and commendations will be captured for data analysis.

CUSTOMER SERVICE TRACKING SYSTEM

The Customer Service Tracking System allows the property to keep a constant monitor on problems, their resolution, and error cause removal. It is a PC-based application that records guest contacts from various sources, classifies guest issues, and provides numerous reports on the captured information. As a guest concern is presented, the guest relations manager (or alternate) completes a guest contact sheet. As the concern is investigated and resolved, the guest contact sheet is updated with limited information, including the origination of the contact:

- associate
- folio
- line 55
- guest letter
- guest phone call
- in-room rapid response form
- guest survey
- walk-up visit

Later, the guest relations manager enters the issue into the database and selects classification codes from a standard issue code table. From then on, by entering the guest name or contact sheet number, the guest issue can be updated or viewed.

The guest relations manager can print reports on types of problems encountered (for the entire hotel or by department), count problems resolved and pending, and report counts by period. This allows repeat problem areas to be analyzed for error cause removal action. Additionally, data regarding the cost of non-conformance, and associate commendations can also be reported. See Figure 3 for sample reports.

The system also tracks how and when concerns were communicated. This allows the success of the collateral pieces to be determined and provides scheduling data for the guest relations manager. The efficiency of handling and resolving problems can also be determined.

Property tracking can provide documentation to justify investments which improve guest visits by tracking frequencies of problems and costs associated with those problems.

MAIL-OUT GUEST SURVEY

The mail-out survey is a key tool in the measurement of service quality. It is a scannable, multi-page form that contains questions on pricing, market research, etc.

In late 1989, a baseline survey was completed to establish benchmark criteria for 1990. Beginning February 1990, surveys are mailed through an outside vendor to 300 guests per hotel per period with an anticipated result of approximately 100 responses per month. Names and addresses are randomly selected but no guest will receive a survey more frequently than once every six

ROOM SUMMARY (Issue Type: Problem)										

Page: 1
Report Date: 06/25/90   From 01/01/90 to 06/25/90

Room	Prob code	Prob Desc	Assc	Fol	Hlp	Ltr	Pho	RR	Svy	Wlk	Total
						Sources					
333	11070	Rate too high	1			3			2		6
333	12010	Room to small		2		1	1				4
Subtotal: Room 333			1	2		4	1		2		10

Grand Total	Assc	Folio	Helpline	Letter	Phone	Rapid R.	Survey	Walkup
	3	5	3	6	4	10	5	1

	Total Problems	Total Pending
	37	7

Problem Trending														

Page:1
Date: 06/25/90   From 01/01/90 to 06/25/90

Problem Code	1	2	3	4	5	6	7	8	9	10	11	12	13	Total
						Periods								
12220							3							3
11150							2							2
14010				1										1
Grand Total	5	6	3	11	4	15	2	1	12	13	15	2	4	

Figure 3. Sample property reports.

months. Surveys are mailed to guests approximately ten days after their registration date.

When surveys are received in the office of consumer affairs, they are scanned to pick up statistics and then separated into batches. The surveys are mailed back to the properties for any necessary resolution within three days of receipt. Letter responses to guests are generated for all surveys processed.

Survey results are reported quarterly. The reports compare the statistical results of the 1989 benchmark guest surveys with the 1990 current quarter and year-to-date statistics as well as comparative reports among properties and divisions.

SUMMARY

Creating the position of guest relations manager was done to establish direct accountability, authority, and ownership for resolution of guest issues.

The in-room rapid response form allows Marriott to see the guests' perspectives right away. By placing these forms in strategic locations throughout the hotel, a consistent message of concern and interest is sent to the guests.

The customer service tracking system is the gel that pulls the customer service strategy together. It is a tool too direct the search for root causes of problems reported through feedback mechanisms.

Through the deployment of the guest relations manager, the in-room rapid response form, and the customer service tracking system, Marriott has been able to obtain feedback faster and then respond to that feedback quickly. The result: customers have expressed that they feel much more of a sense of commitment to customer service from management of hotels with this strategy.

Dana Banks
Assistant Director of Quality

Malcolm Baldrige
**National
Quality
Award**
**1992
Winner**

The Ritz-Carlton Hotel Company: Reducing Service Variability with Human Resources Systems

In 1983, W.B. Johnson Properties, Inc. set out to create the first U.S. hotel group with products and services designed to appeal to and suit the demands of the prestigious travel consumer and their corporate travel and meeting planners, in multiple locations.

Until that time, the luxury hotel industry was fragmented and mostly limited to independently operated hotels. Independent business center hotels provided personalized service in small facilities that were not responsive to corporate meetings, association meetings, or multiple location needs. Some independent luxury resort hotels represented the geographic, historic, cultural, and artistic variations of their regions successfully, but were limited to single locations. Some hotel groups provided products and services that responded to corporate and association travel requirements in multiple locations. However, the highest consumer standards of the travel industry were not continuously applied. Furthermore, because of the people-intensive nature of hotel service interactions, wide service variability existed even in luxury hotels.

Faced with customers who perceived uncertainty in selecting new intangible hotel products and services, and a need for a single supplier capable of high level consistency, the company made a clear commitment to quality.

SITUATION ANALYSIS

The company used every conceivable approach to understand prestigious travel consumers, corporate travelers, and meeting planners. In each approach, a common expectation was evident —highly personalized service delivery from a responsive, caring employee.

Additionally, three other factors of hotel service delivery were addressed:
• the intensity of employee-customer relations
• the variability that can exist in people-intensive service delivery.
• the high frequency and cost of employee turnover in the hotel industry

This analysis led the company to establish its primary quality objective: A service delivery system that prevents variability and reduces customer turnover (both internal and external).

ACTIONS

Since the behavior and performance of the individual employee has a direct impact on the quality of service, the selection of the individual became the priority.

The initial employee selection effort was a simulation of employees interfacing with guests. Potential employees were invited to an informal group gathering where their capability to make contact in a relaxed yet refined manner was evaluated by each senior leader of the company. When a senior leader identified a promising candidate, they would enter the candidate's name and rating on a hidden evaluation board for consensus ranking. The basic criteria was the same as it is today (1) eye contact (2) smile (3) greeting (4) tone of voice (5) vocabulary (6) and a genuine interest, even in strangers.

The evaluations of all the leaders were tabulated and promising candidates were invited to advance through the next stages of the selection process.

SITUATION ANALYSIS

Once our prototype hotels got off to a good start and regular operations processes were functioning, we began to evaluate our performance.

Using the services of independent rating organizations, we compared our quality and customer (guest and employee) satisfaction levels with the best comparative performance to be found. We came to several important conclusions:

1. The quality of our products and services were at industry best levels.
2. Our customer satisfaction was at industry best levels.
3. The rate of employee turnover was below industry best levels (80 percent). However, this rate of turnover caused an estimated loss of 4 million dollars a year.

We studied many possible reasons for this turnover, as illustrated in Figure 1. Once again, we identified the selection of the right employee as the primary preventative measure to lower the high employee turnover rate. To find a better method to select employees and plan a pilot study to test the usefulness of the method became our improvement goal.

ACTIONS

The Ritz-Carlton studied successful employees, identifying the best performers in each job position with the most continuous length of employment. Through this study, we determined specific behavioral traits exhibited by these successful people in their respective positions. With this information, a structured employment interview was developed for each job position. By asking questions that revealed information about the applicant's past behavior, interviewers could more

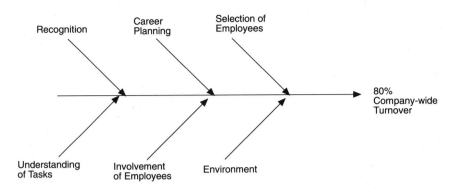

Figure 1. Possible causes for employee turnover.

accurately predict the future behavior of the candidate. This process enabled us to systematically select candidates who had the greatest likelihood of success. Adding an element of precision, a rating scale of one to five was established, with a score of three representing the minimum level performance for hiring.

The next step was a controlled experiment in our Naples, Florida hotel using this new employee designed selection process. Over a three year period we learned that we could significantly reduce turnover by controlling the type of people who were hired for each position. In our Naples hotel, the turnover rate improved from 89 percent to 39 percent in a three year period.

Making the Change

Once we had identified the best known process at that time to reduce turnover, we were anxious to implement the process at each of our hotels and resorts. Our goal was to implement the initial change smoothly as well as learn how to make future changes go even more smoothly. The first step was to develop awareness among our key senior leaders.

The problem was brought to the attention of our senior leaders during a regularly scheduled review meeting. The leaders were briefed ahead of time regarding the study so the champions of the process could stand behind and provide support and guidance. The new process was unanimously approved.

The next step was to plan the implementation precisely. The vice president of human resources was responsible for carrying out the new process. This senior leader began a process to determine who would need to change the way they perform their jobs. Once these individuals were identified, three training issues were addressed: (1) how will they be trained; (2) how will we get qualified trainers; and (3) how will the effectiveness of training be checked. We also did not want to surprise people with change. We wanted to get information to everyone affected by the change. All the senior leaders played a role in getting information to everyone and explaining how the change would affect them.

To increase the likelihood of success, the new selection process was implemented at our next new hotel start-up. This gave our start-up team members an opportunity to learn the process, implement it, and evaluate the quality of the individuals selected.

The use of the new process during the new hotel start-up allowed the individuals responsible for planning the expanded change to address several other key aspects, such as:

1. What might go wrong in implementation?
2. Would the process cause side effects?
3. What if the process is no longer effective after a year?
4. Who will have the authority to make unexpected changes if problems occur?

The vice-president of human resources assembled the final plan to implement the new selection process company-wide. By keeping in close personal contact with human resources directors, constant checks for side effects and backsliding were made.

Initially, we found skepticism with some work area managers. These individuals felt their own techniques were superior to any instrument. By continuing to ask them what they needed to know to feel comfortable with this change, we were able to reduce the uncertainty associated with this new selection process.

EVALUATION OF CHANGES

Before our new process for employee selection was implemented, the annual employee turnover rate for our company was 80 percent with an estimated cost of 4 million dollars a year (for 5 hotels).

Three years after implementing the new process, the turnover rate dropped to 45 percent. This improvement has taken place even though we have opened sixteen hotels during three years.

The improvement has overcome the traditionally high turnover of new operations. With respect to efficiency, this change has saved approximately $12.5 million in waste.

IMPROVEMENT GOAL

Over the next three years, we plan to cut our current turnover rate in half to a rate of 20 - 25 percent. Through a continuing search for the best method of employee selection, we have identified a new standardized process for our company which we find superior to the previous method.

This new process was initiated to enhance the quality assurance activities of The Ritz-Carlton Hotel Company. The quality selection process is an empirical and scientifically validated employee assessment process for the hourly staff. Over twenty years of industry specific data studies have been conducted which helped us create the process.

The new employee selection process has enabled the company to incorporate statistical process control techniques and process implementation audits. By using this process, we not only select the most qualified individuals, but also develop and coach employees on the job.

The quality selection process enables the human resources department to send only those candidates who have exceptional talent for and who fit a particular job into the operations departments of the hotel.

Hiring individuals who have talent for a particular job provides employees with intrinsic satisfaction, especially when they see their talents maximized. And their talent can also be cultivated to achieve near perfect performance. Selecting talented individuals results in motivated individuals and provides the service levels that are expected.

We identified eleven themes, or recurring patterns of thought, feelings, and behavior that remain constant over time. During the interviewing process, each potential employee's ability is assessed, evaluating their strengths in the following areas:

- work ethic
- team spirit
- exactness
- positivite attitude
- learner
- empathy
- caring
- service
- self-esteem
- persuasion
- relationship extension

Once the individual's talents have been identified, our goal is to place people into roles where their individual traits most closely match the talent required for the particular job position. When the fit is right, the employee is able to excel and meet near perfect performance while being inherently satisfied.

Individual talent is never developed without strong relationships and investment, which are developed and enhanced by caring managers and coaches. The Ritz-Carlton Hotel Company believes that quality management is defined as maximizing the effectiveness of assets and resources to achieve the mission of the organization. By understanding the strengths of the individual employees prior to placement, managers at all levels are able to better assist in the development and growth of these individuals.

No single process will always be completely accurate for every person or situation. Therefore, we continue to analyze success by conducting extensive exit interviews when individuals leave the company.

The exit interview results, along with associated data, are examined quarterly to determine if additional improvements in our selection process are needed. In this fashion, The Ritz-Carlton Hotel Company continually improves its selection of employees while significantly reducing the degree of service variability and providing a consistently high quality work force.

Wynne Gannon
Vice President
Ted Kohnen
Corporate Vice President

New York Life: Increasing Productivity and Quality through TQM

New York Life and its subsidiaries provide financial services and products including individual life insurance, group life and health insurance, annuity and disability income products, mutual funds, and pension products. As of 1991 in North America, the Company had over $359.8 billion of life insurance in force and $54 billion in consolidated assets. The surplus to assets ratio, a key figure in evaluating financial strength, is 6.04 percent, one of the highest in the insurance industry. New York Life continues to receive the highest possible ratings from Moody's Investor Service, Standard & Poor's, and A.M. Best.

The home office is located in New York City. In addition to operations in the United States and Canada, the Company has offices in Hong Kong and England. New York Life is licensed to operate in Taiwan. There are approximately 8,200 employees in the United States and Canada.

Focusing on fulfilling our promises to our customers is nothing new at New York Life. For close to 150 years, we have grown and survived difficult economic times because our business is built on customer focused service, developing products that meet our customers' needs, and quality management.

While other companies have learned the hard way that a lack of quality often leads to a lack of customers, New York Life remains firmly committed to developing new techniques and tools for maintaining and expanding superior customer service.

This goal can only be met through a company-wide effort and commitment to excellence. For that reason, New York Life launched a Total Quality Management (TQM) process five years ago, an initiative which taps into our company's greatest resource, our employees, for ideas, energy and vision.

The TQM process is based on three components. They are:

Planning. This refers to the company's annual planning process. Customer comments and requests along with competitive and regulatory information is combined to develop comprehensive long-range plans affecting all operations.

Quality improvement teams (QIT). Employees are trained in a problem solving process and work in groups to address priority issues identified by planners or by the teams themselves.

Daily operations. This is where everyone else in the organization is involved in maintaining the gains that have been accomplished. This is achieved through ongoing monitoring of indicators to assure consistent performance or to investigate the causes of adverse trends.

The TQM process seeks to determine and meet customer expectations, recognize employees as a source of ideas, and strive for continuous improvement.

PILOT IMPLEMENTATION

In early 1988, New York Life began a pilot with eleven employee teams from various departments. The purpose of the pilot was twofold: (1) It enabled the involved employees and their officers to become familiar with quality concepts and statistical tools and techniques; (2) It would prove if employees equipped with the appropriate training could improve performance by focusing on the business processes where they worked before launching a larger effort.

The teams were trained and either given a broad theme to address or determined a theme based on their own experiences. By late 1988, there were team-led results in customer satisfaction and bottom-line profitability. For example, one team focused on policy owner requests for contract changes. The team reduced the number of customer requests processed incorrectly the first time by sixty-three percent. They also calculated that this elimination of work saved $175,000 annually.

COMPANY-WIDE ROLL-OUT

Based on these positive results, New York Life decided to begin to implement TQM by introducing quality improvement teams company-wide in October 1988.

Two important decisions helped insure that the QIT would succeed on such a scale. One, the quality team component of TQM was implemented first so that employees could experience the value of TQM for themselves. Second, a department was created to facilitate the training of employees for teams plus take a hands on approach and work directly with the teams and line management.

THE QUALITY TEAM APPROACH

Before starting a team, an individual is selected by management to be a team leader. The employee attends a four-day training program which includes instruction in problem solving methodology, statistical tools, consensus building techniques, and group dynamics. Classroom training is also available for team members.

Each team has a sponsor who is usually the person the team leader reports to organizationally. The sponsor acts as a coach and a resource to the team. The sponsor and leader discuss possible customer-focused themes and select members who have appropriate technical knowledge. Therefore, team leaders and members are experts in their theme.

The team is also assigned a facilitator experienced in the quality team methodology and tools. The facilitator attends team meetings and consults privately with the leader. The facilitator also coaches the sponsor, when needed, and ensures that the team follows the proven problem-solving process.

The team begins by defining a customer, a theme, and a baseline measure of the theme. They identify the gap between customer expectations and current performance. The focus is narrowed by stratifying data. Root causes are identified prior to the selection of possible solutions. At this point, the team develops countermeasures to attack the identified root causes. Next, the team recommends to management those countermeasures which will be most effective in improving performance. Those approved are implemented and results carefully measured. If the countermeasures are effective, they are incorporated into procedures. The final step of the team process is the evaluation of subsequent actions to be taken by the team. This ensures continuous improvement, a fundamental element of TQM.

TRACKING TEAM RESULTS

Each team monitors improvement by using indicators it identifies. The results employee teams achieved have been impressive. Below are specific examples:

- reduction in rejected mutual fund applications by fifty percent
- reduction in life applications submitted incorrectly by forty-two percent
- $100,000 in annual tax savings for annuity policies
- $100,000 annual reduction in expenses through quicker resolution of dividend questions
- $100,000 saved annually in our Canadian operations by improving utilization of the information system's storage capacity

Another sign of TQM's effectiveness and the impact of empowering employees is in global measures. The aggregate effect of team results has been an increase in policy owner and agent satisfaction since 1988 and reduction in departmental budgets during the same period.

EMPLOYEE EDUCATION AND TRAINING

Most training is provided on an as-needed basis, that is, just in time for a team to begin. Since October 1988, approximately thirty percent of all employees have received training in some aspect of TQM.

New York Life's orientation process now includes an overview of TQM and this represents seventeen percent of the employees who have been trained. This introduction for newly-hired employees began in 1990. It is intended to help employees understand the importance of knowing customers' needs and introduces them to the concept that each employee has customers. This also helps new employees realize the value of a uniform team approach and builds awareness that quality improvement is an ongoing activity in the company.

Twenty-five percent of other employees were specifically trained to be team leaders and another fifty percent trained as team members. The balance of employees trained are company officers who participated in TQM workshops which cover developing customer focused business plans, how to support and coach teams, and how to link department planning to QITs.

EMPLOYEE PERFORMANCE AND RECOGNITION

An integral part of TQM is ensuring its long-term success through recognizing and rewarding employee efforts. Providing quality products and services is an ongoing goal at New York Life and employees know individual success depends on incorporating that idea into their work. Performance appraisal forms contain a section to comment on an employee's contribution to the TQM process. Tickets to sporting and other events are raffled off among quality team members. Company videos and newsletters profile team members and their accomplishments.

National Quality Month is used as another opportunity to highlight employees who have excelled in team efforts. Teams are selected to present and exhibit their improvement stories at a company fair at New York headquarters. Departmental recognition comes in the form of presentations and luncheons. Annual cash awards are given to individuals or teams of employees for outstanding performance.

CONCLUSION

In the years ahead, excellent customer service will separate the winners from the losers in many industries. In the hotly competitive financial services field, where products and prices are often similar, meeting and exceeding customer expectations is very important. It is the difference between life and death in the corporate battle.

New York Life realizes that to maintain a tradition of meeting customers' needs, in order to grow and meet the challenges of our changing business environment, we need to continuously improve our TQM process. Although employees were always considered a valuable corporate resource, the quality team methodology provides a systematic approach to tap that expertise and provide an environment which nurtures professional growth. With a strong infrastructure in place to support the team efforts, we have expanded focus to our planning. Our challenge is to be more proactive in hearing our customers' voices and discover new methods to obtain and use customer information in the early stages of planning, to set objectives, and measure our performance.

Robert F. McDermott
President and Chief Executive Officer

USAA: Employee Satisfaction Equals Customer Satisfaction

Quality is not a program, but a way of life. At USAA, we have taken many actions over the years to help nurture this state of mind in our employees. We planned, organized, hired good people and trained them, provided a great working environment, and gave our employees the best tools available to do their jobs. We see the positive results in many things—from employee absenteeism and turnover rates to national recognition as an outstanding service provider. In spite of our success, we are not content. We continue to seek ways to improve the service to our members.

In 1922, twenty-five Army officers gathered in a small hotel in San Antonio, Texas to address a problem they all shared. Because military officers were highly mobile and perceived to be a higher risk, they often found it difficult to obtain competitively priced automobile insurance from a reputable company. To solve this problem, these gentlemen formed their own mutual insurance company. Today, this company is known as United Services Automobile Association (USAA). As mutual owners, these Army officers agreed to insure each other. They soon added officers from the sister services as well. In 1962, USAA extended the privilege of member-ownership to officers who had separated from military service before retirement. Now all commissioned officers—active, Reserve, National Guard, retired, or separated—are eligible.

USAA'S APPROACH TO QUALITY

Much of USAA's growth has been the result of our approach to quality. Fundamentally, we simply ask employees to apply the golden rule: Do unto others as you would have them do unto you. Through the years quality has become a way of life; a part of the culture where employees accept ownership of the company's values and take personal responsibility for satisfying members' needs. There is a strong commitment to continuous improvement driven by USAA's number one priority of service to the member.

The delivery and follow-through of service, however, has not always been at the level it is today. Before assuming the role of president and CEO of USAA in

1969, I had six months to assess the organization. On the surface, the company was in good shape overall, having penetrated seventy percent of its potential market. USAA had a reputation for fair claims payment, good rates and honest employees. However, after a closer look at member feedback and some of the internal processes that supported the delivery of service, it became apparent that if USAA were to be a world-class company, sweeping changes would have to occur.

In 1969, the term Total Quality Management (TQM) was not in vogue, but common sense and proven leadership practices brought many of the same precepts into our strategy for improvement. It was our desire to orient employees to provide better and more ethical service to our members. We embarked on a mission to institutionalize quality and strengthen a corporate culture that would provide a strong service-oriented foundation which would permeate the entire company. We did not develop a quality program, but instead began a never-ending process of continuous improvement directed at meeting our members' changing needs and expectations. Having quality service and services as strategic directions for all of our plans and action programs led the way to our success and preeminence as a provider of financial services.

Today, the strengths of that culture nicely parallel the Malcolm Baldrige National Quality Award categories of Leadership, Human Resource Development and Management, and Customer Focus and Satisfaction, with a strong commitment to continuous improvement. Even with the advent of TQM, we chose instead to emphasize continuous improvement driven by our external and internal customers' expectations. As a learning organization, we stay abreast of new techniques and processes which have risen from the national quality movement. Exposing our employees to these principles, encourages them to apply many of these quality-related processes to their jobs to better serve our customers.

THE ROLE OF LEADERSHIP

The responsibility for refining and nurturing USAA's value system resides with our leadership—our Board of Directors and our management team. In 1969, one of our first steps as an executive team was to articulate the quality values which we wanted to enhance in the organization. Our current creed and mission statement evolved from the original versions that were developed and communicated throughout USAA. We also developed key precepts, or statements of our commitment and future orientation, to provide guiding principles to USAA employees.

To keep our values in the forefront, each year our Executive Council Evaluates and reaffirms our statements. We then publish them in our Strategic Planning Guidance Document (SPGD). While these statements are the guidelines for the culture we wish to reinforce, words without action are meaningless.

THE ROLE OF PLANNING

You can find the key to turning these values into action in a solid planning process.

An important element of this process was the establishment, in the early 1970s, of our Key Result Areas (KRAs). These are specific areas for measurement of progress and performance. We consider today's KRAs of service, financial strength, product value, resources, growth, and public outreach to be our principal management areas.

Our actual planning process, known as the Resource Management System (RMS), is shown in Figure 1. The process begins with the strategic guidance phase where strategic directions flow from each KRA to provide policy guidance to each division on how to meet KRA goals. These corporate-level directions guide development of divisional objectives, strategies, and action plans. In this way, values serve as the framework for planning and are translated into actions at the operational level where we provide service to our members and each other.

We document the strategic guidance phase of the planning process each year in the SPGD. This guidance then directly influences the business planning phase where we identify and develop the business and marketing assumptions and volumes. We then translate these volumes into resource requirements which also include support requirements such as training, computer systems, research, and communications. Finally, in the financial phase, we allocate resources, project revenue, and consolidate each element into a five-year financial plan.

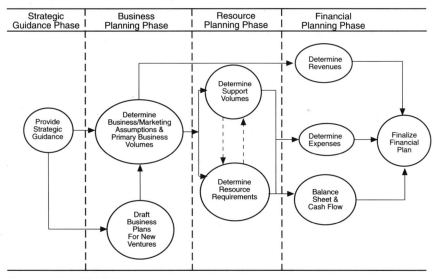

Figure 1. The RMS planning process.

COMMITMENT OF RESOURCES

Providing world-class service has enabled our quality planning to be one in the same with our business planning. Service to our external and internal customers is our number one KRA, and, therefore, *the* priority. We bolster that priority by providing the resources that support service. Without a strong commitment of resources, service to our members would be nothing more than lip service.

The commitment of resources to automate processes used to deliver our services has been a competitive strategy over the past twenty years. In 1969, it took fifty-five steps over the course of two to six weeks to issue and deliver an insurance policy. Through the development and implementation of a Long Range Systems Plan with a price tag of $130 million, we created an automated insurance environment that includes property and casualty underwriting, service, claims, billing, and customer accounting. Now, after a brief telephone conversation with our member, we can issue a policy the same day. This example and the others mentioned throughout this paper, illustrate our commitment to continuous improvement in word and deed.

ORGANIZING FOR CONTINUOUS IMPROVEMENT

As CEO, I chair an executive council which includes my direct reports in both line and staff areas. Our job is to set strategic direction and policy on all issues, including quality and continuous improvement. We address issues, initiate projects, and review and recognize initiatives directed at improving service and quality.

At the next level of this hierarchy, several cross-divisional committees help to translate these strategies and implement policies into plans and programs. For example, the Corporate Quality Committee acts as a communication network and an expediter of processes for continuous improvement. The Corporate Marketing Committee, Executive Steering Committee for Systems, the Quality Circle Steering Committee, and the Corporate Printing and Publishing Group are teams of corporate officers who monitor corporate plans to ensure that they are consistent with executive council policies. Below this level are other related management teams and committees which manage and take action on stated strategies and refer issues upward.

At the foundation of this infrastructure are the hundreds of other employee work groups, quality circles, and a wide variety of teams who actively work quality issues on a daily basis. Figure 2 reflects this hierarchy for improvement.

HUMAN RESOURCE MANAGEMENT—THE EMPLOYEE FACTOR

The most critical responsibility for delivering our service and developing customer relationships lies in the hands of our employees. In 1971, recognizing the importance of maintaining a trained, educated, and motivated work force, we formed a centralized training department that today offers extensive and varied learning opportunities. In 1991, over $18 million was allocated to support that

Figure 2. Infrastructure for continuous improvement.

commitment.

Our employees are not just agents for the company, they *are* the company, and a company is only as strong as its weakest employee. Because of the obvious link between customer satisfaction and employee satisfaction, we have given high priority to developing and maintaining a professional, motivated work force. Simply stated, our philosophy is to treat our employees with the same respect and care that we expect our employees to deliver to our members.

In 1969, however, the USAA infrastructure did not exist to support this philosophy. The annual turnover rate of forty-three percent reflected the job dissatisfaction of the 3,000 employees. We knew we could not develop the culture we had envisioned without first building pride among the employees.

Our outstanding home office facilities have an international reputation and have been featured in numerous periodicals. We have two physical fitness centers complete with exercise equipment and professional exercise physiologists. In addition to these top-notch facilities, we provide three health clinics with sixteen registered nurses at the home office. We also offer annual physicals, Weight Watcher programs, emergency medical care, pre-natal classes, free immunizations, health counseling, and mammogram and cholesterol testing to employees. In 1987, we formed a Wellness Committee comprised of management and non-management employees that meets biweekly to consider all aspects of employee wellness.

In addition, we provide a wide variety of other benefits to employees which enhance the quality of work life including a four-day, thirty-eight hour work week, three Company Stores providing a number of sundry items and services, and an Employee Assistance Program providing confidential counseling services dealing with employees' personal and professional problems. Each of our four major Field Service Offices provides comparable facilities and benefits.

We make every effort to ensure good employees have job security. When reorganizations, automation, or workload changes eliminate positions, employees receive lateral transfers, unlimited job-posting privileges, preferential consideration for vacant positions, and retraining. While they are waiting for a permanent position, they fill temporary needs in other areas.

A critical part of our focus on employees is to encourage an ethic of professional and personal development. We help employees achieve their potential through well-rounded training and development programs. Employee education and training begins with a one-and-one-half-day orientation. During this time, new employees are introduced to the corporate culture, and receive an overview of USAA and its quality definitions, principles, and employee involvement opportunities. Here, we introduce and stress our attitude regarding quality of service to the member as the primary goal.

It is important that our employees be well-educated and trained. We embed customer-focused concepts in all our member-contact training. Leadership education incorporates such concepts as empowerment, coaching, counseling, and recognition. Within our customer relations education curriculum, we have introduced new quality processes to be taught to teams on a just-in-time basis. Newer courses include benchmarking, processes improvement techniques, quality tools, problem solving tools, team building, and facilitation. We average sixty-six hours of annual training per employee with a ratio of one trainer to every forty-six employees. We also strongly encourage voluntary self-development. We provide on-site career counseling and registration, book sales, and evening classes through local colleges and universities held at USAA facilities, and a generous reimbursement program. In 1991, 32 percent of the work force participated in some form of self-development. Strengthening our work force through education enhances the contribution each individual makes to improving the quality of service to our members. It builds confidence in them and enables them to serve our members better.

ENGAGING THE EMPLOYEE

Our employees enjoy an environment designed to encourage innovation and involvement. Beginning in the early 1970s, USAA embraced the philosophy that experienced, highly-trained employees know more about the contents and details of the work they do than anyone else does. Therefore, they are in the best position to make or suggest improvements to that work process. In recognition of this, we have many vehicles through which employees can channel ideas and changes.

We formed our first suggestion program in 1979, and in the spirit of continuous improvement, an employee team revamped it in 1990. The new program provides a centralized clearinghouse for administration of new ideas. Volunteer facilitators assist those who suggest and evaluate ideas, and a point-accrual system for redemption of merchandise is used to recognize submitted and approved ideas. We reward employees each year for the best idea for service to members, service to each other, and service through efficiency.

Some of the best ideas come out of the many teams which are woven throughout our work units. We began Quality Circles (QC) in 1981 and now have over seventy-four active QC. In addition, we have literally hundreds of ad hoc and standing teams used to manage the quality of our processes and systems, to work through problems, and develop opportunities for improvement. Cross-functional and cross-divisional teams have proven effective in breaking down communication barriers and in defining internal and external customer needs and expectations.

Service to the community is another fact of employee development that we encourage. We began a Volunteer Corps in 1983. Last year, the Corps provided over 40,000 hours of public service to local agencies. We have over 800 employees who serve as mentors to at-risk students. Serving others, our members, and each other builds *esprit de corps* and reinforces service as a way of life.

RECOGNIZING THE EMPLOYEES

Key to our success in having dedicated customer-focused employees is our reinforcement of the desired behavior through recognition. Public recognition at USAA comes in many forms such as breakfasts, special luncheons, and parties. Celebrations are held in recognition of educational achievement, community involvement, and completion of projects by teams.

We have found some of the most appreciated recognition comes through our formal employee communication vehicles. Our weekly newsletter, *Highlights,* often captures success stories of employees and teams who have made contributions toward continuous improvement.

A weekly television news program, "First Edition," is another popular way to keep people informed about efforts at USAA. It gives everyone a chance to see the faces of the people who have made a difference. This video program airs throughout the home office and all our Field Service Offices.

Finally, our monthly management meeting is available to all management employees either through attendance or video. We also broadcast it live by satellite to all of our FSOs. Our management meetings have been a very effective way to recognize individual and team improvement efforts, industry awards, and even to acknowledge individual recipients of complimentary letters from members.

All of these initiatives directed at improving our work force have paid off tremendously. In over twenty years, we have brought turnover down to an industry low of 7.1 percent, and absenteeism is a healthy 2 percent. We are able to select only the very best employees by having an applicant-to-hire ratio of 37 to 1. We participate in a survey of insurance company employee attitudes conducted by the Life Office Management Association (LOMA). The recent LOMA 100 studies revealed a high degree of employee satisfaction.

One of the greatest indicators of employee satisfaction is our member satisfaction, which in property and casualty is 98.7 percent. We firmly believe that the quality of the relationship we have with our employees is a key factor in our ability to develop lifetime relationships with our members.

DEVELOPMENT OF LIFETIME CUSTOMER RELATIONSHIPS

To serve our members, we must understand our members' needs and expectations and know if we are successful in meeting those expectations. Our corporate research department performs approximately thirty thousand hours of research annually. It serves each division in developing this customer intelligence using a combination of telephone and mail surveys as well as focus groups. We conduct five major mail surveys each year to track longitudinal information, market share and potential, as well as trends in customer satisfaction and competitive data. We conduct several major phone surveys to obtain our members' attitudes as well as economic insights. We use an independent surveying firm to obtain objective third-party input on our own customer satisfaction as well as the satisfaction levels of customers of other insurance companies. Also, we conduct several special surveys to determine our members' likes and dislikes for new product and service features, the effectiveness of delivery channels, and evaluations of third-party service providers.

Besides what corporate research does, each of the major lines of business conducts random, point-in-time surveys following customer experiences to determine how well we handled a particular transaction. We feed the satisfaction measurements back to the units and, in some cases, to the individuals who performed the service.

Internal suppliers use this same practice to determine how well they are meeting their internal customers' needs. In 1991, we conducted our first internal customer service survey. In this survey, thirty-five internal suppliers joined together to determine overall service evaluations in the areas of courtesy, timeliness, ease of doing business, how well products or services met requirements, and overall satisfaction. These suppliers are now using the data to determine possible training needs and opportunities for improvement.

COMMITMENT TO CONTINUOUS IMPROVEMENT

All of the strategies previously mentioned are examples of our solid commitment to continuous improvement. We are constantly looking for better ways to make a better organization for our members and the employees of USAA. This has included employment of new technology and processes.

Since the early 1970s, we have looked at technology as a strategic weapon, not just a cost center. Through the development of state-of-the-art telecommunications and automation of our key processes, we have enabled employees to better serve our members.

Additional tools and processes for continuous improvement have come out of the quality movement. In the past, we had frequently compared our products and services to others in the insurance industry. We broadened our focus in benchmarking in order to learn from other industries. We developed a formal benchmarking process and a twelve-hour training course for teams ready to embark on a benchmarking study. Teams focused on both business and support processes now look beyond our industry to identify best-in-class companies regardless of industry.

We learn much from benchmarking others and have the responsibility to share and promote what we have learned. Each month, we open our doors in a formal quality orientation to approximately sixty people from all over the world. These people learn how we approach quality and continuous improvement. We share our benchmarking process and other quality improvement tools and then provide our visitors with breakout sessions on customer service, information technology, human resources and training, and marketing.

Outside of direct benchmarking and sharing lessons learned with individual companies, we work with and provide leadership to several quality-related associations such as the American Productivity and Quality Center, the International Service Quality Association, and the Quality and Productivity Management Association. We have also been actively involved in the development of the International Benchmarking Clearinghouse and the upcoming State of Texas Quality Award.

In 1986, we joined a study sponsored by the American Productivity Center (now the American Productivity and Quality Center) to study white collar productivity. One of the offshoots of the study, Family of Measures (FOM), has enabled us to improve the methodology for evaluating and improving the quality of our operational units. FOM is a flexible, continuous evaluation process which enables employees of a unit to determine appropriate measures of quality, quantity, timeliness, customer satisfaction, and resource use. As we gradually deploy FOM through the company, we emphasize that its primary purpose is to measure improvement, not give grades. By providing employees with timely information on performance, without direct reflection to compensation, employees more readily embrace strategies for improvement.

In 1987, we launched a major process improvement program. We structured this program using a modified cost-of-poor-quality study as it related to the payment of claims. Focusing on culture, processes, and personnel, we created a change management unit to facilitate the awareness of the opportunities for improvement, the management selective projects, and the tracking investments and progress.

The program's current focus is on containment of the rising costs of litigation and identifying opportunities to better understand and prudently measure and meet the service expectations of third-party claimants.

A similar effort is now underway which focuses on the other key processes within the property and casualty insurance operations—sales, service and underwriting. This change management process is directed at helping us better tailor our service to what our members expect of us in the next decade.

The first action was to conduct an extensive best practices study where we analyzed and visited companies, both inside and outside our industry, which were known to be excellent in service delivery or best-in-class for a particular process. We also conducted a member needs and expectations study to identify gaps and areas for improvement.

Training in facilitation, team building, and action planning is provided to managers and their front-line employees and challenges them to take greater ownership of their company. They leave the classroom with action plans and the skills necessary to implement them. Most units opt to address work flow and scheduling at first, then branch out into programs to improve USAA's key result areas. The key to the success is not to just generate a few big ideas; it is the cumulative effect of each employee's quest for continuous improvement which generates ideas, and also strengthens employee commitment.

As we move toward the 21st century, USAA will continue to work to improve our service. Although our methods have changed over the years, we remain dedicated to our mission of providing the highest-quality service to our members at a reasonable cost.

Robert Hickerson
Director, Corporate Quality Assurance

Reynolds Metals Company: Don't Forget the Basics!

Quality, as we all know, is the topic of the day—automotive companies, service organizations, retail functions and just about every publication spreads the word about quality in every endeavor.

But, we are missing something—the basics. One of my recent experiences led me to the very impressive offices of one of our qualified suppliers to discuss a massive failure to deliver a product to numerous locations. The lobby walls of the office had the usual awards—local athletic achievements, safety awards, and impressive quality awards for achieving preferred status as a supplier.

Was I missing something? In one hand I had a thick file of this supplier's non-conforming situations, but according to the awards on the wall, this company had excelled in quality. These people were recognized by some of the largest corporations in the world as preferred suppliers.

I was so confused that the receptionist had to ask me twice to go to the conference room for our meeting. In an attempt to correct the situation, the host suggested that a plant tour would assure my company that proper corrective action was in place.

I asked a few simple questions, such as, what calibration procedures were in place—with proof of use? I wanted to see logs, charts, just anything to verify that procedures were in place. Instead, I got the following vague reply, "But we check daily, or weekly, or ongoing, etc." I asked about the procedure for checking incoming materials? There were no procedures.

These were basic, entry level requirements for a beginner's quality system, and yet, they had missed the basics.

BASICS OF A QUALITY PROGRAM

As a former senior examiner for the Malcolm Baldrige National Quality Award, I repeat the Baldrige examination process mentally every time I make visits such as the one just described.

Leadership, information, analysis, strategic planning, human resource utilization, quality assurance of products and services, quality results—where were these ideas in the organization I had visited and which had achieved preferred status? Where was customer satisfaction? I was not satisfied and I had to go to the supplier with our problem and had to inform him that something was out of control.

This example is not a new one. Throughout the national award process there are numerous examples of the basics being overlooked. Maybe these basics were forgotten, due to pressures from customers to show verifiable evidence that statistical process control was used as a tool or that areas were set aside for non-conforming materials.

It never hurts to go back to school and relearn. We must frequently readdress these fundamental issues, even though they may appear to be routine. Basic, mundane tasks that are critical, in more cases than I care to believe, are taken for granted. We must get back to basics, such as calibration, heat treat surveys, the physical condition of all equipment, maintenance (other than routine scheduled items), cleanliness, and physical test equipment.

As an example, heat treat surveys can be properly done to specifications like MIL-H-6088 and AMS-2750. But, how many companies even have copies, much less the latest revision, of these standards. How many companies rely on an outside service company who may or may not be qualified.

Another example is written procedures that identify the process for every step in the production cycle. Only one section (5.2 process and quality control) in the national quality award comes close to examining the processes to ensure that products and services meet design plans or specifications. This in no way faults the Baldrige award, since any good examiner would quickly discover the lack of proper controls.

MORE BASICS

Let's not forget some of the other requirements that we quality people grew up with—corrective action systems, systems to evaluate the current procedures to assure us they are up to speed and doing what we intended, corrective action plans and a proper system for the control of measuring and testing equipment. An indication of inspection status, control of non-conforming material and a method to control specification, drawings and documents is also basic to a good quality system.

An audit we performed at Reynolds illustrated the need to keep the latest copy of all documents. In checking through the files on a production problem, we retrieved the latest production print, went to the production floor, found the material and immediately recognized that the part was made incorrectly. The reason for the production error was that the production people were not using the *final* specifications, but, instead, were using the next to the last version of the specifications. The system was immediately revised by means of the word "obsolete" being stamped on all but the latest editions of specifications.

In any attempt to get back to basics, several tasks should be closely monitored:
• record retention
• control and proper acceptance of purchased goods
• process control

- internal acceptance of the end product
- storage, handling, and shipping procedures
- planning, training, analysis, and reporting
- clearance and reliability of technical information

Have you looked at your procedures lately with the goal of updating them? What an opportunity to rethink and get back to our basic philosophy of what constitutes a good quality assurance system! Back to basics is overlooked in today's environment and needs our attention.

R. H. Walklet
Cadillac Engineering

Cadillac Motor Car: Using Simultaneous Engineering to Ensure Quality and Continuous Improvement

Seven years ago, we introduced a new philosophy at Cadillac and throughout General Motors, one that dealt with how vehicles would be designed, engineered, and manufactured. It is known as simultaneous engineering. While the processes vary among the other GM divisions, the following review will detail how Cadillac simultaneous engineering works for us.

Unlike GM's other divisions, Cadillac is fully integrated, with engineering, manufacturing, purchasing, and marketing all under one management. This means we can initiate a project knowing we have the engineering talent and manufacturing capability needed to make the project a reality. This also means that we can utilize simultaneous engineering for the development and manufacturing of vehicles that are distinctively Cadillac's.

By definition, simultaneous engineering is "a process in which appropriate disciplines are committed to work interactively to conceive, approve, develop, and implement product programs that meet pre-determined Cadillac objectives." The keys to the process are teamwork and communication among the many different staffs. Also, there must be active participation of individuals at all levels of the organization in the decision-making process to ensure that quality and continuous improvement are woven in from the beginning, rather than being tacked on during the inspection process—or worse yet, when the vehicle is in the marketplace.

To appreciate and understand the positive implications of simultaneous engineering, we need to look at how the industry used to develop cars. In the past, we all used a very methodical, sequential process to develop our products. For example, a styling engineer would dream up a car. But once completed, the design would be routed to product engineers who, in some cases, might not be able to fit the available major components within the parameters. The product engineering department would send the designed components to manufacturing, and to our suppliers, who would then have to figure a way to produce what someone else had designed.

The old way of doing business eventually became too costly and inefficient. Too often, one engineering group's idea of feasible was another group's idea of mission impossible. Each time we routed the project, we lost something, both in time and money. We took fewer and fewer risks and our products showed it. By the end, our marketing people, who were not involved in the design process at all, had to go out and sell a product that was not their idea and possibly priced incorrectly for its target market.

Like all manufacturers, Cadillac was and is faced with increasing competition from both domestic and import manufacturers. To remain a strong competitor, we needed to develop a dual focus strategy. In the short term, we had to improve both our products and our processes, and improve in quality, service, and customer satisfaction. Long term, we had to accelerate improvements in product and process so that we could prevent problems before they reached the customer. In analyzing what needed to be accomplished to realize our short- and long-term objectives, we knew that business-as-usual could no longer be tolerated.

In 1985, Cadillac adopted the practices of simultaneous engineering, beginning with management's decision to conduct formalized training to help break down barriers and effect a cultural change that fostered teamwork, communication, and group decision-making. This training began with a series of multi-disciplined off-site meetings by the then Detroit product team staff, to establish the objectives, a general implementation plan, and critical issues to be addressed by the simultaneous engineering teams. These meetings were crucial to the success of our process, since we recognized that our change in culture would require a great deal of time and education for all employees to make it work. Without top management's leadership, support and patience, nothing could be accomplished.

From these and subsequent simultaneous engineering planning meetings came our initial organizational structure, processes, roles and responsibilities. All team members participated in training focused on both the simultaneous engineering process and team development skills, thus reinforcing the team concept as a major contributor to our future success.

Since our reorganization in the first part of 1987, we have expanded simultaneous engineering throughout the entire organization. Cadillac has adopted the pyramid as the symbol of simultaneous engineering (Figure 1). At the base, or foundation, is the Cadillac executive staff, who support and nurture the process to satisfy our customers—at the top of the pyramid.

The role of top management in a simultaneous engineering environment is to sanction the process; to set broad policy and direction; and to provide the environment in which simultaneous engineering can flourish.

Next on the pyramid is the steering committee, comprised of the managers that report directly to the executive staff, whose job is to plan and implement simultaneous engineering policy and direction. They also allocate the necessary resources, serve as liaison to communicate the process to the total organization, and generally monitor and manage the process. Core Steering Committee members meet on a weekly basis to focus on current simultaneous engineering issues and future strategies.

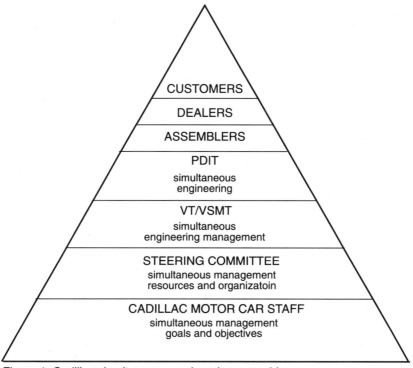

Figure 1. Cadillac simultaneous engineering pyramid.

Next are our vehicle teams, who are specifically responsible for managing all steps of product development of each vehicle program. The vehicle team is comprised of disciplines from every area of the organization, as shown in Figure 2. The roles of the Vehicle Team are: to develop the strategy for a specific vehicle for the business plan horizon; to define the target market and specific demographics; to establish the overall vehicle goals required to meet this strategy; to manage the vehicle content; and to manage the three key elements of a vehicle program— timing, profitability, and continuous improvement of the vehicle's quality, reliability, durability, and performance. In addition to our current product teams, we also have future product and specialty vehicle teams, whose role is to modify the current existing vehicles to meet special market niches.

As we developed the structure of simultaneous engineering, we broke the car into specific vehicle systems and created six Vehicle System Management Teams (VSMTs). These are the Exterior Component/Body Mechanical, Chassis/ Powertrain application, Seats and Interior Trim, Electrical/Electronic Body-In- White, and Instrument Panel/Heating and Air Conditioning Systems.

Figure 2. Sample vehicle team structure.

The role of each one of these VSMTs is to manage their vehicle system, in order to optimize the business decisions that are made in that product area for all Cadillac engineered products, and to continuously improve the process of simultaneous engineering at Cadillac. Each vehicle team works with the VSMTs to develop product program definition and objectives for each model year. The VSMTs and the vehicle teams are in the same layer of the pyramid symbolizing their partnership and interdependency to accomplish the task.

As with the vehicle teams, our VSMTs are comprised of representatives from all functional organizations involved in vehicle development and continuous improvement. VSMT membership includes, but is not limited to, vehicle engineering, manufacturing, financial, assembly plant, materials management, customer satisfaction, vehicle validation, personnel, and suppliers.

Product Development and Improvement Teams (PDITs) are responsible for the actual design of components that make up the six major systems. Each PDIT has varying core memberships, but basically are comprised of the same functional representation as the VSMTs. They have cradle-to-grave responsibility for the production and continuous quality improvement of that system or part.

The membership of each PDIT focuses on all aspects of their assigned portion of the vehicle—quality, cost, timing, technology, reliability, and profitability for all models and model years engineered by Cadillac. Team members work together to make better decisions on future designs, as well as ensuring that our current products meet our customer's requirements. It's just like they are running their own business, because, in fact, they are.

Our suppliers play a key role in our process, which is the focus of General Motors' supplier business relationship. Suppliers chosen through a full assessment process join PDITs and become full participating business partners, working side by side with us. As partners, business decisions on design, materials, and manufacturing processes can be made that benefit both Cadillac and the supplier.

The extension of simultaneous engineering is to enhance the process so that the PDITs support the manufacturing operators...who support the dealers...who support the customer...who is our focus. This support will come as a result of continuous improvement, and by constantly monitoring what our customers are telling us.

Continuous improvement is an on-going, customer-driven process that enables everyone at all levels of our organization to contribute to achieving the primary business goals of quality, cost and delivery. Cutting waste means we can reduce the cost of manufacturing. That means we can offer our products at a more competitive price.

I noted earlier that one of the keys to simultaneous engineering is communication at all levels of the company, not only between functional groups, but also between Cadillac and its stakeholders—dealers, suppliers, and the UAW. One example is our Listening-Post Dealership program that is helping us listen to the voice of the customer. Dealerships are selected on the basis of sales performance, location, customer satisfaction, and other criteria. Each dealership then serves as a listening post on a specific product group, and feeds information on actual reported problems from the customer directly to the responsible VSMT or PDIT. The team then works with the dealership to correct the problem, and works on necessary design changes to prevent further occurrences.

Another key partner is the UAW, which is keenly interested in ensuring that our cars are produced to world-class specifications expectations. We have UAW members involved in the continuous improvement process, visiting dealerships to see the results of their efforts, and reporting findings to the manufacturing plants and simultaneous engineering teams. UAW members participate in our plant manager's meetings, and learn firsthand the customer's perception of quality and the importance of reducing complexity and variation in the production mix. Hourly employees are representing their facility as PDIT members, and bring the voice of the assembler into the vehicle design and continuous improvement processes.

Simultaneous engineering teams work jointly with assembly operators in the plants to solve problems and to obtain insight for future designs. Many of our VSMT and PDIT members have replaced operators on the assembly line to experience how their design was affecting the assembly process. The key benefit of simultaneous engineering is that it allows the total organization to focus on the quality improvement process. It is this focus that will allow quicker turnaround in designing and manufacturing vehicles that respond to market demand. The 1988 Eldorado is a good example of how the process works. It helped bring this product to market two years earlier than would have been possible using the traditional methods. It was redesigned and in the showroom in only fifty-five weeks.

People in our organization now wear two hats—a traditional job-function hat and a business team hat, which encourages everyone involved to operate as if they were running their own business. As a result, Cadillac is becoming their company, not just a place where they happen to work. It's a roll-up-your-sleeves and pitch-in environment, which we encourage by physically locating interdisciplinary team members together, and providing plenty of room for impromptu problem-solving and meetings. Our employees are responding, and the results are being seen in our products.

Breaking down barriers, pooling resources, getting input from those affected by decisions—that is what simultaneous engineering is all about. What started out as a new way of engineering a vehicle has developed into a whole new way of conducting business. We have done more than implement simultaneous engineering, we have created simultaneous management. We have just begun to see the potential of simultaneous management, just begun to scratch the surface of how we can apply the philosophy to everything we do. In the long term, simultaneous management will help Cadillac to maintain the focus on its mission—"to engineer, produce, and market the world's finest automobiles."

Doug N. Anderson, Retired
Director Corporate Quality Services

3M: The Cultural Change at the Chico, California Plant

The quality journey is different for every organization. The direction is the same—the never-ending pursuit of customer satisfaction. But the process and methods differ—even among groups within the same company—depending on where the journey begins and what the driving forces for change are.

3M began its quality journey in the late 1970s with a commitment from Lewis Lehr, chairman and CEO, to focus the company's efforts toward meeting customer expectations. When the Malcolm Baldrige National Quality Award was created in 1987, 3M studied the criteria and felt they were the best guidelines available for developing a systematic approach to achieving uncompromising commitment to customers.

To introduce the process to 3M operations worldwide, a name was needed that would be acceptable throughout the company. Q90s was chosen. Q90s was designed and implemented worldwide as more than a quality process. It is a business strategy for continuous improvement—a way to measure and improve everything 3M does.

Q90s helps every 3M organization assess its strengths and weaknesses, and ensure a focus on customer satisfaction. Using the Baldrige Award criteria, all business and staff units begin the Q90s journey with a self-assessment. Gaps between where they are and where they need to be in order to be world class are identified.

At this point, the journey varies. Each organization develops its own action plan and uses the Q90s tools to meet the particular needs of the group. Tools and the training necessary to use those tools are provided by 3M's Corporate Quality Services and other staff services. Q90s tools include statistical process control, quality function deployment, customer surveys, benchmarking, prioritization, high-performance teams, measurement, and time-compression.

For 3M's Chico, California plant, the journey began when the new plant manager, Lee Bruss reported to work in October 1988. Just two years before, the Chico plant had been two different companies that were acquired by 3M's

Electronic Products Division. The plant designs, manufactures, and markets high-speed data transmission cables and assemblies. A product line of 5,600 different items are supplied to nearly 200 different customers. Most of Chico's products go to the computer industry. Others are used in medical equipment, automatic testing equipment, and telecommunications systems.

When Bruss arrived, the plant had just lost a major customer, but they had also just gained a new major contract from IBM that held the promise of doubling the plant's sales—if the Chico plant could continue to meet the needs of a very demanding customer.

Bruss said, "When I arrived, I found a lot of good people, hard-working people with a lot of brainpower. But they were all kind of pulling in different directions."

When something went wrong, there was a lot of finger-pointing and blaming. People had difficulty working together. They were physically separated into two different buildings five minutes' walk from each other.

The Chico plant in 1988 had a poor safety record, significant quality problems, low in-process yields, a poor on-time delivery record, low productivity and high absenteeism. Departments had a we versus they mentality that stemmed from not seeing each department's work product as an essential part of the total enterprise. A lot of energy was used in defending turf.

INTRODUCING THE 3M CULTURE

Bruss did not see this as a people problem. He saw it as a culture problem. His first priority was to communicate his expectations to everyone at Chico. He worked to build a climate in which trust and respect could grow. Since Chico was new to 3M, they had not yet absorbed the 3M culture—a culture that gives very high value to innovation and entrepreneurship.

In the 1940s, 3M CEO William McKnight established a human resources charter that is the foundation of the company's culture. It is that basic rule of management that makes change a normal part of the company's business.

McKnight said, "As our business grows, it becomes increasingly necessary to delegate responsibility and to encourage men and women to exercise their initiative. This requires considerable tolerance. These men and women to whom we delegate authority and responsibility, if they are good people, are going to want to do their jobs in their own way.

"Mistakes will be made. But if a person is essentially right, the mistakes he or she makes are not as serious in the long run as the mistakes management will make if it undertakes to tell those in authority exactly how they must do their jobs.

"Management that is destructively critical when mistakes are made kills initiative. And it's essential that we have many people with initiative if we are to continue to grow."

As a long-time employee, Bruss had spent more than thirty years in the environment strengthened by that statement. And now he had to convince the people at the Chico plant—starting with the managers—that a well-intentioned mistake would not be punished.

He began to build trust among the managers. And he continued to transfer more of the 3M culture to the plant, including the quality management process.

FACING AN ULTIMATUM

But, as with many organizations, the real driving force for substantive, immediate change came from a customer. In Chico's case, it was IBM Data Systems Division, their biggest customer.

In September 1990, Bruss and two other Chico managers attended a supplier meeting at IBM with a number of other suppliers. IBM made the customer satisfaction issue very simple—starkly simple. IBM told its suppliers that, in the future, they would partner only with suppliers who are actively pursuing the Malcolm Baldrige National Quality Award.

As Bruss and the other managers flew back to Chico, they knew that implementing Q90s was no longer just an excellent idea or an important idea. It was a matter of survival. IBM was their largest customer by far, so there was no doubt as to what their top priority would be when they got back to Chico.

Bruss was excited. "I knew this was going to happen. It was the incentive we needed to get things going. We agreed that we were going to move immediately. We weren't going to wait for anyone."

By a fortuitous coincidence, 3M's Electronic Products Division had scheduled a five-year planning meeting just two weeks after the IBM supplier meeting. Bruss and some of his managers met with other division managers from the headquarters and from Europe to develop a five-year business plan for Chico.

The participants at that meeting developed a vision for Chico and identified several strategic issues. The rapid implementation of Q90s was identified as a critical success factor for the business.

Driven from within 3M to implement Q90s, and presented with an ultimatum to pursue the Baldrige by one of its most important customers, Chico moved into full implementation of the quality management process with a profound sense of urgency.

BUILDING THE TEAM

Fortified by the 3M culture and challenged by the customer ultimatum, the Chico management team went through Q90s training in October 1990. They conducted an assessment of the business unit to determine what needed to be done.

In December, Bruss called a four-day meeting of the management staff to deal with the gaps between where we are and where we need to be. That meeting generated what might be called the positive equivalent of a nuclear explosion. The session was facilitated by two consultants who had also facilitated Chico's five-year business planning session. Nothing was barred from discussion. All elements of the life of the business were discussed. Every manager explained his or her role, responsibilities and departmental issues. Every need, problem, concern, and resource issue connected with the business unit's long-range strategy was listed on sheets of poster-size paper and hung on the walls. And each issue was framed within the context of the Q90s total quality management process guidelines.

After a few days, all the walls were filled with paper. The managers then searched for linkages. This had a strong unifying effect on the group. Seeing all the elements of the big picture displayed on the walls, they were able to grasp at a much deeper level how interconnected were their needs, interests, and responsibilities.

"We came out of that meeting feeling that we have a common task to do," said Ken Rozzell, human resources manager. "We realized that since we're all in it together, the more we help each other, the better off we'll be, and the more we will accomplish. There were some pretty tense moments when people didn't really agree on something and we were able to work those out."

At times, the lack of agreement was in connection with tender topics that had not been talked about for years, or had been swept under the table. All of these were brought out into the open. These were discussed until all affected parties agreed that the matter was satisfactorily resolved. Predictably, this also had a strong unifying effect on the group.

Paul Warner, one of the facilitators, said, "In a meeting like this, you are interested in not only getting answers, but also in the process of getting to the answers. As a result, there are two products. First, there are the reports and other materials generated by the discussions. Second, there is the cross-functional cohesion that comes from the process of solving common problems and forming joint conclusions. It is from this second product that you get the experience of working together in a positive new way. You can use this again and again after the meeting."

ESTABLISHING THE 100 PERCENT RULE

To establish an appropriate climate, the facilitators asked the managers to abide by a very powerful procedural requirement: There had to be 100 percent agreement from all twelve managers on every decision. No eleven-to-one votes were permitted.

That rule ensured that everyone on the management team would be fully committed to the plan of action that came out of the meeting. There was so much at stake that the group wanted to avoid any dissent which could raise obstacles.

"Not having the 100 percent requirement," said Sandy Rykken, process engineering manager, "will totally derail a planning process like that. What you will have is one or two or three people walking out saying, 'Yeah, but that really wasn't the answer, and I don't really agree with it.' If that was the case after our planning meeting, we would have had constant squabbling."

The 100 percent rule was so effective that it is used throughout the Chico organization, "One thing it's no longer OK to have at this site," said Chris Shmatovich, laboratory supervisor, "is someone saying, 'I disagree, but I don't want to argue about it.' All of us have tried this at one point or another. All that does is lead to escalation of the problem at some later date."

SEQUENCING THE PRIORITIES

The most critical application of the 100 percent rule at the December planning meeting was in connection with the prioritization process. This was an extremely challenging activity because of the sheer breadth of things that had to happen in order for Chico to reach its strategic objectives. The huge volume of issues displayed on the planning room walls gave the management team an acute awareness of the sheer magnitude of their challenge.

The Q90s process did not add to the quantity of things to do. Rather, it brought out into the open all the needs and concerns of the business that, as Steve Bohnemeyer, process development supervisor said, "were always floating around in the backs of our minds anyway."

Ron Peterson said, "Seeing all the things we are facing in the business forced us to wrestle the Q90s philosophy into implementation. Everything on those sheets was essential, because they were all tied into our strategic objectives. But we saw that we had far more on our hands than we could handle at one time. We *had* to prioritize."

For the Chico team, prioritization does not mean choosing the few most important things they had to handle and then lopping off the rest. The key at Chico is sequencing—establishing the order and timing in which things must occur.

The Chico team does this in six-month segments. At the December 1990 planning session, the team agreed on what must happen in the next six months, and work began on those immediately. In June 1991, the team reassessed the situation and determined the actions for the next six months. Each action is listed on a planning sheet with the name of the individual responsible for making it happen.

"That's why you have to get every one of your management team in the room at the same time for the prioritization process," Bruss said. "Resources are so tightly allocated, and actions must be so carefully managed, that you must have complete agreement in advance about the plan of attack.

"You have to be able to sit there for however long it takes and hammer it out together," Bruss said. "That's how you achieve the fastest, most effective utilization of the Q90s process."

COMMUNICATING THE PLAN

"After the meeting, we were all pumped up," Rozzell said, "and the production people started saying, 'Well, what are you going to do that's different? How do we know you're serious about this?' So we went out and plastered all our action plans on the bulletin boards and said, 'Here's what we are going to do. So hold us accountable.'"

That was the beginning of an integral part of the Q90s quality management process—communications. "When you are introducing something new," Bruss said, "you have to keep hammering away at it until people are able to understand and accept the change. You must educate and reeducate them until it becomes clear to everyone."

Bruss conducts bimonthly plant meetings at which he presents new programs, progress reports on existing programs, and the overall state of the business. Instead of having one big meeting for all employees which he feels would discourage interaction, Bruss conducts a one-hour meeting for thirty or fewer employees at a time. He repeats the session throughout the day until he talks to everyone on all shifts.

Every week, each member of the management staff holds department and crew meetings to deliver similar messages concerning his or her area. Like Bruss, they realize that it takes a lot of persistent and consistent repetition to establish a new vision for the business. In the early stages of change, there are always day-to-day pressures, operational firefighting needs, that cause people to react in the old familiar patterns.

"You've got to find a way to keep pulling your people back to where they can still see the big picture," Peterson said, "or they will be overwhelmed by the pressures of daily operating demands. Somehow, you've got to find a way to do both—fight the daily fires while still keeping the long-range vision in mind. You must find a way to continue working on the engine while still driving toward the finish line."

Chico also has a weekly speakup meeting. Six employees are selected at random to meet with one manager and one supervisor. The first item on the agenda is Q90s, then questions are answered. The information generated is posted on bulletin boards so everyone at the site knows what happened at the meeting.

"The consistency in what our managers say at the speakup meetings is amazing," Bruss said. "It is consistent because everyone of us on the management team knows where the others are, where they are going, and why they are going there. So, despite the fact that the managers rotate the responsibility for these meetings, the messages are consistent from week to week."

EXPANDING THE TEAM

Communicating the plan was essential for one major reason—to get everyone at Chico involved. Immediately after that first management planning meeting, the management team began referring to itself as the Quality Steering Team (QST). As action plans were posted throughout the Chico facilities, Quality Improvement Teams (QITs) were formed to work on the action plans. The QST meets every week to monitor the progress of the QITs, and to discuss and resolve issues.

Rykken said, "We also review major landmark progress. Change is taking place so rapidly, and our actions have so much impact on one another's departments, that we have to have frequent checks of the situation."

QITs that have completed projects make presentations at the weekly QST meetings. In addition to keeping management informed of progress, it has the added bonus of sustaining the enthusiasm and energy of the teams.

The QST continually seeks input from the QITs. "We have a tremendous need for employee input to succeed," said Peterson. "It's not just a nice thing to do. The business requires it. If we don't get employee input, we won't be able to do the job effectively."

The team atmosphere at Chico is pervasive. "People who used to be very passive, who just came in and did their jobs, now have ownership in what's happening," said Roberta Garner, production supervisor. "They feel they are really a part of what's going on, and it makes a big difference in their attitudes."

"It isn't perfect yet," said Chris Miller, product technician. "But that's OK. It's like working out with weights. There's always some soreness the next day. That means change is going on."

MEASURING THE RESULTS

The Chico management team measures two dozen indices every month, and shares those measurements with all the Chico employees. In just two years, the results were dramatic.

- Attendance, a good measure of employee morale, has gone from 92 percent to 97 percent.
- On-time deliveries have risen from 40 percent to 97.5 percent.
- In-process yields have increased from 50 percent to 87 percent.
- In safety, Chico has gone from one of the worst records in the company to serving as a model for other business units.
- And just six months after that supplier meeting with IBM, Chico was named one of three supplier-partners.

The Q90s process is not complete at Chico—and it never will be. The plant is striving every day for continuous improvement in meeting customer expectations. Bruss continually emphasizes that Q90s is a process—not a program. "A program has a beginning and it has an end," Bruss said. "You come in with a cost-saving program that starts on one date and ends on another, and then you show the results of that effort. Q90s is not that way at all. It's totally changing people's jobs, the way they think about their jobs. And it is a continual improvement process. It never stops. That's the beauty of this whole thing. The relentless pursuit of improvement. You have to hammer away at that idea until people understand, until their mind-set is changed and it shapes the way they are doing their jobs."

For Peterson, "The difference between a program and Q90s is like the difference between a diet and change in lifestyle. When you go on a diet to lose weight, you usually put it back on again, so you are always having to go on diets.

"When your weight loss comes from a change in lifestyle—a change in the way you think about food and the kinds of food you eat—the weight will tend to stay off.

"For us, Q90s isn't just a temporary adjustment in what we do," Peterson said. "It's a lifestyle change—a complete and permanent change in how we think about work, how we set priorities and how we work together."

Gin T. Gan
Quality Assurance Manager

Photo-Sonics, Inc.:
Achieving Quality Results through
Vendor Site Surveys

Photo-Sonics, Inc. originated in 1928 as Acme Tool & Die. Working closely first with Walt Disney and later with other film pioneers, Acme developed unique animation and other special effect motion picture equipment. In the late 1940s and early 1950s, Photo Sonics began developing a variety of 16, 35, and 70 mm motion picture, high-speed cameras and photo-optical instrumentation, primarily for military applications, and later adapted them for industrial and scientific applications.

In 1969, Photo-Sonics developed a 16 mm camera which derived from an airborne camera used to document the effectiveness of air-to-ground weapons. In 1975, a phase lock capability was added to the 1PL camera to allow the synchronizing of the high speed shutter with a reference frequency by means of a unique electronic speed control. Multiple cameras could be set up over a wide field with pictures being taken at precisely the same time. Using this concept, the military has been able to document weapon separations when up to 15 1PL cameras were mounted on the F/18. In 1950, Photo-Sonics developed the 16 mm-1B camera for high speed motion picture photography under high G forces, extreme temperatures, and vibration.

It was at this state of design evolution that NASA began environment testing of the 1PL camera for their five year project to upgrade the photo observation system at the Kennedy Space Center. In its standard form, the camera can withstand 28G of acceleration and high acoustic pressure while maintaining high image resolution at speeds of up to 500 frames per second. It's compact size enables it to fit inside NASA's existing protective enclosures located in the most abusive environments. During the orbiter launch, the camera is subjected to acceleration forces of 25G in all three axes simultaneously and acoustic pressures of up to 160 db.

Despite this abusive operational environment, the only modification required to the standard production camera is to expand the heating range of the built-in heater to accommodate the extreme temperature changes at the launch site.

The product's high quality of design and quality of conformance is realized through absolute control of the manufacturing process, which results in the ability to produce very close parts tolerances with a negligible rate of rework or scrap.

Each mechanical component is designed and manufactured in-house. Chemical processing and electronic and optical components are procured from carefully selected vendors. The company's vendor relationships are consistently maintained by providing vendors with sufficient and timely feedback via immediate telephone communication. Mutual problem solving is done on the spot without an adversarial attitude.

On site surveys are conducted prior to contract award and during the performance of the contract. Many vendors prepare themselves for routine and formal surveys by implementing temporary measures in hopes of qualifying them for the award. It is therefore very important that the quality system surveyor be qualified to perform survey audits by being knowledgeable in all areas of manufacturing, as well as being able to see through these temporary measures. It is imperative to note the following informal criteria as well as the routine survey performance in accordance with MIL-I-45208, MIL-Q-9858, and MIL-ST-45662:

1. To reveal their qualifications and quality consciousness, engage in a brief discussion of the requirements in the request for quote and its process specification with the person who will plan and supervise the manufacturing.
2. Observe the handling, storing and general condition of instruments and tools. Many times planted tools are displayed for survey purposes only.
3. Observe general housekeeping and whether only a temporary cleanup occurred for the survey.
4. Observe the handling of parts being processed, finished parts storage, and workmanship.

From this informal observation, a vendor's capability can be evaluated. It is not necessary to discuss any extensive discrepancies with the vendors, since major corrective actions may not be effectively implemented, within a short period of time, or even during the performance of the contract because the corrective action may be too expensive. In this case, it may be advisable to select another vendor.

The selection, training, and evaluation of new employees is carefully performed by supervisors and managers. Every supervisor and manager is able to perform all tasks within their departmental function with a high level of skill and expertise. This is essential to assure the correct selection, training, and fair evaluation of employees and helps to create employee respect for the supervisor. This in turn creates a positive impact toward product quality and a balanced skill environment which allows strong teamwork. As an example, a problem between first article inspection and production personnel is eliminated if inspection is accepted as a tool of production rather than being seen as a challenge to anyone's competency.

Prior to each machining operation, procedures are reviewed by supervisors. Anticipated problems are identified and necessary prevention methods are discussed and implemented with machinists or operators. Depending on the nature of the problem, engineering, quality assurance, and assembly personnel participate in corrective efforts. Engineers are immediately available when needed for problem solving or material review board actions. When necessary, drawing changes and fabrication planning sheets are revised in a timely manner. Corrective actions to prevent any recurrence are implemented and evaluated for their effectiveness.

Drawing changes required for design change, which may have an impact on manufacturing or on product verification procedures, are discussed with the appropriate personnel prior to incorporation. Necessary machining, assembly, and inspection fixtures are carefully designed without compromise to assure consistent product quality conformance. Formal policies and procedures are held to a minimum and are sufficient to conform to contractual obligations only.

At this time, a vendor's performance rating is evaluated by product quality and timely deliveries, and any discrepancies are addressed to and answered by Quality Assurance Management. In an effort to enhance productivity, cost reduction, and timely delivery schedules without compromising product quality, Photo-Sonics is implementing a system to upgrade its production control function under the direction of the quality assurance department. The new system will also have the capability of obtaining data for quality cost analysis in order to determine cost effectiveness, thereby reducing the internal-external failure cost on an ongoing basis.

Senior management's emphasis on continuous improvement has been implemented through several levels of management and throughout the company. The results can be seen in the uncompromising quality of our product design, engineering, and manufacturing system.

The attitudes and actions of company leadership and front-line management are key factors in creating an atmosphere of positive quality consciousness and teamwork. A result of this cooperative work atmosphere can be seen in the fact that employees have an average of eighteen years seniority with the company.

Over the years Photo-Sonics has received many forms of recognition for its product quality, including an Oscar for the Acme Optical Printer, a special effects motion picture device, and the Scientific and Engineering award from the Academy of Motion Picture Arts and Sciences. Since 1990, Photo-Sonics has been accepted as a member of the Quality Vendor Program conducted by the Defense Construction Supply Center for exceptional quality and delivery performance.

Photo-Sonics has always felt that the backbone of the company is it's employees. Awards of achievement are annually given to fully recognize individuals and remind them that the company's success is due to their hard work. The quality culture at Photo-Sonics, Inc. has been the legacy of its employees for over fifty years. Photo-Sonics, Inc. is dedicated to continuing the company's reputation as a leader in imaging technology.

Valerie J. Smith

SpaceLabs Medical, Inc.: Using Policies, Values, and Measurement Systems to Ensure Quality

SpaceLabs Medical has had to make product quality its top priority since it was founded in 1958. Its first products were vital components of astronaut monitoring systems in NASA's initial manned space missions in the early 1960s. Today, SpaceLabs Medical products are used to monitor patients, many of whom are critically ill, in clinical environments.

According to Chairman and CEO Carl Lombardi, "We initiated the constant improvement approach to our business life because we realized that many of our employees did not relate to the word quality per se. Quality is really an attitude, a way of behaving that we support by simple policies and values that communicate to our employees that we should constantly strive to improve everything we do. We pay strict attention to the quality of every facet of our business—from how the phones are answered to product innovation and excellence to comprehensive, responsive customer service."

SpaceLabs Medical has found, as others have, that the only way to understand how our quality programs are succeeding is through careful measurement—every functional unit of the company utilizes a heavily quantitative approach (which is especially prevalent in the manufacturing operation). As important as measurement and communicating values are, it is equally important to set good examples consistently. If you tell your people that the quality of the product is of highest importance and then take a shortcut to make a revenue number, you will certainly undermine your quality program.

SpaceLabs Medical has built its reputation by focussing on the customer—meeting the customer's expectations—which is a key priority. One way SpaceLabs Medical can anticipate customer expectations is by having each member of the senior management team take responsibility for key hospital accounts. Senior managers, because of their position in the company, can exert influence on the organization to make the improvements and innovations that will help the company best serve its customers.

QUALITY VALUES AT SPACELABS MEDICAL

SpaceLabs Medical's mission statement is as follows:

> SpaceLabs Medical's mission is to be a leading worldwide provider of quality, cost-effective systems that gather, analyze, and present clinical information beneficial to the delivery of healthcare. This mission is to be pursued in accordance with our company values.

This statement is supported and augmented by three significant SpaceLabs Medical documents: operating philosophy, company values and formula for success. All are prominently exhibited on walls throughout SpaceLabs Medical buildings, expressed in internal company communications and sent to prospective employees. They are displayed as posters in all facility lobbies so that visitors can get a sense of the company's guiding principles and beliefs. This distillation of complex ideas into unambiguous, succinct statements provide employees and others with a clear view of how SpaceLabs Medical defines itself and perceives its responsibilities. Not surprisingly, the importance of the customer figures predominantly in each document.

OPERATING PHILOSOPHY

- understand and support SpaceLabs Medical's mission, priorities, and company values
- set clear objectives, plan well, prioritize, measure progress, reassess as needed
- practice systematic and continuous improvement to be the best at what we do
- align personal career objectives with the long-term needs of the corporation
- accept responsibility, admit mistakes, learn, and improve as a result
- manage financial resources in the best interest of the corporation
- reduce politics, bureaucracy, and gamesmanship
- emphasize fundamentals—keep it simple
- have fun

Our commitment to these principles will promote understanding, trust, and respect in the organization as we pursue our business objectives.

COMPANY VALUES

- respect for individuals and the need to develop their potential
- excellence in product quality and customer service
- the importance of technical innovation
- the spirit of persistence and entrepreneurship
- the power of teamwork
- the importance of ethical behavior
- sound financial performance
- the urgency of today and the promise of the future

SPACELABS MEDICAL QUALITY POLICY

The SpaceLabs Medical Quality Policy states:

> It is the policy of SpaceLabs Medical to provide quality products and services that consistently meet the needs and expectations of our customers. Our objective is to be the quality leader in our industry. All management personnel shall ensure that this policy is understood, implemented and maintained throughout SpaceLabs Medical. All employees shall manage and perform all aspects of their work in support of this policy.

SpaceLabs Medical strives to implement its quality policy uniformly throughout the company through the development, execution, maintenance and continuous improvement of the quality functional guidelines and operating procedures, which have been prepared for every major functional organization within the company. The quality assurance organization provides a continuing evaluation of techniques, activities, practices, and related results to measure their effectiveness. The results of these evaluations are provided to all levels of management to ensure that applicable action is taken to meet the specified requirements for quality.

The company takes a systematic approach to the development of its products to ensure that quality remains a top priority. For example, senior management is intimately involved in the decisions made at each phase of product development.

REQUIREMENTS ANALYSIS

Before a new product idea receives approval, a detailed examination of the clinical need, key features required, product strengths, and market impact is prepared and reviewed by senior management.

PLANNING AND SPECIFICATION

After a new product concept is selected for development, a multidisciplinary team of engineers begins to plan, schedule, and specify the actual product. These plans are also reviewed by senior management before authorization of the design project.

DESIGN

The design phase of a product is often an interactive process in which electrical, software and mechanical approaches are discussed, implemented, reviewed, and revised. Extensive testing and review held in the design phase verify that all components of the final system meet their requirements.

TESTING AND CLINICAL EVALUATION

After the product development team has finished its internal testing and verification, another internal group tests the product in a simulated clinical environment to ensure that the product is ready for use with patients. Next, the product is used under SpaceLabs Medical's supervision in an actual clinical setting. The results of both these tests determine the readiness of the product for release.

RELEASE

The first phase of a new product's release usually involves a first product run by manufacturing to ensure that all documentation and procedures are in place. The units from this initial run will often be placed with beta-site customers who provide additional feedback on the performance and utility of the product. After adequate field experience, the product is fully released for customer shipments.

When the product makes the transition from development to manufacturing, the responsibility for preserving the quality designed into the product becomes the first priority of the production force.

SpaceLabs Medical continually monitors field performance of equipment to identify potential areas for improvement and to assure customer satisfaction.

CUSTOMER SERVICE ORGANIZATION

SpaceLabs Medical's service goals to maximize customer satisfaction and performance are accomplished through a major investment in its customer service operation. In the United States, three hundred service personnel are organized to directly serve specific geographical regions. An extensive service support group includes administration, service parts, factory repair, technical support, service training and First-Call™ personnel. Another group supports all clinical information systems implementation. These groups report to the vice president of customer service.

FIRST-CALL™ CENTRAL DISPATCH AND SERVICE MANAGEMENT SYSTEM

Central to SpaceLabs Medical's service commitment is the First-Call™ dispatch and service management information system. Because products are in use around the clock, this system was established to ensure that customers needing service assistance will always reach a member of SpaceLabs Medical's service team 24 hours a day, every day of the year. Customers use a single nationwide toll-free number that is answered by a service dispatcher. Each dispatcher works from an on-line database that provides all the information required to initiate and track a service call: a description of SpaceLabs Medical equipment at the facility, name of contact person, warranty and service agreement information, and special instructions previously conveyed. SpaceLabs Medical promises that a customer service representative will call the customer back within two hours of their call to the dispatcher. Each call is closely tracked until the problem is resolved. SpaceLabs Medical's objective is to have a ninety-five percent fix rate of all problems within the next business day.

First-Call helps customers keep vital patient monitoring equipment on line with minimum involvement by the customer. Because they can initiate service activity with one call, they are assured that their problem will receive prompt and full attention without constant prodding on their part. This frees the customer to turn their attention to other matters. By providing prompt resolution of a service issue, SpaceLabs Medical ensures that equipment downtime, and its resulting impact on critical care unit activities, is kept to an absolute minimum.

Almost all members of the service organization are closely involved with the First-Call™ program. Because the program provides invaluable data, SpaceLabs Medical service management can obtain the information they need to better manage their areas. It allows them to oversee current service activities at national and regional levels so that additional support can be provided where needed.

MEASURING THE SERVICE ORGANIZATION'S EFFECTIVENESS

To help translate customer satisfaction information into quality improvement activities, SpaceLabs Medical constantly measures the effectiveness of its service activities through a customer satisfaction survey program. To ensure strict objectivity, the company has assigned this program to an outside market research firm that calls 100 randomly-selected customers per month. It provides a statistically-valid sample that covers all geographical regions of the United States.

The survey includes service satisfaction questions that probe the customer's experience with First-Call™ response and their feelings about their service issues. If, during the survey, the respondent indicates dissatisfaction with SpaceLabs Medical or a desire to talk directly with SpaceLabs Medical's management, the survey company immediately advises the vice president of customer service. In this way, immediate corrective action or follow-up can be initiated.

The survey provides a level of information that is critically important, which is not given in routine First-Call™ data. This is the *emotional response* to SpaceLabs Medical service. Asking the customer if they want someone from SpaceLabs Medical management to call or if they would purchase SpaceLabs Medical equipment again helps the company determine if a customer is fully satisfied or not.

Each month SpaceLabs Medical is given a report summarizing the data collected. This information is extremely helpful to regional managers—with it they can identify real or perceived problems within their own organizations and work toward specific resolutions. For example, the report may show that an individual service representative is not fully explaining the corrective action taken, so that the customer is not sure that the problem is resolved. The regional manager can use this information to counsel the representative accordingly.

Through a Customer Satisfaction Survey Follow-up Report the Vice President of Customer Service keeps track of every survey participant that wants a manager to call or indicates they will not purchase from SpaceLabs Medical again. This report is routed to regional service managers. A member of SpaceLabs Medical's senior management will then follow-up on the call.

While First-Call is the primary tool used to take care of day-to-day service issues, it is not currently used to determine trends in product reliability. This is done through service reports.

All SpaceLabs Medical service representatives document each of their calls with a service report. The quality assurance manager analyzes these reports to produce statistical data that covers a wide range of concerns. Reports are routed to top management personnel. It is at this level that the SpaceLabs Medical organization determines trends in product problems and identifies product changes that can resolve these problems. A task force meets twice monthly to review these reports and initiate actions that result in product and procedural changes that will lead to increased quality and customer satisfaction.

Daniel T. Koenig
Vice President of Manufacturing

Steinway & Sons: Quality through an Artisan Work Ethic

"Provide customers with the highest quality instrument and services, consistent with Steinway's reputation for excellence, by building the finest piano in the world and selling it at a reasonable profit."

This mission, stated by the company's founder Henry Engelhard Steinway over one hundred and thirty-nine years ago, remains virtually unchanged as the guiding philosophy of Steinway & Sons to this day.

We are in the business of producing pianos for use in homes and in performance venues. We make no distinction in construction based on the intended final customer of the instruments. It is our policy that every piano is built as if the world's finest virtuosos will be performing with them.

This quest for excellence continues to this day. The desire for continuous improvement has its roots deeply buried in the history of the company. Steinway did not allow itself to be satisfied with technical superiority only, but also expanded that drive to be the best in all aspects of the business of making and selling pianos.

Steinway launched its customer service strategy via its Concert & Artist (C&A) program dating back virtually to the origin of the company. Simply stated the C&A program holds that every piano must meet the needs of the performing artist. The philosophy states that taking care of the desires of artists both technically and logistically will have the desired spin-offs for the entire line of pianos produced. Since all Steinway pianos are concert grade, satisfying the high demands of the concert artists will naturally satisfy the entire piano buying public. This is true for technical excellence of the product as well as geographic availability.

The quality strategy at Steinway & Sons starts with senior management's commitment to quality. The company's owners do not claim that every piano is 100 percent perfect, but they do state that the goal to make the product perfect demands 100 percent effort on the part of all employees. To emphasize this point, no piano may be knowingly shipped that is below performance and cosmetic standard, no matter what the financial penalty may be.

Management stresses the importance of high working standards by considering all employees engaged in designing and manufacturing the piano to be artisans. All other employees in support and sales functions, in a manner of speaking, are considered agents of those artisans. In league with the philosophy of artisans, all do their part to produce and sell the instruments. This concept of artisan and supporter of artisans is not a simple concept to explain to new employees. It takes effort to convince people that making high quality products is a goal in itself. The company strives to explain this philosophy of quality first in all aspects of manufacturing and services through a wide variety of methods.

First, the company has a quality credo containing four philosophical points on how people ought to work. They are:

- I will not knowingly accept poor quality work into my work area.
- I will not knowingly pass on poor quality work to the next work area.
- I will not tolerate those who will knowingly do poor quality work or pass it on to the next work area.
- I will strive to learn from my mistakes and reach for perfection in doing my job.

These points form the basis of how all members of the company are to act in carrying out their respective responsibilities. It is in essence the embodiment of the total quality management concept we hear so much of today. It says: know who your customers are, understand their needs, and strive to satisfy them. At Steinway & Sons, the customer is the ultimate user of the piano. But just as important, the customer is also the person who is in immediate receipt of an employee's work. In the long line of clerical, design, purchasing, building, assembly, and test activities that go into producing a piano, the customer is the individual who receives the completed output of work from the preceding operation. Employees are inculcated with this philosophy; satisfy your customer's needs to the best of your ability. This is in essence the artisans' code. True artisans are proud of what they do and are willing to submit it to customers as a testament to the skill and dedication that went into creating that work.

There are three primary methods used by the company's senior management to get the quality philosophy message to its employees. They are the Birthday Club, Quality Improvement Teams, and the Suggestion System. Lets examine the birthday club concept first.

THE BIRTHDAY CLUB

The birthday club is a monthly occurrence where the attendees are employees from all functions of the company who have birthdays that month. The employees are invited to a lunch in celebration of their birthdays. The agenda is a state of the business reported on by every function head—manufacturing, marketing, services, employee relations, and finance.

Each talk, from the function viewpoint, focuses on the need for achieving quality excellence by everyone in order to maintain preeminence in the piano market. Facts and figures are shown outlining the present status and questions are invited from the celebrants. Finally, the general manager answers questions not covered during the specific presentation. This information meeting has proved very useful in getting the quality philosophy before the employees. For example, the manufacturing talk stresses that meeting quality standards is vital and they are second to none in importance. It is meetings of this type that portray, in real terms, senior management's willingness to miss production schedules in order to meet quality requirements. Artisans are assured that while production schedule compliance is desirable, it is not desirable over passing on work that is of questionable quality.

QUALITY IMPROVEMENT TEAMS

The second method employed to communicate the quality philosophy is the quality improvement teams program. This is similar in concept to quality circles. Here, every member of staff from clerk to senior managers are involved in a program to find and implement quality and value improvements with an interesting twist. Cost savings must first be shown to be at least quality neutral. This means savings changes in manufacturing cannot be implemented unless they are shown not to detract from real or perceived quality levels. The major target of opportunity is waste, defined as cost that does not go into the product such as overhead, rework, or set-up time.

Teams are rated in terms of quality points and dollar savings. The teams are competing for annual cash prizes based on various categories. Categories are multiple so all ten teams are encouraged to make contributions to the company's success. Awards are given for the highest total quality points, highest individual quality point idea adopted and highest cost savings total.

The concept of quality points is interesting. The company has created a hierarchy of items that affect the functional and cosmetic aspects of the piano. Team projects are rated against impact on the hierarchy and how well they improve that item. Hence, the scoring system is similar in concept to judging a figure skating competition. The cost savings projects are easier to score. Teams are given credit for savings minus cost to implement. A unique feature of these teams is that they are cross functional and they may attack problems in all aspects of the company's domain.

THE SUGGESTION SYSTEM

The suggestion system is the standard concept of paying for ideas. Here all hourly employees are encouraged to submit ideas to improve the way pianos are designed and manufactured. The company pays ten percent of the first year's saving for all adopted suggestions.

Also, if a suggestion is in the nature of safety, or unmeasurable quality improvements, and the suggestion evaluation committee believes it is a good idea, a merit award is given. Employees are encouraged to submit ideas. The company will even help employees write their suggestions if there is a need to do so. The company wants the suggestion system to be primary in all quality improvement activities because there are significantly more eligible people for this activity than for the quality improvement teams. For that reason suggestions are always given primacy for idea origination and for investigation. While the idea of paying cash for ideas is not new, the nuance of paying for ideas that enhance quality without measurable cost savings is rather unique. Steinway & Sons always, as policy, rewards employees who improve the ability of the company to produce the highest quality instruments.

We have approximately three hundred people eligible for the suggestion system and our participation is above average for such systems, about twenty-five percent annually. We believe our ratio of accepted versus rejected suggestions (forty percent) is also above average.

As mentioned previously not all accepted suggestions are cost improvement, in fact they make up the minority of accepted suggestions, only thirty-five percent. The majority, sixty-five percent, are for intangible quality improvements where calculating savings are not easily done. For example, two years ago we had a suggestion to reduce the number of slots on the music desk from seven to five. The cost savings is insignificant, probably about twenty-five dollars annually. However, by having wider slots, music books and sheet music can be accommodated without sliding. We awarded the suggestor twenty-five dollars for this idea. He was thinking of how we could make the piano better for the customer, and in a small way his suggestion does that. This is an example of how we incorporate this program into the entire TQM program.

We are happy that we have a twenty-five percent participation rate but far from satisfied. Our goal is to achieve a one hundred percent participation rate, and the way we will achieve it is through continuation and enhancement of our current programs. We try to be very visible with the suggestion system. Brightly colored suggestion boxes with blank forms and mail slots for filled in forms are located throughout the factory. Also, posters exhorting the benefits to customer, self, and company are visible around the work spaces.

However, the key to a good suggestion system is its responsiveness. We try very hard to publicize the program and get people to submit ideas. But, if the response time in giving replies to the suggestor is too long, people lose interest and before you know it, the system is dead and buried. In order to maintain interest, we make sure management is responsive. A policy that states each suggestor will be contacted within one week after submittal of the suggestion is in place. Suggestors are told that their suggestions have been received and will be reviewed within the month. At the end of the review period, or sooner, suggestors are informed of their suggestion's status: accept, reject, or needing further review. In any case, suggestors will never be more than thirty days from a status report. This discipline, we found, is very necessary if the system is to flourish.

Internal manufacturing activities are part of the quality strategy too. Technical considerations to assure continuous improvements are pursued as an integrated portion of the strategy. The manufacturing goal is to make the best component parts possible using the most appropriate technology. This enables craftsmen to make the best possible assemblies. The accomplishment of this goal is conducted via technical assessments of manufacturing technology and meticulous training of craftsmen.

Many unknowns in the field of acoustics remain; and it is the company's philosophy that as the unknowns are turned into knowns, all such knowledge will be applied to make the Steinway piano as acoustically perfect as is possible.

The concept of using technology to make the best piano possible is very evident in our approach to making components in our factory. In recent years we have expanded into many aspects of computer integrated manufacturing (CIM). We use the CIM philosophy of integration to ensure that engineering, materials management, and shop operations are well integrated with marketing.

We also use CIM concepts in our scheduling. We want to be able to deliver quality products on time to our customers. To do this we take advantage of manufacturing requirements planning systems (MRP II).

To better supply our customers (both internal and external) we have introduced computer numerical control machines (CNC). These CNC workstations enable us to make component parts much more precisely than was ever possible by manual machines. This means the parts our artisans use for assembling a piano give quantum improvements in the final outcome.

The use of available technologies is very important for us. Our company has thrived over the decades by being among the first in practical applications of technology, particularly in the production end of the business. Steinway & Sons was a pioneer in the use of machine tools to make pianos and will continue to be in the forefront of implementing new technologies. We implement new technologies not for the sake of being progressive, but for the purpose of improving our pianos and making sure that our customers are satisfied.

Continuous improvement also occurs as artisans improve their capabilities to make the piano in accordance with the Steinway design. Operator certification is a process that identifies and documents the method used to do specific operations, and then instructs the operator on the procedure techniques. Finally, operator certification requires that the operator demonstrate proficiency in order to be certified. Once operators are certified, they are given the privilege and responsibility for certifying that work being done at their work stations meets high quality standards.

Continuous improvement at Steinway & Sons exists not only as a philosophy; it exists also in the desire to continuously evaluate quality. A piano is a complex device made up of approximately twelve thousand individual parts. In order for the piano to perform superbly, each of those parts has to be fabricated, assembled, and maintained superbly. However, the best judgment is an independent judgment made by the customer. While customers can and do make excellent subjective decisions on the adequacy of the Steinway piano, they do not make objective, consistent evaluations of the product. These evaluations are necessary to direct continuous improvements. At Steinway & Sons this information is obtained through a weighted point scale system of over 160 specific items that evaluate construction of the instrument . The evaluation is done by a qualified piano technician employed in our retail store. The new piano is examined in this manner with critical expertise. In a manner of speaking the technician is the surrogate expert inspector for the customer. The idea is to constructively criticize and to do it in a way that not only identifies distinct characteristics but also creates a score to determine if we are getting better, staying the same, or getting worse.

The quality strategy goes beyond the factory. While this is obvious, it is instructive to look at some examples.

In a complementary activity to the point scale evaluation just discussed, the company surveys the dealer community and artists. Steinway artists are asked to fill out a user response card following their performances. This survey asks the artist to evaluate the preparation of the piano and how it performed. This information is valuable in two respects: first to measure the quality of preparation service, and second to uncover mechanical problems, if any, that may relate to how the factory did its job in executing the design.

In a different format, dealers are queried about quality standard maintenance. Representative dealers meet with senior management to discuss problems and opportunities of mutual concern. One of the major topics on every agenda is how is the company doing concerning all aspects of quality. These discussions range from minor discrepancies to the evaluation of preparation of instruments for concerts and all items in between. Since this is a partnership, the dealers themselves are also evaluated on their ability to deliver quality service. The goal is for the entire Steinway extended family to deliver quality service to the customers.

Steinway & Sons relates similarly with institutions; e.g. universities, conservatories, etc. These venues purchase multiple pianos and have many in their stable. The company is interested in how these pianos perform. The desire for excellent performance over extensive use is obviously required to maintain our reputation. Therefore, Steinway & Sons maintains close liaison with institutions to service their needs and gain feedback when appropriate. The quality strategy stipulates that problems be solved expeditiously to the institutions' expectations. This strategy is carried out with vigor.

The quality strategy with piano technicians is quite extensive. The strategy emphasizes training, continuing education, availability of genuine replacement parts and lots of communication. Lets examine this phase of the quality strategy.

Training is carried out primarily at the factory by personnel who are expert in piano construction and preparation. Week long training classes are held to teach technicians the proper way to care for and prepare pianos for the consumer. In addition, master technician classes are held to train qualified people on how to prepare pianos for concert service.

Nearly all the trainees are employed by dealers, are on university or conservatory faculty or staff, or are self-employed. Trainees do not have to pay for the first of these classes but are expected to fund their travel and hotel costs. Attendance is by registration reservation and recommendation. Recommendations are usually initiated by the dealer network or institutions.

Since quite often Steinway-educated technicians are our representatives to the piano owner, we depend on them to represent the company competently, hence the desire to train and continuously educate these people.

An important point in helping a technician to obtain repair jobs is the assurance that only Steinway & Sons genuine replacement parts are to be used. This is a significant differentiation between Steinway trained technicians and all others. The company strives to have a forty-eight hour turn-around time from order placement to receipt of parts, for stocked parts. The intent is to maintain the high standards of quality of the instrument. We strive to have Steinway trained technicians, using Steinway parts, maintain Steinway pianos. This way the standard of excellence that is built into the piano is not downgraded.

Reinforcing all the technical support to the piano technician community is extensive communications. The intent is to continuously inform technicians about design, manufacturing, maintenance, and other topics that will make them good spokesmen for the Steinway piano as well to continuously enhance their skills.

The quality strategy extends all the way to the customer, the ultimate end user of the piano. Here, contact is primarily made via the warranty card. Customers register their pianos with the Company and are subsequently welcomed into the Steinway family. They are initially given care instructions and other helpful hints on how to enjoy their purchase.

Periodically they receive newsletters from the company with interesting information about the piano including such subjects as what famous Steinway Artists are doing and news of upcoming concerts. Customers are also periodically asked for feedback on various topics. The company maintains an open door policy with all customers. No communication from a customer is too trivial not to warrant a reply—in some cases by the company president. Steinway & Sons firmly believes that customer satisfaction is paramount and acts on that conviction.

The quality strategy is both internally and externally focused. But more than that, it is a TQM approach which means it is integrated and never concluded. The desire to continuously improve the product and the delivery of service is central to the strategy. We will continue to carry out the quality mission.

Carol A. Weber
Director of Customer Satisfaction

Knight-Ridder, Inc.:
The End of an Error

Sometimes the best of intentions, the infusion of financial support, and the admonitions of top management can still fail to produce positive results for customers. In Tallahassee, Florida, staffers of the *Tallahassee Democrat* learned that teamwork is the key to effecting real change. The *Democrat's* story evolved over several years. It started in advertising.

Advertisers produce the majority of a newspaper's revenue, so it is understandable that great care would be taken in handling ads to assure that they are accurate and represent the advertiser as well as possible.

Advertisers measure the quality of service they receive by the accuracy of the ad, its design (unless they provided it themselves), whether it is placed in a prominent position, and whether it appears on the assigned date. They want easy access to their sales representative, and efficient handling of problems and complaints. They also expect prompt, reliable billing and credit information, and good overall customer service.

Readers, of course, want to see ads for their local stores and they want to see accurate ads—not ads that advertise the wrong product for the wrong price, or have the incorrect date of a sale, or the telephone number with one digit wrong. Handling ads correctly is not only a vital part of an agreement between a newspaper and its client, it is part of the public trust about which newspapers feel strongly—a piece of their overall credibility.

In the late 1980s, feeling pressure to gain market share in the face of increasing competition for advertising dollars, top management of the *Tallahassee Democrat* decided they needed to improve service to their advertisers. The newspaper was logging more than $100,000 a year in billing adjustments caused by running corrected ads free of charge after a mistake was made.

The opportunity for error in handling newspaper ads is enormous. At a paper like the *Democrat,* thousands of inches of ads are handled each night, with each ad passing through dozens of hands. As in most businesses, a certain number of errors was considered acceptable.

Managers had tried over a couple of years to improve their policies and procedures to better serve customers—not just in advertising, but throughout the newspaper. In 1987, they drew up a five-year plan and established various committees to help find new ways of doing business. There was a lot of excitement, some action, but little lasting change.

Then, in August 1988, President and Chief Executive Officer, Jim Batten, called a group of key Knight-Ridder employees together at a special retreat and told them the company had to become more customer oriented in order to meet its customers' changing needs.

To assist in a process of change, Batten pledged that within a year, the company would embark on an extensive customer service survey and that the results of that survey would be used as a benchmark for improvement in customer satisfaction.

Employees now refer to that meeting as a turning point in the way they did business. There was some consternation at first—in fact, in some quarters, downright cynicism. For some, the request that they accept a bold new challenge when many felt they were challenged enough was seen as a passing fad. The country was beginning its slide into what became a full-fledged recession, and belts and budgets were already beginning to tighten. But the CEO's message was a clear directive. Begin putting your customer at the focus of everything you do.

Clearly, the message was heard by the folks at the *Tallahassee Democrat.* They were already focusing on problems with advertisers. Buoyed by the CEO's challenge, they formed more committees, addressed more issues. But they remained dissatisfied with the speed and depth of their solutions.

Then, in the fall of 1989, Batten authorized the expenditure of $600,000 for a company-wide survey of customer opinion. More than 16,300 readers and non-readers were surveyed. More than 5,700 advertisers were quizzed. It was the largest customer survey in Knight-Ridder history.

In Tallahassee, the *Democrat's* top management created a new Advertising Customer Service (ACS) department whose sole aim was to make it easier for customers to do business with the *Democrat.* They set up a one-stop-shopping area where the advertiser could deal with a single person in placing an ad, getting a bill straightened out, or checking on the status of his advertising schedule. Along with ACS, the newspaper poured market survey data, additional resources, and top management attention into a series of projects to provide better and more industry-specific marketing information to advertisers and to get to know advertisers' businesses better so they could serve them better. Advertiser attitudes toward the paper began to pick up. But the ad errors persisted.

The problem was barriers. Over the years, great psychological walls had built up between the key operational departments—advertising, production, and circulation. Meetings set up to work on problems too often degenerated into finger-pointing. The general manager felt that everyone needed a common focus, something that everybody agreed was a problem, to get past departmental territorialism. The focus became those advertising errors.

A new cross-functional committee involving front-line people who had any part in the production of an ad and the handling of the customer was formed. The committee was comprised of ad sales people, designers, typesetters, printers, people from information systems, and finance people who handled billing. Without giving it a lot of thought, Mott had begun to break down the first barrier. Instead of pulling people together, calling them a team and letting them search for problems, expecting them to automatically act like a team, he had identified the most pressing problem and pulled together the people most likely to find answers. Then, he empowered the group.

Mott told the group that he had such faith in them to find the answer that whatever solution they came up with would be implemented. At first, Mott's sincerity was questioned. Front line employees and their managers had never been given such a challenge: find a problem *and* implement a solution? Without a lot of management review? Without months of second-guessing? It could not be so.

Many times the committee met and faltered. At times it looked as though it would disintegrate. The whole thing might have collapsed had it not been for Mott's continued commitment and the work of two facilitators, Doris Dunlap and Billie Smith. Still, walls that build up around departments and divisions do not fall overnight just because of good people and good intentions. It took eight months for this group of employees to really begin working together as the team they needed to be.

"There were arguments. There was finger-pointing. There were even tears," said Doris Dunlap, now Senior Vice President of Administration.

"We had to keep reinforcing the idea that they needed to stop trying to place blame and start concentrating on the customer," said Billie Smith. "We had to take typesetting operators who had worked day after day looking at only what their job required and get them to think about the ad as a product."

To think about an ad as a finished product individualized for a particular customer was a shocking change in approach for those who had looked at ads merely as lines filling up white space on a page.

It was not just the typesetters who needed an attitude adjustment. The whole system needed adjusting. The ad-placing process at most newspapers is daunting even when all goes well. It is a hectic, cumbersome process that provides fertile soil for the growth of self-protective attitudes.

On a typical day at the *Democrat,* a dozen account reps, handling an average of fifty accounts each, would be on the job by 8:30 a.m. In addition to their regular accounts, they are responsible for calls on potential clients and working with the advertising art department to design speculative ads to be used in selling a merchant an idea.

After organizing their day and setting up appointments, most would be on the road by 10:30, visiting advertisers, developing ads, collecting payments, often making extra trips to take ad proofs to the customers for revision and approval. Because of the drive time, delays in making corrections sometimes resulted in the ad not running when it was scheduled.

The ad reps would get back to the office around 4 p.m., then confirm credit approval for the client, sketch a rough layout for new ads, round up art to illustrate it, write up an insert order, write ad copy, and make note of any special requests like color, fancy borders, or cutouts. The original of any repeat ads had to be located in a bank of file cabinets full of old paste-ups.

The ads were delivered en masse to the advertising production area around 5 p.m. There, paper-clipped stacks of scribbled ad orders, sketched layouts, logos, art elements, and advertising copy were dropped into an in-box. Each ad was assigned a number and entered into a computer. Order slips were filled out for each job to be performed, placed into plastic jackets with handwritten routing information, and moved into a production process that would take a single ad through another dozen pairs of hands. Nearly 65 percent of all ads going in the next day's paper were turned in during a one-hour period.

Then, the sales reps went home. Any illegible handwriting, any confusion about whether the advertiser was asking for a number two border or a number four border was left to the designer and typesetter to decipher. Sometimes the ad rep could not be reached with a question. There was no mechanism for anyone in production to call an advertiser directly if a serious error was apparent. Typesetters were not rewarded for actually proofreading ads. They merely typed in what they saw written down by the sales rep. That's why, in one morning's paper, a real estate ad advertised a $40,000 *horse* instead of a *house*. The typesetter or paste-up person might have caught that error and saved the proofreader, who missed it. But that was not their job.

As the group worked together, they began really listening to each other and to each other's problems. They spent time in one another's work areas so they could begin understanding the total ad-placement process. They began to become a team.

Slowly but surely, the new team began tracing the reasons for ad errors. They made a list of sixteen basic errors and another list of the causes. They found that almost 100 percent of their errors were careless ones, occurring because of tremendous time pressures and what they themselves identified as poor attitude. They set about to identify solutions.

They proposed using faxes and phones in sales persons' cars so work could be sent to the *Democrat* plant throughout the day instead of being dumped on the ad makeup department all at once at the end of the day.

An ad designer was assigned to the advertising sales team so that spec ads (a polished version of what an advertiser had communicated to the ad rep) could be faxed to the ad rep who could show it to the client immediately. The same was true for ad proofs. Now, a customer could see a finished product before it appeared, assuring greater accuracy.

Advertising customer service employees—ad builders, pasteup artists, layout artists, typesetters, typists—were taught something about each others' jobs so they could take full responsibility for the total production of an ad.

The team recommended that computers be purchased to allow one compositor to put together a complete ad at one station. Extensive training was recommended to be sure the employees being asked to take on new tasks had the skills to handle the job.

Ad builders, once only concerned with following the instructions on ad dummies, now took responsibility for the entire ad. They read it not just to see if the letters were all in the right place, but to see whether or not they could spot any errors.

The week the team's report was ready coincided with a visit to Tallahassee by Gus Harwell, senior vice president for operations, who oversaw the *Democrat*. The team needed $30,000 it did not have to buy the computer equipment needed to test the theories. All the progress of the past months could have hit a roadblock right then. The team—and *Democrat* management—held a collective breath. But Harwell approved the expenditure—right then—on the spot.

Now that funding was made available, the plan had to work. The ideas were bold, the enthusiasm was high. But could they really reduce errors and improve their advertising clients' perceptions of them?

By the end of their first year with the new process, ad accuracy was running at 99.7%. Adjustments to customer bills, for running ads with problems, were down to a little over $1,000 a month from the average $8,500 they had been running. Those were all good internal figures. But what about the customers?

The *Democrat* began to see measurable gains when classified advertisers were surveyed in 1991. The team compared these results against their past performance and the benchmarking performance of sister Knight-Ridder papers. Advertisers saying they were "extremely or very satisfied" with *service* from sales representatives leaped twenty percentage points from 1989 to 1991. Those "extremely or very satisfied" with the *advertising and marketing information* they got from the *Democrat* (another thrust of the ELITE team program) increased thirteen percentage points. Their improvement scores also went up in the areas of service from dispatch, ad services, and credit and billing.

Beyond the success of the practical solutions was an even more important development—the collapsing of divisional walls. During the course of the project, employees had learned to work together as a team by putting the product and customer—not their own narrow directives—as the focus of their work.

At the *Democrat*, they now call the ELITE team the team that refused to die. The original, highly-charged, group gave way to subsequent groups with the same objective: to eliminate errors. The next target: errors in the *Democrat's* billings.

The *Democrat's* experience so embodied the elements of good customer service that two key people at every other Knight-Ridder newspaper visited Tallahassee to see the ELITE team in action for themselves. More than a dozen of those newspapers now have some version of the ELITE team at work on problems at their own newspapers.

The Tallahassee story shows how Knight-Ridder's total culture is changing to focus more intensely on the customer. We know that customer satisfaction is won or lost in a variety of ways—in simple moments of truth, such as the way you handle a phone call, and in more complicated ways, such as the way you listen to customers and determine their needs.

Some of the main lessons learned about quality efforts and customer satisfaction are that they require:

- total commitment from the top, not just in goal-setting, but in walking the talk, living the example.
- managers to see themselves as leaders of the company, not just as heads of divisions responsible only for their division's performance.
- involvement and empowerment of front line people to identify problems and solve them in a way that will have lasting results. The successful process is both top-down and bottom-up.
- educating employees to see that their responsibility is for the total product, not just their own departmental task.
- providing employees with the training and support they need to get the job done. Employees need to be listened to, involved in the process, and rewarded on the basis of what the company feels is important.
- a shared vision of what needs to be done. Teamwork will evolve when the appropriate people are brought together to focus on a problem or challenge.
- a focus on a particular goal and removal of territorial barriers.
- a means to measure your success. Success that can be seen and celebrated leads to broader efforts, and continuing success.
- listening to customers. Accepting margins of error in areas of constant customer problems is a short path to trouble.
- persistence in the face of the pain of change, for there are few easy fixes for most problems, and cultural change takes time.
- a customer-focused organization, because a customer-focused organization is a learning organization, actively involved in a constantly changing environment, and continually stretching employees' imaginations and abilities.

Contributing to this report were Lee Ann Schlatter, Manager of Corporate Communications at Knight-Ridder, and Publisher Carrol Dadisman of the Tallahassee Democrat.

John Rutherford
Manager of Public Affairs

Kmart Corporation:
Partners for Quality

In the Kmart Corporation's quest for continuous quality improvement in customer service, it is recognized that new and innovative processes need to be developed, improved, and measured continuously to ensure that customer expectations are met and exceeded as a normal course of business. With this belief ingrained in the Kmart corporate culture, processes have evolved and have been developed over the years which assist the Kmart organization in service excellence and addressing customer needs.

From a single Kresge store, established in 1889, serving Detroit, the Kmart Corporation has grown to become one of the largest retailers in the world. With that growth has come a need to handle tens of thousands of items and to make certain that these goods are available for customers in over twenty-four-hundred stores located across the nation.

Talking to customers in focus groups, as well as gathering data from the Kmart Customer Care Network, which includes an 800 number available to shoppers to obtain information, both show that one of the most frequently expressed customer service interests is finding the merchandise available when it is required. With this customer focus in mind, the goals of merchandise flow, investment control, inventory and cost reduction were identified as areas to be addressed in enhancing customer service through having the right goods available at the right time, in the right place, and at the right price.

For any process to work smoothly, it is necessary to consider all partners contributing to the process. Kmart's merchandise flow process has evolved to a system that supplies products from corporate warehouses and ships them to all of the corporation's stores. Partnering with suppliers is absolutely essential for this process to work to maximum mutual benefit, and to have the goods available when the customer is ready to buy.

In 1989, a multi-functional team at Kmart was assigned to work with a corresponding team at Procter and Gamble, one of Kmart's largest suppliers. Knowing that Procter and Gamble and Kmart share similar corporate philosophies on continuous improvement for customer service, this appeared to both corporations to be an excellent opportunity to partner in merchandise flow improvement. Customer-driven continuous quality improvement efforts in the area of service and product excellence are common to the cultures of both companies.

One of the first areas addressed was the customer concern of having merchandise available when it is required. By focusing on flow and inventory turns, it was projected that greater dependability and goods availability could be attained, inventories could be reduced, investments controlled, and costs reduced. In 1989, Kmart warehouse inventories on Procter and Gamble products turned 5.4 times annually. Partnering with Procter and Gamble and adopting practices that were complementary to both companies' systems started with this program in one major warehouse. By the end of 1990, Procter and Gamble goods were approaching 25 turns annually and accomplishing or exceeding all goals. The synergies to be derived from this type of partnering also give birth to numerous other improvement areas.

Gains like these are the results of well thought-out processes and the honest, straightforward sharing of marketing goals by each of the partners. Central in the planning process is knowing and recognizing the customer's needs, as well as the resources available to all the partners in meeting those needs. The examination of tremendous quantities of incoming data was necessary for both companies to form accurate trends concerning consumer needs and to assess the best possibilities for market positioning. From Kmart's point of view, store space and ad space allocations needed to be evaluated based on customer demand for products, opportunity costs, and the consequences of dedicating resources to one product over another. From Procter and Gamble's point of view, production capabilities needed to be considered and product scheduling was extremely important. Kmart's point-of-sale data provided a great deal of helpful information for analysis for both companies. From this data, it could be determined which products were selling at what rate. Further, it could be determined what impact special event sales had on the overall flow of goods.

This approach, however, was not without initial difficulties. The data being captured from the Kmart point-of-sale system was designed to address only the issues that were necessary for Kmart analysis. In partnering with a supplier, adjustments are necessary on the part of both partners in order to allow equipment to interface so that data can be useful to both partners. For example, initially the point-of-sale system concentrated strictly on unit numbers. This, of course, is key information. From Procter and Gamble's point of view, not only are the unit numbers important, but also determining which inventory is being used to create those numbers is of significance. Major suppliers have special promotion and pricing campaigns throughout the year. The impact of these special prices can alter the profitability of a promotion and therefore, when presenting a market plan to a retailer, it is incumbent on the manufacturer to be able to demonstrate that increased sales were not gained at the expense of profit. In fact, in a solid marketing approach, it is critical to be able to demonstrate that both partners are significantly better off as a result of the promotional activity.

By examining point-of-sale data from October 1988, to October 1989, Procter and Gamble identified the data that could be captured from this source, as well as sources for additional data necessary for proper analysis. During this development stage, numerous meetings were held between the multi-functional teams and associates within Kmart and Procter and Gamble. Through this process, both companies were able to better understand the average cost of goods sold, as well as the opportunity costs for both companies.

Partnering with Kmart suppliers is not a one-time event. Rather, it is an ongoing process of communications. Kmart has formed cross-functional business teams which are empowered to affect change and eliminate all non-value-adding costs at all stages of the business cycle. To be fully effective in this effort, it is necessary for all participants in the process to contribute and benefit. Certainly, on occasion there are particular events or areas to be addressed on a one-time-only basis, but the larger body of work is better described as an ongoing modification of business practices to benefit all participating parties.

Distribution analysis is a second area addressed in this mutual exchange, covering merchandise flow and quick response, as it pertains to the ability to respond to customer needs. In 1978, Kmart launched an Electronic Data Interchange (EDI) Program. It was done with the recognition that Kmart suppliers would have to join in the partnering for quality effort to realize all the potential benefits of the system.

EDI allows Kmart and its vendor partners to exchange data required for business functions in a structured, automated manner. These exchanges include sending purchase orders, invoices, shipping notices and point-of-sale data. Together, Kmart buyers and vendor partners are achieving reductions in lead time, increases in turnover of product, and increases in sales for each product line. All participating vendors benefit in time savings and the reduction in mailing, handling, and paper costs. Companies throughout the manufacturing chain are now able to reduce inventories and operating costs. Through EDI technology, vendors are able to automatically generate distribution reorders based on retail sales.

By 1990, Kmart had installed scanning for point-of-sale data capture in all stores. With this in place, the quick response relationship with vendors enabled the development of a purchasing database that allows both buyer and seller to quickly differentiate between fast moving merchandise and merchandise which customers have indicated is not in high demand. Through the automated inventory replenishment system, Kmart's network of distribution centers, which now supplies seventy-five to eighty percent of store merchandise, is able to accelerate turnaround time for orders. In 1990, orders were typically filled in five to seven days. In 1992, Kmart stores receive daily deliveries, and most orders are filled within forty-eight hours. This allows Kmart to address the customer's need for having the right stock in the right place at the right time.

Kmart's Partners in Merchandise Flow program is a bold approach and one in which Kmart empowers its suppliers to place orders and replenish inventory on the data available through quick response technologies. The benefit of this data capture has improved communications on many levels. Kmart views this type of partnering in the use of technologies to meet customer needs as critical for prospering in the future and continually seeks to develop closer relationships with all contributing suppliers.

Having identified merchandise availability at the right time, in the right place, at the right price, as being a key consumer requirement, the Kmart Corporation has developed a vendor tracking report. This enables Kmart to share information with all suppliers on improvement levels achieved in moving goods to the marketplace. Further, Kmart has determined that because its stores are supplied daily from Kmart warehouses, it is advantageous to Kmart suppliers to ship as much of the stores' needs through the warehouse as possible. Not only is it far less costly, but it is a much faster way to move goods from the manufacturer to over twenty-four-hundred stores. It is also the only consistent way to assure forty-eight-hour turnaround on store orders.

Other areas identified for inclusion in the partnering for quality effort are: marketing plans for targeted markets, reduction of unproductive or duplicative items, partnering for advertising efforts, test marketing, and the sharing of consumer research. All these efforts speak to Kmart's ability to respond as fully as possible to customer requirements.

It is the opinion of the Kmart Corporation that the leading retailers in the year 2000 will be those who most fully and accurately respond to the consumer's needs for goods and services. The most effective way to do this is to include all contributors to the process through a partnering for quality effort. The greatest measurable gains to this point have been: a better in-stock position, better turnaround time for goods, investment control, and inventory reduction—all at reduced cost.

Michael Gennett
Divisional Vice President
Customer Service

Lazarus: Quality Control Committee Focuses on Customer Satisfaction

Founded in 1851 in Columbus, Ohio, Lazarus is a chain of thirty-eight department stores based in Cincinnati, Ohio. In 1928, Lazarus purchased Shillito's Department Store in Cincinnati. In the following year, the Lazarus family formed Federated Department Stores, Inc. representing Bloomingdale's, Abraham & Straus Department Stores, and Shillito's. Through the years, Federated had acquired numerous other major retail stores throughout the United States growing to over $11 billion dollars in sales by 1987.

In 1988, Federated was acquired by the Campeau Corporation of Canada. Due to the high amount of debt it required to acquire the company, it could not service its debt, and so Federated filed for Chapter 11 within the U.S. bankruptcy code in 1990.

In February of 1992, Federated successfully emerged from bankruptcy as a publicly traded company on the New York Stock Exchange. Today, Federated is a more streamlined and efficient company. This was accomplished through the combining and sharing of many of the operations and decisions between divisions including buying, credit, and data processing systems.

CUSTOMER SERVICE CONCERNS

Lazarus faced a very serious customer service issue. In 1988, Lazarus had over forty thousand incoming customer complaints predominantly relating to furniture, carpeting, and electronic concerns. The vast majority of these complaints stemmed from a system that was not properly following through on the commitments made to customers by our sales associates. Breakdowns were numerous and customers were regularly disappointed and many times quite angry.

The biggest cause of these customer service issues was that Lazarus was focusing during the 1980s on the merging of four different department stores and a hostile takeover instead of effectively running the business.

For example, in 1982, the Shillito division in Cincinnati was merged with the Rike's division in Dayton. Just four short years later in 1986, Shillito-Rike's was merged with the Lazarus stores in Columbus. The corporate offices were then moved from Columbus to Cincinnati. In 1987, Federated purchased Block's Department Stores in Indianapolis from Allied Department Stores. The end result was four different companies merged together with four sets of executives with four different viewpoints, policies, and procedures. These four department stores had combined sales of nearly one billion dollars along with an operational structure that was antiquated and ineffective in handling a billion dollar business. The warehouses and computer systems in place were designed for a much smaller operation from another day and age.

To compound the issue, jobs were being streamlined and eliminated. Also, decisions being made to rapidly complete the merger resulted in very negative customer service. For example, the merging of the credit files between the various divisions was not properly planned or executed. The result was chaos and confusion for our customers.

In 1988, the hostile takeover of the parent corporation was a further distraction. On January 25, 1988, the Campeau Corporation launched a bid to acquire Federated. Once Campeau had finally acquired Federated after a two and one-half month battle, further streamlining and job eliminations took place.

All of these issues forced Lazarus to focus on these various events instead of running the business and servicing our customers. Lazarus forgot that without our customers, we would not be in business for long.

In early 1989, Federated appointed a new president for Lazarus, Jeremiah Sullivan. Mr. Sullivan re-focused Lazarus on the quality operation of the company.

With all the distractions that had taken place over the past few years, many of the operational and financial components of Lazarus had deteriorated. Mr. Sullivan brought to Lazarus a mandate that every executive was expected to deliver the operational or financial components for which they were responsible. This expectation was higher than it had been in the past. This new direction was a major departure from a traditional hands off approach. One expectation was to reduce the number of incoming customer complaints within a very short time.

The majority of the customer complaints were about furniture, carpeting, and electronics breakdowns. Customers were calling and writing to management about the poor service they were experiencing with missed promised delivery dates, credit breakdowns, and delivery of broken and faulty merchandise. No one was certain as to the exact issues and causes, nor was anyone attempting to resolve them.

THE LAZARUS QUALITY CONTROL COMMITTEE

A quality control committee was formed and chaired by the divisional vice president of customer service. Members of the committee were those individuals responsible for any particular portion of the process required to complete a customer's sale accurately and on time. This included the divisional merchandise managers, director of big ticket selling services, warehouse manager, delivery manager, workroom managers, customer service managers, selected store managers, the director of systems and procedures, and selected credit executives.

The committee researched the various issues causing the problems and then ranked them in terms of their seriousness. Customer complaints were tabulated and categorized by type and number.

The committee was divided into smaller groups, assigned a particular issue, and challenged to design a solution to the problem. Recommended solutions were presented to the full committee who would elect to refine or adopt the solution. The group also discussed the particular solution and how it would affect other pieces of the equation.

The process may not sound unique to solving a business issue. However, remember the executives and the issues that were brought to the table were from four previous companies. Everyone had been used to their own ways of doing things. Additionally, no one member of the committee had ever worked in a billion dollar department store. The sheer size of the business could have been overwhelming. However, that turned out not to be the case. The group realized that Lazarus was a much larger and different company than in the past and new ideas and systems along with a team approach would be needed to bring an end to these issues. The committee had one goal: to reduce customer complaints by fifty percent.

ISOLATION OF THE PROBLEMS

Two major changes took place on the corporate level that helped to bring a resolution to the service issues. These changes were the consolidation of the company's credit and computer systems. Two new sales support divisions were created to standardize the computer systems between the divisions and to centralize the credit function between all Federated divisions. The creation of these two new divisions were important to the quality control committee meeting their goal.

For the first time, we had a computerized system that tied the entire transaction from the selling floor to the warehouse through delivery into the customer's home. This replaced the outdated paper system that had previously been used. The computer system enabled everyone in the process of the sale to have access to the same information and update the system as needed.

The new credit system, established not only electronic credit files for the customer, but a notes section for each customer to file reports about a customer service issue. This system also gave all parties working with a customer access to information about an issue, how it was being resolved, and who was resolving it. This helped us to identify what had been done for the customer to date by the individuals actually resolving the concern.

Another change took place within Lazarus—the consolidation of our warehouses. Previously, each division that had been merged into the new Lazarus had their own warehouses. Once merged, the new Lazarus had small, antiquated warehouses in Cincinnati, Dayton, Columbus, and Indianapolis. The receipt and flow of merchandise resembled a confusing maze.

In 1988, Lazarus purchased a 1,200,000 square foot center. All merchandise receipts were sent to one location for distribution to our stores. The furniture and electronics receipts were shipped to their own separate warehouse location. Our shuttle system within the company now made sense, plus the warehouses had the latest state of the art equipment. All the old smaller, outdated warehouses were closed and eventually sold.

The quality control committee embraced these new systems and the warehousing program. The issues causing our customer service problems were resolved utilizing these enhancements. Once a solution was deemed feasible, it was communicated to the organization and training, if necessary, was provided.

The committee isolated many problems and instituted the following solutions to them.

- consolidating different policies and procedures for handling customer's sales and reporting a customer's complaint to the corporate customer relations office
- cleaning up the poor and dirty condition of the delivery trucks and warehouses
- purchasing the proper handling equipment
- instilling employees' pride in their jobs
- establishing a toll-free number for customers assistance
- revamping delivery to include:
    - training and execution of proper handling and movement of the product
    - using cellular phones for advising customers of their delivery time and also for drivers to call in any customer concerns or errors at the time of the delivery
    - establishing a toll-free delivery number for customers to call one day prior to a delivery to learn the approximate time of delivery
    - establishing regional delivery hubs
    - restructuring the delivery pay and the monitoring of the number of stops by the drivers

- reducing time to install by four weeks
- using a professional carpet measuring service to ensure accuracy of a customer's order
- determining key breakdowns through tracking all returns and sorting each customer service complaint by cause, store, vendor, and specific issue
- establishing a special order system to consistently write a special order item within a specified time period and to communicate instructions for this procedure and for taking non-refundable deposits
- establishing an electronics return policy
- training on the proper packing and movement of merchandise
- establishing a carpet court to determine the cause of a carpet error (did a selling associate mismeasure? or was it an installer's error? Disciplinary action was taken on repeat offenders.)
- establishing a consistent competitive policy by market for furniture, electronics, and carpeting

The results of this process over the past three years have been very productive as well as rewarding. The number of incoming complaints have been greatly reduced, as seen in Table 1.

Table 1. Yearly comparison of complaints totals.

Year	Amount of Incoming Complaints	Change over Previous Year
1987	40,084	
1988	34,473	-14.0%
1989	29,886	-13.3%
1990	18,376	-38.5%
1991	17,810*	- 3.1%
1987/1991	16, 680	-58.4%

*(In 1991, bedding promotions included an automatic return after 30 days of use if a customer was unhappy with the product. These 1,130 returns were not a breakdown but a result of the customer exercising their option offered in the promotion.)

The majority of the complaints today center on customers changing their minds, not being happy with how their product looks, or vendor defects due to poor quality of construction. (The goal is for the latter to be resolved in 1992.)

CURRENT STATUS

Today Lazarus enjoys a reputation with our customers of a near zero defect level of service when buying furniture, carpeting, and electronics. In fact, our furniture and carpet sales increased 24.8 percent in the last six months of 1991. In early 1992, our furniture and carpeting sales were up fifty percent and electronics were up forty-two percent over 1991. This would not have been accomplished if we did not have the operational piece functioning as a team. The quality control committee still meets on a quarterly basis to review the entire process and results.

Daniela Weiss
Senior Public Relations Specialist

TIAA–CREF: Managing Quality at the World's Largest Pension System

A prizefight was the way one newspaper described it: In one corner, weighing in with billions in assets, decades of experience, and over a million clients, are higher education's oldest and largest pension companies, TIAA–CREF. In the other corner, the challengers: a pack of investment companies, insurance companies, and other financial competitors, hungrily eyeing a lucrative market that shows promising signs of opening up.

The year was 1988; the newspaper, the *Chronicle of Higher Education.* But the showdown, as such, has yet to take place. It probably never will. Because, despite its enigmatic name, TIAA–CREF has a very straight-forward agenda — and it's not about fighting for market dominance or sheer growth. Instead the goal is to provide pension programs and insurance coverages that ensure the financial security of people in education and research.

But while the goal is constant, the means of achievement do need to change, as TIAA–CREF's recent experience has shown. Products and services must be continuously adapted and improved since customer needs and expectations change. To sustain a responsive approach, the corporate structure must engender initiative and leadership, and integrate customer satisfaction goals within the operating environment.

This dynamic has reshaped the way TIAA–CREF operates, as illustrated in this case study. Learning how to change, what to change, and when, enables TIAA–CREF to be responsive to its customers.

A LIFETIME PARTNERSHIP

Stability with mobility is the nature of TIAA–CREF's lifetime partnership with a million and a half professors, administrators, research scientists, and other educational employees. Each person has an independent agreement with TIAA–CREF that takes the form of a contract and certificate. These are as portable as a briefcase, enabling career moves among thousands of educational and research institutions, without forfeiture of the accumulated pension benefits. Career mobility also fosters the exchange of knowledge among these institutions, coast-to-coast. They range from Harvard University to the University of Hawaii, from the Rand Corporation to the Center for Molecular Medicine, from the Smithsonian Institution to the Public Broadcasting Service.

A person's pension accumulations, plus earnings, can grow as tax-deferred savings until they are withdrawn from TIAA or CREF (an insurance company and an investment company, respectively, which are not-for-profit companion corporations). TIAA–CREF also provides retirement planning services, individual counseling, tax-deferred savings products and insurance coverages. And, when that person retires, TIAA–CREF offers an income that can never be outlived. For example, one woman who retired at age 63 in 1936 received retirement income until her death at the age of 114 in 1987.

The TIAA–CREF pension system, which preceded United States social security by almost twenty years, was founded to carry forward the vision of Andrew Carnegie. He believed higher education was "one of the highest of all professions"; and, when Carnegie became a university trustee, he was shocked to discover that a clerk in his own steel works often earned more than a professor. Between 1905 and 1908, Carnegie endowed a fund with $15 million to provide free pensions to retired faculty members. Raising the economic status of the profession made it more attractive to young talented people, and older faculty members could now afford to retire, opening up new positions.

But even the Carnegie fortune was not large enough to sustain free pensions over the long run. Consequently, in 1918, Teachers Insurance and Annuity Association was established by the Carnegie Foundation for the Advancement of Teaching with a million dollar grant from the Carnegie Corporation of New York. TIAA pensions are based on defined contributions from the employer and the employee.

Years later, in 1952, a TIAA economist pioneered the variable annuity which, based on investments in common stocks, helps to hedge against inflation during a person's retirement years. To offer this new pension product, TIAA created the College Retirement Equities Fund (CREF). Together TIAA–CREF is the world's largest pension fund, managing over $113 billion in assets.

A STRUCTURE FOR QUALITY MANAGEMENT

In recent decades, the doubling of TIAA–CREF assets every five years reflected its tremendous growth as the leading pension system in higher education. However, its customer services were not keeping pace with changing expectations for broader product choices and more individual autonomy. During the 1980s, a number of college administrators and association representatives were loudly urging TIAA–CREF to add more investment choices, to offer the option to transfer savings to competing investment funds, and to give cash settlements upon retirement or termination of employment.

Fast forward in time, just a year or two later, and even the most vocal critics were becoming satisfied customers. What took place? A re-orientation and reorganization that built the framework for change. That had been the starting goal of Clifton R. Wharton, Jr., who was elected chairman and CEO of TIAA–CREF in late 1986. Wharton's reputation as a big-picture strategist, and his experience as the former president of two of the nation's largest university systems, distilled the skepticism that TIAA–CREF could not or would not change for the better.

The chairman quickly initiated a wide-open style of communication. He and other senior executives phoned and met with people at numerous colleges, universities and other participating institutions to listen to their opinions and criticisms. The recommendations of TIAA–CREF management were then reviewed by a special joint trustee committee appointed by Wharton. Within four months a preliminary draft report was completed. With this in hand, Wharton worked with TIAA–CREF front-line branch managers and benefit counselors to present the findings on campuses across the country, gaining valuable feedback from presidents, business officers, and faculty committees.

"There were those who were absolutely amazed that the draft would be made public, but I said, 'Let people react,'" Wharton recounts. The final report, titled *The Future Agenda,* was published in November. It proposed twenty-six major recommendations, including new investment funds, product flexibilities, increased services, transferability options, and governance changes. Within the first year, fourteen of the major goals were implemented, and the remainder were completed about a year later.

New products and services have been the most visible external signs of change at TIAA–CREF. However, their development required a new internal corporate structure that supports strict accountability standards among the operating divisions, as well as sophisticated budget control and teamwork; coordinated and long-range strategic planning; and an interactive partnership with trustees as well as advisory groups.

Therefore, one of Wharton's first steps was to commission an independent consulting firm to analyze the corporate organization. Following their report, an integrated management structure was developed to replace the old hierarchy that had rigidly separated functions among many divisions reporting to different vice presidents. Today, TIAA–CREF operations are organized into four accountability centers that report to the chairman through the president: Pension and Annuity Services, TIAA Investments, CREF Investments, and Insurance Services. Like profit centers, each one sets strategic objectives over one and three-year periods, conducts regular audits to monitor progress and cost-effectiveness, and has a pay-for-performance policy.

This also became the framework of the major corporate support areas: law, external affairs, human resources, finance and planning, and operations support. And, a new corporate area was created with the specific mission of developing and implementing new products and services, giving the other areas greater latitude to carry out their assigned responsibilities.

At weekly meetings with the chairman, senior executives address policy issues, bringing potential problems to the surface early so they can be handled with greater foresight. Concerns of middle management are brought into open discussion through monthly executive council meetings and quarterly group meetings of all corporate officers. These regular forums have dramatically enhanced internal communications, helping to focus objectives and assign responsibility.

Moving forward on every front, at all levels and across division lines, can only be effective if the moves are in tune with customer expectations in the marketplace. And so the goals of the Future Agenda included the creation of an advisory council of administrators from a range of participating institutions. The advisory council meets quarterly with TIAA–CREF senior managers to share viewpoints from the field and give constructive feedback.

In addition, a Committee on Products and Services was formed to critique the ongoing development, improvement, and marketing of new and existing products and services. This committee is drawn from the diverse group of educators and business people who serve on the TIAA and CREF Boards of Trustees. It is one of several board committees that involve the trustees in specific corporate developments, drawing on their collective expertise in academic affairs and governance; the national economy, corporate finance, and investments; the intricacies of life, health and long-term care insurance; and the philosophy of pensions and meaningful retirement.

QUALITY MANAGEMENT IN PROGRESS

Within this corporate structure, strategic planning and quality management can thrive. Here's a snapshot of how this works. In 1991, having achieved the goals of the Future Agenda, TIAA–CREF was ready to blueprint the next long-range plan. This critical effort began with the preparations for the annual strategic planning retreat where the central theme was customer needs in the year 2000.

A series of white papers were prepared, analyzing customer needs; and, a detailed environmental scan outlined trends in emerging technologies, the capital markets, the competitive marketplace, and the legislative arena, among others. For example, in the education community, enrollment, staffing and salary projections were studied to identify likely areas of growth. Input from customers in the marketplace was obtained through formal research surveys.

Taking a multi-disciplinary approach at the planning retreat, about forty top officers brainstormed and came up with ideas for new products and services, and enhancements for existing lines of business. Afterwards, the attendees ranked specific suggestions by priority, and a Trustee Work Group was formed to review and share ideas.

Within a few months, top priority was given to twelve recommendations, formalized as *Future Agenda I;* these are now being implemented. For example, the proposal for a global fund has been carried out with the 1992 introduction of the CREF Global Equities Account, which offers greater diversification and growth opportunities in the international marketplace.

The principle that every employee contributes to quality service is exemplified by the Service and Technology Oversight Committee and its subgroup, the

Needs Working Group. These groups, drawn from different areas of the company, were established by the chairman to pinpoint changes in customer service expectations, and develop responsive strategies.

Purposely unconventional, the Needs Working Group began their research by interviewing the employees first. "We could've started by doing a customer survey," notes Mike Fegan, vice president and member of the Needs Working Group. "Instead we first tapped into the brainpower and on-the-job experiences of our own employees." About one hundred representative employees were asked to participate in frank, personal interviews where they discussed their perceptions of customer expectations, and outlined the tools they feel are necessary to deliver the highest quality service.

From this exchange, the Needs Working Group distilled 250 basic needs, organized under nine broad business goals. For example, enhanced technology is needed to enable staff to access comprehensive data, instantly, in response to customer requests. Another goal is to target mailings according to the customer's portfolio mix and demographics. This would reduce the mail box clutter that irritates people, while ensuring better response rates to the financial products offered. It requires building a database that can be easily updated with demographic information on customers as well as potential customers.

At this writing, the needs and recommendations for fulfillment are being prioritized. Then, the customers themselves will be surveyed in focus groups and phone interviews. But instead of posing the traditional question, how good is our current service? TIAA–CREF will ask customers, what is your definition of excellence in service, and what kinds of services do you expect? Their responses will crystallize whether or not TIAA–CREF's assessment is on the mark, and shape the timetable of priorities.

IDENTIFYING IMPROVEMENTS: AN ONGOING PROCESS

In many divisions, quality circles tackle the timeless question: can we find an even better, faster or smarter way to perform a service for internal or external clients? Since the early 1980s, these teams have included employees at various levels of operation who are encouraged to identify weaknesses in their own areas and participate in the solution. By volunteering to serve on one of the fifteen to twenty work improvement teams, employees take responsibility for influencing positive changes in the workplace.

Some teams take a service chain approach and bring together six to ten employees from different divisions that contribute to the same product or service. Other teams draw colleagues from the same division, who analyze and resolve issues that are specific to their unit.

Teams meet for an hour each week in a structured forum, sharing the same road-map for change: set the goal; identify and define the problem; generate solutions and present the best one for management approval; develop and implement the plan; and follow up to measure results. To keep the team on track, one person is trained to lead the group through the problem-solving process.

Team facilitators, usually from a different division, provide support and guidance as needed. The facilitator is also a source of additional feedback for the program administrators and operating managers.

One team wanted to streamline the processing of benefit payments. Pooling the multi-divisional expertise of a manager, supervisors and support staff, this team analyzed the work flow and eliminated unnecessary handling steps— reducing costs and the chance for error. Another team included employees who, each month, film and file thousands of records of the premiums received. Their goal—to increase accuracy in filing microjackets—was achieved by simplifying labels, introducing color codes and, most importantly, developing new training tools. Within six months, they cut the number of misfilings in half. Encouraged by these results, they re-examined the process and made additional improvements, reducing the misfilings by an additional thirty-five percent.

An Executive Interview Program, launched in 1990, gives staff a chance to share ideas with officers from divisions other than their own. In informal interviews, employees ask questions, express concerns, and suggest improvements in general business practices, the work environment, benefits, and training.

"The program was originally designed to match an employee to a manager one level higher than his or her own manager," explains Carol Malino, a Human Resources associate who organized the first round of interviews. "With experience, we found that the levels should be more varied, to assure a dynamic exchange between both parties." The discussions have frequently focused on the advantages of more top-down contact, current and emerging technologies, and the company's future. Issues are put on the table for discussion and resolution at quarterly management meetings.

Another kind of dialogue takes place at the Chairman's and President's Lunch every month. Twelve staff members are selected, at random, to sit down with the chairman and the president and informally discuss their questions and concerns. Excerpts from the discussion are published in the corporate magazine so that the information exchange is widely read.

Since feedback from employees is essential in enhancing the working environment, an attitude survey was developed to query staff members about every relevant aspect of their jobs. The results were confidentially tabulated by an outside firm, and then evaluated by TIAA–CREF managers. "We responded with new corporate initiatives, from setting up a trainee program in the systems division to increasing the recycling of paper, company-wide," comments a human resources manager, noting that these and other developments help reduce the rate of staff turnover.

CULTIVATING LEADERSHIP FROM WITHIN
Cultivating leadership abilities within the company is a high priority, and different approaches nurture potential at every level. For example, area managers are encouraged to nominate talented, junior officers for a five-month appointment in the chairman's office, where they observe and participate in corporate operations at the highest levels.

Special assistants work closely with the chairman, attending virtually all his meetings with internal management as well as with trustees. Typically, these officers are specialists in their own fields, such as investment management, accounting, benefit counseling, or law; but they've had less exposure to the other areas of the company. Heightening their understanding of the company's landscape, and applying their talents to different kinds of projects, has long-term results.

To date, all of the former special assistants continue to work at TIAA–CREF; some have switched to other divisions that they learned about during their tenure in the chairman's office. Others have taken on broader responsibilities within their original division. The success of this program has led to a new Summer Management Program, where two supervisors are selected to work closely with the chairman three days a week, attend trustee and officer meetings, and become knowledgeable about different spheres of operation.

TIAA–CREF also invests in an exceptional tuition reimbursement program that pays, up front, for most undergraduate and graduate degree programs, as well as certificate programs that enhance skills and adaptability.

Another low-cost but highly effective program is held, after-hours, at corporate headquarters. Cosponsored by a local college, the curricula hones professional skills, such as how to manage high-pressure situations, communicate effectively, and take advantage of career opportunities.

"Encouraging and developing our staff is also key to the success of our affirmative action program," says human resources officer Carol Nelson. "We emphasize recruitment and development of qualified females and minorities for professional, managerial and officer level openings—positions in which these groups have traditionally been under-represented."

LEADERSHIP IN EXTERNAL COMMUNICATIONS

Fair pension benefits, simplified regulations, and savings incentives like IRAs are some of the issues that bring TIAA–CREF's leadership to Capitol Hill. "We meet with legislators and federal agency officials to discuss pension and employee benefit issues affecting educational institutions," says Diane Oakley, who heads TIAA–CREF's liaison activities. "We also testify at public hearings. For example, at Congressional hearings on new tax legislation, we help present a strong case for modifying certain rules for the education community, based on the distinctive structure of their benefit plans."

This rapport leads to other developments, too. With input from the associations, TIAA–CREF formulated an annual Hesburgh Award that recognizes excellence in undergraduate faculty development at U.S. colleges and universities. "We believe our participants understand TIAA–CREF to be much more than just a provider of retirement plans and insurance. They expect us to share in, and to foster, the high ideals of American education," comments Dr. Wharton. While the award itself bestows a modest $25,000 to the winning institution, TIAA–CREF expects it will stimulate attention and provide proven concepts for preparing faculty for the new demands of the 21st century. In short, it's a competition in which everybody can win.

PUBLIC RESPONSIBILITY

CAPITAL INVESTMENTS

Unlike other institutional investors, TIAA–CREF has its outside trustees (excluding the executive officers) develop and recommend policy positions on shareholder issues for consideration by the full TIAA and CREF Boards of Trustees. These outside trustees work within the Committees on Corporate Governance and Social Responsibility, bringing varied perspectives from academe, business, finance and law.

After a thorough analysis of the issues in hundreds of proxy resolutions, the trustees set guidelines and participate in the decision-making process of how CREF management votes its shares. They are also involved in CREF's initiation of shareholder resolutions, which have ranged from urging corporate withdrawal from South Africa during the 1980s, to taking positions on corporate anti-takeover devices.

This interactive relationship between the committees and the full boards sharpens the focus on vital shareholder issues, which ultimately affects the bottom line for TIAA–CREF participants, since corporations that act responsibly tend to remain competitive over time.

In investing in commercial mortgages and real estate, TIAA considers only those projects that demonstrate superior design, resourceful land use, and harmony with the needs of the community. Environmental audits, on-site inspections, and communication with all federal, state and local agencies ensure the suitability of the property investments.

TIAA also invests in publicly traded bonds and private placement loans to business and industry. In addition to reviewing a company's financial soundness and prospects for earnings growth, TIAA examines its work safety record, product soundness, and regulatory compliance. In some cases, TIAA finances companies that are directly engaged in socially beneficial activities, such as the construction of health-care facilities or the manufacture of pollution control equipment.

HUMAN CAPITAL

Corporate policy encourages volunteer involvement of employees in industry associations, professional organizations, and civic activities since it benefits society and also fosters personal development and satisfaction. Human resource managers are available to assist employees who would like to find volunteer opportunities where they can share their knowledge and expertise, and also learn from the exchange.

One employee points out that when he took a leadership role in a community organization, he learned how to motivate non-salaried volunteers to perform their best. Some of those techniques have helped inspire his management of professional staff at TIAA–CREF.

As a corporation, TIAA–CREF cosponsors the Inroads college internship program, helping exceptional minority students prepare for career positions of leadership. TIAA–CREF also participates in the High School Cooperative Education Program, a work-study initiative, and in the Summer Jobs for Youth Program, which often leads to permanent employment after high school graduation.

And, for the past few years, TIAA–CREF has been active in the Minority Counsel Demonstration Program of the American Bar Association. Through this program, TIAA–CREF provides African-American, Asian-American, Hispanic, and Native American law firms with significant legal work designed to build long-term professional relationships. Majority law firms that work with TIAA–CREF are also encouraged to assign their minority attorneys to TIAA–CREF projects.

THE EVOLVING NEEDS AND EXPECTATIONS OF CUSTOMERS

Every customer is different. While this axiom is true in most businesses, it is a critical factor in understanding how to serve the needs of the education and research community. On one level, there is the plan administrator at the employing school or organization who turns to TIAA–CREF for assistance in designing an appropriate benefits plan, for maintaining the plan, for educating employees about their choices, and for complying with changing government regulations.

Then there's the individual employee who turns to TIAA–CREF for help in clarifying options and integrating retirement planning with other personal and financial concerns. The individual who invests pension savings in TIAA–CREF — the participant — may be just starting a first job or culminating a career. The place of employment could be a private or public university, a teaching hospital or research institute, a museum or an independent school. The participant's financial background could be that of a professor who is a Nobel-prize winning economist or that of a scholar in Greek philosophy. The participant could also be the college president, the building superintendent, or the computer programmer.

Another variable is the benefits plan at the employing institution, which has its own set of choices, options, and features. For example, one institution's plan may offer cashability upon retirement or termination of employment, while another institution will restrict the cashable portion to the employee's contributions.

To address the different needs, some counselors specialize regionally and serve either institutional administrators or individual participants. Others provide services through the toll-free phone centers and correspondence units. The locale of the counselor varies, but the emphasis on responsive service is uniform.

Counselors at TIAA–CREF branch offices spend between one-third and one-half their time on the road, making several thousand visits to participating institutions each year. They conduct workshops for the plan administrators as well as staff meetings, seminars, and personal counseling sessions with the employees. This personalized approach has proved very effective, leading to a demand for even more information and face-to-face contact; consequently, TIAA–CREF has increased the number of available counselors.

This constant presence leads to open discussions of needs, followed by solutions. For example, a Campus Administrative Services system was developed to give institutions direct PC access to TIAA–CREF's network for billing, premium remittance, data retrieval, and plan information. Electronic transmission reduces manual processing and paperwork while eliminating the delays of mailing. Further enhancements are being developed, such as an online calendar of scheduled payment dates, and electronic messaging between TIAA–CREF offices and campus administrators.

TIAA–CREF counselors do not work on sales commissions and are trained to help participants make the decision that is best for them. Every kind of question is fielded from the 30,000 or so participants who call or write to TIAA–CREF each week—from "What is an annuity?" to "How does a bond fund work?" Since customers keep different schedules, the phone centers have evening hours, while automated phone lines provide round-the-clock account information and other services.

Each quarter, a service campaign helps counselors take a fresh look at customer service with the objective of ongoing enhancement of quality. They analyze both complaints and thank-you letters, since it's important to know what delights the customer as well as what does not. The counselors are encouraged to submit opportunities for improvement, which are blueprints for service enhancements. Small prizes are given to those whose suggestions are successfully implemented.

Speed is a critical aspect of service. The acceptable time frame continues to contract with the proliferation of fax machines, overnight delivery, and round-the-clock customer phone lines. As a result, TIAA–CREF has toughened the standards for speed and tracking how well service goals are met. Ten years ago, service was measured by sampling twenty-five cases a month from each benefit area. Today 100 percent of the cases are tracked.

CUSTOMER SERVICE STANDARDS

No matter which information center is called, the customer hears the same greeting: "TIAA–CREF, at your service . . . How may I help you?" This sets the tone for the conversation, where the customer's satisfaction is always the number one priority. This greeting developed from the At Your Service campaign, launched by TIAA–CREF in 1988. An array of internal activities and publications reinforced staff awareness about how best to serve the education and research community, as well as fellow co-workers.

New guidelines were established for handling inquiries, and training sessions for supervisors and staff emphasized responsive, courteous service. A Service Commitment credo was simply worded and framed for every employee, serving as a reminder of the universal principles at TIAA–CREF, namely dedication, excellence, integrity, efficiency, courtesy, and pride in a job well done.

To build on this service momentum, employees have been encouraged to recognize outstanding service by a fellow colleague by nominating him or her for a Star Award. Star employees receive a certificate and are automatically entered into the pool of nominees for quarterly awards. These honorees receive a pay bonus and meet with the chairman. Their varying perspectives on what constitutes quality service are publicized within the company.

The delivery of quality service begins with an intensive three-month training program for counselors, comprising product seminars, role-playing, and job simulations. To test the trainee's speed and accuracy under pressure, some sessions simulate the format of fast-paced game shows such as Jeopardy and the $25,000 Pyramid—except that the questions and answers are about TIAA and CREF investment portfolios, annuity income options, and repurchase agreements. Periodic training sessions throughout the year keep the counselors up-to-date on new TIAA–CREF products as well as regulatory changes that could impact the participants' financial planning needs.

To ensure that all counselors have a thorough knowledge of the industry, TIAA–CREF encourages them to earn professional and advanced degrees in the benefits field. This includes passing the exams given by certifying organizations such as the Health Insurance Association of America, the Society of Actuaries, the International Foundation of Employee Benefit Plans, and the Life Office Management Association. In addition, all TIAA–CREF counselors are registered representatives with the National Association of Securities Dealers.

The counselors are also trained to adapt their language to fit the caller's need. On a literal level, this refers to the multi-lingual skills of the counselors, some of whom speak Spanish, German, French, Italian, Portuguese, Serbo-Croation, Albanian, or Hindi. But on a conversational level, this means the counselor quickly evaluates the caller's unique needs, and adjusts his tone, pace, and vocabulary accordingly.

Ninety percent of the calls are answered within thirty seconds. The phone lines are often monitored by supervisors, who evaluate the counselor's performance based on set criteria such as social sensitivity, communications skills, fact-finding ability, presentation of explanation/solution, response to objections, and call control and closing.

The handling of participants' concerns is considered so important that even the CEO and the president of TIAA–CREF have been known to stop by the counseling centers and observe the interactions.

ABSOLUTE COMMITMENT TO CUSTOMERS

The counseling offered by TIAA–CREF is designed to educate and enable the participant to make informed financial decisions. This is critical as benefit plans are increasingly complex and many institutions simply can not afford enough staff to adequately administer the plans and educate employees on their benefits. TIAA–CREF organizes a wealth of financial information into flexible modules that can be mixed and matched to perfectly fit each audience's age, career phase, schedule, i.e., whether they have thirty minutes or three hours to listen and learn. Following the seminar, attendees are invited to meet privately with a TIAA–CREF counselor who has already reviewed their account information, and can answer specific questions about their retirement planning needs.

"It's the kind of personalized support that many of our participants have grown to expect from us," says Keith Rauschenbach, second vice president. A workbook reinforces the learning process with plain-English summaries of options and investment glossaries that clarify industry terms. Charts illustrate the quantitative aspects, such as how to establish a rate of return objective; and tip sheets anticipate common concerns, such as what to ask before purchasing an investment. Each chapter also lists other information resources, from the National Futures Association to the Institute of Lifetime Learning.

Some of the most popular planning tools are designed to work on a personal computer. One is known as the Retirement Illustration Software System, a customized package that lets the participant project a pension income by factoring in varying economic and financial assumptions.

Another popular package is the Tax Deferred Annuity software, which calculates the maximum amount that a participant can legally tax-defer, based on earnings, length of employment, and other factors. The software can be configured to support most defined contribution and defined benefit plans, including the state pension plans of many large universities; a record of prior tax deferred annuity contributions and other pertinent information is automatically stored. Nearly all of the software packages are made available at no cost to participating institutions.

For those who do not use or have access to a computer, TIAA–CREF also prepares retirement illustrations and tax deferred annuity calculations for participants, upon request.

For those who like to be well-read on financial matters, TIAA–CREF originated a library series which has nine separate handbooks on topics ranging from the specialized, "Comparing TIAA–CREF Income Options," to the evergreen, "Making Sense of Social Security." Within the first two years of issue, 2.5 million copies were mailed, upon request, as well as distributed at seminars and benefits fairs.

In keeping with TIAA–CREF's lifelong commitment to its customers, a specialized newsletter was developed for annuitants, that is, the retirees who are drawing on their pension income. Unique in the industry, the newsletter focuses on topical issues of concern to retirees, including health care and estate planning.

As needs evolve, TIAA–CREF reacts with an appropriate product or service. For example, when the IRS set a deadline for educational institutions to comply with the new nondiscrimination rules (i.e., comparable benefits must be offered to all-level employees), TIAA–CREF was prepared to help, introducing Nondiscrimination-Testing Software and special news bulletins, along with personal assistance from institutional counselors.

Accuracy and ease of use are readily-agreed-upon principles when it comes to information. However, there's less agreement when it comes to the social principles of investing. A few years ago, a number of participants contacted TIAA–CREF and said they wanted their savings invested only in companies that follow specified social criteria, such as companies that do not manufacture weapons, produce alcohol or tobacco, or have economic ties to South Africa.

Subsequent market research by TIAA–CREF showed this kind of fund would be of interest to a relatively small percent of the 1.5 million participants. Nevertheless, with respect for their position, a CREF Social Choice Account was introduced; this balanced fund applies social screens to the investment process. The account has been well-received by participants, some of whom transferred 100 percent of their pension savings into it. The account has also attracted media attention for its competitive rates of return, demonstrating that principal doesn't have to be sacrificed for principle.

OMBUDSMAN FOR DISPUTE RESOLUTION

Even with a strong commitment and track record of quality service, there are still times when things go wrong at TIAA–CREF. Usually the problem can be quickly corrected at the same level where it occurred. However, certain cases require special attention, i.e., varying an existing practice to satisfy special circumstances, or reevaluating a situation because the participant is not satisfied with the outcome. To accomplish this, TIAA–CREF has designated several high-ranking officers to act as neutral, third party ombudsmen.

Reporting directly to the president and the CEO, the ombudsmen examine the problem from a neutral perspective to determine if the customer was treated fairly and what action should be taken.

In one case, a woman had requested a partial lump-sum payment, even though her annuity contract did not allow for it. However, she needed the money to satisfy an (unrelated) equity requirement of her divorce decree, and was in danger of losing her home. The ombudsmen worked with TIAA–CREF's attorneys to have the court modify the divorce decree and, fortunately, the woman did not lose her home.

At this writing, TIAA–CREF remains one of the very few financial services organizations with an extensive ombudsman service for its constituents.

ASSESSING CUSTOMER SATISFACTION

The level of customer satisfaction is measured on an ongoing basis through independently conducted phone interviews with participants (including beneficiaries and annuitants). In 1992, this service quality monitoring program was expanded. Nearly 9,000 participants as well as institutional administrators were randomly selected and surveyed about their specific experiences with over twenty TIAA–CREF services, such as cash withdrawal, the retirement process, the tax reporting unit, and transfers into and out of TIAA–CREF. Almost all of the surveys have resulted in the upgrading of quality control programs, since one of the obvious keys to outstanding service is to do it right the first time.

In a 1989 survey, 89 percent of the respondents found the annuity application easy to complete. Soon after, TIAA–CREF simplified it and enhanced the graphics, too — boosting the satisfaction level several points in a subsequent survey. Service improvements in the Tax Reporting Unit boosted the favorable rating to 82 percent in 1991, up from 71 percent in 1990, and 59 percent in 1989; in Premium Services, the favorable rating rose to 85 percent in 1991, up from 75 percent in 1990.

Behind the higher numbers are significant improvements in procedures. For example, to make it easier for a participant to transfer funds into TIAA–CREF, he or she is now assigned to a retirement planning counselor. This ensures swift, personalized attention for problems or glitches that sometimes develop.

Ongoing service enhancements affect how TIAA–CREF is generally perceived over time. A 1991 image study, conducted by National Research, Inc., used telephone interviews to measure how perceptions had changed since the previous survey in 1984-85. There were 1,500 participants in the study, 20 percent of whom were plan administrators at the institutions.

According to the 1991 results, 100 percent of administrators and 97 percent of participants expressed overall satisfaction with TIAA–CREF. And 74 percent of participants and 84 percent of administrators described themselves as "very satisfied"—the survey's highest rating. That was a sharp increase from the 1984-85 survey, when the results were 57 percent and 70 percent, respectively.

Have TIAA–CREF's new products, services, and flexibilities made a positive difference to customers? The survey results are affirmative. Virtually all the plan administrators and about half of the participants said they were aware of the innovations at TIAA–CREF over the past few years. Among those who were aware of the changes, 70 percent of administrators and 55 percent of participants said it had a favorable impact on their view of TIAA–CREF.

Time is said to be the greatest innovator but, as this chapter illustrates, great strides can be made in almost no time at all. It takes tremendous commitment from a dedicated staff, a supportive board of trustees, and a genuine understanding that quality service is dynamic.

Maurice W. Worth
Senior Vice President—Personnel

Delta Air Lines, Inc.: Excellent Service One Passenger at a Time

Today Delta Air Lines is one of the four largest airlines in the world with annual revenues of $9.171 billion. A total complement of 80,000 personnel operate 2,800 flights each day with more than 550 aircraft to 223 cities in the U.S. and 34 foreign countries along a route system that stretches 560,000 miles from Delhi, India, around the globe to Bangkok, Thailand.

It was not always so. Delta's growth over the past sixty-three years is a story of innovation, of hard work, of determination and above all, dedication to service. Throughout sixty-three years of commercial aviation history and America's economic history, Delta's fundamental belief about service to people, customers and personnel, remain unchanged.

One of the most visible testimonies to Delta's orientation to people, occurred in December 1982, four years into the transition to a deregulated environment. During a downturn in the U.S. economy, several airlines were struggling, others were furloughing personnel and negotiating wage and benefit concessions. Delta had posted a loss. Despite the gloomy business climate and criticism from some on Wall Street, Delta's senior management decided to give their employees a raise.

The response to the raise was a grass roots effort led by three flight attendants in which Delta staff voluntarily contributed $30 million dollars to buy the company's first Boeing 767. What kind of culture encourages 35,000 people to voluntarily purchase a $30 million dollar gift for their company? Why have Delta's three mergers been textbook successful when most other airlines mergers have weakened both airline partners What were some of the ways Delta helped three airline families and 7,800 former Pan Am personnel who recently joined Delta feel at home? How does Delta encourage 80,000 people to consider the customer's needs first?

Delta has always believed that commitment to service is dependent on a mirror effect. Delta personnel treat one another as extended family, and this concern and consideration is mirrored in the way Delta personnel treat customers. Further, Delta believes that providing quality service is a dynamic process that changes from day to day, from flight to flight, and from customer to customer. Because of the dynamic nature of service excellence, the commitment between personnel, leadership, and customers must be considered in each business decision. Delta's dynamic process of service excellence begins with a seemingly innocent slip of paper, an employment application.

Delta hires for the future. A strong profitability record over the years has rewarded Delta with a distinct advantage in the hiring process. The very finest people, the ones most interested in a lifelong career in airline service, submit their first application to Delta.

The employment process is designed to flag a service orientation in an applicant's professional, educational, or community involvement record. The employment process favors applicants who have the potential for promotion, because Delta subscribes almost entirely to a promotion from within policy. Except for a handful of people with specialized skills such as law, everyone is hired in at entry level.

As a result, managers have experienced looking customers in the eye, working directly with them, or handling their luggage or freight. Also as a result of an entry-level experience, supervisors and managers handle problems in the daily operation with empathy. They are willing to help line personnel find solutions to problems in the operation because they have experienced similar situations themselves.

There is a strong tradition of employment security at Delta. The airline business has always been cyclical, and as a consequence during economic slumps, the airline industry has been notorious for furloughing large numbers of people. Employment security at Delta ensures that morale, technical competency, and service expertise are preserved for both the benefit of employee and customer. During economic slumps, extra staffing is redeployed into other jobs. Creative options such as job sharing and voluntary personal leaves are also made available. Delta has not furloughed a permanent employee since 1952.

The management structure of Delta is thin and flat compared to most companies of its size, and leaner than other U.S. airlines. Fewer than 1,500 people, with manager-level or higher titles, lead a total complement of 80,000 staff. Over the past twenty years, it has taken an average of ten years to become a captain at Delta and it is rare for a manager to have less than a decade of experience in the company.

Delta's Open Door policy takes the open door into the workplace. Every twelve to eighteen months, officer-level managers visit each work site and conduct workshop-type meetings with small groups of personnel. Following an update of current and future business, the floor is opened up for comments, questions, criticisms, and suggestions for improvement. The minutes of these meetings are published for each work group and reviewed by senior management. Managers directly responsible for larger groups of personnel, like the 18,000-member flight attendant group, attend these lively workshops year around. These workshops are in addition to a formal President's Team employee suggestion program.

Cross utilization plays an important role at every level of Delta. Airline personnel on special assignment rotate through selected staff positions and return to the line with a broader view of their company. Cross-divisional task forces of line and staff personnel at different levels are brought together to formulate recommendations for change, solve system problems, or plan special events. As a result of a thin, flat management structure, it is not uncommon to find managers ready for promotion, but no slot available. Again, cross-utilization or lateral movement grows management skills.

In addition to aircraft systems training conducted on the ground, flight training conducted in simulator, and check rides conducted aboard aircraft, pilot personnel attend non-technical training sessions that are dedicated to understanding the personal dynamics at work in the cockpit.

The decision-making process at Delta is largely centralized and major changes and decisions must pass the two heads are better than one test. As a result, proposal writing for departmental changes or system improvement is elevated to a fine art.

A Delta tradition that is probably unique among Fortune 500 companies is that there are no budgets. Managers justify routine expenses and major expenses are reviewed by the senior management staff at a weekly meeting. This tradition, a reflection of cyclical profits, has advantages a budget system does not have. Delta's Authorization For Expenditure process has the double advantage of close control coupled with full access to resources, neither of which is available under a budget system.

Delta people are compensated at the top of the industry and some are critical of this tradition. However, Delta has always believed that a strong compensation structure acknowledges the people side of the business, acknowledges the value of experience, and draws and keeps the best people on the team. Delta people achieve higher productivity than their counterparts at other airlines, so salary and wage cost differentials are offset by lower costs in many other areas of the operation.

Perhaps no corporate undertaking can have as great an impact on productivity and service performance as a merger or acquisition. Many airline mergers of the last decade never captured the full synergy of the combined companies. Some endure cultural gaps years later. Yet, Delta's three mergers and recent Pan Am acquisition, all merging union workers into a largely non-union culture have been called remarkably successful by industry analysts. During the Northeast and Western mergers, when there were several months before the operations were merged, Sunday newspapers from the new city were mailed to new personnel. A significant amount of time and resources are spent helping with the logistics of relocating families.

A mentor or buddy system is established in the new work environment. Informal meetings led by coworkers are scheduled before, during and after the merger/acquisition date so that questions can be answered candidly. Senior managers may join these meetings or technical training classes for a personal welcome.

Are there positive, measurable results from expending so many resources on the people side of the equation? The best measurement of passenger satisfaction among U.S. airlines today is the number of complaint letters written directly to the Department of Transportation by consumers. Since 1971 when that reporting began, Delta has maintained the best overall record for passenger satisfaction of any major U.S. airline per 100,000 customers boarded. Delta knows that the only way to achieve the goal of being the best and most respected airline in the world is to deliver excellent service, one customer at a time.

Thomas E. Harmening
Director, Corporate Communication
James Jannausch
Director, Quality Service
Deborah Love
Director, Organization Development

Michigan Consolidated Gas Company: Vision and Values Lead to Quality Service

Which comes first, the push for improved service quality or a company's vision for its future? In many cases, the service quality issue has been approached as a process and one of the outcomes often is the clarification of the organization's vision and values. At Michigan Consolidated Gas Company (MichCon), the process unfolded differently.

It all began in late 1989 when the senior officers of the company peered into the future and asked the question "With the natural gas distribution business becoming more competitive, how can we ensure that customers will come to us by choice?" They concluded the company would have to abandon its mindset of heavy regulation, security and captive customers if it was to prepare for the road ahead. But how do you change a company that at present is in little or no danger of losing its customers due to poor service?

It was a classic case of the no pain, no gain corporate theory. MichCon was not on the ropes and yet had to begin making drastic changes in order to face the more competitive times ahead. It was going to take more than a typical quality service program because the corporate orientation of employees had to change.

As a first step, the company called together its eighteen officers and isolated them at an off-site location for three days in January 1990. The goal was to have the group take a close look at the company and then come up with a vision statement to lead the company into the 21st century.

The officer group discovered that there was significant room for improvement at the company especially in the area of communication between key functional areas. What the group eventually drafted was not only a vision statement, but a set of values designed to guide the company as it strove for that vision.

A VISION STATEMENT CHALLENGED

It would have been simple if the process had stopped there: The company could have issued its vision and values, instructed its 3,300 employees to abide by them and moved ahead. However, one element was missing: employee participation.

The officers decided the best way to have employees buy in to the process was to give each employee a chance to challenge the drafts produced during the three-day officer meeting.

Even a basic decision such as what to name the movement was placed before the employees. A committee from the Corporate Communications Department came up with twelve suggested themes and submitted them to a group of employees selected from all areas of the company.

As it turned out, the transition team did not select any of the suggestions. Instead, they picked the first part of one suggestion and the second part of another. And so the change effort was named: "The Power of You ... Build The Future."

It was then time to roll out the draft vision and values, as well as the overall "Power of You ... Build the Future", to all employees. In planning the rollout, the company faced a problem. MichCon employees are stationed at nearly 100 facilities throughout Michigan. Some stations have as few as three employees.

One way to get to nearly everyone was via satellite. The decision was made to hold the initial televised meeting at some place outside the Detroit headquarters in order to demonstrate to employees that all areas of the company were important.

The kickoff was held in Grand Rapids and transmitted via satellite to eleven other major company locations. Arrangements were made to give all employees access to the meetings or telecasts, including rides to the downlink locations and distribution of videotapes of the event. Additional meetings in Detroit and Grand Rapids over the next three days resulted in well over ninety percent of the company's employees seeing the program. The telecast marked the first time in MichCon's history that all employees were brought together at one time.

Questions were taken from employees at all of the eleven locations and answered on camera during the two-and-one-half hour kickoff meeting. In addition, comment and question cards were distributed to all employees and more than four hundred questions were answered in employee publications over the next eleven months.

Once the kick-off sessions were completed, employees began the process of meeting and challenging the work of the officers. Each group had the chance to discuss the vision and values with an officer.

The challenge sessions took five months. The 262 meetings, held at MichCon facilities generated 6,000 pages of suggested changes, additions and revisions.

Once the revised vision and value statement was finalized, it was ceremoniously unveiled in Howell, Michigan at one of the company's smallest field offices illustrating that even the smallest of stations would need to change.

Each employee was invited to read the vision, review the values and then, if he or she agreed to be guided by them, sign on one of the 3,300 spaces on the document.

A booklet containing a framable copy of the statement, as well as line-byline explanations of the changes made as a result of the challenge sessions, was distributed to all employees.

The company, meanwhile, was making good on its pledge to nail the statement to the door, with plaques of the Vision and Values permanently displayed in nearly all public access areas of offices.

IMPROVEMENT AREAS IDENTIFIED
In the meantime, the officers identified seven elements that the company would need to focus on if MichCon was going to succeed in its transformation: communication, team(work), strategy, recognition, leadership, results, and quality service. The categories were turned over to teams of employees, each led by an officer, and the standards and measurements for each category were defined.

Over two months, the officer-led teams refined the values and devised measurements for them. The measurements set out in the communications to all employees were:
• employee opinion surveys
• the Malcolm Baldrige National Quality Award assessment criteria
• customer surveys and focus groups
• financial and operating results
• random employee interviews and focus groups
• benchmarking other excellent companies
• the performance management annual evaluation system

Quality service was chosen as the first focus area for the company and the decision was made to use the Malcolm Baldrige measures as a guide to improving quality.

The company formed an executive quality council and a small quality service staff to guide and administer the various company departments through the process. *Customer* was defined as anyone—within the company or on the outside—who needs assistance.

Two activities—distribution and public affairs—were chosen from those departments volunteering to lead the drive toward quality service. Both groups formed Operating Quality Service Councils and began setting priorities to determine which customer service processes would be analyzed. Once that was determined, Business Process Analysis (BPA) teams were formed to analyze the processes and then spin off Quality Improvement Teams (QITs) to further study and then actually bring about the changes needed.

The first BPA for example, examined how the department handled public issues having an impact on the company. The BPA recommended—and the public affairs quality council approved—that emerging public issues be assigned a steward to oversee the company's management of the issue.

What emerged was a system that resembled the account executive method used for tracking client accounts at many public relations agencies. The client now has one contact on the issue. The steward serves as the point person and puts together whatever teams and resources are necessary to deal with the issue.

Previously, many clients were uncertain about whom to call for help.

Communication and coordination within Public Affairs also improved. Department employees have more of a sense of what's being done in the department.

In the Distribution department, two of the initial BPAs studied how the company responds to reports of natural gas leaks and how requests for new service are handled. The team studying new service requests included participants from nine different departments and recommended that a cross departmental team handle each service request, considerably expediting the process.

The fledgling quality service improvement program has not been without obstacles. Some employees have said they're too busy with their regular jobs to serve on quality teams. Others have said they just want to do their jobs without interference. Little by little, however, those attitudes are beginning to change.

An employee survey taken in mid-1992 also showed that employees believe that the company is improving. When asked if MichCon had changed in the past year, 56 percent said it had changed for the better. Only 41 percent said it had changed for the better during a survey taken in 1990. Thirty-four percent said it had stayed about the same (46 percent in 1990) and 10 percent (13 percent in 1990) thought conditions had deteriorated at the company.

TAKING THE PULSE

As the company moves to become a customer-driven organization, company media, including weekly and monthly publications, have provided a steady stream of information about change not only at MichCon, but other companies as well. The publications also ran articles about coping with change, including one in which the company's employee assistance counselor stated that being afraid of change is natural and offered tips on dealing with it.

Also produced was an 18-month progress report videotape that offered a no-holds barred look at the progress of the Power of You Build the Future program. The video contained a series of interviews with employees at all levels of the company. While many of the employees stated they had seen some progress toward building a new climate at MichCon, some did not see progress and said so.

One employee said, "the 'Power of You .. Build The Future' simply doesn't mean much right now because it's still in the building stages." Another noted that some employees "are sitting back, waiting and watching others. Some are going ahead and sticking their necks out and some don't care." The video also looked at one supervisor who acknowledged he was having a tough time adapting to the new corporate environment. "No question about it," he said, "this was a very difficult year for me . . . very, very trying."

It is healthy that employees feel secure enough to speak out on camera. It takes an open climate to grow a new one and if nothing else, openness has been established.

The move to improve the quality of client service has now moved beyond the first two groups and is blossoming throughout the company. Other groups are not waiting to be told how to proceed. They are beginning to examine what they can do to improve their customer service as they await the formal program to take place in their areas.

Another benefit of the move to improve service quality has been the site visits to companies MichCon has identified as leaders in providing quality service. It was discovered through this benchmarking exercise that many other companies have faced—and overcome—some of the same obstacles MichCon has faced.

Has MichCon moved from a traditional utility company to an innovative, customer-driven organization? "I believe we've started," said Stephen E. Ewing, MichCon's president and CEO. "But we're not there yet. We don't expect any sudden changes. After all, just as it takes a long time to get an ocean liner to turn around, it takes a long time to get 3,300 people moving in one direction. But once they start moving in that direction, it's hard to stop them. And that's exciting."

J. A. Hultz
*Manager, Construction and
Project Management*

Ohio Edison Company: Quality Improvement through Technical Staff Management

This case study will show how change can be affected through the application of strategic planning encompassing all levels of employee involvement, through customer recognition and support, and through the application of quality goals and processes. The changes discussed here were the result of a three-year program at Ohio Edison Company's W. H. Sammis Power Plant.

The W. H. Sammis Plant, Ohio Edison's largest coal-fired power plant, had a history of lower than desired performance and reliability throughout the 1970s. This case study will present some of the solutions developed to make quality improvements which have contributed to developing reliable and efficient generating units at the W. H. Sammis Plant.

WHY THE NEED FOR CHANGE

The electric utility industry began to experience unprecedented growth after World War II when generating capacity had to almost double every ten years to keep up with consumer demand. This trend continued through the early 1970s. As seen in Table 1, Ohio Edison's system's annual peak load (the maximum hourly demand for electrical energy in any given year) grew from 1715 megawatts (MW) in 1960 to 3053 MW by 1970. These growth patterns seemed to be repeatable and thus, predictable. Larger and larger generating units were built utilizing increasingly complex technology to increase conversion efficiency while meeting the projected need for electric power. As events transpired, however, the growth pattern did not require a doubling of capacity every ten years, nor did technology progress enough to meet the challenges of the large supercritical steam cycle units which were being built in anticipation of the not-to-be realized growth.

THE TECHNOLOGY

In the 1960s, most central station power plants used coal-fired drum boilers that

Table 1. Ohio Edison annual peak
megawatt loads.

Annual Peak Megawatt Loads	
Year	Loads
1960	1715.5
1961	1814.1
1962	1889.5
1963	2036.1
1964	2180.1
1965	2281.0
1966	2506. 3
1967	2590.0
1968	2767.0
1969	2975.0
1970	3053.0
1971	3307.0
1972	3530.0
1973	3810.0
1974	3664.0
1975	3682.0
1976	3817.0
1977	4134.0
1978	4038.0

generated 100 to 300 megawatts. These plants used 2400 psi steam at 1000°F, and are referred to as subcritical units. The technology to control and use this type of power generation unit was within a known envelope. As demands for larger and more efficient units grew in the 50s and 60s, the equipment manufacturers started to market supercritical units as a prime solution to meet future generation growth. Supercritical units generate steam at pressures in excess of 3500 psi at 1000°F. At these pressures steam is in a state that cannot be defined as either a gas or a liquid. It is an unusual fluid that is quite challenging to metallurgy. The technology to contain and control steam at this pressure was not fully developed, and consequently the operating reliability of the supercritical units suffered.

Instead of having low cost, efficient and reliable power, the industry had a technology that required constant modification and repair. The technology also demanded an excessive reliance on the original equipment manufacturers (OEM) for support since the utilities lacked the staffing and expertise to manage the operation and maintenance of the units on their own. The critical skills that were needed included metallurgists, turbine controls experts, electronics and hydraulics experts, computer analysts, and welding engineers. These people were predominantly in the private reserve of the OEMs and were generally not interested in utility employment, and up to this point, the industry had no reason to pursue employees with this type of specialized skill. The skill deficit was also noted in the labor ranks where the employees lacked the training to deal with precision code welding, electronics, computers, or complex maintenance procedures.

THE W. H. SAMMIS PLANT

The W. H. Sammis Plant is a 2220 MW coal-fired power plant located on the Ohio River near Steubenville, Ohio, approximately fifty miles west of Pittsburgh. The Sammis Plant is a comparatively large plant with seven operating units. The first four units, installed between 1959 and 1964, are drum type, subcritical, 2400 psi boilers, each rated at 180 MW. Unit 5, rated at 300 MW, was installed in 1967, and is Ohio Edison's first once-through boiler. It is designed, however, for operating at subcritical pressures (2400 psi). Units 6 and 7, rated at 600 MW each, and installed in 1969 and 1971, respectively, are also once-through boilers, but their operating pressures are in the 3500 to 4000 psi supercritical range. Supercritical steam units store enormous amounts of energy. At these pressures, steam can eat away at steel and defy containment within gaskets and seals.

The interaction of several of the factors noted above caused a significant drop in plant availability and reliability at the Sammis Plant in the 1970s. Among the problems were: underdeveloped technology, lack of certain skills in the work force, lack of a sufficient technical support staff, and rapid addition of different configurations of new units at the same time plant personnel were learning the nuances of the previously installed units. As a result, the annual plant equivalent availability factor (the measure of the actual average plant capacity available to make electricity in a year divided by the theoretical maximum availability) dropped to fifty percent by the end of 1977. This statistic becomes significant when it is noted that a power plant should attain an availability factor of eighty percent or more. The company initiated a major plant modification program in 1978, when an executive level Reliability Committee was formed to oversee the Sammis Plant Availability Improvement Program. This program involved significant capital expenditures, an increase in plant staffing, the creation of an on-site technical support staff, and an effort to improve the working environment of the plant (Carson 1982). The program resulted in a twenty percent improvement in plant availability by the late 1980s.

During this period, the technical staff grew from a handful of production engineers to an on-site engineering staff composed of approximately forty engineers and technicians. They operated primarily in a reactive mode addressing those technical issues that were the result of near-term problems, rather than long-term plant availability.

PROGRAM FOR CHANGE

In the late 1980s, Ohio Edison decided that additional changes were possible at the Sammis Plant. New ideas and approaches to problem identification could turn the Sammis Plant into an even more reliable and efficient producer of electricity. The plant had most of the technical staffing necessary to support this change, but lacked the necessary training and a defined mission. A strategy for effecting further change had to be developed. Key elements addressed accountability, responsibility, cooperation, problem ownership, and customer focus.

The Sammis technical support group consists of a general plant engineer, three supervising engineers, and a maintenance planning supervisor. These five people provide the focal point for directing the allocation of the technical resources to solve the plant's technical problems. They are supported by engineers, technicians and other nontechnical support personnel.

When the decision was made in 1978 to have a large on-site technical support staff, it was assumed that this staff would act like a single, large, multifaceted production engineer, handling performance tests, redesigning systems, specifying equipment, monitoring water quality, and adhering to pertinent environmental regulations. While it is workable for a single production engineer to have ownership and accountability for all of these problems, ownership and responsibility become diffused with forty people acting in different and sometimes conflicting ways.

The first challenge was to change our style. It was necessary to project a professional image if we expected to be treated with the respect necessary to achieve change and improvement at the plant. This involved simple measures such as engineering group representation at all plant meetings dealing with the operation and maintenance of the units; removing graffiti (non-company authorized symbols) from hard hats; issuing standardized coveralls identified with the employees' names; issuing matching jackets for safety awards; holding quarterly meetings to gain feedback on our overall program for change; establishing an open door policy for all; and allowing decisions to be handled at the lowest possible level. Of course, symbolic changes are important, but other more substantive changes were necessary too. These initially included a commitment by supervision to lead by example. The engineering supervisors became partners with the engineers to assist in solving problems no matter what time of night or day of the week. Once they realized that the supervisors were available as needed, the engineers gained more confidence to direct their own projects and ultimately were able to solve a vast majority of the problems without supervisory input. They assumed responsibility and accountability because they knew how to solve problems without direction from supervision, but had the confidence that help from supervisors was available if needed.

The next problem was to define who our customers were and what our mission should be to support these customers. This led to a series of meetings involving the supervisors and many of the more experienced technical people to develop a mission statement based on the customers they identified. The mission statement was distributed to all members of the technical group.

We then proceeded to identify, in the following order, an organizational strategy, an organizational structure to support this strategy, and systems to monitor our performance. It was deemed important that individuals not be identified or slotted on the proposed organizational chart until all of the above efforts were completed. This was necessary to allow for more creative approaches to building an organizational structure that supports an organization strategy rather than a structure that supports the preferences of specific individuals. The results of our efforts were: (1) a significant change in the organization which placed recognition of and support of the customer first, and (2) a requirement that all technical issues be identified on a proactive rather than reactive basis.

Specific personnel were dedicated to generating units (unit engineers) and technical experts were recruited and hired to support the unit engineers. With this change, we were able to quickly establish problem ownership and support in the resolution of most plant technical problems, no matter how complex. The mind-set of the technical staff had evolved from a reactive focus on specific engineering problems to one which focused on all problems which could potentially impact the units' operability.

BUDGETS

In any large industrial organization, budgets dictate the current and future direction of the capital improvement programs. Budgeting, if done properly, is the result of careful planning and cost-benefit analysis. Tradeoffs must always be made in order to get the maximum benefit from a finite pool of money. At the Sammis Plant two separate but complimentary budget systems were developed to coincide with the change in organization. These budgets are referred to as the Five Year Plan and the Two-Cycle Budget.

The Five Year Plan is a long range planning tool that identifies total plant expenditures (maintenance and capital) anticipated over a subsequent five year period. The budgets within the Five Year Plan are developed based on historical and projected future trends.

The Two-Cycle Budget is a capital expenditure budget based on detailed analysis of all critical plant components during periodic plant maintenance outages. The first five year portion of the Two-Cycle Budget feeds directly into the capital portion of the Five Year Plan. The Two-Cycle Budget is based on repair and replacement improvements through two turbine outage cycles and reflects only those capital expenditures related to permanent improvements. At Sammis we have boiler outages lasting approximately four weeks every eighteen months, and turbine maintenance outages lasting approximately nine weeks every five years. These outages present opportunities to conduct detailed quality examinations of various plant components for future repair, upgrade or replacement on a very long range basis. This can result in capital planning for quality improvements as far as eight years ahead, with opportunities to integrate major capital projects into the long-range operating improvement plan for a given unit. The main difference in the five year budget process and the two turbine cycle budget process is that the latter process is based on known or accurately predicted equipment status that projects plant improvements on a total operating cycle basis rather than a five year snapshot.

Another change instituted at Ohio Edison is the use of firm price contracting for the majority of the outage work. This includes not only capital projects but also maintenance work. The use of firm pricing provides better control of budgets; however, its use requires exacting specifications and detailed work scopes.

Historically, the practice was to contract outage work on a time and material (T&M) basis since the full scope of the repairs or refurbishments weren't known until the outage was in progress. With the current practice of doing detailed inspections long before an outage starts (in some cases five years before the outage), we can develop a detailed outage scope and plan, thereby enabling the use of firm price contracting. This has effectively eliminated emergency procurement of long lead time items since we can now develop strategies to competitively bid this equipment based on minimal lead times. The use of specifications subsequently allows the application of quality requirements for supplier and contractor services. These supplier and contractor quality requirements mandate certain steps and processes that we expect from our suppliers. Of course it is not enough to state quality requirements without applying a surveillance and audit program to assure that the mandated quality requirements are being followed. Ohio Edison has a quality assurance group as part of our general office engineering group that provides this service for the plants.

Although we have a significant quality control inspection program, quality must be designed-in and built-in the components rather than inspected-in. The inspection process should only reaffirm the quality of the product. We also have a large laboratory and materials analysis center that is available to the plants to determine failure modes and recommend material or surveillance changes. The suppliers of critical components and materials are subject to prebid surveys, are required to have quality assurance programs, and are well aware of our quality expectations.

Along with improvements in the technical support of the plant, we have also placed added emphasis on the Maintenance Planning group. This group has the responsibility for planning day-to-day maintenance and for developing the detailed plans for future scheduled maintenance outages. The Maintenance Planning group is split into two subgroups; one subgroup is dedicated to units 1-4, and the other subgroup is dedicated to units 5-7. Four to five scheduled or planned maintenance outages occur each year, at different intervals.

As with the engineers, the maintenance planners did not fully understand who their customers were nor their mission. After a series of meetings to develop these criteria, the maintenance planners became owners of all maintenance scheduling and planning. In addition to detailed planning for maintenance outages, we now preplan all forced outage work. Of course this is not always possible if the item that forces the unit off is not anticipated; however, we generally have a feel for the critical path items that will drive the schedule. Prior to critical path management (CPM) of our forced outages, we used a punch list for items that were candidates for repair. The various maintenance departments would select which items they were going to work on and when the work would be done; however, there was little coordination of these activities. As can be expected, the outages were not completed in the minimum time with maximum achievement. With CPM, all parties work according to a plan and achievements are maximized. In addition, we now designate an outage manager for the coordination of all critical path items. These changes allow the plant superintendent to concentrate on solving more important problems rather than having to sift through punch lists to determine what to work on and when to work on it. Lastly, no outage is over until the documentation has been completed, including documentation of as-found conditions, as-left conditions, and lessons learned for application to future outages.

TECHNICAL ACHIEVEMENTS

Building on the changes in technical support and planning philosophy, several plans were developed for future quality improvements. The most significant has been the Boiler Tube Failure Reduction Plan (BTFRP) (Lasky 1990). Because of the age of the units, boiler tube failures were the major contributor to unplanned forced outages. Recognizing this fact, the Engineering group initiated a program in 1988 to collect information concerning the failure probability of all boiler components. This required that we not only review the known past failure history of the boiler components, but we also had to be able to predict life expectancy for components which had no failure history. We were faced with the dilemma of how to predict failure with no history of previous failure.

Part of the company's commitment to reduce forced outage rates involved allowing the engineers to plan detailed nondestructive examinations (NDE) of critical boiler components during forced and scheduled outages. Outages became valuable resources and opportunities for planning future work which, in effect, would reduce forced outages. Through the use of various NDE technologies, quantitative data could be amassed, and through use of computer models and engineering judgment, qualitative estimates could be made concerning a component's future life expectancy. Since the major cause of forced outage was boiler tube failure, the BTFRP became the building block for changing how the Sammis Plant would do future work. The BTFRP was to achieve the following three goals:

1. reliably predict the end of boiler component useful life (with a subgoal of being able to predict end of life two to three years ahead of the first failure)
2. identify the most cost effective repair or modification
3. effectively schedule the repairs or modifications

The above goals were refined into detailed plans which would achieve either a fifty percent failure reduction rate or alternately a 100 percent failure reduction rate. Because it is not cost effective to eliminate all failures in all components, a higher failure rate can sometimes be accommodated if judged to be the most cost effective strategy. Therefore, components which are redundant or which have infrequent failure probability lend themselves to the 50 percent reduction strategy. Through careful analysis based on predicted degradation of certain boiler components, the need for replacement and the optimum time for replacement could be identified. As a result, forced outages could be minimized and budgets would become predictable. In other words—no more surprises!

The BTFRP is a comprehensive quality document requiring dedicated manpower resources to keep current. It is revised semiannually and issued prior to the budget review cycle. The information in this document feeds capital improvement plans, both the Five Year Plan and the Two-Cycle Budgets.

As with most major components in power plants, not all items that cause forced outages can be identified until the primary causes are fixed. Our boiler tube failures masked the fact that our boilers were not tuned for optimum operation. Once the appropriate tube surfaces were replaced in accordance with the BTFRP, the boilers needed to be tuned to prevent future degradation of the tubes.

Combustion tuning involves doing all the right things to make the fire in the furnace optimal for the amount of energy required to be delivered from the boiler and to minimize future damage to boiler components. We now make combustion tuning an important post-outage work item that is essentially the last step in extracting the maximum possible efficiency out of the unit and for allowing long term predictable operation.

Another item that we focused on for technical improvement was the plant heat rate. Heat rate is the ratio of the amount of energy input into the boiler, i.e., fuel BTU value, to the amount of energy converted to electricity that is supplied to the electric transmission network. As the heat rate improves, many subsequent benefits come into play to multiply the overall advantage. With improved heat rate, the plant needs less fuel, therefore, less coal is handled, and less coal needs to be crushed, pulverized, and blown into the furnace. Also removal and disposal of ash is decreased. All of this results in less maintenance and lower end cost to the customer.

To improve the heat rate, there needs to be an improvement in the combustion in the furnace, or in the efficiency of the steam turbine. The turbine takes steam from the boiler, changes the steam energy into rotating mechanical energy, which then drives the electric generator. If the turbine has poor seals, then steam escapes and energy that would otherwise be used to drive the generator is lost. The most significant item in improving the efficiency of the turbine is setting the seals to the tightest possible configuration. This is easier said than done, because if the seals are too tight or if the spin of the turbine has some eccentricity, then the seals can be wiped. A wiped seal causes excessive leakage and thus poor heat rate. Since the opportunity to replace or adjust the seals occurs only once every five years during the major turbine outages, it is imperative that this work be planned ahead of time.

The state-of-the-art in achieving and maintaining tight seals involves the use of a laser to align all components of the turbine. A typical turbine-generator is over 100 feet long and has five or more rotating sections. Therefore, a laser presents unique advantages in achieving precise tolerances (+ or - .001") for alignment.

We started using laser alignment in 1989 with the Unit 7 outage and achieved a significant improvement in both turbine and total plant heat rate. This improvement can be measured in tons of coal burned per year. Unit 7 now burns approximately 110,000 tons less of coal per year at a direct coal cost savings in excess of three million dollars and untold subsequent maintenance cost savings on the coal handling and pulverizing equipment. Looking at this improvement in another way, this unit can now generate approximately forty-five of its six hundred megawatts at no additional fuel cost.

Along with the BTFRP, heat rate improvement, and combustion tuning, other new and innovative methods were adapted on Unit 7. These activities are classified as preventive maintenance and predictive maintenance, and include: live-loading of critical valves; adjusting motor operated valves with a state-of-the-art valve diagnostics machine to assure complete opening and closing; establishing a repeatable and trendable vibration monitoring program; and establishing an oil analysis program that identifies wear particles in critical rotating equipment and looks for misapplied lubricants from which failures can be predicted.

TRAINING

Of course none of the above mentioned changes would be possible without investing in the training necessary for the technical people to do their job. One of the first things we did was to dedicate a significant amount of time and resources to the training effort. The training was aimed specifically at areas where weaknesses were identified and in the application of advanced technology. We also provided specific training to the technical personnel to improve their interpersonal relationship with union and nonunion personnel. A good rapport with the union was deemed essential to the overall success of the program.

RESULTS

The program for change in the plant reliability and efficiency was accepted by the employees instituting the changes. The major reason for this high level of program acceptance was that everyone involved participated in the development of the strategy for change and the institution of the changes. Additionally, responsibility for and ownership of problem solutions and achievement of results were pushed downward. Employees are now responsible for achieving defined goals, and they have the abilities and tools to pursue these goals without administrative hurdles. It would not have been possible to achieve what we did had we not given the employees involved the freedom to do their jobs and a sense of accountability and responsibility for their decisions.

The Sammis Plant is currently completing the first phase of its two cycle capital improvement program. The capital improvement program will continue through 1997; by then each unit will have completed two boiler and two turbine planned maintenance outages. This program includes a capital expenditure level of approximately $30,000,000 per year. As part of this program, the plant has improved the caliber and training of the dedicated operating, maintenance, and technical staffs to complement the plant improvements and to enhance the plant's new reliability level. As a major goal of this program, the plant is dedicated to achieving a forced outage incidence rate of no more than two forced outages per unit per year. This is a significant improvement over our average boiler outage rate of nine or more outages per unit per year prior to the start of this program. However, not all capital improvements have a direct and measurable effect on plant improvement; for instance, new employee offices and locker room facilities have had a significant impact on efficiency, productivity, and employee moral and are deemed a good investment in human resources.

UNIT 7 OUTAGE ANALYSIS

The most recent turbine outage on Unit 7 started September 29, 1989, and finished January 27, 1990. The turbine outage was followed twenty months later with a five week boiler outage beginning in September 1991. The major capital projects included: replacement of all coal burners and igniters, replacement of the two low pressure rotors in the turbine-generator with new ruggedized rotors and associated oil lift pumps, replacement of various boiler tube sections, and replacement of other items which have improved the efficiency and reliability of the unit.

To manage the outage, we put in place certain innovative programs to assure the achievement of our cost and schedule goals. This included the establishment of an outage steering committee which started to develop the philosophy and management approach to the outage six months ahead of time. The outage manager had the authority to do whatever was required to keep the outage moving on schedule. The outage manager, with backing and input from the plant superintendent, was able to break roadblocks and revise work schedules as needed to maintain the schedule.

As mentioned previously, the unit engineer program was also established in 1989, right before the Unit 7 outage. The unit engineer is responsible for coordinating all technical work on a given unit, for capital project justifications, and for coordinating all performance and condition status testing on the unit. This includes nondestructive examination tests which are essential in determining the wear and tear on a modern coal-fired unit. Technical specialists were assigned to the outage team to assist in disassembling and rebuilding of the turbine generator and in developing boiler combustion improvements.

Other outage innovations included the use of plan-of-the-day meetings, weekly project meetings with the contractors and our counterparts from the General Office, and providing around-the-clock engineering coverage of the outage to expedite any technical problems which were holding up the schedule. This engineering coverage was jointly staffed by both General Office and plant engineers. These engineers were temporarily located in construction trailers on the turbine floor adjacent to the work area. The General Office engineers worked on a two week rotation basis and were available on an as-needed basis 24 hours a day during the two week period. This arrangement has worked so well that we have continued to approach all subsequent outages with the same arrangement with the same success.

In 1988 a Systems Analysis Team was also established which studied key systems to determine which were the cause of high probability, high impact forced outages. The team provided a series of recommendations, some of which were implemented during the outage, which will greatly enhance the long-term reliability of the unit.

The outage on Unit 7 provided opportunity to make major changes to the operability and maintainability of the unit. The following provides a brief list of some of these improvements:

- Prior to the outage, the loss of a single coal pulverizer resulted in a 50 MW drop in the rating of the unit. During the outage, the coal burners were replaced. As a result, the unit can now operate at full capacity with one pulverizer out of service and not have to take a capacity rate drop. This subsequently allows for preventive maintenance (PM) of the pulverizers without affecting the plant output. The PM subsequently results in better running pulverizers which results in less maintenance.
- In the first nine months of 1989, we had nineteen forced outages on Unit 7. In the six months prior to the 1989 outage, we averaged eleven days between forced outages. Our Unit 7 went 147 days without a forced outage since the last maintenance outage. (See Figures 1 and 2.)

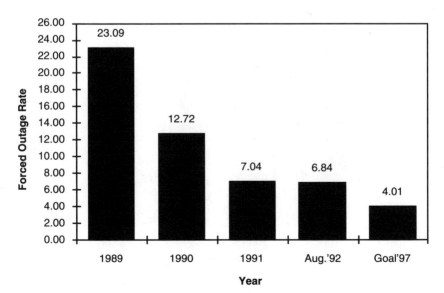

Figure 1. Unit #7 forced outage rate.

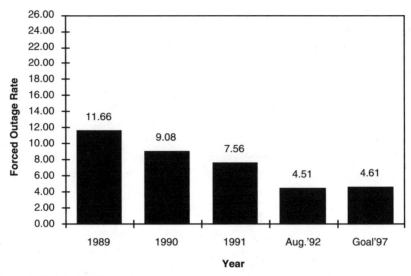

Figure 2. Total plant forced outage rate.

- As shown in Figure 3, the pre-outage heat rate was 10,232 BTU/kWh (year end 1989). The post-outage heat rate was 9,491 BTU/kWh (year end 1990) and has subsequently dropped to 9,375 BTU/kWh in December 1991 (the lower the number, the more efficient the unit.

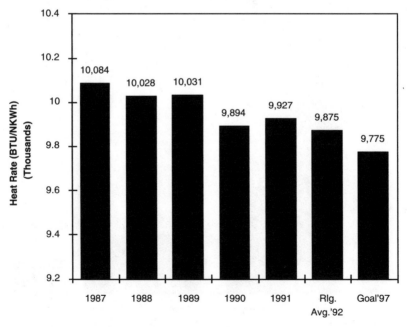

Figure 3. Total plant heat rate.

It has been demonstrated that significant improvements in the operation of Unit 7 have been achieved. A similar program is underway for Units 4, 5, and 6, and even better results are expected. Recently, Unit 5 completed 317 straight days of on-line operation. Although this case study has concentrated only on the changes and achievements of the technical support group at the Sammis plant, many of the improvements noted here would not have been possible without the participation of all plant personnel and the backing of corporate management.

REFERENCES

Carson, J. H. 1982. "Improving Unit Availability at a Large Coal-Fired Generating Station," Ninth Engineering Conference on Reliability for the Electric Power Industry. Hershey, PA. pp. 223-226.

Lasky, C. D. 1990. "Boiler Tube Failure Program Summary," Internal Ohio Edison study. September 29, 1990.

Woodward, M. J. and R. K. Snyder. "Sammis Plant Improvement Study Units 1-7," Internal Ohio Edison study. June 3, 1988.

Part III

Appendices

Appendix 1: The Quality Themes of Leading U.S. Companies

AMERICAN EXPRESS

Theme used within the Travel Related Services Division:

"Quality first"

This theme was adopted throughout the Travel Related Services Division as part of a multi-faceted approach to continuously introduce quality awareness programs and motivate employees toward high quality achievement. The quality first theme was applied to all executive and business stationery, and to numerous motivational prizes and awards. The theme was also exhibited in front of regional operations centers on large banners.

Additional themes were developed for annual, quality awareness month programs at each operating center. A contest was held each year at operating centers to select individual center themes. These contests resulted in hundreds of submissions at the centers. Typical themes included:

"Aim high for quality"

"Quality, the difference is me"

E.I. DU PONT DE NEMOURS & CO.

1. Corporate level theme:

"A great global company through people"

This theme was created by the Chief Executive Officer. It was conceived as an instrument designed to direct the company's focus to what the Chairman perceived to be its four stakeholders: *Customers, Employees, Society, and Stockholders.*

2. Division quality theme at Du Pont Fibres:

"Committed to partnerships that make a better world"

The above theme was developed by a group of divisional executives during a weekend retreat. Techniques used to launch the theme include the following initiatives:

- formal introduction of the theme at their annual, international manager's conference.
- numerous improvement teams were established to find creative approaches toward, effective implementation of a theme.
- created a newsletter carrying the theme as its banner.
- numerous promotional items such as coffee cups, pencils, award certificates, and other items were utilized.

FEDERAL EXPRESS CORPORATION

Federal Express management believes that "themes imply campaigns, and that campaigns end. They do not, therefore, use themes as part of their quality management strategies. *Recognition systems,* it is felt, satisfy their desire to motivate their people to high performance levels.

FORD

Corporate level theme:

"Quality is job 1"

Ford executives indicate that this theme was selected as part of a last ditch effort to save the company from bankruptcy. A crisis had developed in the company during the early seventies as a result of extraordinary increases in fuel prices, double digit inflation, and changes in global competition.

"Quality Is Job 1" was selected to embody the following five-pronged approach toward a new customer orientation within the entire company:

1. Define—Find out first hand clearly what customers want.
2. Commit—Develop a mission, a purpose. Commit yourself to a focus on the customer. Show you care.
3. Design—Develop and implement supporting concepts, programs, and new approaches that respond to customer expectations.
4. Measurement—Stay in touch with the customer and develop effective yardsticks to measure progress at all levels.

5. Improve—Never relax. Adopt the philosophy and develop the environment that builds continuous improvement.

HEWLETT PACKARD

Corporate theme:

"10X"

The above theme was created by the Chief Executive Officer as a challenge to the entire organization to improve quality and productivity by a factor of ten. He said that he wanted his people to totally re-think all functions and processes, and that anything less than a ten times level of improvement goal would not result in significant changes.

HYATT CORPORATION

Quality at Hyatt is delighting guests at every opportunity. It is demonstrating our unique ability to satisfy guests and consistently deliver the Hyatt experience.

Quality at Hyatt is recognizing our people as the key to our success and making employees valuable contributors to the quality process.

Quality at Hyatt is sustaining an attractive return on investment for our owners, while profiting our organization.

Quality—a solid business strategy for delighting guests with the Hyatt experience.

IBM

1. Corporate level theme:

" Market driven quality "

2. Divisional theme IBM, Rochester:

"Rochester excellence customer satisfaction—the quality journey continues"

Both of the above themes are promoted within the company through the use of posters, videos, pins, and other items.

KODAK

1. Corporate level theme:

"Quality leadership process"

The objective of using this theme is to avoid giving employees the feeling that this is the latest flavor of the month program. Promotion of the theme has been accomplished in the following ways:
• published in company newsletters
• given coverage in the current annual report
• corporate quality magazine carries success stories related to the theme
• individual recognition programs covering theme achievements
• use of theme in development of corporate critical success factors

2. Division quality theme:

Individual operating units are given the latitude to introduce their own quality themes. "KP-4" refers to their Kodak Park center and the four imperatives they have established for themselves, i.e.,

"Perfect product—perfect process"

The latter theme was created and introduced by the senior executive at Kodak Park, Rochester, New York. It was used to spur the implementation of key performance measures and to systematically address the issue of cycle time reduction. Each department was then asked to develop action plans toward implementing the theme.

MOTOROLA

Corporate theme:

"Six sigma quality"

This theme draws upon a statistical concept where a six sigma quality level is equal to 99.997 percent accuracy. This theme brings attention to a new objective of achieving zero defects in all manufacturing processes.

The company utilizes this theme in all operations globally, and promotes the concept in its institutional advertising.

WESTINGHOUSE

Corporate level theme:

"You can be sure if it's Westinghouse—we're making sure"

The above theme was designed to capitalize internally on the well known theme that was initiated in 1946. More recently, the company's focus on quality resulted in the internal use of the following theme:

"Total quality performance is leadership in meeting customer requirements by doing the right things right the first time."

XEROX

1. Primary corporate theme:

"Leadership through quality"

The senior management team at Xerox chose the above theme as part of an effort to further the notion that the highest levels of quality performance could be achieved only through a continuous approach or process orientation.

Xerox management believes in providing numerous opportunities for recognizing outstanding quality performance.

2. Secondary theme:

"Team excellence"

This theme is given visibility each year at the company's Annual Teamwork Day where employees, vendors, and customers are invited to participate in celebrations of this concept at three locations in the United States.

Appendix 2: Matrix of Award Criteria Covered by Case Studies

More and more American companies are using the Malcolm Baldrige Award Criteria for self-assessment, planning, training, and as the basis for their quality improvement strategies. It is felt that the award criteria comprehensively integrate all facets of operating a business into a model for continuous improvement of quality products and services. The award criteria are designed to support two results-oriented goals:
• delivery of ever-improving value to customers
• improvement of overall company operational performance

The chart on the following pages is a matrix showing what parts of the award criteria are covered by each of the case studies included in the book. Vertically listed on the left are Malcolm Baldrige examination categories. Listed horizontally along the top, in alphabetical order, are the companies represented in the book. A quick glance at the matrix will show the specific examination categories covered by each company. For example, the matrix reveals that the American Express case study touches on all seven of the examination categories with a heavy emphasis on two of the categories: Leadership and Human Resource Development and Management.

The chart allows for a preliminary benchmark of some of America's most admired companies representing a wide variety of industries. It is provided to assist the reader who is looking for process ideas in a specific category and for comparing procedures among companies within the same industry or differing industries.

It is hoped that the matrix will serve as a useful reference time and time again as companies take a look inward at their methods of operations to identify areas for improvement.

Malcolm Baldrige Examination Categories/Items	American Express	Anheuser-Busch	AT&T Universal Card
1.0 Leadership			
1.1 Senior executive leadership.........................	✓	✓	✓
1.2 Management for quality...............................	✓	✓	✓
1.3 Public responsibility and corp. citizenship......	✓		✓
2.0 Information and analysis			
2.1 Scope and mgmt. of quality and performance data and information...........................	✓		✓
2.2 Competitive comparisons and benchmarks....			✓
2.3 Analysis and uses of company-level data......			✓
3.0 Strategic quality planning			
3.1 Strategic quality and company performance planning process...........................			✓
3.2 Quality and performance plans.....................	✓		✓
4.0 Human resource development and mgmt.			
4.1 Human resource planning and mgmt.	✓	✓	✓
4.2 Employee involvement...............................	✓	✓	✓
4.3 Employee education and training..................	✓		✓
4.4 Employee performance and recognition........		✓	✓
4.5 Employee well-being and satisfaction...........	✓	✓	
5.0 Mgmt. of process quality			
5.1 Design and introduction of quality products and services...............................			✓
5.2 Process mgmt. - product and service production and delivery processes................	✓	✓	✓
5.3 Process mgmt. - business processes and support services...............................			✓
5.4 Supplier quality...			
5.5 Quality assessment...................................			✓
6.0 Quality and operational results			
6.1 Product and service quality results................			✓
6.2 Company operational results.........................	✓		✓
6.3 Business process and support service results...			✓
6.4 Supplier quality results...............................			✓
7.0 Customer focus and satisfaction			
7.1 Customer expectations - current and future...			✓
7.2 Customer relationship mgmt.			✓
7.3 Commitment to customers...........................	✓		✓
7.4 Customer satisfaction determination............			✓
7.5 Customer satisfaction results.......................			✓
7.6 Customer satisfaction comparison................			✓

Cadillac Motor Cars	Centex	Delta Air Lines	Federal Express	Hyatt Hotels and Resorts	IBM	Intelligent Electronics	Lazarus
	✓	✓	✓	✓	✓	✓	✓
✓	✓		✓	✓	✓	✓	✓
					✓		
	✓		✓		✓		
					✓		
					✓		✓
✓	✓		✓		✓		✓
✓			✓		✓		
	✓	✓	✓	✓	✓		
✓	✓	✓	✓	✓	✓	✓	✓
✓	✓	✓		✓	✓	✓	✓
	✓	✓		✓	✓	✓	
		✓	✓		✓		✓
✓			✓	✓	✓		
✓	✓		✓	✓	✓		✓
	✓	✓	✓	✓	✓	✓	✓
✓					✓	✓	
	✓			✓	✓		✓
✓	✓		✓		✓	✓	✓
✓	✓				✓	✓	
✓	✓			✓	✓		✓
✓					✓		
✓	✓		✓		✓	✓	✓
	✓		✓		✓	✓	✓
✓	✓		✓	✓	✓	✓	✓
	✓			✓	✓	✓	✓
							✓
				✓	✓		✓

Malcolm Baldrige Examination Categories/Items	Kmart Corp.	Knight-Ridder	3M	Marriott Corp.
1.0 Leadership				
1.1 Senior executive leadership..........................		✓	✓	
1.2 Management for quality...............................		✓	✓	
1.3 Public responsibility and corp. citizenship......				
2.0 Information and analysis				
2.1 Scope and mgmt. of quality and performance data and information.....................................	✓	✓		
2.2 Competitive comparisons and benchmarks...		✓		
2.3 Analysis and uses of company-level data......	✓	✓		
3.0 Strategic quality planning				
3.1 Strategic quality and company performance planning process...		✓		
3.2 Quality and performance plans.....................	✓	✓		
4.0 Human resource development and mgmt.				
4.1 Human resource planning and mgmt.		✓		✓
4.2 Employee involvement.................................		✓	✓	
4.3 Employee education and training..................		✓		
4.4 Employee performance and recognition........		✓		
4.5 Employee well-being and satisfaction...........		✓		
5.0 Mgmt. of process quality				
5.1 Design and introduction of quality products and services...		✓		✓
5.2 Process mgmt. - product and service production and delivery processes...............	✓	✓		
5.3 Process mgmt. - business processes and support services..	✓	✓		✓
5.4 Supplier quality...	✓			
5.5 Quality assessment....................................		✓		✓
6.0 Quality and operational results				
6.1 Product and service quality results...............		✓		
6.2 Company operational results.......................		✓		
6.3 Business process and support service results...	✓	✓		
6.4 Supplier quality results...............................	✓			
7.0 Customer focus and satisfaction				
7.1 Customer expectations - current and future...		✓		✓
7.2 Customer relationship mgmt.		✓		✓
7.3 Commitment to customers...........................	✓	✓		✓
7.4 Customer satisfaction determination.............		✓		✓
7.5 Customer satisfaction results.......................		✓		✓
7.6 Customer satisfaction comparison................	✓	✓		✓

MichCon	Monsanto	New York Life	Novell Inc.	Octel Communications	Ohio Edison	Photo-Sonics
✓			✓	✓		✓
	✓		✓	✓		
			✓	✓		✓
			✓			
			✓	✓		
		✓	✓		✓	
		✓	✓	✓	✓	
	✓			✓	✓	
✓	✓	✓		✓	✓	
	✓	✓	✓	✓	✓	✓
	✓	✓		✓	✓	✓
					✓	
✓			✓			
		✓	✓	✓	✓	✓
✓	✓		✓			
	✓		✓	✓		✓
			✓	✓	✓	✓
	✓	✓	✓		✓	
	✓	✓	✓	✓	✓	✓
	✓	✓	✓		✓	
	✓		✓		✓	✓
	✓		✓	✓	✓	
✓			✓	✓		
		✓	✓	✓	✓	
			✓	✓	✓	
			✓	✓		
	✓		✓	✓		

Malcolm Baldrige Examination Categories/Items	Reynolds Metals Co.	Ritz-Carlton Hotel Co.	SpaceLabs Medical
1.0 Leadership			
1.1 Senior executive leadership............................		✓	✓
1.2 Management for quality.................................		✓	✓
1.3 Public responsibility and corp. citizenship......			
2.0 Information and analysis			
2.1 Scope and mgmt. of quality and performance data and information...............................			
2.2 Competitive comparisons and benchmarks....			
2.3 Analysis and uses of company-level data......			
3.0 Strategic quality planning			
3.1 Strategic quality and company performance planning process................................			
3.2 Quality and performance plans......................			
4.0 Human resource development and mgmt.			
4.1 Human resource planning and mgmt.		✓	
4.2 Employee involvement.................................			
4.3 Employee education and training..................		✓	
4.4 Employee performance and recognition........		✓	
4.5 Employee well-being and satisfaction...........			
5.0 Mgmt. of process quality			
5.1 Design and introduction of quality products and services......................................			✓
5.2 Process mgmt. - product and service production and delivery processes...............	✓	✓	✓
5.3 Process mgmt. - business processes and support services..	✓	✓	✓
5.4 Supplier quality...	✓		
5.5 Quality assessment....................................	✓	✓	✓
6.0 Quality and operational results			
6.1 Product and service quality results...............	✓	✓	
6.2 Company operational results.........................			✓
6.3 Business process and support service results..	✓		
6.4 Supplier quality results................................	✓		
7.0 Customer focus and satisfaction			
7.1 Customer expectations - current and future...		✓	✓
7.2 Customer relationship mgmt.		✓	✓
7.3 Commitment to customers............................		✓	✓
7.4 Customer satisfaction determination.............			
7.5 Customer satisfaction results........................			
7.6 Customer satisfaction comparison.................			

Springs Industries	Steinway & Sons	TIAA-CREF	USAA	Westinghouse	Whirlpool	Xerox
✓	✓	✓	✓		✓	✓
		✓	✓	✓	✓	✓
✓		✓	✓			✓
	✓		✓		✓	
			✓			✓
	✓		✓			
	✓	✓			✓	✓
	✓	✓	✓		✓	
✓		✓	✓			
✓	✓	✓	✓		✓	✓
✓	✓	✓	✓		✓	
✓	✓	✓	✓		✓	
✓		✓	✓			✓
	✓	✓				
	✓	✓		✓	✓	✓
	✓	✓		✓		✓
	✓				✓	
✓	✓	✓	✓	✓		✓
	✓	✓	✓	✓		
		✓		✓	✓	
	✓	✓				
	✓					
	✓	✓	✓		✓	✓
	✓	✓	✓		✓	✓
	✓	✓	✓			✓
	✓	✓	✓		✓	✓
	✓	✓	✓			✓
	✓	✓	✓			✓

Appendix 3: Job Descriptions

OFFICE OF VICE PRESIDENT, QUALITY

- Implements corporate policy for Total Quality Management (TQM)
- Coordinates communications and awareness activities among senior executives
- Provides visible top management participation in and support of the process
- Reviews and approves the organization of each area's lead team
- Reports progress and achievements of the TQM process to the Quality Council
- Recommends changes and improvements in the process to the Quality Council and coordinates implementation
- Monitors overall corporate TQM process, activities, and results
- Coordinates corporate communication program
- Coordinates corporate recognition program
- Maintains information tracking system and generates reports
- Coordinates the corporate replication program
- Maintains official contact with outside agencies and unofficial network throughout the United States and abroad
- Monitors participation of staff personnel in business Quality Improvement (QI) activities
- Promotes the overall program and encourages a positive climate
- Performs other activities as required by CEO

MANAGER, QUALITY IMPROVEMENT

- Coordinates design, evaluation, and revision of TQM corporate model
- Sits on the corporate Design and Implementation Team
- Coordinates team activities and management reviews
- Advises on major improvement areas and opportunity selection
- Provides needed resources and information to local departments
- Assists in implementation
- Coaches on problem solving and performs internal consulting
- Recognizes team achievements and coordinates corporate recognition program

- Communicates status of TQM program activities throughout the organization
- Promotes the QI program and momentum to Senior Management and the Quality Council
- Teaches QI processes and techniques to Quality Council members and management
- Coaches and supports managers, supervisors, team leaders, and members
- Maintain momentum of program and corporate indicator system
- Participates in business QI activities
- Performs other activities as required by Vice President of Quality

Appendix 4: Award Criteria[1]

1.0 LEADERSHIP *(95 PTS.)*

The *Leadership* category examines senior executives' *personal* leadership and involvement in creating and sustaining a customer focus and clear and visible quality values. Also examined is how the quality values are integrated into the company's management system and reflected in the manner in which the company addresses its public responsibilities and corporate citizenship.

1.1 SENIOR EXECUTIVE LEADERSHIP *(45 PTS.)*

Describe the senior executives' leadership, personal involvement, and visibility in developing and maintaining an environment for quality excellence.

Approach[2] ✔
Deployment ✔
Results

AREAS TO ADDRESS

A. senior executives' leadership, personal involvement, and visibility in quality-related activities of the company. Include: (1) reinforcing a customer focus; (2) creating quality values and setting expectations; (3) planning and reviewing progress toward quality and operational performance objectives; (4) recognizing employee contributions; and (5) communicating quality values outside the company
B. brief summary of the company's customer focus and quality values and how they serve as a basis for consistent communication within and outside the company
C. how senior executives regularly communicate and reinforce the company's customer focus and quality values with managers and supervisors
D. how senior executives evaluate and improve the effectiveness of their personal leadership and involvement

---

[1] Excerpted from the 1993 Award Criteria booklet.
[2] All Items are designated as Approach and Deployment, and/or Results Items. A discussion of these descriptors is given on the last page of this appendix.

Notes:

1) The term "senior executives" refers to the highest-ranking official of the organization applying for the Award and those reporting directly to that official.

2) Activities of senior executives might also include leading and/or receiving training, communicating with all employees, benchmarking, customer visits, interactions with suppliers, and mentoring other executives, managers, and supervisors.

3) Communication by senior executives outside the company might involve: national, state, and community groups; trade, business, and professional organizations; and education, health care, government, and standards groups. It might also involve the company's stockholders and board of directors.

1.2 MANAGEMENT FOR QUALITY *(25 PTS.)*

Describe how the company's customer focus and quality values are integrated into day-to-day leadership, management, and supervision of all company units.

Approach ✔
Deployment ✔
Results ·

AREAS TO ADDRESS

A. how the company's customer focus and quality values are translated into requirements for all managers and supervisors. Summarize: (1) their principal roles and responsibilities within their units; and (2) their roles and responsibilities in fostering cooperation with other units

B. how the company's customer focus and quality values (1.1B) are communicated and reinforced throughout the company, with all employees

C. how company and work unit quality and operational performance plans are reviewed. Describe: (1) types, frequency, content, and use of reviews and who conducts them; and (2) how the company assists units that are not performing according to plans

D. key methods and key indicators the company uses to evaluate and improve awareness and integration of quality values among managers and supervisors

1.3 PUBLIC RESPONSIBILITY AND CORPORATE CITIZENSHIP *(25 PTS.)*

Describe how the company includes its responsibilities to the public in its quality policies and improvement practices. Describe also how the company leads as a corporate citizen in its key communities.

Approach ✔
Deployment ✔
Results ✔

AREAS TO ADDRESS

A. how the company integrates its public responsibilities into its quality policies and practices. Include: (1) how the company determines or sets operational requirements and goals taking into account risks, regulatory, and other legal requirements; (2) a summary of the principal public responsibility areas addressed within the company's quality policies and/or practices and how key operational requirements are communicated throughout the company; and (3) how and how often progress in meeting operational requirements and/or goals is reviewed

B. how the company looks ahead to anticipate public concerns and to assess possible impacts on society that may derive from its products, services, and operations. Describe briefly how this assessment is used in planning.

C. how the company leads as a corporate citizen in its key communities. Include: (1) a brief summary of the types and extent of leadership and involvement in key communities; (2) how the company promotes quality awareness and sharing of quality-related information; (3) how the company seeks opportunities to enhance its leadership; and (4) how the company promotes legal and ethical conduct in all that it does.

D. trends in key indicators of improvement in addressing public responsibilities and corporate citizenship. Include responses to any sanctions the company has received under law, regulation, or contract.

Notes:

1) The public responsibility issues addressed in 1.3A and 1.3B relate to the company's impacts and possible impacts on society associated with its products, services, and company operations. They include business ethics, environment, and safety as they relate to any aspect of risk or adverse effect, whether or not these are covered under law or regulation.

2) Details of the company's process management associated with issues both relevant and important to the company's business should be included in Category 5.0.

3) Health and safety of employees are not included in Item 1.3. They are covered in Item 4.5.

4) The corporate citizenship issues appropriate for inclusion in 1.3C relate to contributions by the company to strengthen community services, education, health care, environment or practices of trade or business associations. Applicants' involvement would be expected to be limited by the company's available human and financial resources.

5) If the company has received sanctions under law, regulation, or contract during the past three years, include the current status in responding to 1.3D.

2.0 INFORMATION AND ANALYSIS *(75 PTS.)*

The *Information and Analysis* category examines the scope, validity, analysis, management, and use of data and information to drive quality excellence and to improve operational and competitive performance. Also examined is the adequacy of the company's data, information, and analysis system to support improvement of the company's customer focus, products, services, and internal operations.

2.1 SCOPE AND MANAGEMENT OF QUALITY AND PERFORMANCE DATA AND INFORMATION *(15 PTS.)*

Describe the company's data and information used for planning, day-to-day management, and evaluation of quality and operational performance. Describe also how data and information are managed to ensure reliability, timeliness, and rapid access.

Approach ✔
Deployment ✔
Results

AREAS TO ADDRESS

A. criteria for selecting data and information for use in quality and operational performance improvement. List key types of data and information used and briefly outline the principal roles of each type in improving quality and company operational performance. Include: (1) customer-related; (2) product and service performance; (3) internal operations and performance, including business processes, support services, and employee-related; (4) supplier performance; and (5) cost and financial.

B. how the company assures reliability, consistency, and rapid access to data throughout the company. If applicable, describe how software quality is assured.

C. key methods and key indicators used to evaluate and improve the scope and management of data and information. Include: (1) review and update; (2) shortening the cycle from data gathering to access; (3) broadening access to all those requiring data for day-to-day management and improvement; and (4) alignment of data and information with process improvement plans and needs.

Notes:

1) This Item permits the applicant to demonstrate the breadth and depth of its quality-related data. Applicants should give brief descriptions of the data under major headings such as "internal operations and performance" and subheadings such as "support services". Note that information on the scope and management of competitive and benchmark data is requested in Item 2.2.

(2) Actual data should not be reported in this Item. Such data are requested in other Items. Accordingly, all data reported in other Items, such as 6.1, 6.2, 6.3, 6.4, 7.5, and 7.6, should be part of the base of data and information to be described in Item 2.1.

2.2 COMPETITIVE COMPARISONS AND BENCHMARKING *(20 PTS.)*

Describe the company's processes, current sources and scope, and uses of competitive comparisons and benchmarking information and data to support improvement of quality and overall company operational performance.

Approach ✔
Deployment ✔
Results

AREAS TO ADDRESS

A. how the company uses competitive comparisons and benchmarking information and data to help drive improvement of quality and company operational performance. Describe: (1) how needs are determined; and (2) criteria for seeking appropriate comparison and benchmarking information—from within and outside the company's industry.

B. brief summary of current scope, sources and principal uses of each type of competitive and benchmark information and data. Include: (1) customer-related; (2) product and service quality; (3) internal operations and performance, including business processes, support services, and employee-related; and (4) supplier performance.

C. how competitive and benchmarking information and data are used to improve understanding of processes, to encourage breakthrough approaches, and to set "stretch" objectives

D. how the company evaluates and improves its overall processes for selecting and using competitive comparisons and benchmarking information and data to improve planning and company operations

Notes:

1) Benchmarking information and data refer to processes and results that represent superior performance and set a "stretch" standard for comparison.

2) Sources of competitive and benchmarking information are of several types, and could include: (1) information obtained directly from other organizations through sharing; (2) information obtained from open literature; (3) testing and evaluation by the company itself; and (4) testing and evaluation by independent organizations.

2.3 ANALYSIS AND USES OF COMPANY-LEVEL DATA *(40 PTS)*

Describe how data related to quality, customers and operational performance, together with relevant financial data, are analyzed to support company-level review, action and planning.

Approach ✔
Deployment ✔
Results

AREAS TO ADDRESS

A. how customer-related data and results (from category 7.0) are aggregated with other key data and analyses, analyzed, and translated into actionable information to support: (1) developing priorities for prompt solutions to customer-related problems; and (2) determining key customer-related trends and correlations to support status review, decision making, and longer-term planning

B. how operational performance data and results (from category 6.0) are aggregated with other key data and analyses, analyzed, and translated into actionable information to support: (1) developing priorities for short-term improvements in company operations, including cycle time, productivity and waste reduction; and (2) determining key operations-related trends and correlations to support status reviews, decision making, and longer-term planning

C. how the company relates overall improvements in product/service quality and operational performance to changes in overall financial performance

D. how the company evaluates and improves its analysis as a key management tool. Include: (1) how analysis supports improved data selection and use; (2) how the analysis-access cycle is shortened; and (3) how analysis strengthens the integration of overall data for improved decision making and planning.

Notes:

1) Item 2.3 focuses primarily on analysis for company-level purposes. Data for such analysis come from all parts of the company. Other Items in the Criteria call for analyses of specific sets of data for special purposes. For example, the Items of Category 4.0 require analyses to demonstrate effectiveness of training and other human resource practices. Such special-purpose analyses are assumed to be part of the information base of Category 2.0, available for use in Item 2.3. These specific sets of data and special-purpose analyses are described in 2.3a and 2.3b as "other key data and analyses."

2) "Actionable" means that the analysis provides information that can be used for priorities and decisions leading to allocation of resources.

3) The focus in 2.3a is on analysis to improve customer-related decision making and planning. This analysis is intended to provide additional information to support such decision making and planning that result from day-to-day customer information, feedback, and complaints.

Analysis appropriate for inclusion in 2.3A could include relationships between and among the following: the company's product and service quality improvement and key customer indicators such as customer satisfaction, customer retention, and market share; relationship between customer relationship management strategies and changes in customer satisfaction, customer retention, and market share; cross-comparisons of data from complaints, post-transaction follow-up, and won/lost analyses to identify improvement priorities, relationship between employee satisfaction and customer satisfaction, cost revenue implications of customer-related problems; and rates of improvement in customer indicators.

4) The focus in 2.3B is on analysis to improve operations-related decision making and planning. This analysis is intended to support such decision making and planning that results from day-to-day observations of process performance. Analysis appropriate for inclusion in 2.3B could include: evaluation of the productivity and cost impacts of improvement initiatives; rates of improvement in key operational indicators; evaluation of trends in key operational efficiency measures; and comparison with competitive and benchmark data to identify improvement opportunities and to establish improvement goals and priorities.

5) The focus in 2.3C is on the linkages between improvements in product service quality and operational performance and overall financial performance for company goal and priority setting. Analyses in 2.3C could incorporate the results of analyses described in 2.3A and 2.3B, and draw upon other relevant data and analyses. Analysis appropriate for inclusion in 2.3C could include: relationships between product service quality and operational performance indicators and overall company financial performance trends as reflected in indicators such as operating costs, revenues, asset utilization, and value added per employee; comparisons of company financial performance versus competitors based on quality and operational performance indicators; allocation of limited resources for improvement among possible projects based on cost/revenue implications and improvement potential; net earnings derived from quality/operational performance improvements; and comparisons among business units based upon quality improvement and its impact on financial performance.

3.0 STRATEGIC QUALITY PLANNING *(60 PTS.)*

The *Strategic Quality Planning* category examines the company's planning process and how all key quality requirements are integrated into overall business planning. Also examined are the company's short- and long-term plans and how quality and operational performance requirements are deployed to all work units.

3.1 STRATEGIC QUALITY AND COMPANY PERFORMANCE PLANNING PROCESS *(35 PTS.)*

Describe the company's strategic planning process for the short term (1-2 years) and longer term (3 years or more) for customer satisfaction leadership and overall operational performance improvement. Include how this process integrates quality and company operational performance requirements and how plans are deployed.

Approach ✔
Deployment ✔
Results

AREAS TO ADDRESS

A. how the company develops strategies, goals and business plans to address quality and customer satisfaction leadership for the short term and longer term. Describe how business plans consider: (1) customer requirements and the expected evolution of these requirements; (2) projections of the competitive environment; (3) risks: financial, market, and societal; (4) company capabilities, including human resource development, and research and development to address key new requirements or technology leadership opportunities; and (5) supplier capabilities.
B. how the company develops strategies and plans to address overall operational performance improvement. Describe how the following are considered: (1) realigning work processes ("re-engineering") to improve operational performance; and (2) productivity improvement and reduction in waste.
C. how plans are deployed. Describe: (1) the method the company uses to deploy overall plan requirements to all work units and to suppliers, and how it ensures alignment of work unit plans and activities; and (2) how resources are committed to meet the plan requirements.
D. how the company evaluates and improves its planning process, including improvements in: (1) determining company quality and overall operational performance requirements; (2) deploying requirements to work units; and (3) receiving planning input from company work units

Notes:
1) Productivity improvement and waste reduction may address a variety of issues including inventions, work in process, inspection, downtime, changeover time and better utilization of resources such as materials, energy, capital and labor.
2) How the company reviews quality and overall operational performance relative to plans is addressed in Item 1.2.

3.2 QUALITY AND PERFORMANCE PLANS *(25 PTS.)*
Summarize the company's quality and operational performance goals and plans for the short term (1-2 years) and the longer term (3 years or more).

Approach ✔
Deployment ✔
Results

AREAS TO ADDRESS

A. for the company's chosen directions, including planned products and services, markets, or market segments, summarize: (1) key quality factors and quality requirements to achieve leadership; and (2) key company operational performance requirements

B. outline of the company's principal short-term quality and company operational performance goals and plans. Include: (1) a summary of key requirements and key operational performance indicators deployed to work units and suppliers; and (2) a brief description of resources committed for key needs such as capital equipment, facilities, education and training, and personnel.

C. principal longer-term (3 years or more) quality and company operational performance goals and plans, including key requirements and how they will be addressed

D. two-to-five-year projection of improvements using the most important indicators of quality and company operational performance. Describe how quality and company operational performance might be expected to compare with competitors and key benchmarks over this time period. Briefly explain the comparisons, including any estimates or assumptions made regarding the projected quality and operational performance of competitors or changes in benchmarks.

4.0 HUMAN RESOURCE DEVELOPMENT AND MANAGEMENT *(150 PTS.)*

The *Human Resource Development and Management* category examines the key elements of how the work force is enabled to develop its full potential to pursue the company's quality and operational performance objectives. Also examined are the company's efforts to build and maintain an environment for quality excellence conducive to full participation and personal and organizational growth

4.1 HUMAN RESOURCE PLANNING AND MANAGEMENT *(20 PTS.)*

Describe how the company's overall human resource plans and practices are integrated with its overall quality and operational performance goals and plans and address fully the needs and development of the entire work force

Approach ✔
Deployment ✔
Results

AREAS TO ADDRESS

A. brief outline of the most important human resource plans (derived from Category 3.0). Address: (1) development, including education, training and empowerment; (2) mobility, flexibility, and changes in work organization, processes or work schedules; (3) reward, recognition, benefits, and compensation; and (4) recruitment, including possible changes in diversity of the work force. Distinguish between the short term (1-2 years) and the longer term (3 years or more), as appropriate.

B. how the company improves its human resource operations and practices. Describe key goals and methods for processes/practices such as recruitment, hiring, personnel actions, and services to employees. Describe key performance indicators, including cycle time, and how these indicators are used in improvement.

C. how the company evaluates and uses all employee-related data to improve the development and effectiveness of the entire work force and to provide key input to overall company planning and to human resource management and planning. Describe: (1) how this improvement process addresses all types of employees; and (2) how employee satisfaction factors (Item 4.5) are used to reduce adverse indicators such as absenteeism, turnover, grievances, and accidents.

Notes:

1) Human resource plans might include the following: mechanisms for promoting cooperation such as internal customer/supplier techniques or other internal partnerships; initiatives to promote labor-management cooperation, such as partnerships with unions; creation and/or modification of recognition systems; mechanisms for increasing or broadening employee responsibilities; creating opportunities for employees to learn and use skills that go beyond current job assignments through redesign of processes; creation of high performance work teams; and education and training initiatives. Plans might also include forming partnerships with educational institutions to develop employees or to help ensure the future supply of well-prepared employees.

2) "Categories of employees" refers to the company's classification system used in its personnel practices and/or work assignments and also includes factors such as union or bargaining unit membership. "Types of employees" takes into account other factors, such as work force diversity or demographic makeup. This includes gender, age, minorities, and the disabled.

3) "All employee-related data" refers to data contained in personnel records as well as data described in Items 4.2, 4.3, 4.4, and 4.5. This includes employee satisfaction data, and data on turnover, absenteeism, safety, grievances, involvement, recognition, training, and information from exit interviews.

4.2 EMPLOYEE INVOLVEMENT *(40 PTS.)*

Describe the means available for all employees to contribute effectively to meeting the company's quality and operational performance goals and plans; summarize trends in effectiveness and extent of involvement .

Approach ✔
Deployment ✔
Results ✔

AREAS TO ADDRESS

A. principal mechanisms the company uses to promote ongoing employee contributions, individually and in groups, to quality and operational performance goals and plans. Describe how and how quickly the company gives feedback to contributors.

B. how the company increases employee empowerment, responsibility, and innovation. Briefly summarize principal goals for all categories of employees, based upon the most important requirements for each category.

C. key methods and key indicators the company uses to evaluate and improve the effectiveness, extent, and type of involvement of all categories and all types of employees. Include how effectiveness, extent and types of involvement are linked to key quality and operational performance improvement results.

D. trends in the most important indicators of the *effectiveness* and *extent* of employee involvement for each category of employee

Note:

The company may use different involvement methods, goals, and indicators for different categories of employees or for different parts of the company, depending on needs and on the types of responsibilities of each employee category or part of the company. Examples include problem-solving teams (within work units or cross-functional), fully-integrated, self-managed work groups, and process improvement teams.

4.3 EMPLOYEE EDUCATION AND TRAINING *(40 PTS.)*

Describe how the company determines quality and related education and training needs for all employees. Show how this determination addresses company plans and needs as well as supports employee growth. Outline how such education and training are evaluated, and summarize key trends demonstrating improvement in both the effectiveness and extent of education and training.

Approach ✔
Deployment ✔
Results ✔

AREAS TO ADDRESS

A. how the company determines needs for the types and amounts of quality and related education and training for all employees, taking into account their differing needs. Include: (1) linkage to short- and long-term plans, including companywide access to skills in problem solving, waste reduction, and process simplification; (2) growth and career opportunities for employees; and (3) how employees' input is sought and used in the needs determination.

B. summary of how quality and related education and training are delivered and reinforced. Include: (1) outline of methods for education and training delivery for all categories of employees; (2) on-the-job application of knowledge and skills; and (3) quality-related orientation for new employees.

C. how the company evaluates and improves its quality and related education and training. Include how the evaluation supports improved needs determination, taking into account: (1) relating on-the-job performance improvement to key quality and operational performance improvement goals and results; and (2) growth and progression of all categories and types of employees.

D. trends in the *effectiveness* and *extent* of quality and related training and education based upon key indicators of each

Notes:

1) Quality and related education and training address the knowledge and skills employees need to meet their objectives as part of the company's quality and operational performance improvement plans. This may include quality awareness, leadership, project management, teamwork, problem solving, interpreting and using data, meeting customer requirements, process analysis, process simplification, waste reduction, cycle time reduction, and other training that affects employee effectiveness and efficiency. In many cases, this may include job enrichment skills and basic skills such as reading, writing, language, arithmetic, and basic mathematics that are needed to meet quality and operational performance improvement objectives.

2) Education and training delivery may occur inside or outside the company and may involve classroom or on-the-job delivery.

3) Trends in the extent of quality and related education and training should provide information regarding coverage of employee categories, including new employees, how much education and training, as well as the basic type and content.

4.4 EMPLOYEE PERFORMANCE AND RECOGNITION *(25 PTS.)*

Describe how the company's employee performance, recognition, promotion, compensation, reward, and feedback approaches support the attainment of the company's quality and performance plans and goals.

Approach ✔
Deployment ✔
Results ✔

AREAS TO ADDRESS

A. how the company's employee performance, recognition, promotion, compensation, reward, and feedback approaches for individuals and groups, including managers, support the company's quality and operational performance goals and plans. Address: (1) how the approaches ensure that quality is reinforced relative to short-term financial considerations; and (2) how employees contribute to the company's employee performance and recognition approaches.

B. key methods and key indicators the company uses to evaluate and improve its employee performance and recognition approaches. Include how the evaluation takes into account: (1) effective participation by all categories and types of employees; (2) employee satisfaction information (Item 4.5); and (3) key indicators of improved quality and operational performance results.

C. trends in key indicators of the effectiveness and extent of employee reward and recognition, by employee category.

Notes:

1) The company may use a variety of reward and recognition approaches—monetary and non-monetary, formal and informal, and individual and group.

2) The evaluation in 4.4B should be segmented by employee category, as appropriate. Employee satisfaction may take into account employee dissatisfaction indicators such as turnover and absenteeism.

4.5 EMPLOYEE WELL-BEING AND SATISFACTION *(25 PTS.)*

Describe how the company maintains a work environment conducive to the well-being and growth of all employees; summarize trends in key indicators of well-being and satisfaction.

Approach ✔
Deployment ✔
Results   ✔

AREAS TO ADDRESS

A. how well-being factors such as health, safety, and ergonomics are included in quality improvement activities. Include principal improvement goals, methods, and indicators for each factor relevant and important to the company's employee work environment. For accidents and work-related health problems, describe how root causes are determined and how adverse conditions are prevented.

B. special services, facilities, and opportunities the company makes available to employees

C. how the company determines employee satisfaction. Include a brief description of methods, frequency, and the specific factors for which satisfaction is determined. Segment by employee category or type, as appropriate.

D. trends in key indicators of well-being and satisfaction. This should address, as appropriate: satisfaction, safety, absenteeism, turnover, turnover rate for customer-contact personnel, grievances, strikes, and worker compensation. Explain important adverse results, if any. For such adverse results, describe how root causes were determined and corrected, and/or give current status.

Compare results on the most significant indicators with those of industry averages, industry leaders, key benchmarks, and local/regional averages, as appropriate.

Notes:
1) Special services, facilities, and opportunities might include: counseling; recreational or cultural activities; non-work-related education; day care; special leave; safety off the job; flexible work hours; and outplacement.
2) Examples of specific factors for which satisfaction may be determined are: employee views of leadership and management; employee development and career opportunities; employee preparation for changes in technology or work organization; work environment; recognition; benefits; communications; job security; and compensation.

5.0 MANAGEMENT OF PROCESS QUALITY *(140 PTS.)*

The *Management of Process Quality* category examines the systematic processes the company uses to pursue ever-higher quality and company operational performance. Examined are the key elements of process management including research and development, design, management of process quality for all work units and suppliers, systematic quality improvement, and quality assessment.

5.1 DESIGN AND INTRODUCTION OF QUALITY PRODUCTS AND SERVICES *(40 PTS.)*

Describe how new and/or improved products and services are designed and introduced and how processes are designed to meet key product and service quality requirements and company operational performance requirements.

Approach ✔
Deployment ✔
Results

AREAS TO ADDRESS

A. how designs of products, services, and processes are developed so that: (1) customer requirements are translated into product and service design requirements; (2) all product and service quality requirements are addressed early in the overall design process by appropriate company units; (3) designs are coordinated and integrated to include all phases of production and delivery; and (4) key process performance characteristics are selected based on customer requirements, appropriate performance levels are determined, and measurement systems are developed to track performance for each of these characteristics

B. how designs are reviewed and validated, taking into account key factors: (1) product and service performance; (2) process capability and future requirements; and (3) supplier capability and future requirements

C. how the company improves its designs and design processes so that new product and service introductions and product and service modifications progressively improve in quality and cycle time

Notes:

1) Design and introduction may include modifications and variants of existing products and services and/or new products and services emerging from research and development. Design also may include facilities to meet company operational performance, and key product and service quality requirements.

2) Applicants' responses should reflect the key requirements of their products and services. Factors that may need to be considered in design include: health; safety; long-term performance; environment; waste generation/reduction; measurement capability; process capability; manufacturability; maintainability; and supplier capability.

3) Service and manufacturing businesses should interpret product and service requirements to include all product- and service-related requirements at all stages of production, delivery, and use.

4) Results of improvements in design and design process quality should be reported in Item 6.2A.

5.2 PROCESS MANAGEMENT: PRODUCT AND SERVICE PRODUCTION AND DELIVERY PROCESSES *(35 PTS.)*

Describe how the company's key product and service production and delivery processes are managed to ensure that design requirements are met and that both quality and operational performance are continuously improved.

Approach ✔
Deployment ✔
Results

AREAS TO ADDRESS

A. how the company maintains the quality of production and delivery processes in accord with the product and service design requirements (Item 5.1). Include: (1) the key processes and their requirements; (2) key indicators of quality and operational performance; and (3) how quality and operational performance are determined and maintained, including types and frequencies of in-process and end-of-process measurements used.

B. for significant (out-of-control) variations in processes or outputs, how root causes are determined, and corrections made and verified

C. how the process is improved to achieve better quality, cycle time, and overall operational performance. Include how each of the following is used or considered: (1) process analysis/simplification; (2) benchmarking information; (3) process research and testing; (4) use of alternative technology; (5) information from customers of the processes—within and outside the company; and (6) challenge goals.

Notes:

1) Manufacturing and service companies with specialized measurement requirements should describe how they assure measurement quality For physical, chemical, and engineering measurements, describe briefly how measurements are made traceable to national standards.

2) Variations (5.2B) may be observed by those working in the process or by customers of the process output. The latter situation may result in formal or informal feedback or complaints. Also, a company may use observers or "mystery shoppers" to provide information on process performance.

3) Results of improvements in product and service production and delivery processes should be reported in Item 6.2A.

5.3 PROCESS MANAGEMENT: BUSINESS PROCESSES AND SUPPORT SERVICES (*30 PTS*)

Describe how the company's key business processes and support services are managed so that current requirements are met and that quality and operational performance are continuously improved.

Approach ✔
Deployment ✔
Results

AREAS TO ADDRESS

A. how key business processes and support services are designed to meet customer and/or company quality and operational performance requirements. Include: (1) the key processes and their requirements; (2) key indicators of quality and performance; and (3) how quality and performance are determined and maintained, including types and frequencies of in-process and end-of process measurements used.

B. for significant (out-of control) variations in processes or outputs, how root causes are determined, and corrections made and verified

C. how the process is improved to achieve better quality, cycle time, and overall operational performance. Describe how each of the following are used or considered: (1) process analysis/simplification; (2) benchmarking information; (3) process research and testing; (4) use of alternative technology; (5) information from customers of the business processes and support services— within and outside the company; and (6) challenge goals.

Notes:

1) Business processes and support services might include activities and operations involving finance and accounting, software services, sales, marketing, public relations, information services, purchasing, personnel, legal services, plant and facilities management, basic research and development, and secretarial and other administrative services.

2) The purpose of this Item is to permit applicants to highlight separately the quality activities for functions that support the product and service production and delivery processes the applicant addressed in Item 5.2. The support services and business processes included in Item 5.3 depend on the applicant's type of business and quality system. Thus, this selection should be made by the applicant. Together, Items 5.1. 5.2. 5.3, 5.4, and 5.5 should cover all operations, processes, and activities of all work units.

3) Variations (5.3B) may be observed by those working in the process or by customers of the process output. The latter situation may result in formal or informal feedback or complaints.

(4) Results of improvements in business processes and support services should be reported in Item 6.3A.

5.4 SUPPLIER QUALITY *(20 PTS.)*

Describe how the company assures the quality of materials, components, and services furnished by other businesses. Describe also the company's plans and actions to improve supplier quality.

Approach ✔
Deployment ✔
Results

AREAS TO ADDRESS

A. how the company defines and communicates its quality requirements to suppliers. Include: (1) a brief summary of the principal quality requirements for key suppliers; and (2) the key indicators the company uses to evaluate supplier quality.

B. methods the company uses to assure that its quality requirements are met by suppliers. Describe how the results of these methods and other relevant performance information are communicated to suppliers.

C. how the company evaluates and improves its own procurement activities. Describe feedback sought from suppliers and how it is used in improvement.

D. current plans and actions to improve suppliers' abilities to meet key quality and response time requirements

Notes:
1) The term "supplier" as used here refers to other-company providers of goods and services. The use of these goods and services may occur at any stage in the production, delivery, and use of the company's products and services. Thus, suppliers include businesses such as distributors, dealers, contractors, and franchises as well as those that provide materials and components.
2) Methods may include audits, process reviews, receiving inspection, certification, testing, and rating systems.
(3) Plans and actions may include one or more of the following: joint planning, partnerships, training, long-term agreements, incentives and recognition, and supplier selection.

5.5 QUALITY ASSESSMENT *(15 PTS.)*
Describe how the company assesses the quality and performance of its systems, processes, and practices and the quality of its products and services.

Approach ✔
Deployment ✔
Results

AREAS TO ADDRESS
A. approaches the company uses to assess: (1) systems, processes, and practices; and (2) products and services. For (1) and (2), describe: (a) what is assessed; (b) how often assessments are made and by whom; and (c) how measurement quality and adequacy of documentation of processes and practices are assured.
B. how assessment findings are used to improve: products and services; systems; processes; practices; and supplier requirements. Describe how the company verifies that assessment findings lead to action and that the actions are effective.

Notes:
1) The systems, processes, practices, products, and services addressed in this item pertain to all company unit activities covered in Items 5.1, 5.2, 5.3, and 5.4. If the approaches and frequency of assessments differ appreciably for different company activities, this should be described in this Item.
2) Adequacy of documentation should take into account legal, regulatory, and contractual requirements as well as knowledge preservation and knowledge transfer to help support all improvement efforts.

6.0 QUALITY AND OPERATIONAL RESULTS *(180 PTS.)*

The *Quality and Operational Results* category examines the company's quality levels and improvement trends in quality, company operational performance, and supplier quality. Also examined are current quality and operational performance levels relative to those of competitors.

6.1 PRODUCT AND SERVICE QUALITY RESULTS *(70 PTS.)*

Summarize trends in quality and current quality levels for key product and service features; compare the company's current quality levels with those of competitors and/or appropriate benchmarks.

Approach
Deployment
Results ✔

AREAS TO ADDRESS

A. trends and current levels for all key measures of product and service quality
B. current quality level comparisons with principal competitors in the company's key markets, industry averages, industry leaders, and appropriate benchmarks

Notes:

1) Key product and service measures are measures relative to the set of all important features of the company's products and services. These measures, taken together, best represent the most important factors that predict customer satisfaction and quality in customer use. Examples include measures of accuracy, reliability, timeliness, performance, behavior, delivery, after-sales services, documentation. appearance, and effective complaint management.

2) Results reported in Item 6.1 should reflect all key product and service features described in the Overview and addressed in Items 7.1 and 5.1.

3) Data reported in Item 6.1 are intended to be objective indicators of product and service quality, not the customers' satisfaction or reaction to the products and/or services. Such data may be of several types, including: (a) internal (company) measurements; (b) field performance (when applicable); (c) proactive checks by the company of specific product and service features (7.2D); and (d) data routinely collected by other organizations or on behalf of the company. Data reported in Item 6.1 should provide information on the company's performance relative to the specific product and service features that best *predict* customer satisfaction. These data, collected regularly, are then part of a process for monitoring and improving quality

4) Bases for comparison in Item 6.1B may include independent surveys, studies, or laboratory testing; benchmarks; and company evaluations and testing.

6.2 COMPANY OPERATIONAL RESULTS *(50 PTS .)*

Summarize trends and levels in overall company operational performance and provide a comparison of this operational performance with competitors and/or appropriate benchmarks.

Approach
Deployment
Results ✔

AREAS TO ADDRESS

A. trends and current levels for key measures of company operational performance
B. comparison of performance with that of competitors, industry averages, industry leaders, and key benchmarks

Notes:

1) Key measures of company operational performance include those that address productivity, efficiency, and effectiveness. Examples should include generic indicators such as use of manpower, materials, energy, capital, and assets. Trends and levels could address productivity indices, waste reduction, energy efficiency, cycle time reduction, environmental improvement, and other measures of improved *overall company performance*. Also include company-specific indicators the company uses to monitor its progress in improving operational performance. Such company-specific indicators should be defined in tables or charts where trends are presented.
2) Trends in financial indicators, properly labeled, may be included in this Item. If such financial indicators are used, there should be a clear connection to the quality and operational performance improvement activities of the company
3) Include improvements in product and service design and production/delivery processes in this item.

6.3 BUSINESS PROCESS AND SUPPORT SERVICE RESULTS *(25 PTS.)*

Summarize trends and current levels in quality and operational performance improvement for business processes and support services; compare results with competitors and/or appropriate benchmarks.

Approach
Deployment
Results ✔

AREAS TO ADDRESS

A. trends and current levels for key measures of quality and operational performance of business processes and support services
B. comparison of performance with appropriately selected companies and benchmarks

Note:
Business processes and support services are those as covered in Item 5.3. Key measures of performance should reflect the principal quality, productivity, cycle time, cost and other effectiveness requirements for business processes and support services. Responses should reflect relevance to the company's principal quality and operational performance objectives addressed in company plans, contributing to the results reported in Items 6.1 and 6.2. They should also demonstrate broad coverage of company business processes, support services, and work units and reflect the most important objectives of each process, service, or work unit.

6.4 SUPPLIER QUALITY RESULTS *(35 PTS.)*
Summarize trends in quality and current quality levels of suppliers; compare the company's supplier quality with that of competitors and/or with appropriate benchmarks.

Approach
Deployment
Results ✔

AREAS TO ADDRESS
A. trends and current levels for the most important indicators of supplier quality
B. comparison of the company's supplier quality levels with those of appropriately selected companies and/or benchmarks

Notes:
1) The results reported in Item 6.4 derive from quality improvement activities described in Item 5.4. Results should be broken down by major groupings of suppliers and reported using the principal quality indicators described in Item 5.4.
2) Comparisons could be industry averages, industry leaders, principal competitors in the company's key markets, and other appropriate benchmarks.

7.0 CUSTOMER FOCUS AND SATISFACTION *(300 PTS.)*
The *Customer Focus and Satisfaction* category examines the company's relationships with customers and its knowledge of customer requirements and of the key quality factors that drive marketplace competitiveness. Also examined are the company's methods to determine customer satisfaction, current trends and levels of customer satisfaction and retention, and these results relative to competitors.

7.1 CUSTOMER EXPECTATIONS: CURRENT AND FUTURE *(35 PTS.)*

Describe how the company determines near-term and long-term requirements and expectations of customers.

Approach ✔
Deployment ✔
Results

AREAS TO ADDRESS

A. how the company determines *current and near-term requirements* and expectations of customers. Describe: (1) how customer groups and/or market segments are determined including how customers of competitors and other potential customers are considered; (2) the process for collecting information, including what information is sought, frequency and methods of collection, and how objectivity and validity are assured; (3) the process for determining specific product and service features and the relative importance of these features to customer groups or segments; and (4) how other information such as complaints, gains and losses of customers, and product/service performance are cross-compared to support the determination.

B. how the company addresses *future requirements* and expectations of customers. Describe: (1) the time horizon for the determination; (2) how important technological, competitive, societal, economic, and demographic factors that may bear upon customer requirements, expectations, or alternatives are considered; (3) how customers of competitors and other potential customers are considered; (4) how key product and service features and the relative importance of these features are projected; and (5) how changing or emerging market segments are addressed and their implications on new product/service lines as well as on current products and services are considered.

C. how the company evaluates and improves its processes for determining customer requirements and expectations. Describe how the improvement process considers: (1) new market opportunities; and (2) extension of the time horizon for the determination.

Notes:

1) The company's products and services may be sold to end users by intermediaries such as retail stores or dealers. Thus, determining customer groups should take into account both the end users and the intermediaries.

2) Product and service features refer to all important characteristics of products and services experienced by the customers throughout the overall purchase and ownership experiences. These include any factors that bear upon customer preference and repurchase loyalty or customer view of quality—for example, those features that enhance or differentiate products and services from competing offerings.

3) Some companies may use similar methods to determine customer require-ments/expectations and customer satisfaction (Item 7.4). In such cases, cross-references should be included.

7.2 CUSTOMER RELATIONSHIP MANAGEMENT *(65 PTS)*

Describe how the company provides effective management of its relationships with its customers and uses information gained from customers to improve customer relationship management strategies and practices.

Approach ✔
Deployment ✔
Results

AREAS TO ADDRESS

A. for the company's most important processes and transactions that bring its employees into contact with customers, summarize the key requirements for maintaining and building relationships. Describe key quality indicators derived from these requirements and how they were determined.

B. how service standards that address the key quality indicators (7.2A) are set. Include: (1) how service standards requirements are deployed to customer-contact employees and to other company units that provide support for customer-contact employees; and (2) how the overall service standards system is tracked.

C. how the company provides information and easy access to enable customers to seek assistance, to comment and to complain. Describe the main types of contact and how easy access is maintained for each type.

D. how the company follows up with customers on products, services, and recent transactions to seek feedback and to help build relationships

E. how the following are addressed for customer-contact employees: (1) selection factors; (2) career path; (3) deployment of special training to include: knowledge of products and services; listening to customers; soliciting com-ments from customers; how to anticipate and handle problems or failures ("recovery"); skills in customer retention; and how to manage expectations; (4) empowerment and decision making; (5) satisfaction determination; (6) recognition and reward; and (7) turnover

F. how the company ensures that formal and informal complaints and feedback received by all company units are aggregated for overall evaluation and use throughout the company. Describe: (1) how the company ensures that complaints and problems are resolved promptly and effectively; and (2) how the company sets priorities for improvement projects based upon analysis of complaints, including types and frequencies of complaints and relationships to customers' repurchase intentions.

G. how the company evaluates and improves its customer relationship manage-ment strategies and practices. Include: (1) how the company seeks opportunities to enhance relationships with all customers or with key customers; and (2) how evaluations lead to improvements in service standards, access, customer-contact employee training, and technology support. Describe how customer information is used in the improvement process.

Notes:
1) Information on trends and levels in indicators of complaint response time. effective resolution, and percent of complaints resolved on first contact should be reported in Item 6.1.
2) In addressing empowerment and decision making in 7.2E, indicate how the company ensures that there is a common vision or basis to guide the actions of customer-contact employees.

7.3 COMMITMENT TO CUSTOMERS *(15 PTS.)*
Describe the company's commitments to customers regarding its products/ services and how these commitments are evaluated and improved.

Approach ✔
Deployment ✔
Results

AREAS TO ADDRESS
A. types of commitments the company makes to promote trust and confidence in its products/services and to satisfy customers when product/service failures occur. Describe these commitments and how they: (1) address the principal concerns of customers; (2) are free from conditions that might weaken customers' trust and confidence; and (3) are communicated to customers clearly and simply.
B. how the company evaluates and improves its commitments, and the customers' understanding of them, to avoid gaps between expectations and delivery. Include: (1) how information/feedback from customers is used; (2) how product/service performance improvement data are used; and (3) how competitors' commitments are considered.

Note:
Examples of commitments are product and service guarantees, warranties. and other understandings, expressed or implied.

7.4 CUSTOMER SATISFACTION DETERMINATION *(30 PTS.)*

Describe the company's methods for determining customer satisfaction, customer repurchase intentions, and customer satisfaction relative to competitors; describe how these methods are evaluated and improved.

Approach ✔
Deployment ✔
Results

AREAS TO ADDRESS

A. how the company determines customer satisfaction. Include: (1) a brief description of methods, processes, and measurement scales used; frequency of determination; and how objectivity and validity are assured. Indicate significant differences, if any, in these satisfaction methods, processes, and measurement scales for different customer groups or segments.; and (2) how customer satisfaction measurements capture key information that reflects customers' likely market behavior, such as repurchase intentions.

B. how customer satisfaction relative to that for competitors is determined. Describe: (1) company-based comparative studies; and (2) comparative studies or evaluations made by independent organizations and/or customers. For (1) and (2), describe how objectivity and validity of studies are addressed.

C. how the company evaluates and improves its overall processes, measurement, and measurement scales for determining customer satisfaction and customer satisfaction relative to that for competitors. Include how other indicators (such as gains and losses of customers) and customer dissatisfaction indicators (such as complaints) are used in this improvement process.

Notes:

1) Customer satisfaction measurement may include both a numerical rating scale and descriptors assigned to each unit in the scale. An effective (actionable) customer satisfaction measurement system is one that provides the company with reliable information about customer ratings of specific product and service features and the relationship between these ratings and the customer's likely market behavior

2) Customer dissatisfaction indicators include complaints, claims, refunds, recalls, returns, repeat services, litigation, replacements, downgrades, repairs, warranty work, warranty costs, misshipments, and incomplete orders.

3) Company-based or independent organization comparative studies in 7.4B may take into account one or more indicators of customer dissatisfaction as well as satisfaction The extent and types of such studies may depend upon industry and company size.

4) The company's products and services may be sold to end users by intermediaries such as retail stores or dealers. Thus, "customer groups" should take into account both end users and intermediaries.

7.5 CUSTOMER SATISFACTION RESULTS *(8.5 PTS.)*

Summarize trends in the company's customer satisfaction and trends in key indicators of customer dissatisfaction.

Approach
Deployment
Results ✔

AREAS TO ADDRESS

A. trends in indicators of customer satisfaction. Segment by customer group, as appropriate. Trends may be supported by objective information and/or data from customers demonstrating current or recent (past 3 years) satisfaction with the company's products/services.
B. trends in indicators of customer dissatisfaction. Address the most relevant indicators for the company's products/services.

Notes:

1) Results reported in this Item derive from methods described in Items 7.4 and 7.2.
2) Information supporting trends may include customers' assessments of products/services, customer awards, and customer retention. (3) Indicators of customer dissatisfaction are given in Item 7.4, Note 2.

7.6 CUSTOMER SATISFACTION COMPARISON *(70 PTS.)*

Compare the company's customer satisfaction results with those of competitors.

Approach
Deployment
Results ✔

AREAS TO ADDRESS

A. trends in indicators of customer satisfaction relative to competitors. Segment by customer group, as appropriate. Trends may be supported by objective information and/or data from independent organizations, including customers. This information and/or data may include survey results, competitive awards, recognition and ratings.
B. trends in gaining and losing customers, or customer accounts, to competitors
C. trends in gaining or losing market share to competitors

Notes:

1) Results reported in this Item derive from methods described in Item 7.4.
2) Competitors include domestic and international ones in the company's markets, both domestic and international.

3) Surveys, competitive awards, recognition, and ratings by independent organizations and customers should reflect comparative satisfaction (and dissatisfaction), not comparative performance of products and services. Information on comparative performance of products and services should be included in 6.1B.

SCORING SYSTEM: APPROACH, DEPLOYMENT, RESULTS

The system for scoring Examination Items is based upon three evaluation dimensions: (1) Approach; (2) Deployment, and (3) Results. All Examination Items require applicants to furnish information relating to one or more of these dimensions.

APPROACH

"Approach" refers to the methods the company uses to achieve the requirements addressed in the Examination Items. The factors used to evaluate approaches include one or more of the following, as appropriate:

- the appropriateness of the methods, tools, and techniques to the requirements
- the effectiveness of methods, tools, and techniques
- the degree to which the approach is systematic, integrated, and consistently applied
- the degree to which the approach embodies effective evaluation/improvement cycles
- the degree to which the approach is based upon quantitative information that is objective and reliable
- the degree to which the approach is prevention-based
- the indicators of unique and innovative approaches, including significant and effective new adaptations of tools and techniques used in other applications or types of businesses

DEPLOYMENT

"Deployment" refers to the extent to which the approaches are applied to all relevant areas and activities addressed and implied in the Examination Items. The factors used to evaluate deployment include one or more of the following, as appropriate:

- the appropriate and effective application of the stated approach by all work units to all processes and activities
- the appropriate and effective application of the stated approach to all product and service features
- the appropriate and effective application of the stated approach to all transactions and interactions with customers, suppliers of goods and services, and the public

RESULTS

"Results" refers to outcomes and effects in achieving the purposes addressed and implied in the Examination Items. The factors used to evaluate results include one or more of the following:

- the performance levels
- the quality and performance levels relative to appropriate comparisons and/ or benchmarks
- the rate of performance improvement
- the breadth and importance of performance improvements
- the demonstration of sustained improvement or sustained high-level performance